THE SPIRITUAL JOURNALS
OF WARREN FELT EVANS

RELIGION IN NORTH AMERICA
Catherine L. Albanese and Stephen J. Stein, editors

THE SPIRITUAL JOURNALS *of* WARREN FELT EVANS

FROM METHODISM

to

MIND CURE

EDITED BY CATHERINE L. ALBANESE

INDIANA UNIVERSITY PRESS

Bloomington and Indianapolis

This book is a publication of

Indiana University Press
Office of Scholarly Publishing
Herman B Wells Library 350
1320 East 10th Street
Bloomington, Indiana 47405 USA

iupress.indiana.edu

♾ The paper used in this publication
meets the minimum requirements of
the American National Standard for
Information Sciences—Permanence
of Paper for Printed Library Materials,
ANSI Z39.48-1992.

Manufactured in the United States of
America

Cataloging information is available from
the Library of Congress.

ISBN 978-0-253-02243-1 (cloth)
ISBN 978-0-253-02255-4 (ebook)

1 2 3 4 5 21 20 19 18 17 16

For all the seekers I have known

I long ago lost a hound, a bay horse, and a turtle-dove, and am still on their trail. Many are the travelers I have spoken concerning them, describing their tracks and what calls they answered to. I have met one or two who had heard the hound, and the tramp of the horse, and even seen the dove disappear behind a cloud, and they seemed as anxious to recover them as if they had lost them themselves.

—Henry David Thoreau, *Walden*

Come, come, whoever you are,
Wanderer, worshiper, lover of leaving,
Ours is no caravan of despair.
Come, yet again come.

—Unitarian hymn, words adapted from Rumi

CONTENTS

ACKNOWLEDGMENTS

THIS PROJECT began the day that I stumbled upon a mysterious ascription in the WorldCat online catalog concerning certain "Journals" of Warren Felt Evans, held at a place unknown. There was no further information, and I did not know how to track what might be related details. When I sought aid, an extraordinarily helpful librarian, Anne Barnhart, at the University of California, Santa Barbara, informed me that the journals existed in manuscript only and belonged to Dartmouth College. Thanks to the UCSB librarian, so began my own life of seeking—for an intriguing manuscript that I had a hunch would contain more than financial information or grocery lists. At Dartmouth, where I turned next, Jay Satterfield, Special Collections Librarian at the Rauner Library, was warm and welcoming. During the summer of 2010, I spent a week pouring over the journals at Rauner, and I was well-rewarded for my efforts. They proved to be a rich repository of Evans's reading, reflection, and transition from one spiritual home to the next, and I thought strongly that they needed to be published. Happily, Indiana University Press agreed. At this juncture, Librarian Satterfield made my life immeasurably easier—and my evolving project doable—by agreeing to photocopy the journals and send them to me.

As I transcribed Evans's flowing Victorian longhand, which was mostly clearly legible, Friend Google continually amazed me with abilities to track down a superabundance of obscure sources—sources that without Google's assistance would have remained unidentified, probably forever. Not to be outdone, my research assistant at the time, Philip R. Deslippe, found a host of bibliographical resources to assist me in coming to terms with Evans as I pondered the wealth in his journals. Later, Dee Mortensen of Indiana University Press and Stephen J. Stein, my co-editor in the Religion in North America series there, gave close readings to my initial drafts of the manuscript transcriptions as well as my draft introduction. The extra pairs of eyes helped enormously, as with their aid I went through my own manuscript again. Their patience with the slowness of my pace was also exemplary. And truly unforgettable at this point, James F. Lawrence, Dean of the Swedenborgian House of Studies at Pacific School of Religion in the Graduate Theological Union at Berkeley, read the introduction against his thorough immersion in Swedenborgian studies as well as general American religious history. His painstaking commentary and identification of relevant Swedenborgian resources—such as, especially, in the case of Horace Bushnell—proved to be true academic treasures. Finally, a generous research fund from the University of California, Santa Barbara, helped to support indexing and illustration costs, and Kay Banning was kind enough to prepare the index.

For all of this help, I remain exceedingly grateful. As authors and editors usually say, though, the results and interpretive tack I have taken remain my own—errors and all. Finally, I need to acknowledge my reigning feline triarchy—Abby, Sashi, and Felicity—who were thoroughly patient with me when I closed the door to my study to spend time alone with Warren Felt Evans.

THE SPIRITUAL JOURNALS
OF WARREN FELT EVANS

Introduction: Warren Felt Evans

WARREN FELT EVANS is not exactly a household name in the twenty-first century. Yet in the late nineteenth century he was an idol and hero for an exuberant and flourishing American subculture. Evans was probably the single individual who most shaped the intellectual and practice-oriented direction of what became New Thought. In book after book, he churned out an evolving creed that incorporated mental healing and very much more. In so doing, Evans brought his initial ideas on the power of mind into touch with new ones from a liberal community of seekers, often disaffected with orthodox Christianity and turning, in combinative ways, toward Asian philosophies and religions as well as the mystical heritage of Europe.

But Evans did not simply absorb and reiterate the metaphysical ideas of others. With metaphysics his and their preferred term for forays into territory beyond the physical—territory in which mystical heritages and newly formed religious combinations blossomed in abundance—Evans was himself a religious creator and a quintessential spiritual seeker. A Methodist lay preacher from 1839 and ordained cleric from 1844, in the years between 1850 and 1865 he kept personal journals in which he reflected on his reading and thought it through in his own way. If Evans had journaled before this time, his manuscripts have not come to light. If he continued the practice after 1865—unlikely because of his escalating career as a healer and author—no manuscript records have been found.

1

I

In the journals Evans kept from 1850 to 1865, though, he often quoted from Wesleyan sources, especially hymn verses that he must have known by heart. In these journals, too, he recorded some details, however sketchy, of his life experience—riveting events that demanded inscription to support memory. So here he wrote of the death, in 1858, of his "darling boy" Osmon, not quite three years old, of "congestion of the lungs." He wrote of visits and letters from his son Franklin, who had gone to fight in the Civil War, and then in 1863, the terrible news that Franklin had been "severely wounded," with his right hand "blown off" and wounds in both legs, "the right leg severely." By April 1864, the continuing narrative of religious change that Evans recorded in his journals became climactic. He inserted the letter he wrote to his presiding elder to send back his Methodist ordination credentials and withdraw from the church. A week later he registered the news that he and his wife had been baptized into the (Swedenborgian) Church of the New Jerusalem.

Founded after the death of Emanuel Swedenborg (1688–1772), the New Church, or Church of the New Jerusalem, grew from 1787 as an English movement based on biblical teachings and the writings of the Swedish seer and scientist. Swedenborg himself came from a Lutheran background, and indeed, by 1718 his father had been appointed a bishop in Skara. Thereafter, the family was ennobled, and the younger Swedenborg pursued and completed studies at Uppsala University even as he functioned as Extraordinary Assessor in the Royal College of Mines. With a fifty-year-long career in the Swedish House of Nobles, he became a Leonardo da Vinci of the north, celebrated for his technological and scientific knowledge and discoveries.

From 1743 and 1744, however, Swedenborg began to receive startling voice visions, leading him in trance to other worlds. Already a prolific writer on philosophical subjects, he had blended them with practical genius (he published titles, for example, such as *Principles of Chemistry* in 1720 and *Philosophical and Mineralogical Works* in three volumes from 1729 to 1734). Significantly, he also incorporated the Hermeticism available to him in Northern Europe until, in fact, he became a theologian. Work after work issued from his pen, most notably from 1747 to 1758 his twelve-volume *Arcana Coelestia*, which encompassed over seven thousand pages. It was here that he articulated in meticulous form his rendition of the ancient teaching of correspondence—"as above, so below"—and applied the doctrine in terms of the biblical books of Genesis and Exodus. Forms replicated other forms in language and in life throughout the vast universe. Worlds, for the mature Swedenborg, replicated other worlds. The idea of a profound correspondence running through all things would influence Warren Felt Evans strongly when he discovered Swedenborg, and it would become central to his Swedenborgian appropriation. So would Swedenborg's ideas of Jehovah Jesus and, consequently, the reality of a divine humanity. And so would Swedenborg's reading of the human world as held in existence by a continuing divine influx and close to the dawn of a new age.[1]

Dominated by the increasing power that Evans found in Swedenborgian theology, his journals yet point toward a high drama of religious conversion and vocational reorientation that occurred only gradually and inch by spiritual inch. Hence, their personal and confessional nature provides an important window into processes of individual religious transition and transformation. Supported by all the spiritual assistance of the Methodist faith, Evans would manage to read himself out of his church, in the process engaging in a spiritual odyssey that would lead him to numerous religious "islands." In fact, Evans—appropriately enough—titled what was most likely his first published book *Happy Islands* (1860).[2] But this is to get ahead of the story.

The external details of Evans's life are simply told. He was born in Rockingham, Vermont, two days before Christmas in 1817. He appears to have had a relatively happy, or at least uninflected, childhood on his father's farm, with an education at the district school. Then, by 1835, according to his own report, he turned his "attention to religious things" and became a Congregationalist. In so doing, he inherited a Calvinist orthodoxy that had softened but that still stressed human sinfulness and divine selectivity regarding salvation—with a theology of predestination that would not easily go away. Meanwhile, Evans attended Chester Academy in Vermont and then Middlebury College beginning in the fall of 1837. The following spring found him at Dartmouth College, where he continued to matriculate until the spring of his junior year in 1839. After that he became a Methodist and began to act as a lay minister.

The denominational switch came with huge theological freight. As a follower of Methodist founder John Wesley, who had incorporated aspects of medieval Catholic spirituality into his teachings, Evans could leave behind the Calvinism of his Congregational legacy. He could open to a view of humanity that was able to embrace much of the spirituality of the Catholic Middle Ages as well as the perfectionism of Wesley himself and later thinkers. These pointed toward a transformation of human nature that was associated with "perfection" in varied and nuanced senses. Evans could rejoice in the freedom, not the bondage, of the will, and he could choose to be saved instead of waiting on God.

And, indeed, Evans did so choose. His reasons for leaving Dartmouth College are unclear—perhaps to secure professional status quickly, which he could do in an acting ministry, and this perhaps because of impending plans to marry. But even before his withdrawal from Dartmouth, on New Year's Day 1839 Evans had preached his first (and trial) sermon on the text "He hath bent his bow, and made it ready" (Ps. 7:12). He had become convinced by the Oberlin theology of sanctification with its perfectionism. Taught by the charismatic revivalist Charles Grandison Finney, professor of theology and later president at Oberlin College in Ohio, the new perfectionist theology had moved distinctly away from Calvinism. Here individuals conjoined their free will to the power of the Holy Spirit to receive a transformative infusion of divine grace; they were restored to the situation of Adam before the Fall. So Evans had opted for a theology of perfection, and the heritage of his new Methodist denomination suited him in a spiritual search that had already begun. By blending Oberlin with Wesleyan perfectionist musings, Evans was creating something new. What Oberlin added to Wesleyan perfection was especially the self-starting message implicit in its language of will. Perfectionism itself, for Evans and so many others, would be a kind of theoretical *carte blanche* for testing the limits of self and spirit, for moving from step to step into new religious territory. Put simply, Methodists like Evans could use their denomination to leave their denomination, as a number of them did.

Now, in June of 1840, though, Evans married Charlotte Tinker, who became his lifelong spiritual partner in his years of religious questing and change. The couple had at least four children—the two boys cited in the journals and two girls who grew to adulthood and survived their father, who lived until 1889. Unlike Osmon, who had died as a toddler, Franklin likewise survived his father. But he was severely wounded in the Civil War, and the elder Evans had bought a press for his injured son and set him up printing periodicals and other materials when he came home. The Evans marriage was apparently quite happy—Charlotte Tinker joined her husband in his Swedenborgianism and then in his healing work. The two of them, we are told, were also "accomplished singers."[3]

Earlier, in typical Methodist fashion, Evans moved from charge to charge in the New Hampshire area that was part of the (Methodist) Claremont District. He had been ordained a deacon in 1844 and an elder in 1847, transferring from church to church at his bishop's behest every one or more years. But he had already been assigned as minister of a church in Peacham, Vermont, only little more than a week after his marriage in 1840. He must have grown in stature among his Methodist colleagues over the years. During his assignment to Concord, New Hampshire, in 1852, where the Methodists had located a divinity school—a precursor to the School of Theology at Boston University—he functioned as a substitute teacher when professors were away.[4] He was erudite in church history, and he also knew the Greek text of the New Testament. Evans, however, never stayed long enough in a place to grow deep roots, and when—as a Conference member—he attended Conference proceedings, he complained of illness and discomfort more than he reported a felt sense of oneness and community. Putting theological convictions to one side, a journal entry in June 1853 explained that Evans became a Methodist "not so much on doctrinal grounds, as from a love for the itinerant ministry." His "youthful heart admired that roving life."

Apparently, though, things grew less than rosy before too long. The same June entry found Evans grumbling, his criticisms probably instigated by a less-than-generous salary but with spiritual concerns also on display. He noted "for a few years past a growing dissatisfaction with some features of Methodism." Methodist piety was "not so uniform" as he wanted it to be, and Methodists had "but little ear for sound instructive preaching." But what he most disliked was "their outrageous financial system, or rather want of system." He had not received enough to support his family the previous year. When he claimed 475 dollars before Conference, was promised it, and therefore reported it paid, he ended with a shortfall of "fifty dollars or more." "A few more things like this would serve to wean me from Methodism," he griped, adding that he would return to the Congregational church if that happened.

Evans was no prophet. Seven years later, still at odds with his denomination, he was telling his journal that "Methodists belong to the old dispensation, and Swedenborgians to the new." In between, the early complaints of ill health became stronger, more afflictive, and more continual. Indeed, after he left the church in 1864 to become a Swedenborgian, he reflected on his decision in ways that made it clear that health issues had trumped financial ones in alienating him from Methodism. Now Evans found divine providence speaking through years of chronic illness that he had sustained, guiding him out of spiritual morass through some very physical ills. "For five years past," he testified, "the providence of the Lord seems to have led me to this result. The failure of my health while preaching at Lawrence. My partial recovery and then after another attempt to preach in the Old Church, the failure of my health again, seemed to me the voice of God, that my labors as a Methodist preacher were by his will closed." His tone was hard and somewhat bitter, if resigned. "My poverty & sufferings while my health would not admit of my laboring, and no help being offered me by the Church for whom I had expended all my energies, served to wean me from it." He had endured "the suspicion of heresy, & even of *insanity*" for the theological views he had expressed in his recently published (Swedenborgian) *Celestial Dawn*.[5] He was hurt by "the cold shoulder" that he was getting from his "brethren."

Evans's decision to become a Swedenborgian, however, represented a significant turning point in a long journey that continued even after. His own "happy islands" metaphor is an apt summary of the spiritual pilgrimage on which he ever seemed to be embarked. Significantly, Swedenborg's teachings on the relationship of spiritual disharmony to physical disease had moved him profoundly, and he pondered and searched in terms of this strand of Swedenborgian thinking, motivated at least in part by his chronic ill health. So it was that, probably around the same time he became a Swedenborgian, he visited the locally famed Phineas P. Quimby, a mental healer in Portland, Maine. The traditional account of Evans's life at this crucial time emphasizes the influence of the Portland healer on him.

Quimby, a former clock maker who had become interested in animal magnetism, had spent a number of years on the lyceum circuit with a younger man, Lucius Burkmar. Quimby would mesmerize the apparently clairvoyant Burkmar, who would in turn diagnose and prescribe for disease. As the relationship progressed and people seemed to get better by following Burkmar's remedies, Quimby became convinced that the real cause for the cure was the mental belief of the "patients." Thus began his transformation into a mental healer or mind curist, a man who could dispense with his partner and now simply sit with patients and let them "see" the truth of their wellness as he saw it. Keeping to this simple procedure, Quimby reportedly had amazing results. Even, it seemed, in shamanic fashion he could heal at a distance.

Evans visited Quimby in Portland at least twice, once probably in 1863 and once perhaps in September 1864, when he chronicled his seasickness on a visit to Bath, Maine, less than thirty-four miles from Portland. Yet his journal makes no mention of Quimby at all, and Evans's reticence about him continued in his published work. It was only in his second mental-healing book that he acknowledged, six years after Quimby's passing, that "the late Dr. Quimby, of Portland, one of the most successful healers of this or any age," embraced the view that the cause of illness was "*wrong belief.*" Changing the belief would, therefore, cure the disease. "By a long succession of most remarkable cures, effected by psychopathic remedies," wrote Evans, Quimby had "at the same time proved the truth of the theory and the efficiency of that mode of treatment."[6] Was the autodidact Quimby someone to be distanced in a quest for professional stature by a much-more-learned Evans? Were Evans's memories fading as the years passed? Have contemporaries and later scholars, often with deep sympathies for Quimby and his formative role in New Thought, overemphasized Quimby's influence on Evans? Or, as his journal entries and early published writings hint, had Evans through his own spiritual journey gradually arrived at conclusions that were similar to Quimby's?

According to the traditional account of Evans's life, Quimby had both helped to heal Evans and instructed him. That would place Evans among a series of patient-students that Quimby had attracted. Among the others about whom we know were Mary Baker Eddy, who later founded Christian Science, and Julius Dresser and Annetta Seabury, who as a married couple eventually became major New Thought leaders in the Boston area. But evidence suggests that in Evans's case it would probably be closer to the mark to see Quimby as a catalyst for Evans's growing sense of vocation as a mental healer and also not as someone who had healed Evans (since he continued to be ill after the time frame of his visits). For example, in a public lecture in 1887, Julius Dresser told his audience that in 1876 Evans had confided to him personally "an interesting account" of his second visit to Quimby. On that occasion, Evans "told Quimby ... that he thought he could himself cure the sick in this way. Quimby replied that he thought he could." Evans took the encouragement seriously. "His first attempts on returning home were so successful that the preacher became a practitioner from that time."[7]

By 1888, though, Evans was remembering the story with a different nuance. He told A. J. Swarts—also once a Methodist minister, and an ex-Christian Scientist—that he (Evans) had never worked with Quimby. In an interview published in his *Mental Science Magazine*, Swarts recounted that Evans "called twice briefly on Dr. Q. in Portland nearly twenty-five years ago, and his interviews satisfied him that his own methods of cure were like those which Dr. Q. employed." Swarts added that Evans spoke "well of him [Quimby], and of all the workers, simply desiring all to be honest and to 'give credit where credit is due.'"[8] Once again, the argument for a parallel path is real. Perhaps there were fading memories, and certainly a realized sense of his own success as a healer may have altered Evans's later narrative. Still, independent scholar Keith McNeil has argued exhaustively that a hypothetical Evans-Quimby relationship, which converted Evans to mind cure and healed him, is largely the artifact of accounts by Horatio (son of Julius) Dresser, William J. Leonard, and other New Thought sources. Most later authors followed these earlier summaries uncritically and never explored counterevidence.[9] With journal entries and pre-1863 published books to lend important corroboration for the McNeil case, a revisionary reading—highlighting the gradualism of Evans's spiritual and vocational changes—becomes yet more persuasive.

Hence, by the mid-1860s Emanuel Swedenborg—and what influence Phineas Quimby offered—were pointing Evans in a similar direction, and Evans was beginning his second profession of mind cure in earnest, bolstered by his new Swedenborgian faith. He also did some preaching as a Swedenborgian missionary and acted as a colporteur, distributing Swedenborgian literature.[10] But his own health issues pointed him insistently toward what became his new way of life—first at Claremont, New Hampshire, and from 1867 in Boston, where he practiced and taught for more than twenty years. Meanwhile, from 1869, the Evanses welcomed patients into their home in Salisbury (Massachusetts) in a kind of domestic sanitarium. Evans took to studying medicine and, according to New Thought minister William J. Leonard, "received a diploma from a chartered board of physicians of the Eclectic School, certifying to his qualifications and giving him the title of M.D." He used the credential "in his circulars, but never in his books."[11]

According to Leonard's sources, too, Evans for many years had endured a fistula and a "disordered nervous system." He had also, during his preministerial studies, experienced a prayer or faith cure in which he had been "healed of a most aggravated and obstinate dyspepsia."[12] Thus the road that led him to mind cure was slow and gradual, and we can catch glimpses at milestones along the way in his journals. By early 1860, for example, he observed there that "faith once gave the mind power over the material world, to some extent. . . . The phenomena of the outward world are effects, the causes of which are in the world of mind." The following year, from a Swedenborgian perspective, he was invoking the "laws of mind" to explain a "conscious communion with the angels . . . effected without a miracle." Still more, when Evans published his Swedenborgian third book, *The Celestial Dawn*, in 1862—as we will see below—he had already discovered, through the Swedish seer, the connection between mind and body. When he joined the Swedenborgian church in 1864, he could allude to the "realm of mind" and its force that operated as powerfully as gravitation. Even Julius Dresser—writing from his perspective as a Quimby disciple—thought that it was Evans's "Swedenborgian faith" that "enabled him to grasp" Phineas Quimby's mental-healing "explanations" so easily and quickly.[13]

Just over a year after joining the church and after his two visits to Quimby, Evans's journal testified explicitly to his discovery of mind cure, with statements of the connection between the mind and disease states and a vision of how healing could happen. "Disease," Evans thought, "should be studied in relation to its effects upon the mind, & then the states of mind that are antagonistic to the disease may be induced, through the spiritual world." Soon Evans could declare categorically that "all diseases originate in the mind. The states of the mind are the body's health or malady." He had gotten the idea from his study of Swedenborg, as a journal entry made clear. Now he was thinking all of this through.

Ultimately, he saw with Swedenborg (and the parallel and unmentioned Quimby) a connection between the state of the spirit and the condition of the body, and, with a driving concern for healing, he went on to address the issue of cure. "If any diseased state of the body is caused by some preexisting condition of the spirit, to induce upon ourselves the opposite & healthy state of mind, will cure the disease." Evans, it turned out, was a metaphysical pragmatist. "If by the Word we have communication with a clime, where disease is unknown, & if through that connection we are linked to the Great Central Life, here is revealed a divine method of cure." It was a method of cure "as available & efficient today as it was eighteen centuries ago."

If Evans's personal journey led him to Swedenborg and the foundational categories that became New Thought, the prodigious and stunning erudition that accompanied him needs to be recognized. His recruitment as a substitute teacher in 1852 for the Methodist Biblical Institute in Concord, New Hampshire, already begins to suggest what Evans's journals make so abundantly clear. He owned, apparently, numerous books, read them voraciously, and retained what he learned with a memory that must have been close to photographic. Immersed in the piety of Methodism, as I already noted, he wrote out hymn verses frequently and seemingly by heart—many of them by Charles Wesley. Other poetry appeared again and again on journal pages.

Much of the material, for the twenty-first-century secular reader, is relatively obscure, and were it not for Internet search engines, many of the sources would be virtually irrecoverable. At times, Evans copied long passages into his journals from the works of Augustus Neander, a nineteenth-century German church historian and theologian whom he much admired. When he did so, at times he cited page numbers but never listed editions. He did the same for the writings of Emanuel Swedenborg after he became enamored of him, and so he did for other writers. He read most of these works in readily available English translations, although he prided himself in his knowledge of New Testament Greek and, in several instances, lettered Greek words into his journals. The same was true for Latin, which he clearly knew.

At first, Evans seemed drawn to narratives of the saints and mystics, whose extraordinary lives provided exemplary data for a would-be mystic. So we read of Bernard of Clairvaux, Anselm, Richard of St. Victor, Raymond Lull, Thomas à Kempis, and Johannes Tauler, among others, as well as of English and Methodist models of sanctity. But his reflections became more focused as he delved increasingly into French quietism. In an about-face from the Arminianized perfectionism of the Oberlin theology with its can-do holiness, with the seventeenth-century Madame Jeanne de la Mothe Guyon and Archbishop François de Fénelon now he would wait on God, stilling himself in a conscious passivity. Later, he would come to reject the pure quietism of this era, but for a time it provided one of the arresting stops on the "happy islands" of his odyssey.

It is not clear when exactly Evans encountered the writings of Emanuel Swedenborg, but it must have been some time in 1858 since his journal betrays its acquaintance with the Swedenborgian language of "Jehovah Jesus" by January of 1859.[14] Looking back on the event, in January 1863 Evans confided to his journal that (years before) while visiting a bookstore in Portsmouth (New Hampshire), he discovered a work that was "rain upon a thirsty soil." This was Edmund Sears's *Athanasia; Or, Foregleams of Immortality*, published in Boston by the American Unitarian Association in 1858. Evans in 1863 wrote that from the first he thought the book to be an answer to prayer. Then, in a moment that became a riveting memory, he noticed that one of Sears's footnotes cited Swedenborg's work on "the Divine Love and Wisdom." Revelation, at least from the vantage of 1863, came quickly. "It was forcibly impressed upon my mind that the views of the book were those of Swedenborg, and that what I had earnestly longed for would be found in him. I accordingly sent to Boston & procured his principal works." What his "soul long yearned for" he had "found."

In a second clue, we know that by the spring of 1860, visiting bookstores in New York City, Evans was attracted to a work by Madame Guyon that contained parallel passages from the writings of Swedenborg. When he attended Swedenborgian church services, though, he was put off by them. He was on his way to the Methodist General Conference, but his visit to the Swedenborgian "temple" occasioned the remark that he had already "read nearly all the important works of that strange but good man, Immanuel Swedenborg." Strange though Swedenborg might be, Evans's fascination with the Swedish theology had persisted and grown and would continue to do so, even as he struggled to become a complete convert. After his visit to the New York City church services, he judged that there was much "of great value" in Swedenborg's writings, though many things were "not new revelations as he claims, but . . . found in all mystic authors." He criticized Swedenborg for being "too coldly intellectual, and too little devotional." The Swedish seer exalted "the intellect" and left "the heart frigid," neglected "prayer," and did not "insist upon communion with God." Still, by early December of the following year, Evans was ready to tell his journal that Swedenborg's writings had "taken a deep hold upon my mind."

Thereafter a floodgate opened. Evans poured into his journal page after page of exposition of Swedenborgian doctrine, all with great enthusiasm and in a state that can be described as luminous. Whereas earlier journal entries often seemed bogged down in ponderous and imitative renditions of medieval and early modern spiritual sources, a new note of authenticity crept into journal pages. By January of 1863, he was recording his growing interest in Swedenborg's teaching on "the science of correspondence," adding that his wife was "pursuing the study" with him. Before he read Swedenborg, he confessed to his journal, he had been "led to study with interest and profit the mystic authors. From Madam Guyon, Fenelon, Kempis, Tauler, Law and others," he had "found something that was valuable. But all was vague and indefinite." Now, though, he could revel that Swedenborg's writings "satisfy both departments of my nature, my Intellect & my Affections. I believed his teachings because I could not do otherwise. I inwardly saw their truth."

II

If Evans used his journals as so many clean white pages on which he could wield a pen to focus his theological and spiritual reflection, he also came to use them as resources for his early published books. In a practice commonly followed by other nineteenth-century authors such as, for example, Ralph Waldo Emerson, he lifted passages, long or short, from these private musings, often generalizing comments and ideas to render them more universal. Comparisons of passages in the journals with those in his first four books published from 1860 through 1864 makes his writing habit abundantly clear.

Evans's earliest work was most probably his autobiographical *The Happy Islands; Or, Paradise Restored* (1860).[15] Here Evans launched a tour and *tour de force* of his journals' pages. The "plot" of this new book was transparent. Intended to "analyze some of the higher forms of Christian experience," *Happy Islands* was actually the record of Evans's own spiritual journey, each island that he, as traveler, visited a stop along the way to the full paradisal bliss for which he yearned. Beginning with the "ancients"—references in Homer, Plato, and Plutarch to certain "Fortunate or Happy Islands" ("*Insulae Fortunatae, or Beatae*")—Evans went on to explain his personal quest for these fabled lands. He became, as he said, "fully convinced that they were not merely the abode of immortals, but were somewhere in this world." He thought that "the spiritual state symbolized by them" belonged "to this earthly stage of existence." And he stated from the first that "the voyage to the Happy Islands" was "not so much a movement through space, as a movement of the soul towards God." In this frame of mind, he reported that he had come "in contact with a person who had long resided in the Happy Islands," and now the search had become sharpened and more focused.[16]

Who that person was remains something of a mystery. Returning from a camp meeting in Springfield, Vermont, in September 1859, Evans had recorded his meeting there with a lay Congregationalist from Boston who had exhibited a passionate interest in sanctification and apparently held forth on the theme quite intensively. Evans remarked that he had "never found a person with a richer experience in the things of God." Meanwhile,

in his memorable visit to the Portsmouth bookstore, Evans had purchased not one, but two copies of Sears's *Athanasia* and presented one to
"a brother in the ministry." Still, he had probably visited the bookstore in
1858, and the 1859 meeting with the Bostonian does not quite square with
the "brother in the ministry" for whom he had purchased a second copy
of Sears's book. And certainly, his developing correspondence with Swedenborgian Sampson Reed pointed to a close spiritual kinship between
the two, but that friendship blossomed years after Evans had begun his
island journey.

Whoever the unknown way-shower was, Evans was heartened and inspired by meeting a resident of the islands. He began looking for a boat,
visiting seaports to find a vessel that was headed in the direction he sought.
To no avail. Now he understood that he must make his pilgrimage alone.
So he researched "all the information it was possible to acquire, as to the
distance of the isles, their longitude and latitude, and what would be necessary for the voyage." He acknowledged that he "needlessly feared" it
"might be a long one" but that he had "embarked on board a boat named
the Resolute, at a city and harbor called Semivivum [half-alive]." Leaving
the place of the half-living, Evans's boat was launched, and he was on his
way.[17] By the time he reached his destination, though, he could confess
that the trip was "unnecessarily protracted and difficult." He detailed, for
readers, the seven (was this deliberately the invocation of a mystical number?) islands he visited—all with Latinized allegorical names in a style
that transparently echoed John Bunyan's *Pilgrim's Progress* of 1678, as did
much else about Evans's journey. Now, though, the Reformation theology
expressed through Bunyan's Everyman character called Christian, had
been transformed from the moralism of its original ethos into a mystical
expedition into the unknown. Catholics were no longer the fearsome presences that they were in the Bunyan allegory. In fact, in certain versions of
their spirituality, they were venerated inhabitants of the isles.

So Evans told readers at some length of his visits to "Staurosis, Anapau-
sis, Plerophoria, Euphrosyne, Teleia Agape, Eleutheria," and "Henotia"—
which, he explained, stood for "Entire Consecration, Rest, Full Assurance
of Faith, Fulness of Joy, Perfect Love, Liberty, and Divine Union." He
hastened to add that the islands "were not situated far from each other,
and the passage from one to the other was easy." Circling "Henotia, or

Divine Union" from "nearly equal distances," he confided, "below the surface they were united, and constituted but one system."[18] As Evans made his serial way to island after island, it was clear that his entire work was predicated on the theory of correspondence fundamental to the Swedenborgian theology that he had already begun to embrace. Each island conformed in its external natural features to an inner state of the soul. Nor was Evans reserved in painting these soul features for readers, displaying the romantic attention to the natural world so apparent in his journals.

On Staurosis (Entire Consecration), for example, he was met by a "Divine Man" on the beach of this "least lovely" of the islands, shaped as it was "in the form of a cross" and "surrounded by high and precipitous rocks" with "no verdure." The island had to be visited because it "contained the only harbor accessible to ships," and so Evans found himself, aided by his divine companion, making his way to a summit that "appeared wholly inaccessible." The Divine Man caught Evans when his foot slipped and sometimes carried the weak but resolute pilgrim. The summit at last gained, Evans felt that he had come back to "the sweet home whose image had followed him in all his roamings." What followed was a description of the "sequestered vale" and "large flat rock in the shape of an altar, covered with a downy moss, and standing in the midst of flowers," where Evans rested.[19]

In this state of repose, what should surface, in veiled and metaphorical form, but the "altar theology" of Methodist lay theologian and revivalist Phoebe Palmer, whose well-known *Way of Holiness* (1845) expounded her own brand of perfectionism.[20] "While resting upon this altar, there sweetly float out from the soul into the listening ear of a present God the words, 'Here, Lord, I give myself away. I present to thee my body, and my whole inward being, a living sacrifice, holy and acceptable in thy sight.'"[21] After the altar gift, when Evans stood refreshed, he beheld the startling sight of a "perpendicular rock, which was like polished marble" and "rose to a great height." He saw an inscription plainly visible near the summit "deeply cut in large gilt letters, and surmounted by a golden cross: 'Here I relinquish all, and take God, the infinite and uncreated Good, for my sole portion and inheritance.'" The inscription went on to some length, and Evans's divine guide informed him that it was the "New Covenant" and that anyone who wanted to live in the islands needed to subscribe.

Indeed, the mountain itself was blanketed with names, some of which were "familiar." "There were seen engraved in the solid rock the names of Anselm of Canterbury, Bernard of Clairvaux, Raymund Lull, Thomas à Kempis, Tauler, Ruysbrock, Fenelon, Madame Guyon, John and Charles Wesley, Mr. Fletcher and his devoted wife, Elizabeth Rowe, Hester Ann Rogers, Carvasso, Bramwell, Payson, Bunyan, Baxter, and innumerable other honored and sainted names."[22]

The list was mostly a catalog of authors cited with veneration in Evans's private journals. He had quoted a number of them and recounted the opinion of others. Etched in rock and recorded in a work for public dissemination, Evans's devotional reading had acquired a proclamatory power that could reflect and legitimate his choices not only for others but for the author himself. In keeping with the theory of correspondence, Evans's *Happy Islands* held a mirror to his soul and magnified its discoveries as he traveled, like a veritable journeyman of the spirit, from isle to blessed isle. Still more, he was explicit and didactic about his epistemology and its cosmological significance. On the island of Euphrosyne or Joy, for example, he told readers that there was "a certain experience of heavenly life and bliss which is symbolized by a lofty mountain." He hastened to add, echoing his mid-December 1858 journal, that "according to the correspondence which subsists between things in the natural world and the spiritual world, mountains signify a great elevation in the moral and spiritual condition of man." It was, indeed, "an elevation of the soul above the common level of its natural action to a higher plane of spiritual activity and enjoyment."[23]

As early as July of 1850, Evans had climbed a mountain near his home and then confessed to his journal that he had always since childhood "loved to wander in the solitudes of mountains" and "delighted to pray on their lofty tops." In terms that make the Staurosis episode translucent, he remarked that there was "scarcely a mountain or high hill in Eastern Vermont or the South-Western part of N. Hampshire, upon which I have not given myself to God in an everlasting covenant." That very afternoon he had "found near a large oak tree, a flat stone, laid upon another stone. It was laid there by the hand of God as an altar." What followed told already of an altar theology that—whether influenced by Palmer's 1845 *Way of Holiness* or not—was foundational. "Upon this I prostrated myself after taking off my shoes, rendered thanks to God for his good Providence, which has watched over me all my days; and upon that rude altar I gave myself anew to Christ."

Meanwhile, the metaphor of rushing water, so basic to New Thought and made so memorable in Ralph Waldo Trine's much later *In Tune with the Infinite* (1897), already appeared throughout Evans's *Islands.* Thus, on Plerophoria or Assurance—a "favorite resort"—he called God "the ground of all existence" but also "the fountain of all life." He went on, in almost Emersonian terms, to declare that "the life of a soul, or an insect, is a stream flowing from that Fountain: and were it not continually supplied from its Source, it would flow away and cease to be."[24] The earlier Emerson, hardly a stranger to the doctrine of correspondence, had affirmed essentially the same. In his often-quoted "Over-Soul," he told readers that when he watched "that flowing river, which, out of regions I see not, pours for a season its streams into me, I see that I am a pensioner; not a cause, but a surprised spectator of this ethereal water."[25] The later Trine would not be outdone. The "Divine current" flowed through us all, he averred, and for the sick one, whose body was like a trough clogged with muddy water, all that needed to be done was to "open the trough to a swift-flowing stream of clear, crystal water." That done, "in a very little while even the very dirt that . . . collected on its sides and bottom" would "be carried away."[26]

So Evans's theory of correspondence was itself part of a grand flow— a stream of spirituality that had descended through the times. Moving behind the message was the Swedish seer Emanuel Swedenborg, whose teaching of a divine influx that permeated the universe and human life had left an abiding legacy—one that Evans, as we have already seen, would increasingly adopt. Always, the influx managed to shape reality as it flowed, replicating the eternal world of the divine. On the island of Teleia Agape (Pure Love), Evans could proclaim that "this world, so grand, so glorious, seems but the outward robe of the higher spiritual world." It was "a heavenly veil, tremulous and wavy," thrown by the Creator over "his inner and more perfect creations." "In the Happy Islands," he explained, "all outward things were arranged in exact correspondence to their spiritual state." "All discordant sounds had ceased," since "harmonious sounds" symbolized "divine order in the affections of the soul." "Nature," Evans effused, "seemed a vast harp, struck by angel fingers, which expressed and offered up to God the sweet harmony of holy souls."[27]

The Swedenborgian theory, however, had a practical consequence, as it would for the later Trine. By the time Evans's book was being published in 1860—several years before his encounter with Quimby and before Evans had become a thorough Swedenborgian—he had arrived at the basic belief that constituted mind cure. On the same Teleia Agape on which he was enthusing in romantic vein about angel fingers striking the harp of nature, he had driven his point home in a more pragmatic direction. If there was "a closer connection between the world of mind and the outward world than many suppose," and if the island was home to no "ravenous beasts, or venomous reptiles," with "every poisonous weed . . . expelled from the land," there was more. Evans noticed, significantly, that "life was greatly prolonged in this blessed clime, and diseases were fewer than in any other part of the globe." He went on to observe that "a large portion of the diseases which assail us have their origin in the mind." Invoking Christ as "the great Physician," he named his divine work to be "to heal every form of mental disease, and thus to diminish the ailments of the body." The body lived "from the spirit" that had "put it on," and thus the "mind in its different states" was "the body's health or malady."[28]

Evans could hardly have been clearer, and if it took him a period of years to realize fully the implications of his island voyage, the territory had already been marked. We need not follow him further in the isles of bliss to see them as a kind of high-minded raid on his journals that turned them inside out. The process and the purloined material gave him the assurance he sought and always seemed to need so deeply. In a new and transformed setting, journal materials functioned as a public affirmation of the validity of Evans's insights and their spiritual authority.

III

Very probably, Evans's second book—and the one that, on the face of it, seemed most congenial to Methodist spirituality in its perfectionist and proto-holiness wing—was *Divine Order in the Process of Full Salvation* (1860).[29] The publication was brief—only forty-eight pages in print, and in actuality it might be considered an extended pamphlet. In a journal entry in February 1861, Evans himself recorded that the previous year he had "published a small work" and gave its title. His attraction to a theology of perfectionism and sanctification was apparent. The work began with a visionary proclamation that "the Holy Spirit and the Providence of God seem to be moving the members of all Christian churches to seek a higher and deeper experience in religion than that usually obtained." The present Christian mind, he asserted, was characterized by "a restless craving for an unrealized good." Abstraction and the third person fell away quickly as Evans continued, telling readers that the reason he and they went away from God empty was that "we are in no condition to receive the divine good." He complained of a Christian church "not sufficiently in sympathy with the celestial world where praise predominates," but he also warned that "emotional bliss" was not the same as "holiness" and had "no moral quality."[30]

Caught in the dilemma of a failing institution and a flagging soul, Evans was ready to announce a way out, which—as we shall see—had been inspired by none other than Emanuel Swedenborg. "Our first step in the process of full salvation," he declared, was "the renouncement of our own will as the rule of life" (this, tellingly, a different emphasis from his previous Oberlin perfectionism). When that was accomplished and we had "given our all to God," the next step was "to exercise an appropriating faith." In language that echoed the proto-holiness theology of Phoebe Palmer, Evans called for "laying our whole being upon the altar." "We are to see to it that the sacrifice is kept on the altar, and then never to yield this point."[31] Evans here was on target with what he had taken from Oberlin perfectionism. He wanted to renounce his will and yet use it—keeping his sacrifice on the altar without yielding the point. Palmer herself had claimed an experience of "entire sanctification" in 1837, and after that she became a missionary for perfectionist belief and practice that left a role—as in the Oberlin theology—for the human will. In her well-known "altar theology"—which helped to shape *Happy Islands*, as we have seen—she spelled out the steps to be taken to reach an experience of sanctification/perfection. In Palmer's reading, the message of Jesus could be found in Matthew 23:19 with its pronouncement that "the altar sanctifies the gift." She reasoned that if she offered her body as a living sacrifice upon the altar, God would yield to her strong desire and render her holy.[32]

First came the individual's consecration to God. Then came the firm belief that God would be faithful to his promise to sanctify what was consecrated. Finally came the witness to the miracle that God had wrought. Evans was in effect concurring. "With humble, loving obstinacy, moment by moment," he urged, "we are to believe and trust that Jesus, according to the virtue of his name, continues to save us."[33] As his work progressed, the discourse community with which it was overtly linking itself became ever more visible. He invoked the "higher Christian life" as "a life of full consecration and assurance," and he looked to the sanctified in "pious memoirs" or "living testimony" to discover the process of full salvation: "We shall find the process in every case to be this,—CONSECRATE ALL, AND BELIEVE."[34] Evans was, in fact, echoing the language of William E. Boardman, which inaugurated the "higher-life" movement in Presbyterian, Congregationalist, and Baptist churches. Boardman's book *Higher Christian Life* had appeared in 1858 with its announcement that conversion was merely the beginning of the Christian life.[35] What continued after that was sanctification, and it came gradually throughout a person's spiritual journey, empowering the individual, through the grace of the Holy Spirit, for a life of service and mission.

Still, Evans had managed to conflate the *active* passivity of Palmer's altar-bound surrender and Boardman's higher life with the quietism of none other than Archbishop Fénelon. Continuing to distrust the message of his feelings, Evans generalized private musings from his journal to argue that full salvation might "exist when we have no emotion, when the soul is plunged into the night of naked faith." His journal had continued with the reflection that "naked faith" was "the purest form of Christian love" and was "what Archbishop Fenelon aimed to realize." In his 1860 *Divine Order*, though, the "very essence of love" had been modulated to become acceptance of "the will of another as our will," willing "that their pleasure be done and not ours." Unlike emotion—"an unsubstantial vapory cloud" and "a mountain of vapor"—love that was "a state of the will" existed as "a mountain of granite."[36]

Beyond this, Evans was making connections that, provoked into fuller consciousness, would become a theology of New Thought. God, who was "love itself," had "a necessary and eternal property . . . to communicate divine good to his creatures." Nothing could stop the divine action "but our want of capacity to receive." The "assurance of faith" brought "full salvation," and it was "the glory of the human soul, that it was made to be a receptacle of the divine life and the divine good." "Faith" was the "channel" through which it flowed.[37] Evans was stating, in Christian terms, what would become the proverbial law of attraction. Good begot good; to the person who had, more would be given. When the gift had been experienced and full salvation was at hand, confessing the new condition, as in Palmer's third step, became "an act of praise."

Yet Evans could not acknowledge, with Palmer, a single act of "entire sanctification."[38] Rather, like Boardman and the higher-life movement, he saw the process of "full salvation" as gradual—a pilgrim's progress through thickets of spiritual dullness and sin. There was "a difference between sanctification in its incipient stage, or infancy, and holiness as a confirmed habit of the soul, a fixed spiritual condition." At first, "an effort" might be "required to do duty." The will had "not become fully fixed in a new direction." However, "at length, when the law of habit . . . had time to act," then he and others would "become rooted and grounded in love,—confirmed and strengthened in all goodness." Finally, "the soul's bent of sinning" would be "destroyed," and the "death of self" would be "complete." There were, he explained, "two degrees" to the sanctified life, like "the two apartments of the temple," and conversion launched an entrance into the first. But even the movement into the second, which might technically be "full salvation," was not enough. The soul could not "merely cross the threshold of the holy of holies, and then stop." Rather, "it must advance perpetually farther inwards towards God, who dwells there, and lose itself more and more in the divine presence."[39] Evans, like a significant number of others in the Wesleyan perfectionist and proto-holiness movement, was entertaining his quietist friends Archbishop Fénelon and Madame Guyon.

Indeed, Patricia A. Ward, a French and comparative literature scholar with a personal background in the (holiness) Church of the Nazarene, has uncovered a series of connections between continental quietist spirituality and the holiness movement. Wesley himself, noted Ward, published a fifty-volume *Christian Library* in Philadelphia from 1819 to 1827, with excerpts and summaries of devotional spirituality and autobiography that included the continental quietists. "This approach to reading," wrote

Ward, "was to influence many of his American followers, especially those who became part of the holiness movement." "The language of 'rest,' or stillness, so prevalent in Quaker, Methodist, and holiness hymns and writing, represents the often-unrecognized impact of Quietist spirituality on the vocabulary of American religious experience."[40]

Yet for all the holiness-quietist connection, sitting in the next room was another secret guest at the theological table. The overt message was clear: Evans had invoked a series of ideas congenial to the higher-life movement and, alongside, a related quietist overlay that reflected a devotional trend not unknown in Methodist and proto-holiness circles. Covertly and without acknowledgment, though, Evans's views echoed those of Emanuel Swedenborg. In a lengthy journal entry in December 1861 (well after the publication of his book), Evans extolled Swedenborgian teaching under six headings. In the last of these, he let out the book's large secret. "We are taught in the doctrines of Swedenborg, that there is a divine order in the process of a soul's salvation." Criticizing "the current popular teachings of the day in times of revival," Evans thought that "appeals" were being made "to the selfishness of the heart." So the "outward life" was "changed from self-love." But that was not enough for the now-Swedenborgian Evans. Instead, he declared, "our first duty and the first step in the process of our salvation, after coming to the knowledge of evil, is to combat it and put it away as a sin against God." Once the soul achieved this, it became "receptive of good which flows in from God through heaven." Evans stressed that humans had all they needed to put themselves in the correct disposition toward God. "It belongs to man's free will or free agency, to do this, and he must do it *as of himself*; but all the while acknowledging that it is of God, from whom all good proceeds."

There had been cognitive dissonance to be sure between, on the one hand, Boardman's higher life, Palmer's altar theology, as well as the earlier will-oriented Oberlin perfectionism and, on the other, Madame Guyon and Archbishop Fénelon. Evans had tried to bridge the theological gaps, perhaps better than his predecessors, with language. The fact remained, though, that the idea of "divine order in the process of full salvation"— which Evans found so compelling—came from Emanuel Swedenborg. It was clear that his pamphlet/book was a theological work in progress, in which Evans was trying to integrate all of his intellectual sources with one another. It was also clear that he had hidden the Swedenborgian aspects of his work from a public whom he had correctly intuited would not be inclined to accept them. Instead, he had cloaked his views in a mantle of pseudo-orthodoxy or something closer to it than Swedenborg, hoping to convert readers to the new ideas. The Swedish seer, he had surmised, would be an unwelcome visitor in the spiritual and theological homes of most of his readers.

IV

If Evans had combined American proto-holiness sources with French quietism and a closet Swedenborgianism in *Divine Order*, Evans presented journal material oh-so-carefully. By 1862, thoroughly immersed in Swedenborgian doctrine and already an undercover convert, he published a third book based on his personal musings. *The Celestial Dawn*, like *Divine Order*, tiptoed around the name of Emanuel Swedenborg, never explicitly citing Evans's theological mentor even though the work prominently referenced his other journal heroes. Here were William E. Boardman of *Higher Christian Life* fame and Roman Catholic Francisco de Losa, companion and biographer of the mystical Gregorio López, whom John Wesley himself had admired. Here alongside them was ambiguously nonconformist and nonseparatist Puritan minister Richard Baxter, whose *Saints' Everlasting Rest* Wesley had abridged. And here, too, were Irish Methodist convert Thomas Walsh, who walked city streets rapt in prayer and interiority, as well as the enigmatic German Dr. von Cölln. Those with theological savvy apparently were not fooled. Still, even with—as noted above—the icy and censorious reception the book got in non-Swedenborgian quarters, it must have done well enough because it was reprinted two years later.[41] Reformulating basic Swedenborgian theological themes in terms of his own spiritual odyssey and the reading practices that had supported it, Evans was ready to offer a comprehensive religious vision to his readers.

As in Swedenborg's teaching, the vision was thoroughly interior, and yet it was emphatic as an affirmation of human worth in the world. Citing the *Higher Christian Life* (close enough to the Oberlin and Methodist perfectionism with which he began), Evans used Boardman's trinitarian teaching with its acknowledgment of the divinity of Christ. But Evans took the teaching to a Swedenborgian place that turned orthodoxy into heresy. "It will be seen," he wrote, "that the Son is not another God beside Jehovah, but is the Father brought nigh to us." Boardman would no doubt have agreed that far. In the context in which Evans had inserted this reflection, though, orthodox things had gone decidedly awry. Already Evans had been instructing readers on the "Divine Humanity of Jesus" and how heaven had been brought closer by it "than it could be by angels or spirits." Now, instead of the old dispensation—"a dispensation of angels"—the "Divine Humanity" was "the medium through which the celestial influences descend." "Jehovah Jesus" was "the only living and true God."[42] As we have seen, Evans had confessed to Jehovah Jesus as early as January of 1859 and had called Jehovah Jesus the only living and true God—with the entire Trinity within him.

Like Swedenborg, Evans had emptied the fatherhood of God into the sonship and emptied the sonship into humanity. In so doing, he had turned the perfectionism of his past inside out, elevating human life and its projects to a quasi-divine status. This the writing practices of his journals had helped him to accomplish. The process was reflected yet again when Evans cited Charles G. Finney with a lengthy quotation from his *Guide to the Savior*.[43] By 1855 in its third edition, Finney's work provided earnest instruction for attaining to the "entire holiness of heart and life" that its subtitle promised. Evans had been drawn to Finney's reflections on the "spiritual meaning" of the Bible and how it faded in and out of view depending on whether or not the Christ light was present with which to read it. And once again, Evans had inserted Finney's words—which appear nowhere in his journal—into a consummately Swedenborgian proclamation of interiority.

It was through the "Divine Humanity" that the "children of God" could find that "the abyss of truth in the divine word" became "luminous to depths never before penetrated." For those in the "sensuous world," instead, the mind penetrated "the external letter, the mere exterior cortex of truth, to the arcane, or hidden meaning within."[44] Evans had successfully brought Finney into a new Swedenborgian setting that no doubt would have astounded the revivalist himself and that might be construed as politically inspired to reach a certain type of reader. But the easy amalgamation provides insight into the work that Evans's journaling was doing for him—bringing old saints together with new ones, easing a passage into previously unknown territory that now could be called a spiritual home. This even with Charles Finney in absentia in journal pages.

Still, if heaven had to be "an interior state" before it could be "an external condition," for all the mysticism Evans, like Swedenborg before him, was pulling readers back into the present world. Heaven needed to be sought in "a domain of thought," and "material substance" could not "be spiritualized." To make his point, Evans could enlist the Scotch commonsense philosophy of Dugald Stewart on the certainty of the existence of mind as well as the subjective idealism of Bishop George Berkeley on the nonexistence of materiality.[45] True enough for Evans. Still more, "to be in heaven" was "to be in a state of celestial love," as a quoted Charles Wesley hymn served to underline. In the midst of such love, the world *was* the reflection of divine reality and, much as for Jonathan Edwards, shadowed it forth. Natural creations were "types of things in the heavens" and "copies of celestial realities." Indeed, in the parables of Jesus "by the laws of correspondence the lower creations" were "made to image the higher." The Epistle to the Hebrews, too, recognized and declared "the correspondence between earthly and heavenly things."[46]

As in the emerging theology of Evans's journals, however, correspondence in *Celestial Dawn* led to affirmation and affirmation was transmuted into power. Perry Miller in the mid-twentieth century had remarked of Edwards's manuscript "Images of Divine Things" that it was "nothing less than an assertion of the absolute validity of the sensuous."[47] Nearly a century earlier than Miller, Evans saw a connection that was inverted but nonetheless real. Mental states affected "the appearance of the external world" and tended "in some degree, to adjust the outward universe in harmony, both in appearance and reality, with our spiritual condition." The "outward world" would be "in correspondence with the world within."[48] Once again, as in his private journals, Evans was bringing readers to the doorstep of mind cure. From an idealist perspective that had begun by negating the substantiality of the material world, he had entered by the back door to affirm matter's plasticity before mind. He had implied a human ability to manipulate the world of matter in directions more pleasing to the mind's and heart's desire. The heavenly world, in the end, led back to this one. *Celestial Dawn* was opening a door to empower readers through the Swedenborgian theological affirmation that Evans had worked so laboriously to develop in private. "In a completed regeneration," Evans proclaimed, humans would be in "the New Jerusalem state." Now they would experience "the dawn of the heavenly morning," with their "spiritual vision . . . purged" and with souls "flooded with the light of a celestial day." The state began now. As Evans's later life would attest, its calling card was mind cure.[49]

V

Evans came fully out of the closet with his fourth book based on journal materials. *The New Age and Its Messenger* (1864), a slim volume with a scant 110 pages, stood as an unabashed paean to Emanuel Swedenborg and an apology for his teachings.[50] Evans had complained to his journal at the end of 1858 that "men, and even the Church" were "buried in the things of sense" and "floundering in the dismal swamp of materialism and Saduceeism"—to the point that the "spiritual world" was "a *terra incognita*, an unknown land." An uninflected literalism in Christian teaching as he experienced it had by this time become for him, as his words suggested, a spiritual materialism, and he was on a mission to find a remedy. Instead of stereotypical Sadducees—the strict literalists of his religious imaginary—Evans longed for a "genuine rationalism" as "the point of transition to a spiritual state." This would constitute the path from human fallenness to true spirituality. From it, humans could rise to the truly spiritual condition in which the angels existed, with faith "not the result of a slow process of reasoning" but instead "an intuition, a spontaneous inward perception." Here "celestial love" predominated, and the angelic intellect flew "out from their love."[51]

In early 1861, Evans's journal had attributed this intuitive state not to angels but to a human person earnestly seeking advancement in "divine knowledge." "Such a one," he had written, "sees in the divine Word what others look for in vain. God reveals his revelation to him. The seals are broken, and the Book opened." When such an individual thirsted for "truth" as a way to promote "the spiritual good of others" rather than "for the gratification of self," the path to divine "wisdom" opened. Now the seeker saw "truth in its own divine light, receiving it not by reasoning, but by intuition." If so, Evans had reconsidered the theme by the time he made his private musings public in *New Age*. The use and reworking of journal material filled the pages of the new book, but now—unlike in *Celestial Dawn*—the material was clearly identified as Swedenborgian teaching.

Meanwhile, echoing his journal, an early chapter of *New Age* inveighed against a "modern Pythonism" abroad in the land, contrasting it with Swedenborg's "open communication with the spiritual world." Given his cultural context, Evans was no doubt referring to the contemporary phenomenon of mass spiritualism that had flourished throughout the 1850s. Swedenborg's experience and his teaching were, in their "moral influence," as distant from such attempts at contacting the spiritual world as "heaven" was "above hell." Swedenborg's transmissions came "like a beam of heavenly light in our darkness; the other like the dark and deadly vapor of the Stygian lake." The latter made "Christ a mere man, and God a *principle* and not a person," and so was "a refined materialism and atheism." By contrast, Swedenborgianism found "in Christ the one only Deity, the personal and living God." Swedenborg's teaching introduced the "soul to an all-satisfying communion with Him."[52] Seen in the light of the long evolution of Evans's own spiritual search, his orthodox (anti-Pythonistic) protest and theological declaration of certainty are ironic. In the years after 1865—for which no journals have been found—Evans's published books would reveal a pilgrim whose theological horizon changed significantly as the years passed and as he caught sight of a spiritual landscape that would become early New Thought.

Now though, in 1864, Evans was searching the scripture in light of Swedenborg's law of correspondence. In the process, he quite strikingly echoed Emerson's statement in a well-known chapter on language in his little book *Nature* (1836), which also shared Swedenborgian roots.[53] Evans was attempting—like Emerson—etymological constructions to make his point. The "Word of God," he said, was "written according to . . . correspondence, and all natural things [were] significant of spiritual things." With a foray into ancient Greek and Latin linguistic constructions (Emerson had adhered to English-language meanings and had focused on more general "moral or intellectual fact"), Evans drove home his

confessional message. "The great discovery of Swedenborg, and the grand
characteristic of his system" was "the science of correspondence, without
a knowledge of which the deep spiritual significance of the Word enclosed
within the enveloping letter, cannot be understood."[54]

As in his journal, Evans was explicating the "three distinct senses in
the Word"—the sensual/natural, intellectual/spiritual, and intuitional/
celestial. This was pure Swedenborgian teaching, and Evans acknowledged it so. With Swedenborgian finesse, he proclaimed to readers that
"the second coming of the Lord" was "not to be into the natural world, but
out of the Word." Still, Evans managed to gather some of his journal heroes
into a quasi-Swedenborgian fold, explaining that "the mystic authors, as
Fenelon, Madame Guyon, and Tauler, have had glimpses of this spiritual
significance," even if, sadly, "they had no fixed principles of interpretation"
and "groped like blind men along the wall."[55]

Moreover, as in his journal, a person's spiritual enemy was "the *proprium*." Evans had thoroughly castigated this aspect of the human condition, quoting Swedenborg himself in a journal entry in late 1860. The
point of worship, Swedenborg had instructed, was to enable the devotee
to remove "his *proprium* (or self-hood) which prevents influx and reception" and which "hardens his heart and shuts it." Now, in *New Age*, Evans
changed the context, calling death itself "a conscious and vital union of
our personality with the living God" and "the extinction of the *proprium*
or selfhood."[56] Yet hope flourished for the possibility of a different way
of life especially through a "prayerful perusal of the spiritual writings of
Swedenborg." Then a person would discern the difference between "apparent and real truth." Hence, Evans could celebrate the dawn of the "New
Age," when the mind would be elevated "to a higher range of thought."
"Conceptions" would be raised "from the position where only *seeming*
truth" could be "apprehended, to that higher plane where truth" shone
"in its own uncreated light."[57]

Evans continued to wax enthusiastically throughout his slender volume, which in many ways reaffirmed what he had already declared so
forcefully in *Celestial Dawn*, but now with a significant nametag attached.
Especially, though, as his book's title announced, Evans was proclaiming
the New Age that Swedenborg had heralded well over a century before late

nineteenth-century Theosophists would announce a New Age to come. Evans, as cosmic optimist, already presaged the New Thought affirmative prayer that he would later articulate and promote. With the effusive writing of his longhand journal to support him, now his printed pages could speak a New Age into being. The New Age was "to be characterized by a vivid faith in the reality of life beyond the grave," and it was distinctly a "New Age of the Church." Even more, Evans could, with Swedenborg, move beyond the earth as he knew it to understand God "as the God of *all* worlds." This was the view of the deity that belonged "to the New Age" and was "one of the glories of the New Jerusalem." Swedenborg, in his mystical travels, had visited other planets—with belief in reputed life in other parts of the universe *au courant* in the cultural circles in which he moved. Evans, in turn, was on board for the journey in his own spiritual imaginary. "The extension of the human race, in countless numbers, to all the earths in the stellar universe," he enthused, served "to make man think less of himself as an individual, and thus to weaken that deep-seated love of self," which was "the root of all evil."[58]

VI

Evans had left his journals behind. Like Swedenborg who had visited so many new spiritual realms, Evans would continue to be a seeker as he published book after book—six of them, with a seventh manuscript never published—on the good news of mental healing.[59] Here was New Jerusalem, indeed, and as the years passed, Evans did not need the Swedish seer so insistently to lead him. In fact, a departure from the purer Swedenborgianism of the late journal years grew ever more obvious. As early as *The Mental-Cure* (1869), Evans's work was revealing his eclectic departures from Swedenborgian orthodoxy. As Keith McNeil has noted, the Swedenborgian *New Jerusalem Magazine* published a review of the book that was decidedly chilly. Although *Mental-Cure* had been published by the Swedenborgian-friendly house of H. H. and T. W. Carter, the unnamed *New Jerusalem* reviewer opined regret. Evans's book could not be regarded as "a successful attempt to throw new light upon the cure of disease from the revelation of spiritual laws made to the New Church, but rather as in sympathy with what is hostile to the church." The "general tenor of his book" seemed "more akin to Spiritism than to the New Church."[60]

Still more, Evans had long been enamored of the idealism of Bishop Berkeley, and his presence in *Celestial Dawn* has already been noticed. As Keith McNeal perceptively tells, in his 1881 *Divine Law of Cure*, Evans declared that he had become a "convert to [Berkeleyan] idealism more than two score years ago."[61] This would have placed Evans's conversion during his college years at Dartmouth. If so, in following Berkeley, Evans had long held the view that matter did not exist independently from perception and that matter's apparent existence bore the imprint of the divine Mind. Indeed, Evans's unpublished manuscript in the National Library of Medicine in Bethesda, Maryland—which exists in two notebooks with Evans's tentative titles inscribed for each—reveals the profound impact of idealism on his continuing thought. He called the first volume "A Practical Application of the Ideal Philosophy to the Cure of Disease" and the second "Occult Science of Medicine: A Practical Application of Idealism to the Cure of Disease."[62]

Yet for all the Swedenborgian reviewer's grumbling that the Carter house had produced a dubiously Swedenborgian work and for all the eclecticism and Berkeleyan idealism of Evans, H. H. Carter brought out Evans's last three books. Moreover, Evans's friend Robert Allen Campbell, writing in 1888 (the year before Evans's death), described him in print as "an honored member of the New Jerusalem (or Swedenborgian) Church of Boston"—this "for the past twenty-five years."[63] Even with the Swedenborgian affiliation though, a glance at Evans's final work, *Esoteric Christianity and Mental Therapeutics* (1886), suggests how far he had traveled as he neared the end of his long years of pilgrimage.

Unlike the books Evans published during the era of his journals, this one leaves off the "Rev." that during those years had preceded his name. Although in the late 1860s and early 1870s he was still using the title, later works—unless they were reprints—had eliminated it.[64] Evans had abandoned his clerical identity. A lead article in *The Christian Science Journal* for August 1886 lambasted Evans in a scathing review that revealed much about the distance he had traveled. Signed only by "A Christian Scientist" (Mary Baker Eddy herself?), the piece charged that perhaps no previous theory of the last decade "equalled, in presumption and absurdity, this mad attempt to force Christianity (the hope of the whole human race) into the farcical groves of Occultism." Evans's book had "set before the public gaze a pantomime" with characters who were "dead priests, magicians, and old-time philosophers, whose special hypotheses perished in the same centuries with themselves." "To suit the author's purpose and create faith in an enigmatical Deity," accused the anonymous reviewer, "myths of antiquity—legends, fables, superstitions, long-exploded tricks—are exhumed, musty and rank, or empty as air. These are clad with Eastern prestige, and linked to modern skepticism, credulity, ignorance, and relish for humbug."[65]

Minus the venom, the Christian Science reviewer was not all wrong. Reading from the testimony of an enemy, we can discover a Warren Felt Evans who had traded Swedenborg for what, said the reviewer, looked "like a twin of Theosophy."[66] By 1885 and his book *The Primitive Mind-Cure*, Evans had become thoroughly enamored of Madame Helena Blavatsky and her theosophical fellow travelers. That work had already flamboyantly blended Western philosophy and Asian writings with Hermeticism. The tradition that grew around the pseudonymous texts of the early Christian era called the *Corpus Hermeticum* (attributed to Hermes Trismegistus, ancient priest of the Egyptian Thoth) achieved a commanding presence not only in Blavatsky but also in Evans. Upon this mystical catch-all, he had built a new scaffold for his idealism, toughening it to become more uncompromising than in previous renditions. Blavatsky's *Isis Unveiled* had appeared in 1877 with its excavation of Western Hermeticism, to which she added generous doses of Hinduism and Buddhism.[67] Evans clearly agreed.

Now, in 1886 and *Esoteric Christianity*, Evans's preface was telling readers that the author intended his work "to aid the student of Christian Theosophy to explore the inner realm into which his own spirit opens." His first chapter alone had referenced Plato, Hermeticism, Hindu adepts, Egyptians, Chaldeans, and the Jewish Kabbalah in the service of theological construction.[68] Indeed, years of combinative thought and practice had yielded an Evans who raided the world's spiritual closets unabashedly. Yet, albeit the Christian Science attack, Evans called his work *Christian* Theosophy and managed to stay in his own mind Christian. He brought the selective wisdom of a global assortment of religious seers and societies to the New Testament—still in the process finding that "the religion of Jesus Christ" stood "apart from all other religions." This was because Jesus—as "an incarnation of the universal Christ"—could "lodge himself, and incorporate and repeat himself, in his true disciples."[69] Still more, for all the theology, the passion that inspired and drove the book was practice. Like all of Evans's volumes after the years of his journals, this one subjected mental healing to a strenuous exercise in legitimization through the intellectual synthesis with which Evans dazzled readers.

Perhaps the most striking way to see how far Evans had traveled by the time he wrote *Esoteric Christianity* is to compare his final views of Christ and God to those in *The New Age and Its Messenger* from twenty-two years before. There, as already noted, he had inveighed against those who made "Christ a mere man, and God a *principle* and not a person," thoroughly horrified by "a refined materialism and atheism." Now, though, he had upended the Christ of biblical tradition by turning all humans into divine beings and finding the Christ within them. If the way to be saved was to "believe in the Lord Jesus Christ," Evans assured readers that "the Lord, and the Jesus, and the Christ, are all in man as the centre of his being."[70] Christ was not a *mere* man because all people were divine in nature—gods walking the earth. In his own way, Evans was careful. Each individual was "not God, but *a* god" and a "personal limitation of the Universal Spirit," yet still "possessed of all the attributes of its parent source," among them "omniscience and omnipotence."[71] Still, whether God or a god, Evans's human being represented a radical separation from the Swedenborgian *ur* text with which he had begun.

If humans were elevated by this Christology, Christ was surely leveled—not a mere man but still a lot like other people. Evans exalted the "inner I" and "the ever-identical Self." "This unchanging, undying, and identical self is my spirit," Evans affirmed. It was "that which Jesus calls in himself the *I am*, and it is that alone which can say of itself, I Am." And this, reiterated Evans, was in all of humankind. "Now it is evident that Jesus said this of himself as man, for he knew what was in man." For Evans, the human "inner unchanging *Ego*" was "the Christ within us, whose divine name [was] Ehejah, or I Am, that is the One and the Same." God came to "personal manifestation in the spirit of man."[72]

As with Christ, so with matter. Instead of "refined materialism and atheism," Evans upended matter as he told readers that "in its reality and inmost essence" it was "divine." Only when it took dominion over spirit did it become evil. But matter "in itself, and in its place" was *an invisible, divine, and immortal substance.*" It was "the correlative of spirit—a manifestation of spirit."[73] This matter was also different from what people called matter, which was "unreal and an illusion." Still, Evans's divinized matter was—well—matter. He had collapsed materialism and atheism in a kingdom of God that came "in us, and with saving power." Here "spirit and matter" were "no longer at war" but became "one *substance*," and the "phenomenal" was "absorbed into the real"—akin to the highly complex dualism and even "integrated monism" that Swedenborg taught.[74] Was this a realized panentheism? Was it a moral and mystical fusion that left the illusion of separateness behind in a commanding affirmation of unity? Was it, under its skin, actually pantheism?

Evans did not say, but his attempt to craft his spiritual vision—with threads hanging and rough edges showing—had moved him well beyond the Swedenborgian theology that pervaded his final journal years. He had even, at one point, matter-of-factly corrected his Swedish mentor, saying that Swedenborg had "improperly called perception" what Evans now knew as intuition.[75] And while he elsewhere cited Swedenborg, referring, for example, to his "grand science of correspondence,"[76] it was evident that Evans had vastly expanded his vision. Swedenborg's voice was one among many in a staggering array that brought Theosophy and even Western philosophy together with a reinscribed Christianity. Evans, it seemed, was bringing everything he had read and pondered into an encyclopedic attempt at grand synthesis.

That his last paragraph quoted "the leader of the Brahmo Somaj, or Church of God, in India" spoke volumes about how far he had come. The many-paths-to-heaven's-gate message could be read as Christian triumphalism or as its inverse—an erosion of Evans's earlier-affirmed Christian exceptionalism. "The Spirit-Christ spreads thus forth in the universe as an emanation from the Divine Reason, and you can see him with the eye of faith underlying all the endless varieties of truth and goodness in ancient and modern times. . . . Scattered in all men and women of the East and the

West are multitudinous Christ-principles and fragments of Christ-life, one vast and identical Sonship diversely manifested."[77]

VII

Evans would die three years later, his life as a seeker ended. More and more accounts have come to light to suggest, however, that he was not alone in his seeking. Given this observation, we may well ask what it was about Evans's life (and perhaps that of others like him) that constituted him *so radically* a seeker—a seeker who needed to reinvent spiritual connections endlessly and to keep leaving provisional pasts behind. What turned Evans into an eternal spiritual discontent, a journeyer who had to turn over one stone after another to see if any mystery remained? Why did he not mellow as he aged, bury his discomforts, and settle quietly into orthodoxy? We can never know for sure. We can, however, perhaps begin to answer by comparing him to another nineteenth-century seeker who yet managed to end his spiritual journey in tenuously orthodox ways and to remain within a traditional Christian fold.

This second seeker is Horace Bushnell, well-remembered New England liberal theologian and pastor of the mid-nineteenth century and a man who displayed remarkable similarities to Warren Felt Evans. With a life span from 1802 to 1876, Bushnell was fifteen years Evans's senior and died thirteen years earlier. Thus the two both lived into their early seventies, and they were roughly contemporaries. Bushnell—from a solid middle-class family with a stable domestic life—spent his childhood in rural northwestern Connecticut, not too far from Evans's rural Vermont. With a Methodist father and Episcopalian mother, Bushnell received an Episcopalian baptism because that denomination ran the only church in the village of Bantam, where the younger Bushnell was born. Later, in New Preston, Bushnell's parents joined the Congregational church with its lingering Calvinism, even as their farm and wool-carding business went through a period of economic uncertainty that affected their son as well. Traditional Calvinist views of a sinful humanity and the predestination of the elect must have resonated with the anxieties of the Bushnell household's everyday world with all its ups and downs.

After graduating from Yale College in 1827 and a series of false starts in teaching, journalism, and law, Horace Bushnell—already reared in Christian orthodoxy but distanced from much of it—experienced conversion. Significantly, though, it was only when his "heart" overrode his "head" at Yale that his personal religious turn brought him to the door of the Congregational church and to Yale Divinity School. Thereafter the New Haven West Association in 1832 licensed him to preach, and the following year the North Church in Hartford called him as pastor. He remained there until 1859 when ill health forced him to resign. So Bushnell's story was largely a tale of Connecticut Congregationalism.[78] Twice a Yale professional school graduate (law and divinity), he had found his spiritual home in the tradition to which his parents had introduced him. By contrast, Evans, as we know, never finished Dartmouth, left Congregationalism for Methodism, and continued his learning through a voracious reading habit. Perhaps here lay the beginnings of difference.

Still, both seemed to experience contentment and deep satisfaction in family life. Both men married happily and, with children, enjoyed solid domestic moorings as adults. And both also mourned the loss of children. If Evans lost Osmon when the child was not yet three, Bushnell had experienced the death of his infant daughter Lily in 1837. Later, in 1842, his only son died after developing, according to his surviving daughter Mary Bushnell Cheney, "alarming symptoms of brain-disease."[79]

Likewise, the intellectual and spiritual journeys of the two men led them in manifestly similar directions. Both came to theology from distinctly pastoral perspectives, and both made religious—and Christian—experience central to their concerns. Both likewise sparked controversy and endured ostracism from clerical colleagues in their respective denominations. Bushnell published his provocative *Discourses on Christian Nurture* in 1847, arguing for a gradualist and "organic" vision of Christianity with home and family at its center. In the era of the evangelical, with its revival-bound model of instant conversion, Bushnell's stance proved to be at odds with the regnant ideology. He did not help matters much when, in 1849, he published *God in Christ* with its "Preliminary Dissertation on the Nature of Language." Here he championed the metaphorical essence of all language, questioning the possibility of fixed and precise verbal formulae to express the fundamentally inexpressible. The book sparked what became in effect a heresy trial among various denominational associations within the Congregational fold. Bushnell was finally saved when, after significant sparring and squabbling among these associations, his own North Church ended matters in 1852 by withdrawing from any association to become independent.[80]

Like Evans, Bushnell provoked increasing dismay among the orthodox with his published views. Two years after *God in Christ*, as if matters had not become sufficiently controversial, Bushnell published still another book that raised eyebrows. *Christ in Theology* (1851) only underlined his metaphorical arguments about language in order to explain them.[81] Here one comment (which surely would have delighted the later Evans) invoked Hermes Trismegistus admiringly—an Egyptian "even twenty centuries before Christ" who "in the depths of nature, and apart from the aids of revelation" verified the intimate connection between heaven and earth.[82] The same year, when Bushnell began delivering the set of lectures at his North Church that later became his book *Nature and the Supernatural* (1858), major spiritualist theologian Andrew Jackson Davis attended the first lecture and was drawn to Bushnell's words. The topic gave Davis "much pleasure," and he applauded Bushnell, too, for approaching it "considerably unlike the method pursued by most clergymen." The Congregationalist minister used "*reason* or judgment" and addressed "the *corresponding* faculty in the mind of the hearer."[83]

Bushnell, in fact, was a man in the middle. He straddled the line between the stiff-upper-lip Anglo-Protestant orthodoxy of his day and a loose and diverse network of metaphysical seekers (among them, increasingly, Warren Felt Evans) with their alienation from conventional religion. Hermes Trismegistus and celebrations of nature signaled all the forbidden lands into which Evans was happily venturing by his later years. Meanwhile, Bushnell was no occasional visitor. Like Evans, he was deeply committed to Christianity even if, unlike Evans, he stayed loyal to his denomination. Yet Bushnell's preference for organicism and his declaration in favor of metaphor pointed to his analogical habit of thinking. The law of correspondence reigned in Bushnell's spiritual treasury, with heaven and earth understood as one fused and unified whole and clairvoyance and precognition alive and well. It is perhaps no accident that past Bushnell criticism has consistently read him as a mediating figure, albeit with views of mediation that never venture into metaphysical territory.[84]

Bushnell himself, however, talked the talk of metaphysicians and also, with his mystical inclinations, like Evans, he walked their walk. Congregationalist though Bushnell remained, he counted proto-metaphysical figures as dialogue partners and friends—men like Cyrus Bartol, Theodore Parker, and George Ripley, all associated with the Transcendentalist movement. He may even have known Emerson slightly.[85] Unlike Parker, who eschewed miracles, Bushnell's world lay open to the unexpected, counting miracles part of nature and available in everyday life. In his *Nature and the Supernatural*, Bushnell trumpeted the magical in ways that resonated with American metaphysics. In its inherent epistemology, magic existed as the mode of action that followed logically on the theory of correspondence. If everything in the world was related to some other/larger reality, then what was to stop the one from acting on the other? Bushnell implicitly demonstrated a high comfort level with the connection.

His book recounted exemplary miracles to testify to the "supernatural"—something outside the cause-effect chain in nature and "producing in the sphere of the senses, some event that moves our wonder, and evinces the presence of a more than human power." Curiously, an impressive number of his "miracles" targeted cases of clairvoyance—a faculty of intuitive discernment of which metaphysicians were fond because it enacted the doctrine of correspondence. We can, in fact, imagine Evans shaking his head in agreement as Bushnell told the story of Arthur Howell, a cleric who, encountering a funeral procession, knew without a doubt that the dead woman had been falsely accused of a crime. Howell recounted for mourners what the deceased woman had said to her minister before she died and stated categorically that soon her innocence would be manifest. Her minister, who was there, acknowledged what Howell declared, and later—as Howell had predicted—her character was cleared.[86]

Bushnell waxed with enthusiasm on "cases of definite premonition" that were "reported so familiarly and circumstantially, as to make a considerable item in the newspaper literature of our time." He affirmed "prophecies" that were "so often and particularly fulfilled, as to be the common wonder of the merely curious" and extolled "dreams" that often foreshadowed facts "in a manner so peculiar, as to forbid any supposition of accident under conditions of chance."[87] Evans would not have disagreed.

Still more, the two men had both experienced the uncanny through mystical experience. Evans's journals testify to his own unitive episodes in a resoundingly Christian context. Bushnell could theorize mysticism, as would Evans, and had also known it. By elevating oneself to "a steady contemplation of the spiritual," he affirmed, a person could feel himself "no longer a clod, but a particle of the divine nature"—not unlike Emerson's famous declaration about being "part or particle of God." Indeed, Bushnell, during his years at Yale, worn out with study one night had remained "wide awake" in his bed with his body "rising and floating in the air" for an hour or two. He could not touch the bed and started believing he had died and was voyaging "to the world of spirits."[88]

On another front, both Bushnell and Evans had been reading some of the same material and had been significantly affected by it. Like Evans, for a while Bushnell was attracted to French quietism. He attentively absorbed Archbishop Fénelon, and he came to know Madame Guyon through Thomas Upham's biography of her.[89] Evans would cite the same Upham biography in journal entries in June 1857 and likewise would cite Upham's *Life of Faith* (1852) in 1857 and again in 1862. Similarly, for both quietism was linked to experiential themes that leaned in a proto-holiness direction as both men turned toward a spirit-filled reading of the Christian life. We have already seen Evans's early embrace of Oberlin perfectionism and his later familiarity with themes that emanated from the work of Palmer and Boardman. During his Methodist years, it might be said, Evans was ever yearning for a "higher Christian life." Bushnell, in turn, left an unfinished manuscript on the Holy Spirit. His recent biographer Robert Bruce Mullin has argued that the Hartford pastor can be seen as both "a proto-liberal and a proto-Pentecostal."[90]

Bushnell's basic insight of the "analogy of being"—developed from the metaphorical views of language taught by his Yale professor Josiah Willard Gibbs, Sr.—resonated with Swedenborg's theory of correspondence that had so transformed Evans. Congregationalist Bushnell's declaration in his "Preliminary Dissertation on Language," the long discourse that stood at the head of *God in Christ*, did not directly appeal to Swedenborg. (Evans had himself been initially unwilling to acknowledge Swedenborg, as we recall.) But the Swedish seer's rippling effect, through Emerson and other literary sources, would not go away. There was, thought Bushnell, a "logos in the form of things," and the "outer world" functioned as a "vast dictionary and grammar of thought" and was likewise "itself an organ throughout of Intelligence." Within the world as we knew it, "God, the universal Author," could be found "EXPRESSED every where, so that, turn whichsoever way we please, we behold the outlooking of His intelligence." Since this was the case, "the whole universe of nature" was "a perfect analogon of the whole universe of thought and spirit."[91]

Still more, Bushnell was directly in touch with Swedenborg's theology, even if he was more measured and analytic regarding it than the converted Evans. In fact, Bushnell admitted to the portrait painter Frank (Francis) B. Carpenter—attracted to Swedenborg in later life—that the Swedenborgians professed to like his books very much. Moreover, Bushnell recalled that he had first been drawn to Swedenborg by hearing of his doctrine of correspondences. But, he continued, departing from Evans, "there was broader and better ground for this doctrine than was found in Swedenborg's statements or theories." When Carpenter confessed his inability to "place" Swedenborg, Bushnell responded by saying there were "but two ways" to regard him. "His claim to open knowledge of the spiritual world must either be admitted, or he must be placed by the side of other theological writers." Without hesitation, Bushnell opted for the second choice—and he also made it clear that he did not enjoy reading Swedenborg. He owned many of Swedenborg's works, but—again unlike Evans—found their style so cumbersome, repetitious, and dry that, according to Carpenter, "he could hardly have patience to read." There was "nothing aggressive" about Swedenborgianism, Bushnell thought, and so "it could never be preached successfully."[92]

Despite the line in the sand that Bushnell, so differently from Evans, had drawn between himself and Swedenborg, the similarities with Swedenborg remained. Just as Bushnell had remarked, too, Swedenborgians continued to notice. Tellingly, for example, Benjamin Fiske Barrett—who would be called in his Bowdoin College obituary "head of the progressive wing of the Swedenborgian church and perhaps the most eminent clergyman of this denomination in the country"—wrote at length on Bushnell. In his apologetic *Cloud of Independent Witnesses* (1891), the prolific Barrett argued for the Swedenborgianism of a series of prominent ministers, and he ranked Bushnell among the chosen. "It is not generally known that Dr. Bushnell was a reader of Swedenborg's writings," explained Barrett, since in all his work Bushnell mentioned Swedenborg only once. "But," Barrett went on, "his writings furnish ample evidence not only of his familiarity with, but of his cordial acceptance of, all the principal doctrines of the New Church as revealed through Swedenborg." Barrett followed assiduously with the details of his claim, quoting copiously from Bushnell's writings.[93] In *tour de force* fashion, he overlooked the rich and multiple sources of Bushnell's ideas, but the effect of citing doctrine after doctrine in basic agreement with Swedenborg cannot be gainsaid.

With "the whole universe of nature" an analogy of "the whole universe of thought and spirit," like Evans, Bushnell did not stop with theory. Ideas such as these found experiential ground in his delight in the natural world. As Evans's journals demonstrated for him, Bushnell found the footprints of divinity in nature. He experienced, on occasion, extraordinary illumination and a sense of the presence and power of God. On one trip to Mount Washington, New Hampshire, in 1835, for example, he wrote home to his wife, Mary, about "every step" opening upon "something glorious." "Surely I see God as I never did before." On another journey, to Niagara Falls in 1853, he pondered the water rushing down as "this tremendous type of God's eternity and majesty." His "soul revelled" as never since he was "a conscious being." Formerly closed into "concentric shells of brass or iron," now he had begun to "break through one shell after another, bursting every time into a kind of new, and wondrous and vastly enlarged heaven." (In a striking coincidence, Evans's journals contain a pasted-in newsprint article that he wrote extolling the wonder of the Falls and the sense of the divine they inspired in him.) And six years before he died Bushnell wrote to Mary in 1870 from Lake Waramaug, Connecticut, in a state of profound exhilaration. "O my God! What a fact to possess and know that he is! . . . I never thought I could possess God so completely."[94]

For both Bushnell and Evans, too, such experiences of exaltation and connection with deep spiritual moorings were juxtaposed with continuing physical weakness and ill health. Evans's chronic suffering had kept him out of the pulpit time after time or led him barely to drag himself into it, as we have seen. Bushnell had his own private plague—"throat trouble" that continually assailed him, preventing him sometimes from preaching, and eventually forcing his resignation from the Hartford church. He died of consumption. Like Evans, however, Bushnell pursued the spiritual path of his choosing whatever his physical complaints, and he used the spiritual as an implicit ally in overcoming sickness. And like the route that Evans took, Bushnell's path skirted what some chose to call pantheism.

Because humans possessed a supernatural inheritance, as Bushnell's *Nature and the Supernatural* testified, they could operate out of the realm of what he called "Powers." Different from nature's stock trade in "Things" as part of the world of cause and effect, Powers could change Things, altering and re-creating them. All the things that humans could do—like building houses or writing books or establishing constitutions—were the result of their participation in the supernatural, the world of the Powers. Such participation meant that humans could join with God in divine eruptions into nature—in what Bushnell termed the miraculous, as we have already seen. As David Smith observed, "every person" constituted in Bushnell's view "a miniature neo-Platonic God." Or, in Christian terms, awakening to one's "normative being through the influence of Christ" transformed one incrementally into "a vehicle of divine life for others." And as William Johnson pointedly noticed, nature and the supernatural did not exist as "two realms worlds apart." Rather, they came together as "co-factors in the one system of God," with both of them "functions of the divine."[95]

Yet, unlike Evans, Bushnell refused to see the implications of his own theology—preferring instead to hurl denials at pantheism and pantheists even as he affirmed his "one system of God." Evans, as we know, was far more comfortable venturing into theological forbidden land as the years passed, leaving it to Mary Baker Eddy and her followers to throw missiles along with his former Methodist colleagues. So at this point we have a parting of the ways, a stance of denial for Bushnell and of affirmation for Evans. We are at the crux of the matter, at the heart of what made the two men—so very much alike—also so profoundly different. How explain what happened on these separate life journeys? Can we make sense of the divergent paths the two ultimately took by invoking genes and DNA? Can we attribute the disparity to uncertain and murky factors in antebellum as over against postbellum America? Can we find some emotional upheaval in one or both men to chisel away at their difference? Why was one man a seeker who stayed home and the other a *radical* seeker who kept on leaving?

VIII

Whatever the potential for explanation in some of these questions, one social factor stands out as a major *dis*similarity in the professional life of each man. Despite his ill health and his travels, Bushnell remained (literally) firmly attached to one congregation—his North Church in Hartford. He stayed Congregational *and* wearing the mantle of a particular pastorate in a particular place. By contrast, Evans, as a committed Methodist, "rode" small-town circuits, moving from place to place, as his bishop instructed, every few years. By definition, the Methodist system did not allow a pastor to put down deep or permanent roots anywhere. As a minister, Evans was a sojourner in each small town, ready to move on as commanded. His second manuscript journal is instructive in providing a telescoped summary of some his relocations at its start.

In 1840, when he married Charlotte Tinker, Evans was appointed to Peacham, Vermont, where he remained a year. In 1844, the year he was ordained deacon, he was stationed at Goffstown, New Hampshire, again for a single year, and after that, it was Pembroke, New Hampshire, for two years. By 1847, when Evans was ordained an elder, he was stationed at Rindge, New Hampshire, for a year—followed by two years in Marlow, once more in New Hampshire. Then, in 1850, he was appointed to another New Hampshire town and pastored the church in Newport for two years. Thereafter, Evans's second manuscript journal lists the small towns to which he was appointed and gives some sense of his emotional response to each move. It must have been a grueling experience time after time to leave familiar scenes and friendships, and protective defenses must have gone up willy-nilly to shelter him from loss. It is likely that part of the defense system would have been a cultivated detachment from new people and situations—a willingness to let them in just so far and no more. And if Evans might have learned to be wary of getting too close to people and places, his search for intimacy would lead within.

The peripatetic style that organized his physical and social life was something he originally loved. Recall his initial attraction to Methodism because his "youthful heart" was drawn to the "roving life." Indeed, the other side of the itinerant story is that the roaming that drew him must have supplied—or resonated with—a mental template. Here was a grid that could be filled in not merely in outer terms but also in the life of the mind. Thus, Evans could internalize external circumstance in ways that made intellectual and spiritual change seem normal and movement from one internal spiritual station to another a continuing part of the inner life. In short, Methodism contributed to seeker culture for Evans not only by gifting him with a theology of perfection but also by institutionalizing a life of movement that made it usual and expected. Methodism also nudged the mover toward finding within the roots that could not grow deep in the outer world because of the constant movement. It likewise corroborated for him any presentiments he already had toward following in this inner direction.

Still other forces were at work in Evans's world that contributed to seeker culture in general and, increasingly, made it more likely that even seekers who stayed home would become, like Evans, *radical* seekers who ventured into new territory. For one, as R. Laurence Moore has argued, science and secularization were the twin realities that challenged orthodox religion. Even if—as Moore has suggested—the hold of both on the popular imagination has been exaggerated, Americans were living in the afterlight of the years that Fred Somkin once called the time of the "unquiet eagle."[96] They were experiencing the off-key ambiance of a new world coming and an old one dying, while the sectarian spirit seemed to rise to ever greater heights and a pervasive unease spread. After the early industrial revolution of the 1830s and 1840s, new forms of technology had opened expansive vistas in both practical and imagistic ways. Still further, in the age of progress, Americans lived in motion, propelling themselves from place to place, buying cheap land, and forging new lives that promised blessing but also uprooted them from traditional moorings. After the Civil War, as a forcefully united nation shuddered through lingering trauma, the emotional disquiet of the antebellum years only escalated. Now, in the time that, in a novel, Mark Twain and Charles Dudley Warner named the "gilded age," historian Paul A. Carter could see an era of spiritual crisis.[97]

It is, of course, difficult to suggest straight-line connections between new forms of knowledge and the expansion of seeker culture. But there are large questions about possible relationships. What did spreading knowledge of Darwinian evolution have to do with the growing number of seekers? And what about the burgeoning challenge for orthodoxy of biblical criticism emanating from Germany and elsewhere? What did the growth of professional disciplines in history, anthropology, and comparative religions have to do with the erosion of traditional faiths? How much, really, did the increasing availability of Asian texts and their messages impact a generation of spiritual seekers?

Beyond that, outside the world of the mind and the production of texts, what about new social realities and their ways of ruffling established patterns? How much did the waves of immigrants pouring into the late-century United States create a climate that relativized old mores and mindsets? How did the phenomenon of urbanization and the percolation of its arrangements and ideas into small-town America change things? How much did an (already noted) ever-increasing social mobility add to the equation? Did the moves out of small towns and, especially, into cities upset traditional orthodoxies? Did a new secular peripatetic style—as populations moved more and more to follow job opportunities or assignments—make the Methodist itinerant style seem a prediction of the future? Did increasing industrialization and the practical technologies that arose—like the telephone and the incandescent lamp—have repercussions that would move beyond the practical? Did new medical discoveries and healing modalities alter the way people saw religion? What about the spread of popular psychology that, as Donald Meyer would have it, reconstituted the religion of seekers? What about the business model that he also identified—the gift of corporate America to a new set of spiritual leaders?[98]

We will never fully know the answers to these questions. But the collective changes in the second half of what Gilbert Seldes once called the "stammering century" had to make their mark on what people perceived and felt and what they did about it.[99] Even if much of the intellectual upheaval of the times affected elites more than nonelites, change was in the air, and rumor swirled in the nuances of language even in the newspapers and in the commonplace cultural mores and habits that were quietly eroding older ways of being. Many—if not most—dug in and insulated themselves by immersion in received tradition or reinvented tradition, with changes softened into near-invisibility. Bushnell surely fits in here. On the other side of the aisle, the birth of fundamentalism also was not that far ahead of this era. Some, however, and not a few, pursued ever-evolving quests to new inner places for spiritual solace and security in changing times. Warren Felt Evans was among them. Much more than many others, Evans—like Bushnell—was a thorough intellectual. Beyond that, Evans's Methodist peripatetic lifestyle only underlined the spiritual climate of search he must have experienced. Both as a major leader of the emerging New Thought movement and as a singular representative of a growing spiritual style, he left journal materials that shed important light on his culture and his times. The light they shed on the past gives perspective, too, on our own religious culture in the twenty-first century. In fact, Evans's unease and that of others in his era might be described as something of an inauguration for what would become for many in our time spirituality-as-usual. Untold numbers among those whom sociologists have labeled the Nones (denying affiliation with any religious tradition or denomination) belong to Warren Felt Evans's tribe. They are "spiritual" but not "religious."[100] In reading his story, we get evocative clues to our own.

A Note to Readers

AS EDITOR, I discovered that even in the ordered and relatively intelligible Victorian longhand of Evans's journals, numerous issues concerning transcription arose. Accordingly, I made a series of editorial decisions to regularize presentation of material and simplify reading.

First, Evans's spacing in the journals is erratic. He left more space between journal entries sometimes than other times, and occasionally he left entire pages blank. Instead of preserving these differences, I have regularized spacing. When his blank spaces signaled a lapse of many months (or, in at least one case, about three years), I have placed a content note to alert the reader. When he did not indicate a long time lapse with a blank space, I have also alerted the reader. Furthermore, I have omitted blank lines within individual journal entries, even when the blank indicated a change of theme. The presence of a new paragraph itself points to an obvious shift in focus. Moreover, for reading convenience, date entries have been printed in boldface. Underlining, when it occurs in the text, is Evans's own.

On another front, Evans sometimes introduced new paragraphs flush to his left margin, sometimes indented them, and sometimes inserted the first word of a new paragraph ambiguously between the left margin and a normal indentation. I have regularized all paragraphs with standard indentations. In some cases, Evans also made long marginal notes. I have used his asterisk or caret to indicate these. However, I have introduced a new paragraph to signal the end of the interpolation. Evans often quoted poetry as well, and such quotations have likewise been regularized. And I have italicized the titles of the books he cited (either in full or in a brief working title), whereas Evans himself simply capitalized the first letter of most words in the title.

It was sometimes a judgment call whether an ink mark on a page was a punctuation mark or simply Evans resting his pen. If the mark made some sort of sense I kept it; if not, I ignored it. Likewise, it was sometimes difficult to tell a comma from a period. If the grammatical structure required one or the other, I used the appropriate mark. Where Evans used two different punctuation marks serially in a way that seemed not intelligible, I omitted the second one, as, for instance, in the case of a semicolon followed by a colon. I have also regularized the placement of punctuation marks in certain situations. For example, Evans would habitually write a date—as in, say, "Oct. 18.th"—with a period placed before the "th" or a period placed directly under the "th." I have adopted standard punctuation and placement practice in such instances but have retained many of his sometimes erratic date punctuation practices. Meanwhile, I have regularized Evans's punctuation placement for a period or comma in relation to a quotation mark or an end parenthesis, so that the placement of the period or comma comes before the quotation mark or end parenthesis when so required. Similarly, I have regularized quotation marks within quotation marks, so that they appear as single rather than double marks in conformity with standard usage. And I have regularized quotation marks in general, so that double quotation marks are used when Evans uses quotation marks for material taken from literary sources. However, when Evans omits all quotation marks in citing a source, I have let his usage stand, except when clear identification of material as a quotation demanded punctuation marks. Likewise when he clearly ends a sentence with a comma, I have maintained the comma splice without introducing an awkward "sic."

In the content of the journals themselves, Evans usually—but not always—employed characteristic nineteenth-century spellings; words like "developement," "fulness," and the traditional abbreviation "Jno." for the Gospel of John come immediately to mind. I have kept Evans's usages in these and other instances without comment. Again, Evans frequently employed parentheses in the journals, as if bracketing out material for future use in writing projects. The practice seems to be a product of his habit of rereading journal entries. To complicate matters still more, he many times employed a beginning parenthesis without its partner or an end parenthesis in the same way. I have not tried to second-guess him about where the missing parenthesis might be placed but have let the irregular usage stand. In the matter of quotation marks, where a missing quotation mark was obvious, I placed it in square brackets; where it was not obvious, I have again not tried to second-guess him.

I have also tried not to trouble the reader with the excessive use of "sic" to indicate Evans's writing errors and misspelled words. Where not overly intrusive, in some instances I have used brackets—[ ]—to add a missing word or missing letters to a word or to supply a corrected word or missing punctuation. Where Evans himself crossed out a word, I have indicated that by placing the word in braces—{ }—*before* the word he settled on. However, when he corrected an error, I have eliminated the error without notice. When Evans inadvertently repeated a word or phrase—such as "the the" or "in preaching in preaching"—I have let it stand. On occasions when the grammar was problematic, I have supplied a note to suggest the best construction.

Journal I (1850–1857)

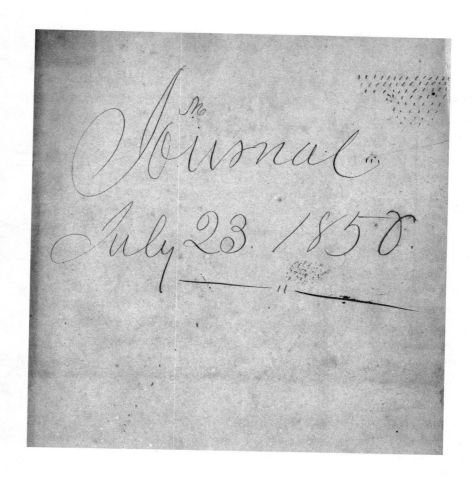

Ms Journal
July 23. 1850.

July 23, 1850. Newport N.H. At our Conference in May, held in New Market, I was appointed to this place. I am the first Methodist preacher ever stationed in Newport village. Some {fifty}[1] 25 or 30 persons, members of the Congregational Church, withdrew their support for their preacher, and subscribed for Methodist preaching, and sent to Conference for a preacher. This secession originated in a difficulty among the singers, some three years since. It was taken up by the Church, and resulted in this rupture. I hope God will make the wrath of man to praise him. A Methodist Church is much needed in the place. Many souls will go down to hell, who might have been saved, unless there is one. We have hired the use of the Universalist Chapel. Our congregation has been large & respectable, numbering thus far, about three hundred souls. I should rather have begun on a smaller scale, for I do not suppose that I, or an angel from heaven, can succeed in holding all these people. In the name of God I go against this host. Wilt Thou, O Lord, deliver them into my hand? Our Sabbath school numbers about one hundred teachers & scholars. Some two or three persons have been converted as the result of our meetings. I have felt at times a burden upon my soul sufficient for an angel to bear. It has seemed as if God would tear me in pieces. But I can say in the language of King Asa, "It is nothing for thee to help, whether with few or many. Help us O Ld, for we rest on thee."[2] Amid all my trials of mind my health has been poor. But God has enabled me to visit much fr house to house. I have called upon about one hundred families. May there be from this some ripe fruit.

July 24. Last evening we had a class meeting at our house, and one person who has been converted since I came here, joined the class. May she be faithful unto death. This morning I visited three families. Had some peace and comfort in laboring for Christ. May I not live in vain. I am still oppressed with dejection of spirit. May God help me to conquor this state of mind. I have often prayed since I came here that God would adapt me to the work he has for me to do in this place. I have recently read a work entitled "Methodism in Earnest" which gives an account of the labors of Rev. Mr Caughey in Great Britain, which resulted in the conversion of 20,000 souls.[3] I have been much pained with my own want of success. It often seems to me that I labor in vain; but I hope to live in my influence after I am dead. It has sometimes appeared to me that I shall soon finish my course unless I am better. After my work is done I do not wish to stay. My hope of heaven is bright and strong.

"Hope like the glimmering taper's light,
    Adorns and cheers the way,
And still as darker grows the night.
    Emits a brighter ray."   Goldsmith.[4]

July 26. (Have just returned from visiting a mountain which stands some two or three miles N. West of my residence. It is said that God loves the mountains. True it is, that some of the most remarkable events recorded in the Bible, took place on their summits. I have always since my childhood loved to wander in the solitudes of mountains. I have delighted to pray on their lofty tops. There is scarcely a mountain or high hill in Eastern Vermont or the South-Western part of N. Hampshire, upon which I have not given myself to God in an everlasting covenant. They stand and raise their venerable forms, in the blue heavens, as monuments of my consecration to Christ. This afternoon I found near a large oak tree, a flat stone, laid upon another stone. It was laid there by the hand of God as an altar. Upon this I prostrated myself after taking off my shoes, rendered thanks to God for his good Providence, which has watched over me all my days; and upon that rude altar I gave myself anew to Christ. I called earnestly upon God who gave the law to Moses on Sinai, & who vindicated his own character upon Mt Carmel, by sending down fire upon the sacrafice of his servant Elijah, to invest me with power from on high, and to give me a deep & lasting influence over the minds of men. It was good to be there. I was in the mount with God. Returning home I felt my heart burn within me. My spiritual strength has been renewed.)[5] (In the West from where I stood, Ascutney is seen, on whose top fifteen yrs ago, all alone I knelt and prayed.[6] In the dim distance behind this were seen the Green Mts of my native state.[7] They are the home of freedom. I felt like repeating to them the address of Tell to the mts of Switzerland.[8] In the East stood old Kearsarge, a giant among pigmies.[9] To the North I caught a glimpse of the White Mts. All these I take to be witnesses of my consecration to Christ. It is also written in God's book of remembrance. May my covenant never be forgotten. O how I pant to be a burning and shining light. On all the hills around my fathers house I have prayed for this. This has been the burden of my prayer upon every eminence around Chester Academy, or Dartmouth College. May those prayers be answered while I live or after I am dead.)

In the evening we had a prayer meeting at our house. One soul was converted to God.

July 28th. Had some freedom in preaching. In the morning I preached on the Temptation of Abraham. In the afternoon I used Mat 12:41.[10] The preaching of Jonah and its effects upon the Ninevites: In the evening I preach in a schoolhouse on Isa 5:4. and showed that God had done all he could do to save men.[11] We had a solemn time. I hope impressions have been made on some hearts as lasting as eternity. I enjoy myself much in the Sabbath School. It is an important institution. For the last three yrs about 21,000 have been converted in the Sabbath Schools of the M.E. Church. This is a great religious fact. There are in England 250,000 S.S. teachers and 2,000,000 of scholars. In the U. States, 500,000 teachers, & 3,000,000 of scholars, making in both countries 750,000 teachers & 5,000,000 of scholars. Let these scholars take hold of hands and stand three feet apart, they would reach 2840 miles. From Boston to Liverpool via Halifax is 2550 miles. These children might connect the two countries by a Sunday School telegraph.

Aug 5. 1850. Last Sabbath was our Quarterly meeting. We had an interesting day. In the morning I baptized a man by immersion. On Saturday evening we had had a good prayer meeting at our house. Two persons rose for prayers. God has been good to me. I have had some communion with God. (I wish to "rise to all the life of God." (I have made during the quarter 140 pastoral visits. May God water the seed sown.)

Aug {6} 8. Today bought me a horse, for which I pay seventy five dollars. I have much needed a horse & carriage. I have been under the necessity of walking in all my pastoral visiting. This had made me much hard work.

Aug {8} 6. This evening had a class-meeting at our house. One young lady was converted to God. May she be kept by the power of God <u>through faith</u> <u>unto</u> eternal salvation. She was deeply affected on account of her sins.

Aug 11. Had much liberty in preaching today. In the morning I preached on Phil. 3:13, 14.[12] (In the afternoon an Episcopalian minister, Rev. Mr Presby, from Mississippi, whose father is a member of my congregation, preached for me from these words: "These things I command you that ye love one another." It was a good sermon, practical and evangelical. I afterwards learned that he was a slaveholder. Had I known it before I would not have admitted him to my pulpit. May God have mercy on him, and help him so to love his slaves as to deal justly with them, & make them free.)

Aug 13. It is the evening of our class meeting, but being a very stormy time no one has come in. May God carry on his own work. I have not enjoyed that sweet peace of mind, which I sometime have, but Christ is all my hope & trust. I have lately read an account of the life of Swartz.[13] The secret of his eminent usefulness in the cause of Christ, is, he was wholly consecrated to God, by a pious mother. Few men have ever labored more for Christ or will receive a brighter crown.

Sep 2. 1850. Since I have written in my Journal, I have visited at my father's in Rockingham. Found it pleasant once more to visit my native place. I returned Aug 31t, the [day] on which Prof. Webster was hung.[14] Thought of him much on the way, especially when the time set for his execution arrived. He was hung for the murder of Dr Parkman of Boston. Yesterday I had a very good day in preaching. Since our Quarterly meeting, two souls have been converted. May the Lord carry on his work. Have had some seasons of peace in believing. My trust and hope are all in Christ. On the 23d of Aug nine men, heads of families, joined the M.E. Church, from the Congregational Church. They seem to be good men & real Christians. As they could receive no letter from their Church were under the necessity of receiving them without. They were received in full connection.

July 19th 1851.[15] It has pleased God in his good Providence to return me to this station. The last year was a year of prosperity, and I hope of usefulness. I trust I have not lived in vain. I returned to Conference fifty six members. I have seen the salvation of God during the present year. One Saturday evening I earnestly besought God to give me fruit on the following

Sabbath. In answer to prayer one soul was converted & others awakened. I do pray God that I may see more fruit this year than last.

I have just recovered from a short but severe sickness. I was attacked with an erysipelas in my right foot.[16] At one time it suddenly affected my whole system. It occured to me at first that I was dying[.] I felt myself sinking. It seemed very much like death. But this passage was suggested to my mind while I was committing my spirit to Christ, "I was brought low & he helped me."[17] Last Sabbath I was confined to my house. It is the first Sabbath I ever lost from ill health, though I have often preached when I was sick. Through the mercy of God I still live. May I live to his glory. Tomorrow I hope to preach. May Christ stand by me.

July 20. Today attended meeting at the Baptist Church. Was not able to preach. May God give me strength once more to cry "behold the Lamb."[18] I love to preach Christ & the cross. It is hard work for me to hold my peace. May it please the Lord to give me more than my former strength. I will spend it in his employ. I have been greatly afflicted with a want of sleep. I not slept only about three hours in twenty four for a week. Sleep is the gift of God. "He giveth his beloved sleep."[19] It is a choice gift, equally valuable with our daily bread. I have read not long since of a man in China who was condemned by the government to suffer death by being kept from sleep. After some days, he entreated of his guards to put him to death. He lived in great agony eighteen days.[20] I would as lief go without food as sleep. Wesley[21] had the power of putting himself to sleep any time. It seems to have been under the control of his will. He gave his beloved sleep. If God would give me that power, I would value it more than a monarch's crown. Will he not give it me? Lord help. Great Redeemer, is it not the purchase of thy blood. I cast myself upon they mercy. Disappoint not my trust. Fail me not, in my time of need.

Sept 26. 1852.[22] It has pleased God to call me to labor this year in Concord.[23] I have been here about three months. It is a hard field. There are backsliders and lukewarm professors enough to curse a whole nation. I have preached with great weakness. I have carried into the pulpit a load of bodily infirmities, enough to cause me to sink in any other work. Sometimes Christ has stood by me, and the rush of the divine energy into my soul has raised me above all my weakness. The last two years have been the most useful of my life. I have often prayed that this year I might be more useful still. O Lord come to my help. Stir up thy power & come and save me. Make me adequate to this great work.

Feb 13. 1853.[24] Today is our last Quarterly Meeting for the year. In three months, the Conference year will end. I have most earnestly prayed that my ministry might this year be more useful than any previous year. Yet I have seen but little fruit of my labors. I know not that a single soul has been converted to God through my labors, in this place. I would not spend my strength for nought. I have preached as plain & pointed as I ever did. I have not attempted to preach for the sole edification of the Professors of the Biblical Institute, nor the students, nor of Bishop Baker, who has been one of my hearers most of the time.[25] I have been saved most of the time from the least embarrassment in consequence of their presence.

Yet to day God has humbled me. He laid me in the depth. All my bones are broken. I have suffered more mental distress than I ever did before in so short a time. I have been embarassed in every thing I have done. I could not read a notice without my flesh quivering with fear. In passing the sacramental elements I could hardly utter a word. In making the last prayer, I could not proceed, and soon finished. It was a time of greater horror, than any person, as it seems to me, ever suffered out of hell. Such feelings are unworthy the ministerial office, and make me ashamed of my self. More fierce temptations have assailed my soul than I ever met before. I have felt terribly angry with myself. Profane thoughts have wanted to find a lodgement, in my heart. I have been dreadfully shaken. But my God will deliver me. It ill becomes an ambassador of God to tremble like dry a [a dry] leaf in the wind. God called me to the ministry for some nobler purpose than to quail before the face of clay. I have felt at times that my mind was not in the ascendancy—that it was not dominant, but was crushed beneath the weight of mind in my presence. I hope I am not always to feel that I am imprisoned beneath such a mountain. God will give me strength to upheave the mass that is piled upon my soul, and to trample it under my feet. I pray God to give me nerves of iron, and a tongue that shall be a sharp sword to the enemies of the cross. Instead of being as weak as a sick girl, whose nerves are thrown into a tremor by the rustling of a leaf, I want such a mental power, and such a dauntless valor, that I can look {the devil} Satan in the eye, and cause him to turn pale, and fly tremblingly back to hell for very teror. God give me power from on high. This day will be a crisis with me. I have felt that my fears and embarassment are to end forever. O my God bring me not again to so fiery a trial, lest I fall. Break not the bruised reed. Give me a gigantic vigor of mind that shall hold my hearers in chains, and draw them to the cross of Christ. Infuse a part of thine own creative energy into my soul. Prop up my will with thine own omnipotence.

God has most powerfully revived his work in Newport, my former station. Up to this time 137 have joined the Methodist Church, 60 the Baptist, and more than fifty the Congregationalist. It is a great work. I have greatly rejoiced at the glad tidings. O that I could see such a work in this place.

March 10. 1853. I have enjoyed deep and sweet communion with God since I last wrote in my journal. I have resolved to be holy, to present to God my whole being as a living sacrafice holy & acceptable to God. It is now spring. May my soul be renewed.
"And see where surly Winter passes off,
Far to the North, and calls his ruffian blasts;
His blasts obey, and quit the howling hill,
The shattered forest, and the ravaged vale;
While softer gales succeed, at whose kind touch,
Dissolving snows in livid torrents lost,
The mountains lift their green heads to the sky.["]26

May 22. 1853—   **Concord N.H.**
On the 11th of this month our Conference commenced its session at Newport. We had a very pleasant session. It has pleased Providence to return me to Concord. I hope my labors may tell upon the extension of the kingdom of Christ. The day after my return, I was siezed with a very violent attack of fever, but immediately sent for a physician, and succeeded in throwing it off. It has left me very weak, so much so: that I did not deem it advisable to attend Church. I am at home, and enjoy sweet communion with God. Jesus is my all; heaven is my home. I hope that during the coming year, I may grow in grace, and become more assimilated to the image

of Christ. I hope to have more to do with Christ, than I have had the last year. Unless each successive year shall leave me better, more heavenly-minded, more Christ-like I am not fully answering the end of life. I pray that my life may not prove a failure. I do hope, through Christ, at length to reach the goal and be crowned. I long more than ever to be useful as a minister; but if I do not <u>see</u> the fruit of my labor, I may see that the cross of Christ is exerting its saving energy upon my own soul. I may realize that I am steadily growing in piety. O for a heart that beats in unison with God, a soul in sympathy with the world's Redeemer—

May 24. I have enjoyed this day some peace & sweet communion with God. I found it good to draw near to him in my closet. I have had ardent desires to be eminently pious. How sweet it is to feel a conscious union with Christ. May the blessing of the Father, Son, and Holy Spirit be upon me. I would commit the keeping of my soul To Christ.

May 25. Am exceedingly weak in body; not able to walk about in visiting from house to house. I trust the inner man may be renewed day by day. Have had during the day some gleams of peace. May the Lord restore me again to health, that I may be strong to labor for him—

May 26. Spent the day mostly in preparing the Minutes of Conference for the press. I published them last year. There is more labor this year than last in preparing the manuscript. The names of all contributors to the Missionary Cause from fifty cents and upwards are published, according to the Discipline—

(In the evening enjoyed a sweet season in reading the word of God. It is sweet to my taste. There is no reading which so improves the heart as the reading of the Bible. Other books may teach a man what he does not know, but this makes him wise unto salvation.)

May 29. This has been a day of great peace. It was our first Quarterly Meeting for the year. In the morning we held a love feast.[27] The presence of God was manifest. A converted Jew, who had come to study in the Biblical Institute, spake and acknowledged Jesus as the Messiah, & only Savior of sinners. It is interesting to hear one of the sons of Abraham acknowledge

God, and Jesus Christ whom he hath sent— In the forenoon I preached from the words, "My meat is to do the will of him that sent me and to finish his work."[28] I wish to record to the glory of God, that I was divinely assisted, I was was weak in body, but felt strong in God. It has been to me a day to be remembered.

May 31. Went to the west part of the town to visit a woman, not expected to live. Conversed and prayed with her. Visited a{nother} dying man also, found him humble & aparently truly penitent. Visited in all eight families. Enjoyed much peace. Had rest in the cross of Christ.

June 1. To day the legislature commenced its session. At ten o clock I heard a class at the Institute in Ecclesiastical History, Dr Dempster has gone to attend the Black River Conference.[29] Expect to hear the class for several days. Enjoy myself much in the exercise. History has been with me for many years a favorite study. I find Christ in it. It is full of Christ.

June 2. A great gathering in Concord; for what purpose few could tell. Took a seat in the Legislature, and heard the Governor, Dr Noah {H.} Martin read his annual message—a very sensible state paper, with the exception of first part, which was a glorification of New Hampshire.

June 3. Today heard my class in the Biblical Institute. In the evening visited two families. Enjoyed much peace & communion with God. Had a conscious & vital union with Christ.

Saturday June 3. Heard my class in the Biblical Institute— God is good to me today. (About sixteen years ago I was converted to God in Rockingham Vt.) I connected myself with the Congregational Church of the place, a Church for which I have always retained a strong affection. I afterwards left that denomination & connected myself with the Methodist Church; not so much on doctrinal grounds, as from a love for the itinerant ministry. My youthful heart admired that roving life. I have found in myself for a few years past a growing dissatisfaction with some features of Methodism. The piety of Methodists is not so uniform, as I wish it was. There are exceptions to this, but this is characteristic of the denomination. They have but little ear for sound instructive preaching. But what I most dislike is their outrageous financial system, or rather want of system. (The last year I have not received enough to bear the expenses of my family. Before Conference I was promised my whole claim, $475, and so reported my claims paid. But there will be a deficiency of fifty dollars or more. A few more things like this would serve to wean me from Methodism, and cause me to seek a field of usefulness in some other denomination.) Should I ever leave the Methodist Church, I should go back to the Congregational from which I came. I pray God to guide me by his unerring Providence. My great desire is that I may not live in vain; that I may leave my mark upon the world. May God be with me and direct me. Jesus, who has called me to the work of the ministry, has promised to be with me always. I hope to live in communion with him through life, and then obtain through grace an immortal crown.)

June 4. Sabbath. I have preached three times to-day—enjoyed great peace. Have been conscious of divine help. In the morning I especially enjoyed myself in preaching from 2 Cor 4:10. Always bearing about in the body the dying of the Lord Jesus that the life also of Jesus might be made manifest in our body— After showing in what sense the Christian exhibits the dying of Christ, (I showed that it was the design of the Gospel to reproduce the life which Christ lived in the life of the believer—)

June 5. Was very solemnly affected by hearing of the death of Ira S. Watkins[.] He graduated from the Biblical Institute last November. He had entered Union College.[30] He was drowned in the Mohawk,[31] together with another young man. The boat was upset by a sudden squall of wind. I had been intimately acquainted with him from his youth. He was a young man who was sincerely pious, and was qualified to fill a certain sphere of usefulness. He was at the time of his death engaged in preaching on Sabbath afternoons to the boatmen on the Canal, a work for which he was well fitted. It is a mysterious Providence which has removed him. But he has gone. "Friend after friend departs."[32] They have fallen around me "like leaves in wintry weather."[33] Peace to his memory. Long will he live in my heart. He has finished his course. He has reached the goal & is crowned. I shall see him again.

June 11ᵗʰ. Another week has gone. Its successive hours have fled, and I am one week farther onward in the voyage of life. I am not entirely satisfied with the labors of the past week. I have not visited enough. My forenoon has been occupied at the Institute mostly, and has taken up much time that I should have devoted to my pastoral work. I need every moment the merits of Christ's death. On that death do I rely. Christ is all. He is my refuge from the curse of a broken law.

The past week has been one of much religious enjoyment. It has been marked by providential and gracious blessings, for which I am grateful. May another week if I shall see it be more usefully spent. May it be more pleasing to God and more satisfactory to myself.

June 12. Have been divinely assisted to preach. In the forenoon I preached from John 15:5.[34] On the union of Christ and believers. In the P.M. on the omnipresence of God. In the evening I preached again in the west part of the town. It has been a good day.

June 13. Feel, the effects of the last Sabbath's labor.

June 15, 1853.
X15.[35] (This evening married my wife's sister, to Mr Alfred Brigham, who graduated at the Biblical Institute last November.)

[June] 17. Visited a few families, in the forenoon. I have devoted some leisure moments to the reading of Knapp's Christian Theology.[36] It is the best work I have ever seen on theology. It has been my practice (for some time past on procuring a new work, before commencing to read it, to kneel before the Lord with it, and pray that its perusal may be sanctified to my intellectual growth and spiritual progress. All knowledge I consecrate to the service of God, and hallow by the cross of Christ. May God make me a workman that needeth not to be ashamed— a successful minister of the New Testament.)

[June] 18. Visited during the week sixteen families. May some fruit attend my labors.

[June] 19. Sabbath. In the morning I preached on John 13:7.[37] My subject was: The future will explain the mysteries of the present. I enjoyed myself much in the discussion of that theme. Perhaps my sermon may have been more intellectual than would suit many of my hearers. My congregation, with the exception of the students and Professors are not so far advanced intellectually as to require meat. They must be fed like babes with milk—

June 26. Today it has been somewhat uphill work to preach. My throat is inflamed so that I cannot speak with ease. Yet I have preached as well as I could. I rest the result with God— May the Head of the Church water the seed sown— I have aimed at his glory.

(I find within me a growing dissatisfaction with the M.E. Church. Still I think I was led by Providence to connect myself with it— Whether Providence designs that I should continue my connection with it I know not. This is one of the things hidden in the undeveloped future. God I trust will lead me right. I give myself up to follow the leadings of Providence. It is my purpose to do nothing rash. As the pillar of cloud moves, I will follow on— O that my soul may have union with Christ. I want to live usefully, and then if it may please God, I pray that I may lie down in the midst of my friends and die in peace. I feel a strong hope that I shall reach heaven at last. He who has begun a good work in me will carry it forward till the day of Christ.)

June 30. This is the last of another month. Day by day, hour by hour it has fled. It is numbered with the years beyond the flood. It has been to me a good month. I have enjoyed profound peace in God & rest in the cross of Christ. I have had some conflicts, and much peace. The Lord pardon the past and help me for the future.

Claremont Oct 4th 1856.[38]

After two years labor in Lisbon I find myself in Claremont. I have been here about three months. My whole term of labor in Lisbon was a series of inward struggles; my soul being like a bird that had wandered from its nest— In the month of April I started for the General Conference which was held at Indianapolis, Ind. My journey out and back was to me both interesting and profitable. Since my stay in Claremont I have been striving to realize the higher forms of Christian experience; especially have I prayed for the baptism of fire, the gift of power.[39] Some souls have been converted. I have been seeking complete union with God in Christ. Have felt an ineffable nearness to him; at times my soul has seemed to be blended with his infinite and everywhere present Spirit—to be bound up in the same bundle of life with the Lord my God. Two or three weeks ago I purchased the *Imitation of Christ* by Thomas á Kempis, and have derived much spiritual nourishment from it. It has been to me a precious volume.[40] For two weeks not a shadow passed over my mind. My soul lay floating on the ocean of the divine presence. All things were full of God. Every thing spake only of God. But the last week I have felt an inward schism— A misty veil has been between my soul and God, not sufficient to conceal him wholly, but I have seen him but dimly.

I am now reading the *Life and Christian Experience* of Madam Guion.[41] I have found in it, among some things that seem to me not right, many profound views of the Christian life. Notwithstanding all the errors of popery, and her imperfect views of faith, she realized a deep Christian experience, and enjoyed the blessedness of a divine union. The manner in which she was led to a more profound Christian experience has been blessed to my own good. After relating to a certain religious person her strivings after God, and her want of success, he replied, "It is, Madam, because you seek without, what you have within[.] Accustom yourself to seek God in your heart and you will find him." "Alas," she exclaims, "I sought thee where thou wast not. It was for want of understanding these words of thy Gospel, The kingdom of God cometh not with observation, neither shall they say lo here, or lo there; for the kingdom of God is within you."[42] My soul I hope will be the realm of love. He that dwelleth in love, dwelleth in God and God in him.[43]

X[44]

Oct. 10. Last evening was an era in my Christian experience. After retiring to rest I felt an unspeakable nearness to Jesus. In prayer I felt to desire and to ask for nothing but Jesus; and he manifested himself to me as he does not to the world. . I could not sleep till past midnight, so filled was my soul with the divine presence.

My dear wife entered into rest, and felt the sweetness of divine union.

I have learned that peace comes not by struggling— it is only when I cease to struggle and drop into the arms of Jesus that my soul finds rest. My heart has become the temple of God. It is there I worship him.

Oct. 16th. Since I last wrote in my journal I have felt much of the Goodness of God towards me. I have felt at times some inward disturbance, which has given place to a divine rest. Never did my soul enjoy more of God than for some weeks past. His gifts and graces do not now satisfy; my soul demands himself. I am beginning to answer the end of my creation in enjoying God. I felt a sympathy and union with all holy spirits in the universe— I have longed to commune with such spirits as Neander—[45] I can easily see how the worship of saints could spring up in the Church.

I have taken much comfort in reading Bloomfield's Greek Testament.[46] I read the Greek Testament with almost the same facility as the English.

I find my habits of abstraction of much service to me in living a hidden life. Geometry and the study of ancient languages discipline the mind so that it can easily retire within itself, and shut out the world and worship God in the inner sanctuary of the heart. I find in my heart some ardent longings to be dissolved and be with Christ, in a world all purity, all intellect, all bliss. Never did earthly things seem more empty and vain. I have learned to despise the vain pomp of the world—all its heartlessness, its senseless fashions, its honors and its wealth. They are all shadows. God is the only substance— May my union with him become more intimate. I have longed to become fixed—to be no more variable—to be formed in the image of God's immutability.

Oct 18th. Spent some time in reading my favorite author, Neander, after critically reading in Greek a chapter in the first epistle to the Corinthians.

I find language weak to express my inward experience. I have been led to the conclusion that there are three grand stages [stages] in the progress of a soul in the knowledge of God. 1. God apprehended by faith—a belief more or less strong that God is and that he is a rewarder of them that diligently seek him. 2. The demonstration of reason. My reason rests in the a priori argument. Ever since I read M. Cousin's *History of Philosophy*, my reason has been as certain that God is as I am that the three angles of a triangle are equal to two right angles.[47] 3. Direct intuition—a realization of the beatitude, "Blessed are the pure in heart for they shall see God. Christ has said if any man love me he will keep my words, and my Father will love him and we will come unto him and make our abode with him."[48]— God in the most intimate union and intercourse with {him} the soul. This spiritual intuition of God, (I hope it is not saying too much) I have reached. I see him only as the pure in heart can see him.

This is what the Platonic philosophy aimed to realize—but failed—to rise above all sensible forms, and contemplate the Absolute, the Inefable the <u>one</u>. It is only in Christianity that this aim of philosophy is realized— In my contemplation of God, I find no form floating before my vision. So in contemplating heaven I am raised above all sensible images—all those <u>anthropopathic</u> notions of God which cling so tenaciously to the mind are swept away.[49]

I love to be elevated above all sensible objects—and to dwell in a world of pure ideas—a world all intellect and all love. I still see through a glass darkly, then face to face.[50]

I find my soul a kind of <u>microcosm</u> a little world by itself. Into this I often retire to worship God. In the noisy world around me in the boisterous ocean of human life surging, foaming, roaring around me, I find a Patmos to which I banish myself, to commune with the Alpha and Omega, the first and the last.[51]

To some extent I have felt my soul raised above the forms of worship, as set times for prayer. I have spent days when every breath was prayer, and the whole inner life one constant flame of devotion. May I ever enjoy this holy <u>sabbatism</u>, this rest that remains for the people of God.[52]

Oct. 19. Sabbath— I have felt today more inward disturbance than for several days. There has been no consciousness of guilt; for with godly sincerity I have aimed to please God. My heart has been a <u>vacuum</u>, an <u>aching</u> void. Yet my trust is in God, and he does not seem to have forsaken me. The Christian life is a reproduction of the life of Christ. (It seems necessary that the soul should pass through all the states of Christ. His infancy,— we are to become as little children in order to enter into the kingdom of God— his poverty, his labors and persecutions, his triumphal entry into Jerusalem, and we are to taste something of the deep soul-agony of Gethsemane, and Calvary—"My God why hast thou forsaken me."[53] We shall experience a withdrawal of all sensible divine comfort, and the soul will be thrown upon its own resources. This is the severest trial of the whole Christian life. To rejoice that we are made partakers of Christ's sufferings, is the hardest lesson that a Christian has to learn, yet it may be learned at the feet of Jesus—.)

I hope that from all my internal struggles which I have passed through in past years a rich harvest of Christian experience may be gathered, and may I henceforth abide in the peace of God— May my faith & love ever grasp a present God.—

Oct 24. I have felt a desire to take an advance step towards heaven. The work of my redemption has gone forward by successive stages or <u>stadia</u>, just as that work has progressed in the world. I pray that I may advance another step nearer to God. (For twenty y[e]ars I have been in the service of God, and yet
"A point my good, a drop my store,
Eager I ask, I pant for more.)"[54]

I have commenced the practice of fasting. It is necessary in order to gain the control of the lower nature, what is called in Scripture the <u>flesh</u>, the πςευχγ [ψυχή]; which is to be subjected to the {πρα}πνευμα, the intellectual and moral nature.[55]

I have observed of late that the profoundest feelings of the genuinely Christian heart,—of a heart admitted to the blessedness of a divine union and fellowship—demand for their expression the highest form of poetry.

Sober prose is too frigid, too tame; poetry is the natural language of inspiration; it is also the appropriate language of the pure in heart. Mr Charles Wesley's hymns on full redemption more nearly meet the wants of the soul than any other uninspired compositions I have ever seen. (They express, so far as the poverty of human language can express, the ineffable longings of the soul after God, and the bliss, the calm repose of being lost in him. If there is language in heaven by which they communicate with each other, what a language that will be! It will be such poetry—the poetry of feeling—as earth never heard; it will be language that can express "a far more exceeding and eternal weight of glory.)"[56]

(There is a stage of Christian experience, an infantile state, which language is adequate to express; and such a soul may fear that it expresses too much. And there is a stage of Christian attainment & culture, a peace that passeth all understanding,[57] and all expression. There is a prayer that maybe [sic] clothed in appropriate words and there is a prayer that must be offered in silence—if offered at all. Language faileth here. The whole soul is one desire.)

Oct 27. Yesterday in Church I enjoyed <u>sweet</u> communion with God. In the forenoon I preached on 1 Jno 4:18. There is no fear in love, but perfect love casteth out fear, because fear hath torment. I trust I spoke from an inward experience. In the P.M. I preached from Isa. 38:1. Set thine house in order &c—[58]

(I have felt today what my soul has craved—a clearer consciousness of God, a more heart felt sense of the divine presence. In my search after a more vivid intuition of God, the words of Christ came with emphasis to my heart—"I am the way, the truth, and the life. No man cometh unto the Father but by me."[59] In Christ the only point where the Deity & humanity ever meet and blend, I found God. The veil through which I behold him was made thinner and more transparent than ever. Christ was presented to me as the <u>Truth</u>. He is the only <u>substance</u>, in opposition to shadows, and types. In him centers all wisdom and knowledge. Whoever has Christ formed within, has the essence of all knowledge & all truth.)

He is my life— He is that eternal life which was with the Father and was manifested unto us— (He is the Life & Light of the world. All things that live, live in him. He is the Life of souls. I have been led to pray that my whole being—my soul in its very texture, and every fibre and atom of my body may be penetrated with this principle of divine life):

"Let life immortal sieze my clay,
Let love refine my blood;
Her flames can bear my soul away,
Can bring me near my God."[60]

I have tried to cut loose more fully from the earth, to make a clean sweep of every worldly interest, to cast the world away and to throw myself upon the Providence of God for my wealth, and to seek in communion with God all my bliss. My soul reposed in its divine source, It was attracted to its proper center and became still. (Rest in Christ, the repose of a soul) fixed upon that blissful center, was presented to my mind under the image of a boundless ocean, with all its clouds and storms cleared away, & its waves and restless heavings subsided into a motionless placidity. Over it was seen nothing but the blue concave filled with a mild light, which rested upon the sea and illumined its surface. No sun or moon, or stars were seen; no land appeared in view. Far out of sight of the world, and all its false show, & out of hearing of its noise, a cross was seen to float on the surface of the calm waveless deep, and on it a sleeping infant, with nought to disturb its innocent repose. Such rest have souls in Christ. "Come unto me all ye that labor and are heavy laden and I will give you rest. Take my yoke upon you and learn of me, for I am meek and lowly in heart and ye shall find rest unto your souls."[61] Jesus, I come. I find in thee what I have sought in vain elsewhere. Ever give me this holy quietism, this heavenly Sabbatism; a rest so profound, so far below the world, in the abyss of Deity, that nothing external can disturb. I would gladly retire to the sacred solitude of my heart, and shut out from my soul the image of every thing earthy, and live alone with thee. But I must go out into the world and breast its storms. But in thee I have peace.

"Thy power I pant to prove,
    Rooted and fixed in love;
Strengthened by thy Spirit's might,
    Wise to fathom things divine,
    What the length, and breadth and height,
What the depth of love like thine.

    Ah! give me this to know,
    With all thy saints below;
Swells my soul to compass thee:
    Pants in thee to live and move;
    Filled with all the Deity,
All immersed and lost in love."[62]

Oct 31. Have been much blessed in reading my favorite Neander. Have thought of the invisible Church, and felt to love it. My knowledge of the Platonic idealism, has here subserved my spiritual progress. In Creation, Plato taught, that God first formed the plan as it were, conceived the ideas of things—just as an architect first forms an inward conception of the edifice and all its parts. Then he aimed to <u>realize</u> these ideas, or archetypes as far as possible in the external or actual world. To rise to the contemplation of these pure and eternal ideas is the highest attainment of science, and is the end of Platonic abstraction. Platonic love—it is the conception of one of the profoundest minds of the old world—is the love, not of that which [is] visible to the outward senses, but of the idea which that outward object only imperfectly represents.

In the new creation proceeding from Christ & Christianity, we are to carefully distinguish between the ideal, as it existed in the mind of Christ, and its actual realization in history and in the present time. I think I have learned to love the <u>ideal</u> Church with all my heart. It is worthy to be loved; it is amiable. All obstacles to love are here removed. We are to take from the Church all its imperfections, all its moral deformities, and then how pure the flame of love towards it. We then love it with pure heart fervently. It is the "holy Catholic Church," the pure and spotless bride of Christ. The ideal Church, as it existed in the mind of Christ, is seen in Eph. 5:25–27. "Christ loved the Church, and gave himself for it, that he might sanctify and cleanse it with the was[h]ing of water by the word, that he might present it to himself a glorious Church, not having spot or wrinkle or any such thing, but that it should be holy and without blame"—αμωμος, so perfect that Momus the god of ridicule, could find no blemish in it.[63] Christianity, has been struggling against the the sensualism and depravities of the world to realise this divine ideal for 18 centuries. Has it failed? No, Christianity knows no such word as failure. Christ does not aim at impossibilities. He surveyed the work in all it[s] length and breadth, and depth and height before he undertook. Of such a Church, as a visible outward organism, as a sect, as a name or denomination, there has been no {such} historical realization. (But there is an <u>invisible</u> Church, which has existed in every century, which is pure and spotless. This is the body of Christ; Christ dwells in it, and pervades it as the soul does the body. Out of this Church there is no salvation. Christ is the door. It is the holy of holies of the visible temple. Much impurity may connect itself with the outward apparent Church; but none can belong to the inner invisible Church, who are not united to Christ by a vital faith working by love, and to each other in the common fellowship or partnership of a divine life. This whole train of thought has been suggested by reading the words of Jovinian, in

Neander. (vol 2. p. 275.) (["]The Church founded on hope, faith, and charity (love) is exalted above every attack. No unripe member is within it—all its members are taught of God. No person can break within its enclosure by violence, nor creep in by fraud."[64] Here he speaks of the invisible Church.)

(Plato wrote over his academy the sentence—["]Let no one enter here who is ignorant of Geometry."[65] Over the inner, invisible Church, is inscribed— No one enters here but by faith & love.)

I love that pure Church. I thank God that I have been enabled to arise from sensuous and earthy images to its contemplation. Any other love of the Church often leads to bigotry: & it is only a selfish partyism. I apprehend that to rise from the love of the outward, visible Church, to the love of the inner, invisible Church, inclosed in the former as the soul in the body, is the highest form of brotherly love. The flame ascends pure and without smoke or earthy vapors.

"The faithful of each clime and age,
This glorious Church compose;
Built on a rock with idle rage
The threatning tempest blows."[66]

Nov. 3ᵈ. Requies in sanguine Christi. Rest in the blood of Christ— A calm tranquility— The peace of God, and the rest of God. Have enjoyed something of the infinite repose of the divine mind. In Christ Paradise is restored—the principal element of which state was a holy fellowship with God.

When God is mine and I am his,
Of paradise possessed,
I taste unutterable bliss,
And everlasting rest.[67]

(God is Light— Christ is Light, and in him is no darkness at all. Have desired an experience of Christ, as celestial Light. I long to bathe my soul in those waves of light that roll from the throne of God.)

Nov. 4. It has occurred to me that everything of real and permanent value in all preceding dispensations has passed down into Christianity, and there become the property of all real believers. The prophetic state was not to be confined to the old dispensations, and to be done away in the new. What was the essense of that state? It was not the prescience of future events. There could be prophecy without any predictions. But it consisted in the intuition of God—(an unclouded consciousness of God within.) The senses were called off from outward objects, the soul retired into its inner sanctuary, the holy of holies, and held converse with God. All other voices were silenced, the whole universe was dumb, and God alone spake to the soul. This holy converse with God was enjoyed in the paradisiacal state. It was enjoyed by the holy patriarchs, Abraham[,] Isaac and Jacob. The Jewish prophets, that succession of holy un-worldly men, heard the voice of God within. Now it is characteristic of Christianity to render universal what was only the privilege of a few in the previous dispensation. All Christians are priests. The privilege of entering the most holy place, enjoyed by the high priest, is now given according to St Paul to all believers. (So the intuition of God and the blessedness of divine internal converse, which was granted the Old Testament prophets, is now the privilege of all the pure in heart. It is now perhaps more spiritual than it was then, but not less real and certain.

As the system of divine revelation now stands out in all its divine completeness, we are not to look for any new communications of truth. God will speak generally in the language of his written word, and always in perfect harmony with it. In stillness and silence, in the sacred retirement of the closet, the still small voice may yet be heard, in the sweetest of all harmonies. In the deepest solitude the holy soul is not alone. In the center of an inaccessible, desert, in the most {distant} desolate island in the ocean, the soul has all it needs for its complete bliss. In fact the more abstracted it is from the world and its images, and the more the soul can retire into itself, the sweeter will be its fellowship, with the Father and with the son.

I pant for a holier worship. I would not stand without in the outermost court with the profane, nor stop in the stop in the sanctuary, where the great body of {the} believers adore, but my faith would knock at the door of God's inner sanctuary, and if sprinkled with Jesus' blood, he will open the door and let me in. There I may enjoy a more spiritual intercourse than Moses did in the burning bush—a converse free from {every} all sensuous representations. Cannot God directly impress the soul without the intervention of the senses. Does not the holy Spirit often do it? (May

I ever live in speaking distance with the Great Shepherd, so as to hear his voice. One word from thee, My Jesus, is worth a volume without thy voice. Thou art the Truth. Communicate thyself to my soul.)

How truly does the devout Kempis say; "If thou withdrawest thy attention from outward things, and keepest it fixed upon what passeth within thou wilt soon perceive the coming of the kingdom of God, for the kingdom of God is that peace an[d] joy in the Holy Ghost, which cannot be received by sensual and worldly men. (All the glory and beauty {and} of Christ are manifested within, and there he delights to dwell; his visits there are frequent, his condescension amazing, his conversation sweet, his comforts refreshing, and the peace that he brings passeth all understanding.")[68]

This holy internal converse, which constitutes the essence of the prophetic state, has been enjoyed not only by Kempis, but by Madam Guion, Carvasso,[69] and many others. The soul will never rest short of this. It is not enough to see God by reason's eye in the dew drop, or in the heavens, or in all the operations of nature, or marching at the head of the centuries in history. By faith we must grasp the God we seek, and hear him inly speak.

Nov. 8. Have desired to experience the exquisite and intensely pleasing emotion which accompanies the morally beautiful. A susceptibility of the emotion of the beautiful is one of the original powers of our nature. God has made the most ample provision to gratify it. But created beauty does not fully satisfy the soul. The feeling grows with that on which it feeds— It soon outgrows the finite, the transient, the earthly, and demands for its rest the infinite. (No tongue can describe the refined pleasure which arises in the soul when one can rise to the contemplation of the infinite beauty of the divine character.) It is a bliss no sensual mind can taste. The love of the beautiful may exist in several degrees. In its lowest stage it is the love of the beautiful in art; a still higher degree is the love of the beautiful in nature, in God's works. But the highest stage which the soul may reach, is the love of moral beauty, the το καλον, of the Greeks.[70] Most happy is that soul who can contemplate the uncreated beauty of the divine mind. He will then ever pray, "Let the beauty of the Lord our God be upon us."[71] Also with David in Ps. 27:4. ["]One thing have I desired of the Lord, that will I seek after; that I may dwell in the house of the Lord, all the days of my life, to behold the beauty of the Lord." Isaiah represents the felicity of the celestial state, to consist in the gratification [of] this refined emotion. "Thine eyes shall see the King in his beauty."[72]

In Christ every feeling of the heart may find the center of its rest. This pleasing power of our souls need not wander through the works of God, to find something that may satisfy this innate love of the beautiful. (Beauty in nature is but a ray from Christ—who is the Rose of Sharon, the Lily of the valleys, & the "fairest among ten thousand" and the one altogether lovely.[73]

I would give myself up to gaze upon the ineffable beauties of God in Christ. O that I could see him as he is. Jesus, unveil thy beauty to my inmost soul. Let the beauty of thy character be transcribed into mine. (Give me a heart that is an exact copy of thine.)

Nov. 9. While I lay awake this evening I enjoyed a manifestation of God to my soul. Had a clearer conception than ever before, of the manner in which all things are present to the mind of God, and how all things exist in the divine Mind, and must be immediately present to his consciousness. Creation was not a going out of himself. Things started to life within the mind of God, and outside of that nothing exists, or can exist. God is not only present with every thing in the universe, but every thing is in him. Every thing is distinct from him, yet nothing is separate from him, or independent {from} of him. I live in God and move in him, and in him have my being. If I pray to him in the most distant corner of the earth, or in profound silence in my own closet, He must hear it; for my very thoughts occur within the infinite circle of the divine Mind, and they must be as much present to his consciousness as to my own. (Our very thoughts are heard distinctly by him in eve[r]y point of boundless space. Every atom and every world is present to the divine consciousness.)

I am beginning to realize the profound import of the words, abiding in God, and God abiding in us.[74]

Nov. 12. Read five chapters in the Gospel of John in Greek. This is the most important of all the Gospels. It was truly called by the Fathers, "the Spiritual volume, the Pectus Christi,["] the heart of Christ. Here is divine philosophy, hidden wisdom, which is to be spoken among the perfect, or the fully instructed, and which God preordained unto our glorification before the world was. The single Gospel of John is worth more than all the speculations of the Greek philosophers, from Thales to Proclus, without setting a slight value upon them. Here philosophy explores the abyss of Deity. Yet all is simple while it is profound. Its deep spiritual import, has been opened to my mind—

[**Nov.**] **24.** Yesterday being the Sabbath was to me a good day. In the P.M. I preached on Jno. 14:27. Peace I leave with you. My peace I give unto you. Not as the world giveth, give I unto you. I hope my labors were not in vain.

For some time past, I have enjoyed a sweet consciousness of God. My fellowship has been with the Father & with the Son. I have had a vivid intuition of both the Father & the Son; but have been unable to realize in the interior of my heart a consciousness of the Holy Spirit as a distinct person in the Holy Trinity. My intellect has been convinced, but my heart has not felt that same uni[o]n with the Holy Ghost as with the Father & the Son. I was led to pray that I might be instructed on the nature and offices of the Spirit, and that I might have an inward experience of the whole Trinity— My prayer has been—O the great condescension of God—in a good degree answered. My inward consciousness of God is now complete. The Three in One, the Triune God, has been pleased to manifest himself to me. The Holy Ghost takes the place of Christs material presence. (He has been sent into the world as {the} another Comforter, who shall be in us, and abide with us forever.) The Divine Paraclete, is the medium of communication with the Father & the Son. It is only in him the soul has access to either. (He is the great Teacher. He leads into all truth.) It was profitable for the Church that Christ left the world, as to his material presence, because, on his departure he sent the Paraclete. (See Jno 16:7–15)[75] Tittmann, an eminent German commentator, well remarks. "The Holy Spirit effected much more in them, (his disciples) than Christ himself had done, (see v. 12, 14, 16.) imparting to them a more complete knowledge of the Savior, than what he himself could communicate, and also many other excellent gifts, necessary for their apostolic function; supplying to them eloquence irresistable, the power of working the most illustrious miracles, for the confirmation of their testimony concerning Jesus, and rendering their timid minds invincible to all the terrors, of their adversaries."[76] Says

Euthymius, "It was the pleasure of the Holy Trinity, that the Father should <u>draw</u> them to the Son, that the Son should <u>teach</u> them, and the Holy Spirit should <u>perfect</u> them. Now the two first things were already completed; but it was necessary {that} for the third to be accomplished, namely the being perfected by the Holy Spirit."[77] To be perfect in the Scripture sense, is to be fully initiated into the mysteries of the Gospel. It is to rise from the lowest elementary principles, to a maturity and fulness of Christian knowledge. (Heb 6:1.)[78] This can be reached only under the powerful tuition of the Holy Spirit.

Nov 27. Thanksgiving day. Preached at 11 AM on the Hand of God in American history.

In the evening in my study experienced a state it is not easy to describe— I can give it no name, better than losing myself in God—a kind of annihilation, or suspension of all the powers of my soul. I was only conscious of naked existence— there was no emotion of any kind, no desire, no joy, or conscious peace, no feeling, no misery, no guilt—no thought, no imagination. I was conscious of nothing but simple being. My will was lost. It was not a trance, nor an ecstacy. It was not an unhapy condition. It was an inconceivable stillness—a silence like that which reigns without the bounds of creation in empty space. Does it proceed from a closer union with god? Is not this loss of all emotion, something like the state of the Infinite Mind? I apprehend it is a passing into God, a passing into the pure divine. It seemed a purely spiritual state, almost a disembodied state, for the senses were closed, Yet I repeat, it was not a trance. My divine Teacher has shown me that an emotional state is not the highest in religion. He who seeks the state of ecstacy, {as the} and is satisfied with nothing but the intoxication of emotion, has not fully lost himself. He is not wholly unselfish. (Union with God, which is a very different thing from ecstacy, is the end at which a Christian should aim.)

Nov 30th 1856. Sabbath. Have walked today by <u>naked faith</u>. Have had little feeling of any kind—[79] Preached as well as I could— Had a sincere desire to do good to sinners. (I feel that I am nothing.) Have not felt so constantly those blissful and fervid emotions, as I have heretofore. Have an impression that God is disciplining my soul for a higher and holier flight into the enjoyment of the Deity. He is purifying my love from all taint of self and earth. The love that follows a state of naked faith is the purest form of Christian love. It has less of self in it. It is what Archbishop Fenelon aimed to realize; a disinterested love, a love of <u>order</u>, of <u>absolute beauty</u> and <u>perfection</u>, superior to every agreeable sensation, and which can act in the absensence [absence] of all the sensible pleasures and consolations of grace.[80] It is the love of God for his own sake. It is perfect love. My soul for some time past has seemed to me like the deep blue canvass of the heavens in a clear, still winter day. There are no clouds or tempests in it. No sun, moon or stars, nothing on which the sight may rest. Nothing but the deep blue. There are stars which revolve in the infinite depths of space; yet they are apprehended only by faith. My soul is like the heavens at such a time. I have no feeling, no emotion, on which my faith may lean. Yet it still holds to God. It grasps a present Deity. And I am conscious in the profoundest depths of my heart of a refined satisfaction with God. It is not an emotion. Yet it is present to consciousness when I narrowly search for what is in my soul. It is <u>naked faith</u>, working by pure love. It is a seraphic flame, a flame that ascends without smoke or earthy vapor. It is still, and silent. A state of naked faith, if the soul does not falter, and if the will holds the soul, emptied of all emotions and desires, in the presence of God, is a profitable state. But how many stumble and fall here, when the divine Shepherd leads them into the desert to wean them from themselves and the world. When he has purified me I shall come forth like gold. Our God is a consuming fire even to his people. The rustiest piece of iron when cast into the furnace, becomes bright and white in the flame. The soul cast into the flames of the divine love, has its earthiness burned off. When my soul is completely emptied, God will fill my emptiness with his fulness.

He never suffers a vacuum. What the earth does not fill in our hearts, he fills with himself— I long to love him as angels do. My soul has some sweet drawings towards the heavenly state. It is held in a state of equalibrium between two moral forces—a desire for the saints rest, and a desire to advance the kingdom of Christ on earth.

The earth was covered yesterday with a mantle of snow—an emblem of purity— How white and stainless! Would that my soul was as white—

Winter drives the soul in upon itself for enjoyment. It hides the earth in a mantle of purity. May this be the best winter I have ever seen.

Dec. 1ˢᵗ 1856. In my closet this evening found myself unable to pray vocally or even in a whisper. Offered up my prayer mentally. This is the sweetest form of prayer. It has one advantage over vocal prayer—the mind is more concentrated, or recollected. The soul abstracts itself wholly from the sensible world, turns inward upon itself, and adores God in the inmost chamber of the heart. This is worshiping God in spirit and in truth, which is well pleasing to him. Prayer is the contact of the soul with the Infinite Spirit. This is true prayer. Yet perhaps few persons can practice that perfect abstraction which is necessary to mental prayer. Few can wholly leave the outward world and retire into the chamber of the soul and shut the door—shutting the world out, and God in. In mental prayer, the mind is not inactive, but acts more vigorously than ever. Its desires being formed by the indwelling Spirit, it asks only for things God is willing to grant. It is the Spirit itself speaking within. The soul is in the immediate presence of the Deity. (How sweet it thus [is] to leave the world, and be present with the Lord. It is next to going to heaven. It is heaven begun.)

Dec. 27. Have earnestly sought for power—from on high—power in the pulpit. I think I see where that power which the apostles received on the day of Pentecost lies. As the atmosphere is the medium through which the outward word reaches the sensorium, and conveys an idea to the mind; so the everywhere present Spirit of God is the medium through which the truth reaches the heart of the hearer. The Holy Spirit is not only the medium through which the soul communes with God & with Christ; but it is only when we speak in the Holy Ghost that we can convey our thought and feelings into the inmost soul of those who hear us. This is the demonstration of the Spirit, power from on high.

Dec. 29. Last evening (Sabbath) we had a larger number to our prayer meeting than had been seen for several years. It was a time of solemn impressions. I pray God to deliver the multitude into my hand. One soul has recently been converted. Others are serious.

This evening in my closet I earnestly besought Christ to send the Comforter, the divine Teacher, to instruct me fully as to what constitutes the power from on high. I despaired of ever learning the truth on that subject by my own investigations; and threw myself at the feet of the Paraclete, who spoke to my heart, as follows: "It is not by might nor by power, but by my Spirit, saith the Lord. Be ye clean that bear the vessels of the Lord; (for holiness is power, and is necessary that I may dwell in the heart. Knowledge is power, truth is power. (Study to show thyself approved unto God a workman that needeth not to be ashamed. Have faith and hope. Said I not unto thee, if thou wouldst believe thou shouldst see the glory of God?) Said Paul, when I am weak then I am strong. Naked dependence on God, a feeling that thou art nothing, and God is all, is an element of power— Glory only in the cross of Christ, for the preaching of the cross is the power of God & the wisdom of God— Be sin[c]ere, earnest, solemn. (So live that men may see God in thee, as the glory of God shone in the face of Moses, so that the children of Israel could not steadfastly behold him. I have ordained thee that thou shouldest bear much fruit. I will make thee the father of a great multitude.")[81]

(Amen. So let it be done to thy servant. Good is the word of the Lord. Every word that proceedeth out of the mouth of the Lord shall surely come to pass.)

Jan. 2ᵈ. 1857.

Find my heart panting for a deeper experience of divine things. Read in Neander's *His. of Christianity and the Church*, respecting the Abbot Joachim, who was thought to be endowed with the spirit of prophecy. Neander remarks: ["]A certain faculty of prophecy seems implanted in the spirit of humanity; the longing heart goes forth to meet beforehand great and new creations, which it needs in order to the attainment of its objects; undefined presentiments hasten to anticipate the mighty future." (Vol. 4. p. 216.)[82]

The essence of the prophetic state, is an inward experience of God—a conscious union with the Deity. The more intimate this divine fellowship is, the more the sanctified soul, partaking of the divine nature, will find the past and future meeting in the present—the future and past subsisting now. Such a soul in its knowledge will antedate the intuitions of the eternal state, and may catch a shadowy glimpse of future events, especially great movements in the kingdom of God. Perhaps in a future age, when the Church shall enjoy more of the Spirits influence, and a more intimate and conscious union with the Head, the prophetic spirit will reappear in the world. (Certain I am that the experience of the Church at the present time, falls far below the New Testament standard.)

Jan 6. Last Sabbath enjoyed some freedom in preaching in preaching from Luke 16:4. I am resolved what to do. I showed the relation of a strong purpose to the Christian life—making holiness to consist not in excited involuntary emotions, but in a fixed bent of the will in the direction of God & heaven. I trust there may be some fruit unto life eternal.

In the evening I felt a deeper sympathy with the Savior on the mount of Olives weeping over Jerusalem, and with the unutterable soul-agony of Gethsemane, than I ever before experienced. I felt no anxiety regarding my own salvation, but an intense desire for the salvation of others. Though the state of the Apostle Paul, (Rom 9:1–3) was not fully reproduced, yet I reached a position where I could comprehend him.[83]

Today I have profound rest in Christ— Glowing love often fills my heart— I have an ineffable craving for inward communion with God. All outward services are unsatisfactory unless they bring me in close contact with the infinite Source of all good. There is an hour when the soul alone with God, transcends these earthly bounds, leaving reason far behind; desires truth, not through obscure types and visible symbols, but by direct communication from its sempiternal source in the bosom of God. It is a flowing of the pure divine into humanity, which is fitted to be receptive of it. These lofty ecstatic flights of the soul into the realms of pure truth are worth sometimes years of study. The ideas the soul then rec[e]ives may be in a measure, though not always perfectly, reproduced and committed to paper. I often pray for the indwelling of that eternal Wisdom, the living Word, which is spoken of by Solomon as the companion of God in the solitude of his own eternity. (I am fully convinced that Wisdom & Christ & Heaven are one.)

Blessed is that man whose desires soar beyond all created good to God, the uncreated and eternal good— I can say with Raymund Lull, (born in the island of Majorca, anno 1236)[84] "The spirit longs after nothing as it does after God. No gold is worth so much as a sigh of holy longing. The more of this longing one has, the more of life he has. The want of this longing is death. Have this longing and thou shalt live. He is not poor who possesses this; unhappy the man who lives without it."[85]

I have thought as I have studied the history of the Church, that the piety of the eminent Christian teachers of the mediaeval period, say in in the eleventh and twelfth centuries was of a deeper type than since the Reformation. Such persons as Bernard of Clairvaux, Anselm, Richard a Sancto Victore,[86] Raymond Lull and others, are truly lights, shining in a dark place. The attempt to follow Christ in evangelical poverty, one of the prevailing ideas of the times, led them farther in self-renunciation than many at present go. No one ever loved Christ with a more glowing love than Raymond Lull. In speaking on the inefficacy of pilgrimages, how finely does he say, "Often have I sought thee on the cross, and my bodily eyes have not been able to find thee, although they have found thine image there and a representation of thy death. And when I could not find thee with my bodily eyes, I have sought thee with the eye of my soul; and, thinking on thee, my soul found thee; and when it found thee, my heart began immediately to warm with the glow of love, my eyes to weep, my mouth to praise thee."[87] It is not by roaming through the world that the longing soul finds Christ. He reveals himself within. How often have we vainly wished that we could walk with Christ as his apostles did, and enjoy his <u>bodily</u> presence. Vain wish! The flesh profiteth nothing. The spirit is everything. (Our spirit may enjoy as close a fellowship with Christ as those did who actually "handled the Word of life."[88] In spirit we as often as we please walk with him to Emaus while he talks with us by the way & our hearts burn within us.)[89]

Jan. 8. There is nothing from which my soul shrinks with greater horror than from the thought of losing the enjoyment of God, and coming down to the ordinary Christian position, where the soul is filled with earthy sensuous images. I realize the truth of the couplet:
"Tis worse than death my God to love,
    And not my God alone."[90]
"If a soul" says Bernard of Clairvaux, "has once learned and obtained from the Lord, the power of turning inward upon itself, of panting in its inmost depths after God's presence, of continually seeking the light of his countenance—I know not a whether such a soul would consider the suffering of hell itself, for a season, as a greater punishment than—after having once tasted the bliss of this spiritual direction, to be turned

back again to the allurements—say {not} rather, to the hardships, of the flesh."[91]

Contemplation. The highest aim of the eminent Christian teachers of the middle age was contemplation—the contemplation of God. Plato had taught the world to rise from the sensible, the mutable, the earthy, to the love & contemplation of the immutable and eternal. The state of contemplation was with many an ideal state after which they longed without realizing it.[92] Others professed to reach this exalted Christian position.

It was a pure and holy state. Sin which separates between God and the soul was removed. Self was renounced and crucified. God was loved for what he is in himself—as the Most Perfect Being.

It was a state of abstraction—a withdrawal of the soul into itself from the sensible world. In peaceful abstraction from all created things, the soul was occupied intently with the idea of God. This idea filled the whole soul to the exclusion of everything else.

"Plunged in the Godhead's deepest sea,
And lost in his immensity."[93]

Bernard (born anno 1091) marks three stages or positions in the Christian life— The third and last stage is "where the spirit collects its energies within itself, and, as far as it is divinely sustained, divests itself of things human, to rise to the contemplation of God. At this last stage, the man attains immediately to that which is the aim of all aims, the experience of the divine. To the same point the other two stages tend but by a longer way. That which is highest cannot be taught by words, but only revealed through the Spirit. No language can explain it; but we may by prayer and purity of heart attain to it, after we have prepared ourselves for it by a worthy life."[94]

Richard de St Victor, distinguishes three stages of religious development. That in which God is seen by faith; that in which he is known by reason; and that in which he is beheld by contemplation. He says: "To the first and second stages men may ascend; but to the third they can never arrive except by ecstatic transportion of the spirit above itself. The soul raised above itself, beholds things too high for reason in the light of the Godhead, where the thinking reason retires back." (Neander's *His. of Christianity &c* vol 4. p. 412)[95]

It is to be remarked that this state of contemplation, as it was called, is the point where faith begins to be lost in sight, or more correctly where faith becomes intuition, the highest form of faith. Faith is the substance, or confident expectation of things hoped for, the evidence—the convincing proof or demonstration—of things not seen.[96] Its office is to give us a knowledge of things that lie beyond the circles of sensation. Intuition is its highest form. This is the only form of faith which belongs to a future state. But the contemplative spirit may even in this life soar upward leaving the earthy and sensible behind, and antedate the intuition of the life eternal. It is an inward consciousness of God—

The state of contemplation is identical with that of the Quietists, who made such a stir in Spain & France in the latter part of the 17th & early in the 18th centuries. Michael de Molinos, a Spanish priest, taught in a book which he published in 1681, entitled the *Spiritual Guide*, that the highest state in religion consists in the perfect tranquility of a mind removed from all external and finite things, and centered in God, and in a pure & perfect love of the Supreme Being for his own sake—as intrinsically lovely, independent of all his dealings with us— (See Mosheim's *Eccl. His.* vol. 2. p. 219)[97] Madam Guion & Archbishop Fenelon embraced the same view, and the former fully realized it in her experience. This quietism, this sacred repose of the soul in God, is what St Paul calls the rest of God— entering by faith into his rest— This silence of our own wills, and desires, and absorption into the Deity, so that our whole being is consciously penetrated & pervaded with an omnipresent God, is what St Paul calls "being filled with all the fulness of God," and St John denominates dwelling in God, & God dwelling in us—[98]

The abbot Joachim,[99] (died between the years 1201 & 1202) in his ardent longings to see realized in the actual world the New Testament ideal of the Church, looked forward to the future, which he doubted not would be a time of all-satisfying contemplation, taking the place of that learning which dwells on the letter and finite conceptions of the understanding, and which by the inspiration of love penetrates the abyss of knowledge in the Divine Mind. He thought that the work of redemption was to pass through three successive stages corresponding to the three persons in the Trinity. The times of the Old Testament belong especially to God the Father; in it, he revealed himself as the <u>Almighty</u>, by signs and wonders. Next followed the times of the New Testament, in which God, as the Word, revealed himself in his wisdom, where the striving after a comprehensible knowledge of mysteries predominates. The last times belong to the Holy Spirit, in which the fire of love in contemplation will predominate. As the letter of the Old Testament answers to God the Father, the letter of the New Testament more especially to the Son, so the spiritual understanding which proceeds from both, answers to the Holy Spirit. These three ages of the Church he thought represented by the three apostles, Peter, Paul, and John, the latter representing the contemplative position. He looked forward to a time in the future developement of the Church, when there would be no need of religious teachers, for every man should be taught of God— Then the prophecy of Jeremiah, that God himself would be the teacher of men, and put his law into their minds and write it in{to} their hearts would be fulfilled.[100] Contemplation would be the prevailing state of the Church. His views, are at least ingenious. (See Neander. Vol. 4. pp 220–232.)[101]

This high Christian position was thought to be the special gift of God, and not to be obtained by any strugglings of the spirit; and yet it would not be reached without ardent longings for it. The soul in its deep {long} craving for God, can say, "My soul thirsteth for thee, my flesh longeth for thee in a dry and thirsty land where no water is." (Ps 63.)[102] ["]As the heart [hart] panteth (or brayeth) after the water brooks, so panteth my soul after thee, O God. My soul thirsteth for God, for the living God; when shall I come and appear before God." (Ps. 42:1.2.) And with Job. "O that I knew where I might find him."[103]

In the *Meditations* of Guigo, (see Neander, Vol. 4, p. 413) he seems to have apprehended the way in which the soul must reach this state of inward communion with God—[104] It is not by inward struggles to break the fetters of the spirit; we must cease to struggle and sink into divine rest— In the above work it is said, "The way to God is easy, for a man walks in it by unburdening himself. It would be hard were it necessary for him as he went, to take up a load. Throw off then every burden, by denying all else, and thyself."[105]

Philosophy in all ages has had it as its highest aim to unite the soul to God. This has been connected with pantheistic speculations, but still it indicates the deep craving of the soul for that union with the Deity which is effected only in Christ and Christianity. The old Indian or Hindu philosophy placed the supreme good in "a state of abstraction by which the soul separates itself completely from nature, and even a state of annihilation resulting from absorption into the <u>substance,</u> (which is God.) These are considered as states of perfect repose, supreme felicity, and the definitive object of science." (*His. of Philosophy*. Vol. 1. p. 60.)[106] The annihilation here spoken of cannot be a cessation of existence, for that could not be a happy state. Madam Guion calls her highest state, a "prof<u>ound annihilation,</u>" not that she ceased to be, or lost her individuality.[107] She only lost her <u>selfhood,</u> by the union of her will to God.[108]

Pythagoras taught that ['']the complete salvation of the soul is its transformation into God. Delivered from the multiple and variable, it is absorbed into the absolute unity.' (*His. of Phil.* Vol 1. p. 109)[109] Plato also aimed to lead men, by abstraction from the sensible world, to rise to the contemplation of eternal ideas, and their substance which is God.

The Alexandrian philosophy founded by Plotinus, (born AD 202) professed to conduct the soul to an intimate union with the Deity. Plotinus, Porphyry, Proclus, each professed to have intercourse with the gods.[110] Their philosophy taught that true science results from divine illuminations, from an intimate presence of God in the soul.

Jan. 28th. Since I last wrote in my journal[111] I have passed through a painful sickness of two weeks continuance. Some four or five sinners have been converted. The Church, at least many, seem to be inwardly thirsting for full redemption.[112]

I have found the *Saints Everlasting Rest*, even this side the immortal shores— Mr Baxter, in his *Saints Rest*, seems to have had a clear view of what constitutes the rest of a soul; but he is deficient in confining it so exclusively to a future state.[113] The apostle in the epistle to the Hebrews shows that we may enter into that rest by faith. "For we that have believed do enter into rest." (Heb. 4:3.) This rest: is the enjoyment of God— The soul in this life may attain to the enjoyment of the Supreme Good.

Mr Baxter defines the saints rest to be—"the most perfect state of a Christian, or it is the perfect endless enjoyment of God, by the perfected saints, according to the measure of their capacity"—(See Chap. I. sec 2.) Just before this he earnestly exhorts the reader—"that he {set his} take God in Christ for his only rest, and fix his heart upon him above all." In another place he says that "those who seek this rest, choose God only for their end and happiness. He that takes anything else for his happiness is out of the way the first step."[114]

Such being the nature of the saints rest, it may be enjoyed in this life; but will be more perfectly in the heavenly state. That soul which has learned to rise from things seen and temporal to the enjoyment of the internal presence of God is no stranger to the bliss of the immortal state.

Jan 29. Have been reading Baxter's *Saints Rest*, and have reaped some spiritual profit, especially from the last few chapters, on leading a heavenly life on earth. There can be no doubt that Baxter was experimentally acquainted with the highest forms of Christian life. He reached that maturity and ripeness of Christian character denominated in the N. Testament perfection. He was evidently acquainted with "the soul-ravishing exercise of heavenly contemplation," and enjoyed a living fellowship with God.[115] He says in Chap XI. Sec. 4. "As the noblest of creatures, so the noblest of Christians, are they whose faces are set most direct for heaven. Such a heavenly saint who hath been wrapped up to God in his contemplations, and is newly come down from his views of Christ, what discoveries will he make of those superior regions! How high and sacred is his discourse! enough to convince an understanding hearer that he hath seen the Lord, and that (no man could speak such words except he had been with God. This, this is the noble Christian. The most famous mountains and trees are those that reach nearest to heaven, and he is the choicest Christian whose heart is most frequently and delightfully there.) If a man have lived near the king, or hath seen the sultan of Persia, or the great Turk, he will be thought a step higher than his neighbors. What then shall we judge of him that daily travels as far as heaven, and there hath seen the King of kings, hath frequent admittance into the divine presence, and feasteth his soul upon the tree of life! (For my part I value this man before the noblest, the richest, or the most learned in the world.")[116]

The above was drawn from the depth of his own heart. How often has my own soul been ravished with delight, when I have transported myself from this dark world, to the heavenly sphere, where I have seemed to walk with God high in ["]the climes of bliss."[117] Upon my bed in the darkness of the night, I have bathed my soul in waves of celestial light. My soul at times has been transported to the suburbs of the New Jerusalem. In this heavenly contemplation it is important, as far as may be done, to banish all material, sensuous images from the mind, that our foretaste of heaven may have less of earth in it, and more of the pure spiritual bliss enjoyed by glorified spirits. The more complete our abstraction from things seen and temporal the more divine will be the bliss of the soul in this sublime exercise.

Mr Baxter seems to have had a clear conception of the privilege of the purified soul in enjoying the inward presence of God. The more holy a person becomes the nearer and sweeter is his communion with God. A soul in union with the Deity is paradise restored. He says, "When man's heart had nothing in it to grieve the Spirit, it was then the delightful habitation of his Maker. God did not quit his residence there till man expelled him by unworthy provocations. There was no shyness or reserve till the heart grew sinful, and too loathsome a dungeon for God to delight in. And was this soul reduced to the former innocency, God would quickly return to his former habitation; yea, so far as it is renewed and repaired by the Spirit, and purged from its lusts, and beautified by his image, the Lord will yet acknowledge it as his own; Christ will manifest himself unto it, and the Spirit will take it for his temple and residence. So far as the heart is qualified for conversing with God, so far it usually enjoys him." (Chap 13. sec. 19.)[118]

Jan 31. Enjoyed at times today a sweeter intercourse of spirit with Christ than I ever before enjoyed. I have recently been much impressed with a passage of the Epistle to the Hebrews, Heb. 2:11, 12. "For both he who sanctifieth and they who are sanctified are of one; (father) for which cause he is not ashamed to call them brethren, saying, I will declare thy name unto my brethren; in the midst of the church will I sing praise unto thee."[119] I have looked upon Christ, and God in Christ as most closely related to me, bound to me by the ties of consanguinity. Jesus is my elder brother. My soul has had most familiar intercourse with the God-man. With John I have reposed my head upon his bosom; and he has returned my love. My soul has embraced him, and he has granted me the kisses of his mouth, (Song of Solomon, Chap. 1:2).[120] I have exercised believing thoughts of the love of God and of Christ to me. Have made his perfections to pass before me, and have tried to banish all jealous thoughts of him. This passage in the *Saints Rest* has been blessed to good: (["]Ever keep thy soul possessed with believing thoughts of the infinite love of God.) Love is the attractive of love. Few so vile but will love those who love them. No doubt it is the death of our heavenly life to have hard thoughts of God, to conceive of him as one that would rather damn than save us. This is to put the blessed God into the similitude of Satan. When our ignorance and unbelief have drawn the most deformed picture of God in our imaginations, then we complain that we cannot love him nor delight in him. This is the case of many thousand Christians. Alas, that we should thus blaspheme God and blast our joys. Scripture assures us that 'God is love,' 1 Jno 4:16, 'that fury is not in him,' Isa. 27:4; that he hath no pleasure in the death of the wicked, but that the wicked turn from his way and live, Ezek. 33:11. Much more hath he testified his love to his chosen; and his full resolution effectually to save them. (O that we could always think of God as we do of a friend! as of one that unfeignedly loves us, even, more than we do ourselves; whose very heart is set upon us to do us good, and hath therefore provided for us an everlasting dwelling with himself.") (Chap 12. sec. 19.)[121]

It is important that my soul have correct conceptions of the divine character and nature. If I look upon God as anything but the most perfect Being; If I draw a distorted picture of God in my imagination, which looks no more like the true God, than the golden calf of the Israelites at mount Sinai resembled Jehovah, how can I love him. I do not love God but a creature of my imagination, an idol my hands have formed. (May the Holy Spirit, the divine Teacher, take of the things of God and Christ and show them unto me.)

Feb. 2ᵈ. 1857. Have been for some time past deeply impressed with the <u>allness</u> of God, and the <u>nothingness</u> of the creature. It seems to me that the fundamental idea of Scripture is, that God is all in all; and that God is in Christ reconciling the world unto himself. I can sympathise with the feeling of Madam Guyon when in that profound little book, *The Short and Easy Method of Prayer*, she asserts that there are but two truths in the universe—the All, and the <u>nothing</u>.[122] This may look like pantheism—and it does express the profound truth that underli[e]s even pantheism. Pantheism is only truth perverted. (God is all; but all things are not God.) To say that the universe is God is to utter the contradiction that the finite is the infinite. The universe however vast it may be, may still be conceived to be greater, and hence it does not answer our idea of God, who is so great that nothing can be conceived to be greater or more perfect. The universe manifests God, but does not exhibit the whole of God. There is much of God that is not in it. It does not exhaust God. The heavens, even the heaven, of heavens, cannot contain him. To say then that these created things are God, which things are finite and limited, is to say there is no God. It is blank atheism, whatever name it may assume. All things exist in God: They were created within the infinite circle of the Divine Mind. They are upheld by a constant exercise of the same power that formed them, so that preservation is a continued creation. Nothing exists without God. Withdraw God from anything, and it ceases to be. Take away the substance, and the shadow it casts disappears, or is annihilated. Thus God is all and in all. What is my soul? All its powers are the gift of God, and are the result of the divine presence. Everything in it which is good comes from God—is an emination from God; is a ray from the Father of lights. Its continuance in existence for an hour depends upon the will of God. God only hath immortality. My soul could no more exist without the constant presence and power of God, than it could have created itself from nothing. And what is true of my soul is true of everything—the worm and the angel, the atom and the world. God originates and continues all things, and they all exist in him—within the limits of his infinite & everywhere present Spirit. He is the sea of being—the infinite substance.

There is a state of soul, an intimate union with God, and rest in God, which may be called annihilation. The soul views God to be all, and itself, and all creatures comparatively nothing.

"Plunged in the Godhead's deepest sea,
And lost in his immensity."[123]

Not as the drop of fresh water, which falls into the ocean, becomes a part of the ocean, and loses its own individual existence. The soul annihilated still exists. It is even the highest form of existence. It is consciously living in God—having no desires out of God, willing nothing but what God wills. It is the death of self. ["]I am crucified with Christ, nevertheless I live; yet not I, but Christ liveth in me." ["]Ye are dead & your life is hid with Christ in God."[124] The earthy and sensual, once the ruling element of the soul, is now dead, and buried in the grave of Christ. The old Adam expires in agony on the cross. God in Christ {only} alone lives in my soul. That which is peculiar to me, that which constitutes myself, has ceased to be. God is all. I am nothing. I live because Christ lives. If he should cease to be, I should cease with him. My life is so bound up with him, that to separate us, would be death. My soul has sometimes plunged so deep into the abyss of Deity, as to lose sight of the creatures, and even of myself—so as to see nothing but God. The more intimately a soul is united to God, the more it sees things as God sees them. A soul submerged in the Godhead, and from the depths of God, looking out upon the creatures, sees their nothingness, and God is all. "All nations before him are as nothing; and they are counted to him less than nothing and vanity." Isa. 40:17.

That devout and un-worldly man, Thomas à Kempis, had an experience of a state of annihilation, or of the soul losing itself in God. He says, "Dearest Jesus, spouse of my soul, supreme source of light and love, and sovreign Lord of universal nature! O that I had the wings of true liberty, that I might take my flight to thee and be at rest! When will it be granted me, in silent and peaceful abstraction from all created being, to taste and see how good thou art. O Lord, my God! When shall I be wholly absorbed in thy fulness! When shall I lose, in the love of thee, all perception of myself; and have no sense of any being but thine." (*Imitation of Christ*, p. 148. Gould & Lincoln. Boston 1855.)[125]

If I have in me any goodness, it [is] not mine, but God's. He only is good. My sins and earthly desires, these were mine; but they have ceased. What was mine, is now no more. Is there love in my soul? Is Christ all the world to me, and is all my soul love? Love is of God. He that loveth dwelleth in God & God in him.[126] It is my glory to say "I am nothing; Christ is all." My soul has panted for this annihilation of self, that in "peaceful vacancy" I might be lost in the enjoyment of God[127]— Let all inordinate desires cease in me. Let me lose my selfwill. O that I might ever say in the center of my soul,

"May thy will, not mine, be done;
May thy will & {thine} mine be one."[128]

I have longed to die unto myself. Often has my heart prayed:
"O that I might now decrease!

O that all I am might cease!
Let me into nothing fall;
Let my Lord be all in all!"[129]

As confined flowers instinctively seek the sun, so my soul continually turns to God. The whole current of my thoughts, and my whole inner life, flows in the direction of the Supreme Good. It requires no effort to think of God; but demands an effort of will to think of anything else. The moment I find myself unoccupied, my soul is wrapt up in the contemplation of God. Even when my hands are employed my thoughts are with him. My soul sometimes in its weakness almost tires of this contemplation, and says with the spouse, "Stay me with flagons, comfort me with apples; for I am sick of love." (Canticles 2:5.) To think of anything else so much as I do of God would be unendurable. My soul would sink under it. But this action is rest. For the deepest repose a soul can enjoy consists in the sweet and constant action of all the powers of soul & body in the enjoyment of God. How much my soul blesses him, that his grace has taught me to rise from the enjoyment of the creatures, and even of his gifts, to the enjoyment of himself. I rejoice more in this than they that divide the spoil.[130]

Feb. 9. My soul has suffered for a few days past some inward disturbance, yet I have had all the time access to God. I want to rise to the enjoyment of true inward liberty, in which my soul detached wholly from all the creatures, and dependent only on God, and released from every anxious desire, and completely satisfied with the uncreated Good, shall repose in heavenly tranquility. O that my life might flow onward every day like the rivulet through the vale, reflecting from its surface the heavens above.

I have wished to rise to the enjoyment of a fulness of joy—to have the joy of Christ fulfilled in me. But I would rejoice only in the Lord, and joy in the God of my salvation.

Feb. 16. Yesterday (Sabbath) was a good day. In the evening five or six souls started for heaven. God is answering my unceasing prayer. O for power from on high.

My soul at times has joyed in the God of my salvation. How often, blessed Redeemer, have I mused upon the sweet words in thy prayer in Jno 17:20–23. "Neither pray I for these alone; but for them also that shall believe on me through their word; that they all may be one, as thou, Father, art in me, and I in thee, that they also may be one in us—that they may be one even as we are one—I in them and thou in me, that they may be made perfect in one."[131] Here thou prayest that the same union, the same perfect oneness which subsists between thee and thy Father, may exist between me and God. I should never have presumed to have hoped or asked for this, if thou hadst not prayed for it. I could never have thought so great a dignity & blessedness to be possible if thou hadst not here declared it. Surely it cannot be presumption for me to ask for what thou hast prayed. These are thine own words dear Jesus. I adopt them as my prayer. Make me one with thee. Dwell in my heart, and let my whole being be wrapped up in God. O that I might be joined to thee and be one spirit with thee. 1 Cor. 6:17.[132]

Let me not only be justified by faith, but enjoy union with the whole Deity through love. I in thee, & thou in thy Father, that we all may be one. O Jesus, draw closer the bands that join my soul to thee. I can say at times with my whole heart "I am my Beloved's and my Beloved is mine.["] Cant. 6:3. My heart has leaped for joy that this whole universe is mine—all thou hast and art is my undivided portion. What more can I want.

My blessed Jesus, sometimes speaks to my heart. Yesterday after returning from preaching with my mind much disturbed, I entered my closet, and there in solitude and silence, I heard him inly speak. I asked for words of comfort. And it came with living freshness, as newly fallen from the lips of Jesus, "Lo I am with you always— I will never, never, never, leave thee nor forsake thee. Thou shalt sit with me upon my throne.["][133] No one can tell the sweetness & power with which these words came to my heart. It was the divine Paraclete or Comforter calling to my remembrance all things which Christ has said unto me. At such times the words of Jesus come with the vividness of a new revelation. But all other voices in the soul must be hushed to silence— self love must cease to speak, the jarring discord of passion, and inordinate desire must no longer be heard. The senses must be closed and the outward world excluded. Then in this holy stillness, how sweet to the ravished inward ear is the divine music of Jesus' voice. As the high priest consulted the Urim & Thummim, so my soul often retires to this inward oracle, and there sweetly converses with God with heavenly, yet awful familiarity.[134] Yesterday in my closet I felt that the Father, Son, and Spirit, and holy angels were with me, and in that divine society and fellowship I had an earnest of heavenly rest.

This evening at my house one sinner yielded to be saved by grace. Two young lads also seemed to be touched by the Spirit of God. One young lady who was converted Sabbath Evening was present and prayed.

Feb. 18. Have thought much lately of that great mystery of the Gospel, God manifest in the flesh— The <u>hypostatical</u> union, as it is called, by which the human nature of Christ was taken up into the divinity has shown the possibility of the perfect union of our souls with God. Christ in his human nature, like the first Adam represented the whole of human-ity; and when that nature was taken up into an eternal union with the Godhead, it prepared the way for the {eternal} oneness, or unification of my soul with the Deity. The incarnation of Christ is the greatest truth the human mind ever contemplated. It is the profoundest mystery in the uni-verse. Why an infinite being should love so low an object—why infinity should love any thing less than an infinite object—is incomprehensible. But why God should take our nature up into himself, and that forever, as he has done in Christ is a love that passes knowledge. In the incarnation we see a <u>huminization</u> of the the divine, in order to the <u>deification</u> of the human. The Deity becomes a son of man, that I might become a son of God. The union of the man Jesus, with the divine nature, was that which prepared the way for the union of all redeemed souls with God, "that in the dispensation of the fulness of times he might gather together in one all things in Christ, both which are in heaven, and which are on earth; even in him." Eph. 1:10. The apostle declares that God has predestinated us unto <u>sonship</u> by Jesus Christ to himself. Eph 1:5.[135] For when he took up that nature which was our representative into himself, he took my soul with it. The first fruits of this eternal union with the fulness of the Godhead I may, even in this life, enjoy, and do enjoy. How far God came down to invite me to a divine fellowship with him! My heart leaps to embrace the offer and in Jesus I lose myself in God. He has brought heaven and earth, God and man together.

I most cordially agree with the following remarks of Dr Ullmann in his *Life of Thomas à Kempis.* "To enter into fellowship with God, the chief good and fountain of blessedness, and <u>to become one with him</u>, is the basis of all true contentment. But how can two such parties, God and man, the Creator and the creature, be brought together? God is in heaven and man on earth; God is perfect, and man sensual, vain, and sinful. There must, therefore, be mediation, some way in which God <u>comes</u> to man and man {comes} to God, and both unite. This union of man with God depends upon a twofold condition, one negative and the other positive. The negative is that man shall wholly renounce what can give him no true peace. He must forsake the world, which offers to him so much hardship and distress, and whose very pleasures turn into pains; he must detach himself from the creatures, for nothing defiles and entangles the heart so much as impure love of them, and only when a man has advanced so far as no longer to seek consolation from any creature does he enjoy God and find consolation in him; he must in fine die to, and and deny himself, and wholly renounce selfishness and self-love, for whoever loves himself will find, wherever he seeks, only his own little, mean, and sinful self, without being able to find God. This last is the hardest of all tasks, and can only be attained by deep self-acquaintance. But whosoever strictly exercises self-examination will infallibly come to recognize himself in his mean-ness, littleness, and nonentity, and will be led to the most perfect humility, entire contrition, and ardent longing after God. For only when man has become little and nothing in his own eyes, can God become great to him, only when he has emptied himself of all created things can God replenish him with his grace."[136]

The positive condition is also stated. "Not only must a man become free from the world, the creatures, and himself, but God must impart himself to him, in order that he may thenceforth live to God. The two things, however, being dependent upon each other, and taking place simultane-ously, cannot be effected by man alone, but are brought about essentially by God, and through divine grace."[137]

The rule of Kempis, which deserves to be written in gold, was, "<u>Part with all and thou wilt find all</u>.["][138] These are only the echo of the words of Christ: "Except a man forsake all that he hath he cannot be my diciple."[139] He must give all to Christ and then receive all back in and with Christ. Self-renunciation is the basis of all spiritual perfection. Renounce thyself and all, and believe in Jesus Christ, and thou shalt be fully saved.

Feb. 19th. As my soul once searched for knowledge {divine} as for hidden treasure, now I seek for wisdom. Wisdom is the soul of knowledge. Knowledge without it is empty wind; it is worldly in its origin, and leads the soul to the world. How vast the difference between the meek wisdom of a divinely illuminated mind, and that mere secular knowledge which is wholly disconnected from God, and falsely called science. Unless knowledge leads my soul to God, the universal center, it is worthless and unsatisfying. True wisdom comes from God and leads to God. It is not a native of earth, but comes down from heaven, and draws the soul to the seat of its rest. It does not enter the soul through the senses, but it [is] a high and divinely bestowed knowledge, imparted to the soul in union with the Deity. It contains in it holiness, divine freedom, and peace. It includes in it the chief good, "for which every man, by virtue of the deepest and inmost want of his nature cannot but long."[140] This heavenly Wisdom, for which my soul longs, was the companion of God in the solitude of his own eternity before he created the world. Then it filled the divine Mind with infinite happiness; and surely its possession cannot but make my soul full of the purest bliss. (See Prov. 8:22–29.)[141] The soul must soar above the world to find the fountain of this pure wisdom. It is a hidden mystical wisdom which none of the princes of this world know, It is the wisdom of God in a mystery—which we speak only among them that are perfect, and which God ordained before the world unto our glorification. 1 Cor 2:7.[142]

It is not merely knowledge but the inward essence of all intelligence. It is obtained only by direct communication of the soul with God; the mind thus becoming divinely illuminated. It cannot be obtained by books merely, at least not from the outward letter, nor from the senses, nor by reasoning. It is by retiring into myself, by withdrawing into the depth of my being, that the pure, essential truth flows from its eternal Source into my soul. By purity and prayer—the prayer of stillness—the soul is merged in that celestial light in which God dwells, and which interpenetrates my whole being. As the divine presence moves over the abyss of the soul, it gives vitality to all the germs of wisdom which are hidden in its depth. These become fruitful. What a weight of meaning do the Scriptures then contain. A verse becomes a volume. All our previous inquiries have only ruffled the surface; now we see its meaning stretching away down into infinity. Before the soul obtains this baptism {into the} of divine light in reading the words, "The light shineth in the darkness and the darkness comprehendeth it not."[143] Christ is the Word of God, the Eternal essential wisdom of the Father. Paul declares that Jesus Christ is the power of God & the wisdom of God. 1 Cor 1:24.[144] He is made unto us wisdom. 1 Cor. 1:30.[145] I will ever be a scholar in his school and sit at his feet and hear his words.

This evening in my closet I felt a closer union with God than I ever before experienced. I had a clearer sense of an indwelling Deity than ever before. To reproduce my ideas and commit them to paper is exceedingly difficult, and even impossible. But my soul will always remember that precious season of the commingling of my Spirit with the Father of spirits. I found the center of my soul, on which I sweetly rested. I saw the difference between my soul and Christ's in respect to the indwelling Deity. In him dwelt <u>all the fulness</u> of the Godhead.[146] In my soul, (it so appeared to me) dwelt only a portion of the Deity, that portion which fills the space occupied by my being. This was the Soul of my soul, and filled my interior as my spirit does every part of my body. Yet at that point, which seemed the blissful center of my being, I was put into communication with the whole Deity. My soul, emptied of all desires, and passions and cares, was only conscious of existence in God, and a pure, and it seemed almost angelic love. It was a new era in my interior life—the soul taking an advance movement into God. It was an ineffable flowing together of the divine & human. The creature losing himself in the Creator. O the heavenly sweetness of that holy hour. Never did I so comprehend the meaning of those words of Christ— "If a{ny} man love me he will keep my {commandments} words, and my Father will love him and we will come unto him and make our abode with him." John 14:23.

Feb. 28. Another month has passed away. It has been a month of much religious enjoyment, and sweet peace.

In reading in Plutarch, I find that he believed that it was not unreasonable a good man should hold converse with the Deity. He says in the Life of Numa, that there were many who were thought to have attained to superior felicity, and to be beloved in an extraordinary manner by the gods. "And indeed it is rational enough to suppose, that the Deity would not place his affection upon horses or birds, but rather upon human beings, eminently distinguished for virtue; and that he neither dislikes nor disdains to hold conversation with a man of wisdom and piety."[147] Thus speaks the heathen philosopher Plutarch. Surely it would [be] most unreasonable to suppose that the redeemed soul, the noblest work of God, should be cut off from all conscious communication with the infinite Source of its being. To say that a soul cannot have a conscious fellowship with the Father of spirits, is to say that it cannot attain the highest bliss of which it is susceptible, nor answer the end of its creation.

March. 8. Preached today from Rom. 8:2. and Mat 16:24.[148] In the afternoon enjoyed some freedom.

My soul still longs for the calm happiness of unbroken fellowship with God. In a sermon of the great Doctor Cudworth, he quotes the following, which my own experience confirms. Deus ipse, cum omni sua bonitate, quatenus extra me est, non facit me beatum, sed quatemus in me est— ["]God himself with all his goodness, so far as he is without me, does not make me happy, but only so far as he is in me."[149] It is in a sober and qualified sense God incarnated in my nature, after the image and pattern of Christs incarnation that can satisfy my soul. My heart cries out to God with the holy Kempis, "Make me one with thee in everlasting love."[150] I feel a silent and powerful attraction toward the Universal Center, and willingly fall into its current, and would be absorbed and lost in God. Self will is the only thing that prevents this divine union. In fact it is the only thing in the universe that is opposed to God, or to which God is opposed. Every thing else is subject to him, the atom and the world, and all animal natures. Self will is the root and essence of all sin. Sin in its ten thousand Protean shapes, when reduced to its ultimate analysis is only self will. The very beginning of the Christian life is the renunciation of our wills—the entire abnegation of self. Deny thyself and take thy cross, is written over the gateway of Christs religion. How reasonable is this precept. There was a period when there was no will in the universe but the will of God. He dwelt alone in the solitude of empty space. It is not reasonable to suppose that he should create a being to act entirely independent of him. There should now be no will but his in the world. All other wills should be one with his. In heaven to which my soul hastens, and for which it longs, there is only one will. All other wills are merged and lost, blessed Jesus, in thine. Thou hast taught me what it is to reign with thee, to sit with thee on thy throne. It is not to govern under thee any part of the universe, but to have my will one with thine. There whatever the soul wills, it has, because it wills only what thou dost will. And to have what we will, is absolute monarchy, which cannot exist in this state of being; for no earthly monarch has his own will in every thing. But in heaven my redeemed soul will have exactly what it wants, for it will desire nothing except what thou, my good God, shalt will; And every thing which thou dost will must come to pass. This is the hidden meaning of being kings and priests unto God. The pious Anselm, (born at Aosta in Piedmont in 1033. Died 1109) clearly apprehends the blessedness of that closest of all unions—the union of the divine & human will—which is the prime element of the heavenly state. He says—"My dear brother, God calls and asks you to bid for the kingdom of heaven. This kingdom of heaven is one whose blessedness and glory no mortal eye hath seen, no ear hath heard, and no heart of man can conceive. But that thou mayest gain some idea of it, take the following illustration. Whatever anyone who is thought worthy of reigning there wills, that, whether in heaven or on earth, is done; and whatever he does not will, is not done. For so great will be the love between God and those who are to be in this kingdom—and of the latter one towards the other—that all will love each other as they do themselves, and God more than they do themselves. Hence no one there will be disposed to will anything else than what God wills, and what one wills all shall will, and what one or all may will, God shall will. It will therfore be with every individual and with all, with the whole creation and with God himself, as each shall will. And thus shall all be perfect kings, for that shall be which each wills; and all will be at the same time with God as one king, as it were one man, because all shall will the same thing, and what they will shall be. God from heaven asks you to bid for such a good. Does any inquire, for what price? He is answered, He who will give the kingdom of heaven, demands no earthly price; and to God to whom belongs everything that exists, no one can give what he had not. And yet God does not give so great a good for nothing; for he gives it to none who do not love it; for no one gives that which he dearly values to him that cares nothing about it. Therfore love and possess. Finally, since to reign in heaven, is nothing else than to be so united by love into one will with God, all holy angels and men, as that all at the same time possess the same power, love God more than thyself, and thou beginnest already to possess what thou wilt have there in a perfect manner. But this love cannot be a perfect one in thee, unless thou makest thy heart free from all other love; for like a vase which, the more you fill it with water or with any other fluid, will hold so much the less oil, so the heart excludes this love in the same proportion as it is carried away by some other love." (Neander's *His. of Christianity* &c vol. 4. p 366, 367.)[151]

One of the greatest blessings I ever received from my good God, is the power to love him. This my soul prizes above all my intellectual powers. How truly does Fenelon say that "the greatest of all the gifts that he can make us, is that love which we ought to have for him. When God loves us so much as to make us love him he then reigns in us; he then forms our life, our peace, our happiness, and we already begin to live by his life."[152] A susceptibility of exercising love is one of the most valuable powers of our nature. But to prevent this emotion from being a source of disquietude and not of rest to the soul, the object loved must be of sufficient worth and excellence to answer the vastness of the capacity. Love soon stretches itself beyond every finite creature. It is an emotion that was made for God, and nothing less than infinite moral beauty can give it rest—can afford it room to expand and exert all its vigor and activity. When the most perfect being is the object on which it rests it may expend all its energy. To confine our love to the creatures will be to experience an unsatisfied craving continually, and will be a source of more torment than peace. Wouldst thou then, my soul, be happy? Love the Infinite Good. Love all other things, even thyself only for his sake, and thou shalt find rest.

Again love is restless without the presence and possession of the object loved. When the beloved object is far removed, the soul feels the pang and chasm of separation. How happy then are those who love Him who can never be absent from them; who is nearer to us than we are to ourselves. It is only a conscious union with God that can satisfy the soul. Love must possess God or never be at rest. It is disinterested and asks no reward except the possession of the object loved. And this, if it be sincere, and perfect, it always has. It is not in our nature to love an object and not desire to possess it. The {loves} soul that loves God requires God in return. It never can rest until it can say with the spouse from an inward sense and experience, "My Beloved is mine."[153] Hence God inwardly speaks to all souls who perfectly love him, as he he did to Abraham, "I am thy exceeding great reward."[154]

"This God is our God forever and ever."[155] To create a soul to love God, and yet ever to keep that soul in the distance, is to make a being who is restless and miserable, from the necessity of his nature and situation: But I thank him whom my soul loveth, that he has infinitely shortened the distance between himself and my poor worthless being— It is thought by some philosophers that in the physical world no two bodies ever actually touch however near they may seem to approach to each other. But the holy soul comes into actual contact with the infinite Spirit, for God is above all, for the universe cannot contain him; he is through all; for his essence pervades all things; and he is in us all who love him. He is in our soul as our souls are in the body.

March. 11. I can say with Mrs Elizabeth Rowe. "I love my friends, my vital breath and the light of heaven are dear to me; but should I say I love my God as I love these, I should belie the sacred flame which aspires to infinity. 'Tis thee, abstractedly thee, O Uncreated Beauty, that I love; in thee my wishes all terminate; in thee, as in their blissful center, all my desires meet, and there they must be eternally fixed: It is thou alone that must constitute my everlasting happiness."[156]

I have thought of the struggling of the older philosophies to reach {the} a calm repose in the bosom of God. Ever since man was driven out from Paradise, the soul of humanity has cast a long, lingering look back to that divine fellowship it then enjoyed. This secret craving of the soul after re-union with the Deity is seen in some of the systems of the Hindu philosophy. The desire to return to the All, and to be absorbed in the divine substance, which pervades some of these systems, is but an instinctive, though perverted longing of the human spirit after an interior and eternal unity with the Father of spirits. It needed only the light of the Gospel to conduct it to the enjoyment of the highest bliss of which human nature is susceptible. Says Schlegel in his *Philosophy of History*, page 160, that in order to free themselves from transmigration, "They had recourse to philosophy—to the highest aspirings of thought towards God—to a total and lasting immersion of feeling in the unfathomable abyss of the divine essence. They have never doubted that by this means, a perfect union with the Deity might be obtained even in this life, and that thus the soul, freed and immancipated from all mutation and migration through the various forms of animated nature in this world of illusion, might remain forever united with God. Such is the object to which all the different systems of Indian philosophy tend—such is the term of all their inquiries. This philosophy contains a multitude of the sublimest reflections on the separation from all earthly things, and on the union with the Godhead; and there is no high conception in this department of metaphysics, unknown to the Hindoos. But this absorption of all thought and all consciousness in God—this solitary enduring feeling of internal and eternal union with the Deity, they have carried to a pitch and extreme that may almost be called a moral and intellectual self-annihilation."[157]

They erred in looking for a union with God which should destroy the personality of the soul. The union which Christ prays the Father to grant his followers, is a being made one with him, as he and his Father are one. The three persons in the Trinity are not one in such a sense as to destroy their distinct personality. I cannot sufficiently thank God that I have the Gospel of his Son which has revealed to me the summum bonum,[158] after which philosophy searched in vain—

April. 20ᵗʰ 1857.[159] God has not left me. He leads me beside the still waters and into green pastures.[160] O thou whom my soul loveth, let me rest with thee, where thou leadest thy flock at noon:[161] The presence of God everywhere is no more a mere theory, an article of my creed, but an internal and experimental reality. My soul is breathing out continually after God. In my closet this evening he revealed himself to my heart with ineffable sweetness. My faith grasped a present God.

Claremont May 9ᵗʰ 1857.[162] Since I last wrote in my journal I have attended Conference at Lawrence Mass, and have been re-appointed to Claremont. I have an intense desire to come to the people in the fullness of the blessing of the Gospel of Christ. I walked out this afternoon to a beautiful pine grove not far from my residence, and prostrated myself upon the ground, and consecrated all my activity to the service of Christ. I besought him who met Moses at the burning bush, and empowered him to execute his commission in the deliverance of the people of God to go up with me in the work of the ministry. I earnestly besought Christ, who gave the fullness of the Spirit's influence to his apostles on the day of Pentecost, to invest me with the same Pentecostal power—to lay his hands upon my head and ordain me that I might bring forth much fruit. He revealed himself to my soul with heavenly sweetness. O that his Spirit might fertilize all the germs of power that lie hidden in the depth of my being, and bring me out more prominently and usefully. Human applause I do not desire—it is an empty shadow. But my prayer is to God for a fruitful ministry. Give me a holy unction that enchains a congregation, and brings them willing captives to Christ.

It is my purpose to take my point of departure for heaven anew. Thanking God with all my heart for the experience and mercies of the past year, I will from this hour seek a holier fellowship with Christ, and a deeper work of God in my heart. The past year has been the best of my ministry; may the year to come be filled up with a richer experience of divine things, and a sweeter, clearer consciousness of the internal presence of God with me. Shelter me O God, from every storm. Strengthen me in every duty; and give me to partake thine own infinite repose.

May 21. As it was in the days of Christs earthly mission, so now, there are three degrees or different stages of faith in Christ. ["]On the lowest stage stood those,["] according to Neander, (*Life of Christ*, page 138) ["]who, instead of being drawn to Christ by an undeniable want of their spiritual nature, inspired by the power of God working within them, had to be attracted by a feeling of physical want; and by impressions made upon their outward senses. Yet like his heavenly Father, whose Providence leads men to spiritual things even by means of their physical necessities, Christ condescended to this human weakness, sighing at the same time, that such means should be indispensable to turn men's eyes to that which lies nearest to their spiritual being. 'Except ye see signs and wonders, ye will not believe.'["]163 Jno. 4:48.

In the second stage of faith, there was some sense of spiritual need drawing the soul to the Messiah, and some power of discerning spiritual things, but their religious feelings were debased by the admixture of various sensuous elements. This was the condition of the apostles, before their religious feelings were purified by continual personal intercourse with

Christ, and the imparting to them of the plenitude of the Spirit's influence on the day of Pentecost.[164]

A ["]loftier stage of faith was that which, proceeding from an inward living fountain, did not wait for miracles["] addressed to the outward senses ["]to call it forth, but went before and expected them as natural manifestations of the already acknowledged God. Such a presupposed faith, instead of being summoned by the miracles, rather summoned them, as did the pagan centurion, whom Christ offered to the Jews as a model— 'I have not found so great faith, no, not in Israel.'["][165] Such a faith does not arise from any thing outward, and rests not upon any outward signs, or sensible appearances, but upon an invisible God, of whose existence and power the soul has an inward consciousness. Blessed are they that have not <u>seen</u> & yet believed.[166] Thus said Christ to Peter, who in a happy moment recognized in the son of man the Son of God—who by a spiritual intuition recognized beneath the servant form, the hidden divinity, and was led to confess the Messiah,—"Blessed art thou Simon Barjona, for flesh and blood hath not revealed it unto thee, but my Father who is in heaven." (Mat 16:16,17.)[167] By flesh and blood we understand human testimony, and all mere outward evidence. Happy the man who can recognize the divine presence, independent of all outward things, who is elevated above {all} the external world and carried out of the sphere of sense. Who thus not only finds God in the hidden depth of his being, but beholds him without form or parts, sees him without the intervention of any sensuous images—and—what do I say—knows him without even a name, that is, as something which no name can express. This is the highest position of faith— Ruysbroch had a clear apprehension of it when he speaks of its being the highest stage of spiritual developement, "when we have the feeling and inward consciousness beyond all knowledge and science, and of a certain infinite, fathomless unknown; when we are dead to, and rise above all the names which we give to God or to creatures, or pass beyond them into something eternal transcendent, which is incapable of being designated by any name, and lose ourselves therein; and when above all the exercises of virtue in us, we perceive and experience a certain eternal repose, wherein there is no activity; and above all blessed spirits, an infinite and immeasurable bliss, in which we are all one, and this unity itself, so far as it is possible to the creature, is the same that blessedness is in itself"—[168]

He who attains to such an apprehension of God, and intuition of the divine nature, so as to see him who is invisible, needs no sensible sign or outward evidence. How rich in blessedness are those moments, when the soul transported beyond the sphere of sense, loses itself in the depths of God, yet so as {not} to retain a consciousness of the self-subsistence of the creaturely spirit. Where the two are made one so that both retain all the attributes that belong to each. Such an hour of holy fellowship is worth an age of a life of mere sense.

The highest evidence of God's existence at least to my own mind, is not derived from outward things. It is true the outward world was made to glirify [glorify] God, that is to proclaim the perfections of the divine nature; yet if every material thing in the universe were annihilated, and there was nothing in empty space but God and myself, I should have the highest evidence that he existed. In fact the laws of my spiritual being are such that I cannot avoid the conception of the absolute and the infinite—the most perfect Being. This, if it be only a conception of the pure reason gives me only the idea of the absolutely perfect being, which is as far as philosophy generally goes. But when, through a moral harmony subsisting between my soul and the divine nature, I am brought to an inward union with, and experience of God, he is no longer merely an idea, but the living God. He is not only apprehended by reason, but felt in the depth of the soul where he dwells as in the most holy place of the temple. I apprehend the more spiritual a soul becomes—the more it is released from the bondage to sense—the less that person will rely upon the outward world for the proof of the divine existence. The popular argument derived from the marks of design, or contrivance, everywhere observable in nature, and which is an argument so well adapted to a meterial way of thinking, will give way to a more ideal & spiritual proof.

May 22. The true ideal of the Christian life we see realized in Christ, its divine source. In him there were combined in perfect harmony and in exact proportions the contemplative, and active life. A life of contemplation, unless it be molded by the influence of the performance of the duties of Christian love, is apt to degenerate into a gloomy aceticism. But I apprehend that one of the defects of the Christian life of these times, is a want of silent contemplation. Men shun solitude. They seek for bliss too

much out of themselves— Martha who was cumbered with much serv-
ing, {and} has more representatives than Mary who is the symbol of the
contemplative life. If the character of the two could be merged into one,
it would present the Christian life in its completeness and perfect moral
symmetry. I wish to copy in this respect the life of Christ, and avoid any
one-sided developement of Christian character.

May 30. It has appeared to me that the union of the soul to God, may exist in different degrees, as is the case between two created minds. There
may be a oneness of desire. The soul may desire what God desires. This is
the lowest stage or degree of union with God. A second stage is where the
soul <u>loves</u> the same that God loves, and hates the same as God hates. In
this state of sympathy and harmony of the affections with the character
of God is found a closer union & fellowship. But the most perfect union,
and one which includes the two states above mentioned, is a union of the
will with the will of God. In two created spirits where the wills are at variance, so that what one wills the other does not will, they are farther from
oneness than the opposite poles of the earth. When the will is lost in the
will of God, and the soul can say from its inmost depth, "Lo, I come to do
thy will O God,"[169] and can pray the Lord's prayer in its full import, "Thy
will be done in earth as it is done in heaven." then it is joined to the Lord
and is one Spirit with him.

But this perfect harmony of the human & divine wills, can be reached
only in one way—by the love of God & of Christ being diffused through the
whole soul, and penetrating the whole being. Pure & perfect love, the love
of God supremely and for his own sake, and with all the soul's capacity, carries the will along with it, as saith the apostle Paul, "The love of Christ con-
straineth us."[170] This love has its root in faith, and can arise only from faith.
But though it has its origin in faith, which in the mental economy sustains to
it a causal relation, yet it also reacts upon faith—affords it appropriate nourishment, and strengthens it. Here is the philosophy of inward holiness—

My own soul pants for the higher unity. I am consumed with an intense and undying craving for intimate communion with God. I do enjoy
God. He is near to me, and is in me; but I pray for a total and lasting
immersion of my soul, in the Godhead's deepest sea. Open thy heart,
blessed Jesus, and take me in. My desires are knocking at the door of thine

inner sanctuary. Open to me the door, and admit me within, and sup with me & let the feast be everlasting love.

June 6ᵗʰ, 1857. My experience for some time past has not been characterized by strong emotions of joy. At times, and often, I have enjoyed a divine peace and rest; yet for much of the time, I have walked by faith alone. I am more and more convinced that the essence of religion, the very highest position in the divine life, is not made up of changable emotions, but of a destruction of our selfish will—so that our will without losing its individual existence and activity perfectly harmonizes with the will of God, just as two well tuned musical strings, mingle their sounds into one. This loss of our selfish will exerts a great influence upon the desires. In order to enjoy the profoundest repose of soul, we must cease to desire anything which is not included in the will of God. I have been laboring to reach a position in the Christian life, where I shall desire nothing but that which the present moment affords—a state of entire satisfaction and contentment. First I give myself wholly to God, and take him for my only portion, and implore him in his love and unerring providence to manage all my interests for me, and grant me all that may be necessary for my highest holiness—to give me all that joy & peace, and sweetness of his love diffused through my whole being, and all those inward & outward crosses which may be necessary to this result. Then I will recognize in the divine arangements of the present moment exactly what I need, and find then and there the the sum and satisfaction of all my desires. Nothing more disturbs the inward calmness of the soul, than a restless craving for something we do not possess. I have in a present God, and in that divine order of things which his providence has arranged for the present moment all I can need. Why should my soul wander abroad for more? In him is all. He is my all in all. I have in him all that I can find in wealth, or honor, or health, or society & friends, or home or country. At times when I fall upon my knees to pray I can ask only for him—cannot pray for any particular thing. If that particular object is contrary to God I do not desire it; if it be less than God, it will not meet the wants of my inmost nature. At such times my heart can only say:

"Give me thyself, from every boast,
From every wish set free;

Let all I am in thee be lost,
But give thyself to me."[171]

In such an hour I experience a fulfillment of the words of Jesus, in John 16:23. "In that day, ye shall ask me nothing"; that is, such is the fulness of the soul lost in God, that at such a time it has nothing to ask, nothing to desire. "In that day ye shall have nothing to ask me,"—is the rendering of Bloomfield and the best commentators[172]— The hardest lesson the human heart ever learned, is that which the apostle Paul acquired— "I have learned in whatsoever state I am, therewith to be content."[173] In the school of Christ, I will learn the same. I now take take my position at thy feet, my blessed Jesus.

June 17th. I fully concur in the remark of Archbishop Fenelon in his *Maxims of the Saints*, as translated by Upham: "Those souls which have experienced the grace of sanctification in its higher degrees, have not so much need of set times and places for worship as others. Such is the purity and strength of their love, that it is very easy for them to unite with God in acts of inward worship, at all times and in all places. They have an interior closet. The soul is their temple, and God dwells in it."[174]

One reason why they do not need fixed times and places of worship so much as persons in the first stage of Christian life, is because they are not moved in their heavenward way so much by influences lying out of themselves, as are beginners in religious experience. They are impelled by a principle of life deep seated within. Yet such persons are more punctual in their attendance upon the ordinary means of grace, such as public & social worship than others. When providentially deprived of them, they can live without them. Yet both for their own good and for the good of others, they should be found in their places in the public congregation and the more social means of grace. I find wherever I am, with the greatest facility, my soul retires inward upon itself, and there adores God. I do not, as formerly, restlessly go abroad in search of him my soul loves and adores, inquiring of every thing I see, "Where is God my Maker who giveth songs in the night?" but I find him in my heart.[175] Even amid the noisy multitude, I erect a closet in the center of my soul, and retire into it to pray. There God in an ineffable manner meets me, and unites my soul to his. My soul cannot as yet sustain itself for any considerable length of time, in this perfect forgetfulness of the external world, and abstraction from the things of sense, and contemplation of the <u>pure divinity</u>. Yet there are moments rich in a heavenly experience, when I am lost in the depths of God. It is not a state of excitement, of strong emotions; it is not a state of ecstacy, or rapture; but a moment when the whole soul is pervaded with calmness and peace. It partakes of the rest of God, in its union with him.

June 18th. In the contemplation of God, I am able to think of him, without form or parts, or without the intervention of any sensuous image. This is what is called by some writers on inward experience, being occupied with the <u>pure</u> divinity. The idea of God is purely spiritual in the sanctified and contemplative mind. It is not marred by any image borrowed from the senses. It was the remark of St Augustine, "that the capacity of the soul is such, as to enable it to have ideas independently of the {senses} direct action of the senses; and, which, therefore represent things that are not characterized by extension and form, or any other attributes that are visible and tangible." (*Life of Madam Guyon*, by Prof Upham, vol 2. p. 236.)[176]

He does not truly know God who contemplates him as having any of the properties of matter. In contemplating God, I do not stop with his attributes, as his wisdom, power, truth, goodness. These are not God himself; they are only qualities or attributes of God. We may form an idea of matter or mind, distinct from the qualities or attributes of either. So of God. The very idea of an attribute implies the idea of a substance or subject to which the attribute belongs. I know God, and love him, abstracted from all material images, and even from all names and attributes. This idea of God is simple and indefinable. I am afraid that some people do not love the true God, for they do not truly know him; but they love and worship God as possessing form, and many of the properties of matter. This is rather an image of God than God himself. The purest love to God is that which unites the soul to God without any sensuous image intervening. The highest knowledge of God is that which is internal and spiritual in its origin, and which views him without form, as the all pervading substance—as that which is "above all, and through all, and in all." (Eph. 4:6.)[177] {Yet} But few rise to this higher knowledge. Few become free from the bondage of sense. Yet it is better to know God through the aid of the senses than not at all. This early and imperfect knowledge may constitute the basis of that which is spiritual. In the progress of the soul its <u>sensualism</u> may gradually give place to a refined <u>idealism</u>. First that which is earthy; then that which is heavenly. Pure or perfect love is the best school in which to learn what God is. It is only by loving him that we come really to know him. "He that loveth not, knoweth not God; for God is love." 1 John 4:8. When the soul rises from the earthy to the heavenly in the knowledge of God, and loves him as he is, and for what he is, how seraphic is the flame. "This is the true God and eternal life. Little children keep yourselves from idols." (1 John 5:21.)[178]

July 9th 1857. I have been much occupied of late with the study of the noble science of Botany. Have become much interested with it. There is no science which exhibits more of God—his wisdom, & his superabundant goodness.

My flesh and my heart still cry out for the living God. At times my heart has been inclined to sadness. My soul is wearied to death with everything but Christ and communion with him. At times I sweetly rest in Jesus. The language of my heart is;
"O that I could, with fovored [favored] John,
Recline my weary head upon
The dear Redeemer's breast:
From care and sin, and sorrow free,
Give me, O Lord, to find in thee,
My everlasting rest."[179]

Aug 7th. The thought has occurred to me that the Holy Spirit is not only the source of all holy tempers and feelings in the Christian heart,—hence called fruits of the Spirit—but he is also the animating principle of nature. The laws of nature in the growth of the vegetable world, are the mode of his operation. The mysterious principle of life proceeds from him. He is in a certain mitigated sense the soul of the world—the <u>animus mundi</u>. The motions of the universe proceed from him. That the Holy Spirit is the animating, life-giving, and controlling principle in the physical universe, seems to me to be inferentially taught in the Scriptures. The Holy Spirit moved upon, or <u>brooded over</u> the original chaos. Gen. 1:2. This brooding over the chaotic mass, is thought by some to have suggested, to the old theologies the idea of a "first-laid egg," out of which all things were formed. The Spirit reduced the formless mass to order and harmony, and imparted vital energy— "By his Spirit he hath garnished the heavens." Job. 26:13. By the word of the Lord were the heavens made and all the host of them by the breath of his mouth. Ps. 33.6.

In a sublime passage in {the} Ps 104:27–30 this doctrine is more directly asserted. Speaking of the creatures the psalmist says:

["]These {all} wait all upon thee, that thou mayest give them their meat in due season. That thou givest them they gather; thou openest thine hand, they are filled with good. Thou hidest thy face, they are troubled; thou takest away their breath, they die, and return to their dust. Thou sendest forth thy Spirit, they are created: and thou renewest the face of the earth."

The same truth is at bottom of the passage in Isaiah, where in poetical and prophetic language, {where} under the figure of a desert becoming clothed with verdure, he announced the calling of the gentile world to the privileges of the Gospel. "Until the Spirit be poured upon us from on high, and the wilderness be a fruitful field, and the fruitful field be counted for a forest." Isa. 32:15

The subjection of the animal world to the control or governance of the Holy Spirit is taught in the sublime prophecy of {the} Isaiah respecting Idumea, though perhaps looking farther.[180] After speaking of various wild beasts, as dragons, owls, satyrs, and vultures, who should inhabit the solitudes, where once stood the populous cities, he says "No one of these shall fail, none shall want her mate; for my mouth it hath commanded, and his Spirit it hath gathered them.["] (Isa. 34:13–16.)[181]

"The grass withereth, the flower fadeth; because the Spirit of the Lord, bloweth bloweth upon it. Surely the people is grass."[182] The word spirit here may be thought to mean wind or breath, and refers to the withering simoon, or blast from the desert.[183] Yet it is so called because that blast itself goes forth at the command of the Spirit of God, and proceeds from him. Behold in another passage of prophecy, the animal world under the governance of the Spirit: The law of instinct in animals which is as uniform in its operations as gravity, is the mode in which the Spirit controls the kingdom of animated nature. "As a beast goeth down into the valley, the Spirit of the Lord caused him to rest; so didst thou lead the people, to make thyself a glorious name." (Isa. 63:14.)

It is the Spirit that quickeneth, or giveth life. His omnipresence clothes the earth with verdure, and garnishes or beautifies the heavens. {Even our slumber} He still broods over the world, which his power & presence restored from chaos. He governs also in the world of mind. "There is a spirit in man, and the inspiration of the Almighty giveth them understanding." (Job 32:8.) As all knowledge comes from him, so every holy motion of the soul, its inward pantings for God, its heavenly breathings and aspirations, its fulness of joy, and sacred repose, are all inspirations of the Holy Spirit. Its joy, love, peace, long-suffering, gentleness, goodness, temperance, fidelity, are only fruits of the Spirit. Even our slumbering dust shall be animated by the life-giving Spirit. ["]If the Spirit of him who raised up Jesus from the dead dwell in you, he that raised up Christ from the dead, shall also quicken your mortal (or dead) bodies by his Spirit which dwelleth in you."[184] The Spirit then in the economy of the holy Trinity, is the energizing principle in the physical and mental world.

May my soul be like a well watered garden, yea like Eden itself, where the creations of God's Holy Spirit shall abound and flourish.

Sept. 2ᵈ. 1857. God is still the center and rest of my soul. "Rest not a moment without the felt presence of your God," says Richard Watson.[185] An inward consciousness of God, a sense of the divine presence within, is the privilege of all Gods people. The sanctified soul has a power of discerning God. The way it does this is beyond expression; yet blessed are the pure in heart for they shall see God— David Hartley, notwithstanding his materialistic bent of mind, recognizes the power of the mind to do this, and appropriates to it the term theopathy, and pronounces it a right and beneficial mental condition.[186] God is everywhere in space. And must his existence be to us a mere opinion? Can we not have his felt presence? Tauler in one of his sermons thus truly and eloquently says: "I have a power in my soul which enables me to perceive God; I am as certain as that I live, that nothing is so near to me as God. He is nearer to me than I am to myself. It is a part of his very essence that he should be nigh and present to me. He is also nigh to a stone or a tree, yet they do not know it. If a tree could know

God, and perceive his presence as the highest of the angels perceives it, the tree would be as blessed as the highest angel. And it is because man is capable of perceiving God and knowing how nigh God is to him, that he is better off than a tree. And he is more blessed or less blessed in the same measure as he is aware of the presence of God. It is not because God is in him, and so close to him, and he hath God, that he is blessed, but because he perceives God's presence, and knows and loves him; and such an one will feel that God's kingdom is nigh at hand."[187]

How finely does the devout Fenelon, archbishop of Cambray, point out the way in which we are to find God. Addressing the Divine Being he says: ["]Thou art, then, (and I am enraptured with the thought!) continually at work in the very center of my being; invisibly thou workest there, as a laborer digging mines in the bowels of the earth; thou dost all, and the world perceives thee not; it attributes nothing to thee. I myself was once wandering astray, in vain attempts to find thee, at a great distance from me; I was drawing together in my mind all the wonders of nature, that I might thus form to myself some image of thy greatness; I was going to inquire after after thee of thy creatures; and I never thought of finding thee in the center of my heart where thou never ceasedst to dwell. No, my God, we need not dig into the heart of the earth, nor pass beyond the seas; we need not, as thy holy oracles tell us, fly up into the heavens to find thee; thou art nearer to us than we are to ourselves."[188]

In another place he also says: "As for me, O my Creator, with my eyes shut to all external objects, which are but vanity and vexation of spirit, I will find, in the most secret recess of my heart, an intimate familiarity with thee, by Jesus Christ thy Son."[189]

To thus know God, not merely as the God of nature ordering all the movements of the material universe, nor as the God of Providence and revelation, but as a God dwelling in us as in the most holy place of the temple, is eternal life.

Sept 24. I have enjoyed of late much sweet communion with God— at times my heart has been filled with love to God— Love is the principle of holiness, and the highest bliss of the soul. The heaven of heavens is love. The power to love God is the greatest gift bestowed upon human nature. It is the crowning blessing of infinite goodness. He who loves nothing but himself is in the profoundest misery. It is the essence of hell. To love anything out of ourselves makes the soul happier. But to love Jesus & to be conscious that he loves us is to feel the holiest and happiest emotion of the human heart. O the bliss, the heavenly sweetness of that hour when Jesus alone is loved! It is heaven come down to earth. It is Paradise repaired. A soul consumed with the love of Jesus, droops in his absence like a flower smitten with an autumnal frost. Where perfect love reigns the soul cleaves to Jesus. The thought of separation is a pang in the heart. To be separated from him is the most dreaded hell. Life without him would be a desolation, & the universe a gloomy solitude. The highest ideal of heavenly bliss is {to} an eternal union with him—to be where he is and to be like him. When he is present all is well. Pain is sweet, labor is rest, and death itself, as the messenger to summon & conduct us to his presence, is welcome. When he is absent from the soul, a vacuum is left which the whole universe cannot fill. All comfort withers and dies. The least adversity or cross is insupportable—

He who loves God according to the full measure of his capacity is as happy as his nature will admit. "It is the image and little representation of heaven; it is beatitude in picture, or rather the infancy and beginnings of glory." (Jeremy Taylor.)[190] In Paradise where Adam was, this was the law. "Thou shalt love the Lord, thy God with all thy heart, with all thy soul, and with all thy mind, and with all thy strength, and thy neighbor as thyself.["][191] This is the old commandment, and the new commandment, and the sum of all the divine commandments. It is all the law and the prophets. All other graces are only different forms of love. Under proper circumstances and in a fitting opportunity it becomes patience, or meekness, or chastity or temperance, or zeal. It is the soul of every virtue. All real virtue is an outgrowth from this root. He who loves in the proper degree, will be right in everything else. It is the bond of perfection, and the fulfilling of the law.

But what is perfect love? It is sincere love, true love. Dissembled love is like painted fire. It is not love only in outward appearance. Perfect love is lodged in the center of the heart. It is perpetual and constant. If it should cease for a moment is [it] would not be perfect. It does not come and go like the tide, but ever flows on like a majestic river. It is not a passion but a principle; not an emotion merely, but a state of the will. A child may love his father, or a parent may love his son when he is not even thinking of {them} him. Other thoughts fill the soul, other cares occupy his whole attention. Yet love never ceases even for a moment. As soon as the thought of the endeared object gains admittance, then love is felt. Before, it existed as a state of the will. The highest form of love is not a mere emotion. Pure love has been called "loving without feeling, just as pure faith is believing without seeing."[192]

It is supreme love. If there be in the universe, any thing which we love as much or more than God, any thing we more highly prize, our love is defective, and not perfect. In a mitigated sense, perfect love is loving God alone. All other love is so small in comparison as to seem nothing. The love of God has swallowed up all other love. Everything else is loved in him and for his sake.

It is a grateful love. The soul goes forth in thankfulness to its divine Benefactor for all his mercies, for all those precious emanations from him we have enjoyed. It loves him for his amazing goodness to us. This gratitude, though it has reference to the gifts of God to us, is not selfish. As Mr Hervey has said, "There is something in it noble, disinterested, and generously devout."[193] It is an effort of the soul to express its appreciation of the divine benefactions. It existed in Paradise when man came pure from the hand of his Maker; it will be perpetuated in heaven where God is all in all. Grateful love in the perfected heart becomes ceaseless praise. Just as the distant waterfall in the silence of the night continually murmurs its song to the stars above it, so the ear of God forever hears the low breathings of {love} grateful praise proceeding from the heart where perfect love reigns. This form of love must be stronger in the Christian heart than it was in the Paradisiacal state. Adam never felt in Eden the glow and rapture of that love, where much has been forgiven. The pardon of many offenses, which had deserved death, binds the soul to its merciful Redeemer in stronger ties, than creation did, or could. He loves much to whom much is forgiven.

Look at the woman in the house of Simon the Pharisee. Luke 7:36. et seq.[194] Wicked she had been, notoriously vicious had been her life. But at length she began to feel a sense of alienation from God, and was pained at the sight of the abyss which her sins had opened between her and the Holy One. She felt the bitter pangs of repentance, and an intense desire for salvation. Convinced of sin, groaning under its crushing weight, goaded by an awakened conscience, and hoping to obtain balm for her wounded heart, she threw herself at Jesus' feet, moistened them with her tears, wiped them with her hair, and anointed them with the costly ointment. Attracted thus to Jesus for rest to her burdened soul, he lifted from her heart the mountain of despair, pronouncing her sins, which were many, all forgiven. How glowing was her love, more than Adam felt in Eden. The greater had been her sins, the more profound had been her desire for salvation, the more she valued the gift of pardon, and the more ardent was her love to her Redeemer. She loved much for much had been forgiven. This is the law of our nature. To rescue from a great evil is more highly prized than the bestowal of a great good without any previous experience of evil. The free gift is of many offenses unto justification. The pardoned and sanctified sinner is bound to God by the most endearing ties.

Perfect love has respect also to {the} degree. "Thou shalt love the Lord thy God with all thy strength.["][195] This is said to the child, the peasant, the philosopher, the angel. Each is to love God according to the measure of his capacity. Perfect love, is love diffused through our whole being— Every other emotion of the heart is tinged with love; it is the warp and woof of every emotion. The life of such a soul is bound up in the same bundle of life with the Lord its God. Prayer and praise are no more an effort[,] {but an} a labor, a task, but a spontaneity. As fire ascending seeks the sun, as rivers flow to the ocean, so love breathes out itself in ceaseless prayer. Love hidden in the inmost depth of the {heart} soul prays without ceasing, even when the mind may be occupied with other things. The whole life is prayer, one constant flame of devotion. The way to heaven is no more uphill. Heaven is brought down by love on a level with the soul. The current of nature is turned and flows toward the cross. Christ makes such a heart his constant habitation.

It is the love of God for his own sake as the most perfect Being. We love the Lord because he first loved us. "I love the Lord," says David, "because he hath heard my voice and my supplications." Ps. 116:1. The consideration of God's goodness and bounty to us in his providence, and especially the great love wherewith he hath loved us in our redemption by the cross, may be and most commonly is the first motive of our love to him. But this is only the beginning and not the perfection of love. The soul may love God for his own excellency independent of all his dealings with us, and above all the consolations of his grace. May not a parent love a child, or a wife a husband independent of all their faults, or good deeds. The being is abstracted from all his <u>accidents</u> and loved for his own sake. Thus God loves the sinner. Thus we are commanded to love our enemies. The man is placed in front of all his evil doings, and his humanity, abstracted from all its evils which do not belong to its essence, is loved for its sake. We love the idea of man which that person so imperfectly exhibits. Thus as children we {imitate the} become followers of God, who maketh his sun to rise on the evil and on the good, and sendeth rain on the just and on the unjust. God loves in the wicked only that which is the work of his hands, the pure humanity without the unseemly accretions or additions which sin has made to it. When we thus love our fellow men, we are perfect as our Father in heaven is perfect. Mat. 5:43–48.[196]

Thus we may love the pure divinity of God, abstracted from all his dealings with us. This does not exclude the lower forms of love, but includes them all. We love God not merely because he is a means of our happiness but because he is what he is.

Says Abelard. (A.D. 1108) "Whoever seeks in God, not himself, but something else, does not in reality love <u>him</u>, but that other thing. xxxxx[197] O that we might have so upright a disposition of heart {to him} towards the Lord, as to love him far more on his own account, because he is so good in himself, than on account of the benefits which he brings to us. So would our righteousness render to him what he claims, that, because he is supremely good, he should be supremely loved by all. Fear and hope of reward are but the first step in piety: The fear of the Lord is the <u>beginning</u> of wisdom; but the perfection of it is the pure love of God for his own sake."[198]

Perfect love casts out fear. "There is no fear in love but perfect love casteth out fear.["] 1 Jno. 4:18. Here are two different mental conditions, fear and love. They cannot coexist in the same heart. Much of the misery of this life is referable to fear. There is no emotion that more disturbs the soul, and is so opposite from this calm repose and tranquility which are characteristic of the purified nature, as fear. It is said by St John, that it hath torments.[199] Did I wish to punish a person as severely as possible, I would subject him to the dominion of fear. I would keep [him] in in a constant state of alarm, and apprehension of some evil. There should be in his heart a fearful looking for of judgment and fiery indignation which

should devour the adversaries. {Perfect love} Fear exists in many different forms. It assumes Protean shapes. It is sometimes anxiety about the
future. Perfect love casts it out by creating in the soul a supreme desire
for God. Such a love asks for nothing but the object loved. In God we find
all the needs of the soul met. It casts out the fear of man, that is a slavish
fear of losing the favor and good opinion of our fellowmen. A consciousness of perfect safety is connected with perfect love. It is convinced that
nothing can harm us if we be followers of the Good One. It places little
value on the good opinions of men. They are idle wind. The frowns of the
world are nothing, and it weeps in secret places at the emptiness of human applause. The favor of God is all. The fear of death is cast out, though
the love of life may linger. Death becomes the point of eternal union with
God. It gives boldness, "liberty of speech," in the day of judgment. The
fear of the wrath to come is swalowed up by the hope of glory. That which
is supremely loved cannot be feared nor its presence dreaded. Hence the
slavish fear of God, which clings to the unsanctified nature, is absorbed
by a filial confidence. All these forms of fear, which are the offspring of sin
and black night are destroyed, and the whole soul pervaded with calmness
and peace.

Perfect love gives directions to the thoughts. God becomes the center
of our thoughts, as we naturally think of that which we love most. As the
magnetic needle when it has been pulled aside from its proper direction,
vibrates for a moment back and forth, and then settles down in {upon} its
natural position pointing north, so the mind occupied necessarily for a
season with other thoughts, as soon as it is left to itself fixes itself upon its
divine center. It requires no effort to think of God; but demands a volition to call off the thoughts from him.[200] It is one of the laws of our nature
that love influences the will so to act as to please the object loved. Hence
says Christ, {this} If ye love me keep my commandments.[201] Perfect love
is perfect obedience. Obedience is more a state of the heart or will than
an outward act.[202] But this state existing within, it spontaneously {pass}
flows out into the external act when the occasion permits or demands. It
contains the germs of all good actions.

Sept. 26. Have felt for several weeks my heart to glow with divine love.
I would rejoice in the Lord always. I have chosen God for my sole portion

and inheritance, and I would not convey an impression to any, that he who has such an inheritance could be dissatisfied with it. Let those who have nothing but this world be melancholy and wretched. How poor is their condition. How rich is his who has nothing but God. In him he has all. Then will I rejoice in the Lord always, and in everything give thanks.[203] It is important that I <u>delight</u> myself in the Lord. Then will he give me the desire of my heart. That is a soul, which seeks its sole hapiness in God, shall have all it desires. For in such a state it desires only God, and possesses him. To <u>delight</u> myself in the Lord is one of the sweet ways of overcoming temptation. There is a saying of St Anthony, quoted by Jeremy Taylor, which seems to contain an important truth of Christian experience— "There is one way of overcoming our spiritual enemies; spiritual mirth, and a perpetual bearing of God in our minds—"[204]

(**Oct 25th**. This has been a Sabbath of some comfort, and of some freedom in preaching. Have not felt that inward disturbance which has sometimes followed from the pulpit. In watering others my soul has sometimes been dry. Today I have had inward freedom; my soul has not been jostled from its center, but sweetly rests in Jesus.

I have thought there is a way to preach, and to preach the most effectually, and yet it will not exhaust the body or mind, but will invigorate the whole system, and prolong life. It ought not to be unhealthy to proclaim the truth. May Jesus grant me the secret of so preaching as even to preserve my health and life.)

Nov. 7th 1857. I find it has been characteristic of all persons eminent for piety, persons who have attained the highest results of Christian experience that they have lived in the presence of God, and in the enjoyment of inward communion with him— "Let us," says Mr Fletcher, "shut our eyes to the gilded clouds without us; let us draw inward, and search after God, if haply we may find him." (Benson's *Life of Fletcher*, p. 335.)[205] The state of mind {by} in which the soul is fixed intently on God, while it is called off from all other things, has been denominated recollection—a state identical with that of contemplation as it was named by the Christian teachers of the middle ages. This state has been well described by Mr Fletcher, who says: "Recollection is a dwelling within ourselves; being abstracted from the creature, and turned towards God. It is both outward and inward. Outward recollection consists in <u>silence</u> from all idle and superfluous words; and a wise disentanglement from the world, keeping to our own business, observing and following the order of God for ourselves, and shutting the ear against all curious and unprofitable matters. Inward recollection consists in shutting the door of the senses; in a deep attention to the presence of God; and in a continual case of entertaining holy thoughts for fear of <u>spiritual idleness</u>: —Let it be calm and peaceable; and let it be lasting." (Benson's *Life of Fletcher*, p. 87.)[206] In this state of abstraction from all created things, God is in an ineffable manner directly present to the soul. The soul is <u>collected in itself</u>. The thoughts and affections and desires instead of being divergent in every direction, are drawn in from the circumferences, and consolidated around some center, and that center is God. (Upham's *Life of Faith*, p. 427.)[207]

This abstraction from the creatures makes the heart a solitude where God dwells alone. The soul by a kind of divine enchantment is fixed intently upon God, and loses sight of all the creatures, {and} even of itself.

The state of recollection is essential to the highest form of Christian experience. It was enjoined upon Abraham in the command— "Walk before me and be thou perfect." David also expresses an experience of this state when he says "I have set the Lord always before me." Ps 16:8. Happy is that man whose habitual state is one of inward recollection. God becomes his familiar companion. Prayer is the natural breathing of such a soul— God is never absent from such a heart. He abides in it as his perpetual home. His communion with God is sweet and constant. Such a man was the Rev John Fletcher, of Madeley.[208] Mrs Fletcher remarks, that "It was his constant practice [endeavour] to set the Lord before him, and to maintain an uninterrupted sense of his presence. In order to this, he was slow of speech, and had the greatest government of his words. Indeed, he both acted, and spoke, and thought, as under the eye of God. And thus he remained unmoved in all occurrences; at all times and on every occasion possessing inward recollection. Nor did I ever see him diverted therefrom on any occasion whatever, either going out or coming in, whether by ourselves or in company. Sometimes he took his journies alone; but above a thousand miles I have travelled with him; during which neither change of company, nor of place, nor the variety of circumstances which naturally occur in travelling, ever seemed to make the least difference in his firm attention to the presence of God. To preserve this uniform habit of soul, he was so watchful and recollected, that to such as were unexperienced in these things it might appear like insensibility. But no one could converse in a more lively and sensible manner, even on natural things, when he saw it was to the glory of God. He was always striving to raise his own, and every other spirit[,] to a close and immediate intercourse with God." (Benson's *Life of Fletcher* p. 333.)[209]

The power of retiring inward, {there} & in the profoundest depth of our being to perceive and enjoy the divine presence, is one of the principal instruments of Christian perfection. He who becomes mature in Christian experiences must be delivered from the distraction of his senses, and the roving of his imagination. He must walk in the presence of God. Alas how few in this age live within themselves. I am afraid there is an increasing tendency to externalize religion.

Journal II (1857–1865)

Chronology of my Life.

I was born in Rockingham Vt, Dec 28 1817.

In June 1835, turned my attention to religious things and connected myself with the Congregational church.

Fitted for College at Chester (Vt) Academy, and entered Middlebury College, Sept 7 1837, in the following spring went to Dartmouth College where I remained until the middle of the Junior year.

Jan 1st 1839, Preached my first sermon at Bellows Falls, from "He hath bent his bow & made it ready." Also connected myself with the M.E. church. Had previously embraced the Oberlin view of Sanctification.

June 21st 1840, was married to Miss Charlotte Linker of Chelsea Vt, and in the session of the N.H. Conference held in Chelsea July 1st 1840, was appointed to Pincham Vt. Remained one year and located.

Joined Conference again at the session in Portsmouth July 10th 1844. July 14th 1844 was ordained Deacon by bishop Hamline. Was stationed at Goffstown N.H. where I remained one year.

In 1845, was stationed at Pembroke where I labored two years.

At the Conference in Northfield N.H. May 23d 1847, was ordained an Elder, and stationed at Rindge N.H. Remained one year. The two following years labored in Marlow.

At the Conference held in New Market May 1850 was appointed to Newport, where I labored two years. From that time my journal shows where I have preached.

Journal Dec. 31st. 1857.[1]
W. F. Evans.
Claremont N.H.

Chronology of my Life.[2]

I was born in Rockingham Vt. Dec. 23^{d} 1817. In June, 1835, turned my attention to religious things and connected myself with the Congregational church.

Fitted for College at Chester (vt) Academy, and entered Middlebury College, Sept. 7th 1837. In the following spring went to Dartmouth College, where I remained until the middle of the Junior year.

Jan. 1st 1839. Preached my first sermon at Bellows Falls, from "He hath bent his bow & made it ready."[3] Also connected myself with the M. E. Church. Had previously embraced the Oberlin view of Sanctification.

June 21st 1840, was married to Miss Charlotte Tinker of Chelsea Vt, and in the session of the N.H. Conference, held in Chelsea July 1st 1840, was appointed to Peacham Vt. Remained one year and located.

Joined Conference again, at the session in Portsmouth, July 10th 1844.

July 14th 1844 was ordained Deacon by bishop Hamline.[4] Was stationed at Goffstown N.H., where I remained one year.

In June 1845, was stationed at Pembroke[5] where I labored two years.

At the Conference in Northfield N.H., May 23^{d} 1847, was ordained an Elder, and stationed at Rindge, N.H. Remained one year. The two following years labored in Marlow.[6]

At the Conference held in New Market May, 1850, was appointed to Newport, where I labored two years. From that time my Journal shows where I have preached.[7]

1857.[8]

Claremont Dec. 31st 1857. In a short time another year expires. May my sinful nature expire with it. May the old Adam in me die, and all things belonging to the new life in Christ live and grow in me— I can never deem the work of my salvation complete until I do good without effort, just as the sinner does evil. In the 2^{d} Chapter of Isaiah, the prophet in speaking of the age of the Messiah, says: "It shall come to pass in the last days, that the mountain of the Lord's house shall be established in the top of the mountains, and shall be exalted above the hills; and all nations shall flow unto it." Isa. 2:2. As the torrents of the mountains, as the rivers in the valleys, flow to the ocean from the law of their own nature, so the soul fully redeemed <u>flows</u> toward the mountain of God's holiness from its own inward impulse. It is not impelled merely by a sense of obligation, but through the attractions of love it silently and calmly moves in the line of duty. The degree of ease with which one does what is right, is the measure of the degree of our redemption.

I find the following among the maxims of Lao-tseu, a Chinese philosopher who lived about 600 years before Christ— "Men of superior virtue are ignorant of their virtue. Men of inferior virtue do not forget their virtue. Men of superior virtue practice it without thinking of it. Men of inferior virtue practice it with intention."[9] In the highest stage of our personal redemption, our whole inward nature is transformed, the current of life <u>flows</u> spontaneously in the direction of God and heaven. The thoughts, desires[,] affections, and even the will all tend of their own accord towards their natural center. Such a soul does right without a struggle, without an effort, and sometimes without knowing it. He is not driven by conscience to duty, to secret prayer for instance, like a slave to a task. His nature <u>flows</u> in that direction. He acts in accordance with the law, and yet is not pressed by the law. He is impelled not by the pressure of law, or the demands of conscience merely, but his nature, his life, is to do what the law demands. His soul has recovered its native freedom—the freedom of angels and of God.

"All the rivers run into the sea, yet the sea is not full; [un]to the place from whence the rivers come, thither they return again." Eccl. 1:7. (The time will come when the multitudes of the world will <u>flow</u> unto the mountain of the Lord's house, not like the Euphrates in a great, rapid, and impetuous current, roaring and dashing; but the ransomed spirit shall flow to God, like the gentle Siloah, whose waters go softly. Isa. 8:6.7.)[10]

Jan. 2. 1858. With the first beginnings of the soul's restoration, the appearance of outward nature is changed. How often is the remark made that all things seem to be new. The new moral creation within is reflected upon things without, and there seem to be new heavens and a new earth, because we behold them through the medium of new feelings, and see them from a different stand-point. The harmony of the restored moral nature with the with the outward world deepens with the progress of the redeemed spirit in holiness. It sees in the beautiful, moving forms of the earth the emanations of the beauty of the Lord, and sees all things to be full of God— The successive seasons, with the beauties and harmonies belonging to each, are exhibitions of the Deity.

> ["]These as they change, Almighty Father, these
> Are but the <u>varied</u> God. The rolling year,
> Is full of thee. Forth in the pleasing Spring
> Thy beauty walks, thy tenderness and love.
> Wide flush the fields; the softening air is balm;
> Echo the mountains round; the forest smiles;
> And every sense, and every heart is joy.
> Then comes thy glory in the Summer-months,
> With light and heat refulgent. Then thy Sun
> Shoots full perfection through the swelling year:
> And oft thy voice in dreadful thunder speaks;
> And oft at dawn, deep noon, or falling eve,
> By brooks and groves, in hollow-whispering gales,
> Thy bounty shines in Autumn unconfined.
> And spreads a common feast for all that lives.
> In winter, awful thou! with clouds and storms
> Around thee thrown, tempest o'er tempest rolled,
> Majestic darkness! on the whirlwind's wing,
> Riding sublime, thou bid'st the world adore,
> And humblest nature with thy northern blast."[11]

The earth though sympathizing with the moral disorders of mankind, still exhibits traces of its original perfection, some lingering marks of its Paradisaical order and bloom. It is this which accounts for the fact that in the language of two of the most highly polished nations of the old world, the universe is designated by words signifying <u>order</u> and <u>elegance</u>, (κοςμος, and mundus.)[12] Pythagoras, who seems to have had a keen sense of the harmonies of nature, is said to have been the first of the Greeks who applied the word κοςμος to the material universe. (See Hulsean *Lectures*. p. 194.)[13] Enough of its original beauty gleams through its present disorders, to convince us that it was not made to be the abode of sin, and of beings made miserable by sin. "The earth, arrayed in verdure, adorned with flowers, diversified with hill and dale, forest and glade, fountains and running streams, engirdled with the ocean, over-canopied with heaven; this earth, so smiling and fruitful, so commodious and magnificent, is altogether worthy of its Maker; and not only a fit habitation for man, created in the image of God, but a place which angels might delight to visit on embassies of love." (Montgomery's *Lectures on Poetry*. p. 52.)[14] These beauties can be appreciated {only} and enjoyed fully only by those who are pure in heart. Sin blights and blasts the fair scene. It draws a veil over the beautiful creations of the divine hand. But the earth is full of divine radiance, and the relics of its original adornment. The redeemed spirit, adjusted in harmony with all that is divine, finds them on every hand. It now,

"Makes musis [music] with the common strings, With which the world is strung, and makes the dumb

Earth utter heavenly harmony.—["]"[15]

How often in silent contemplation, with the soul in communion with a present God, have I heard,

"The low sweet voices of a thousand streams,

Some near, some far remote, faint trickling sounds,

That dwelt in the great solitude of night

Upon the edge of silence."[16]

Jan. 24. Had a greater struggle of soul this afternoon after meeting than I ever before experienced. I joined my soul to Christ by living faith, and thus merged in Jesus, I went to the throne of the Father, who always—hears him. I felt as if I should die unless my prayer was heard. In the evening we had a time of power, such as I have not seen since I came to Claremont. Three souls were converted—

Jan. 27. My mind is unusually active, I am not troubled with wandering thoughts, with such as wander from God. My thoughts naturally move towards him, and fix themselves upon divine things. I almost tire of this divine contemplation. Sometimes I fall into a <u>divine slumber</u>. The soul ceases all effort in thinking; all desire is silenced; and the mind looses itself in the depths of God. Earthly images fade away, and the soul sweetly floats inward from the circumference, and becomes tranquilly fixed on its divine center. This divine slumber is necessary to the rest of the powers of the soul, and to recruit its energies. The spirit sleeps in God— Does not the Psalmist refer to this when he says of God that "he giveth his beloved sleep." Ps. 127:2. Fenelon remarks in his *Pious Thoughts*, "That the presence of God calms the spirit, gives a peaceful slumber and repose, even during the daytime, and in the midst of all labors."[17] How sweet thus to rest, with the mind free from all disturbing emotions, and desires, and all active thought, and to fall into a divine slumber— I love to hide in the secret place of the Most High from all care and anxiety, and in inward silence to sympathize with the repose of God—to sink into the bosom of the Infinite Life, and become still. There are times, after long continued thought and exertion, as in preaching, when the soul needs not bliss, but asks only for rest.

This holy slumber is not to be a permanent state, but only as the soul needs repose. "There remaineth a rest to the people of God."[18]

Feb. 27th 1858. At times my soul has had a clearer sense of the <u>allness</u> of God than I ever before experienced. One night on my bed my soul lost itself in the All— It seemed to me that there was nothing but God—that he was the life, the support, the substance of everything which exists. I thank God for rest in the all-pervading Deity. This inward consciousness of God, this living and moving in the divine element, has made all times and places alike. Every day is exalted to the dignity of a Sabbath, while the Sabbath is not lowered to mere secular time. Sometimes I find formal prayer to be an impossibility. I enter my closet, fall upon my knees, hold my soul in the divine presence, but have no special burden of prayer, no particular requests to make. I can only sweetly rest in the will of God, while my heart from its inmost center silently breathes out the prayer, the holiest in earth or heaven—

May thy will, not mine be done,
May thy will and mine be one.[19]

Prayer is becoming with me an inward life— The soul in a ceaseless current flows out after God. Its desires silently flow into the mind of God, and the thoughts of God flow into my soul. There is a community of feeling between my heart and the God it adores. In this holy fellowship with Christ we have all things common.

March 7. Sabbath— In the evening three persons presented themselves as objects of prayer. May they all find rest in Christ.

March 10. I have found the true riches—at least I have discovered where they are to be found. He is infinitely rich who desires nothing. Many persons are esteemed rich who are not really so— Says the devout Charles How— "I take him to be the only rich man, who lives upon what he has, owes nothing, and is contented. For there is no determinate sum of money, nor quantity of estate, that can denote a man rich; since no man is truly rich that has not so much as perfectly satiates his desire of having more. For the desire of more is want, and want is poverty."[20] But nothing can meet the large desires of the soul but the possession of the infinite and un-created Good. The soul that is satisfied with God and desires nothing else is unspeakably rich. If I delight myself in the Lord, he gives me the desires of my heart. I have found this blessedness in some good degree— How sweet has been my fellowship with God for a long time— In the solitude of my own being I commune with him—

"Within his circling arms I lie,
Beset on every side."[21]

I have been blest with the "season of finite good," and have found gold tried in the fire.[22]

March 19th 1858— There is at present a more extensive revival of religion in the country than has been known for a long time; New York city is especially the scene of a most powerful work of God.[23] The popular current has been turned towards the cross, and the masses are flowing towards the house of God. Prayer has been offered that this saving influence might sweep over the place like an an overwhelming flood of life and glory. My own soul has been much burdened with an intense and incessant desire for a general outpouring of the Holy Spirit. Yet I would constantly rest in the will of God in this matter. O that his salvation might go forth as brightness. Let my cry come before thee my king and my God; for unto thee do I call.

March. 26— In order to abide in the peace of God, I find it necessary to banish from my heart all jealous feelings of God, and to maintain a constant assurance that he loves me, and desires my highest good. (God is not only good, but he is goodness itself—he not only loves me, but he is pure unbounded love itself. Such a being is not subject to any sudden caprice of passion or feeling. His love is not a transient feeling but an unchanging nature. He loves me even when I am fearful he does not, and when unbelief has forced a barrier between my soul and his infinite Spirit.)[24] It is only a want of affectionate confidence {that} in him, that prevents my enjoying him at all times. Nothing can separate my soul from him it adores and loves but unbelief, a want of that confidence, that loving trust in him, which hath great recompence of reward. It was unbelief that removed man from the paradisiacal state. When faith becomes an undoubting assurance of God's unchanging and everlasting love, Paradise is repaired, and the soul restored to a perpetual and blissful intercource with his all-pervading Spirit. The soul can then say :

"Where'er I am, where'er I move,
I meet the object of my love."[25]

It is to be borne in mind that my unbelief makes no change in the divine mind, but puts my soul in such a moral position that I cannot enjoy God. Faith is the essense of the fillial relation; it is the principle of sonship. "We are all the children of God by faith."[26] It is faith which opens the heart, and the infinite Spirit flows into it; as says Christ, "Behold I stand at the door and knock. If any man hear my voice and open the door I will come in unto him, and will sup with him, and he with me."[27] Here is a sensuous image of spiritual delights. To feast with Christ, to recline at the table of God, is to share the bliss of God, and to drink from the infinite fountain of God's own pleasures. This is more than the fabled <u>ambrosia</u> and <u>nectar</u> of the Greek mythology. It is a peace unknown to the sensual mind—a joy unspeakable. The attitude of Christ before the door of the heart, calling with his voice, and knocking to arouse the slumberer within, indicates a desire on his part to enter. His appropriate habitation is not the temple, not the house made with hands, but the human soul. When free will ceases all resistance to his entrance, he comes in, just as when an artificial embankment gives way, the ocean overflows the land. When we cease to bolt him out as a thief, and invite him in as a friend, he will come in and spread the feast of God, the hidden manna.

Earthly monarchs have in various parts of their dominions royal palaces, erected and maintained in order, for the residence of the king, when he visits those parts of his empire. But he can dwell in only one at a time. The soul is a palace of the Divinity. It is God's royal abode. But he can dwell in all souls at one and the same time. For while he is the being who is above all and {in} through all, he is also in all. He can without removing from place to place, dwell in all hearts. The indwelling of God in the soul, is the great mystery of the Gospel. How often is it brought to view. "I will dwell in them, and will walk in them; and I will be their God, and they shall be my people."[28] The interior of soul, far within the outward walls of sense, is the home of God, just as much as the white house at Washington is the proper abode of the president. God does not desire to dwell in the solitude of empty space, but in the holy heart he finds an abode of his delight. But alas other gods besides the Lord have usurped the throne of our hearts. But they are out of their place, as much as the image of Jupiter was, in the days of Antiochus, upon the altar of God in the temple.[29] Alas men have defiled the temple of God, with the "broth of abominable things." But "him who defileth the temple of God will God destroy."[30]

The proper residence of the soul is in God, as the proper abode of God is in the soul. Every living thing has its native element and place of abode adapted to its nature and powers. Some occupy the ocean, some the air; some find a happy abode amid the frozen snows of the north, others on the burning sands of the equatorial regions. But every thing which God has made has its appropriate habitation, out of which element or locality it cannot be fully blest. The proper habitation of a human soul is God. Thus says David— "O Lord thou hast been our dwelling place in all generations." And in another place he says— "He that dwelleth in the secret place of the Most High, shall abide under the shadow of the Almighty."[31]

March 29th. This morning at 8 1/2 o'clock, our darling boy, Osmon C.B. Evans breathed his last, aged two years and nine months. He died of congestion of the lungs, with which he was attacked but three days before. Much did he suffer, and now he sweetly rests. He filled a great place in our hearts and in our family. He had become greatly endeared to us all. We thought we saw in him the developement of a gentle and generous disposition. One of the most marked characteristics of his tender mind seemed to be a passionate love of the beautiful. This night an awful silence reigns in our house, which seems almost as terrible as his previous groans and screams. We bow with submission to the unerring Providence of God which has removed him, though our hearts feel desolate and afflicted.

April. 9ᵗʰ. Since the hand of Jesus broke off a slip from our family tree, and transfered it to the heavenly Paradise, I have felt a sweet attraction to the world of the blest. I love to think that with my loved boy I shall range the heavenly plains and explore the celestial city. His pure spirit has returned to God, and in God I still find him, and through God I feel a sweet sympathy of soul with him. My inward ear still hears him say, "Ozzie love papa—Ozzie love mamma!" Love can never die. It is as immortal as the source whence it emanates. Love is of God. His blessed spirit is in the care of Jesus. His death has made me a wiser and better man—

I have recently enjoyed a deeper consciousness of the love of God, his boundless and everlasting love than I ever before reached. It has left a heavenly savor behind it, but it is difficult to reproduce and describe the impression in words. There are ineffable experiences, such as the weakness of language cannot express. I have found that my growth in the spiritual life has gone forward by new manifestations of God to my consciousness, and every successive stage of that growth has been based upon, and preceded by, some new and enlarged view of God— The enlarged view I was enabled to take of the love of God, has let me deeper into him, and sunk my soul one degree lower down into "perfection's height."[32] It seemed to me that God's love was co-extensive with his infinite presence. Long have I found God so near to me that I could not move without moving in him. His presence extends through all space. I am floating in the depths of the ocean of the infinite Life. But that life which pervades all things in that happy hour seemed to me to be love—a love boundless and eternal, and pervading and filling the whole extent of unlimited space. My soul seemed like a particle of glittering dust floating in a boundless & tranquil ocean of light and love, extending to infinite heights and depths in every direction from the point I occupied. I had a glimpse, such as my weakness could bear, of the love of God which passes knowledge.[33] To bathe my soul in that ocean forever—to float beneath its waveless surface—will be the fulfillment of my proper destiny. God is love.

Lawrence Mass. June 1st 1858. God's unerring providence has placed me in Lawrence. I have been here about four weeks. But all places are alike, for God is the habitation of my soul. I long at times to burst through the limitations of time and space, and dwell with an ascended Christ in the limitless abode of an omnipresent Deity. Christs ascension was not an asent through space, so much as it was an ascent in the altitude of being. His human nature is emancipated from its material bonds and limitations, so that he can fulfil his promise to his disciples, "Lo I am with you always, even unto the end of the world.["][34] The heaven in which he dwells is not so much a place to be entered from without, as a spiritual condition to be developed from within. So of the original Paradise. I have ardent longings to be emancipated into God.

I have felt of late the deep importance of the Spirit's influence in the developement of the kingdom of God. I see why it was that the very words of Christ are not preserved in the Gospel, and why Christ, like Socrates, left no fixed and written formula of his doctrine. It was to leave room for the progressive developement of Christian truth, under the superintendence of the Paraclete or divine Teacher, the Spirit of truth. It is the office of the Paraclete to vitalize and unfold the germs of truth which the evangelists have collected in the several Gospels. It is the remark of Dr Von Cöl[l]n of Germany, that "The simplest sentence {which} that ever fell from the lips of Jesus, contains a depth and fulness of meaning, which we can never boast of having fully mastered, even with all the aids of Philosophy and History."[35] Every sentence contains the germ of an infinite developement. Under the influence of the Spirits presence, the outward letter, becomes illuminated, like characters written with invisible ink when exposed to the heat of the fire. It is only by the divine Comforter that we can get anything more than a mere surface knowledge of the Gospel. He who is in the communion of the Holy Ghost, is in union with the Spirit of truth itself, and drinks in truth from {the} its fountain and source. I am trying to study the Gospel at the feet of the great Teacher. May he more fully illuminate the abyss of truth, and give me a glimpse of its heavenly mysteries.[36]

July 1st. I am more and more convinced that God is the only good. All things without him and separate from him would be a poor portion for my soul. O for a profounder rest in the bosom of the Infinite God. Let me lose sight of all else, even myself. God is my all. In this world I am poor; in him I am rich. I have all and abound.

"When God is mine & I am his,
    Of Paradise possessed,
I taste unutterable bliss
    And everlasting rest."[37]

Sept. 30. At times for some weeks past my soul has been drawn by love's sweet force to Christ. Never have I felt a stronger attraction towards him. I sometimes feel a sweet impatience (Alas—the feebleness of human language) to be with him where he is, to be free from all these finite limitations and restraints of sense, and to be set free in infinity and eternity. O that God would give me grace to rejoice in him always. The more holy a soul becomes, the more it will be inclined to praise the Lord. As its redemption advances, thanksgiving will be more and more blended with its supplications, until as it nears the celestial state, there will be a transition from special supplication to praise, unceasing praise. Just as rivers when they approach near the ocean begin to partake of the qualities and attributes of the ocean. Before a soul is fitted fully for the celestial state, it must learn to rejoice in the Lord, independently of all temporal things. It must joy in God alone, for it will soon be removed from all temporal conditions, from all the things that are seen. It must be prepared for this abstraction from material and sensible things. To rejoice in affliction is one of the highest preparatives for an immaterial state, or a purely spiritual condition. Affliction of some kind becomes a necessary discipline for a heavenly state. The darker the night of trial, the sweeter will be the song of the soul's triumph; just as music has stronger charms when it floats on the midnight air. O that a ceaseless flame of holy praise, and spiritual joy, as quenchless as the fires of heaven, might rise from my soul to God. The apostle commands me to blend thanksgiving with supplication, when he says "Be careful for nothing; but in every thing by prayer and supplication, with thanksgiving, let your requests be made known unto God."[38] But as I advance in the triumphant progress of my redemption to the frontier of the celestial kingdom, praise becomes the predominant element in my prayer. Prayer is a divine symphony made up of these four parts, thanksgiving, supplication, confession, and intercession. But in the holy soul, praise, like a lofty tenor overpowers all the other parts, and is heard above their more feeble strains. "O for a gust of praise," said the dying Fletcher, "to fill the whole world."[39]

David expresses the idea of rejoicing in the Lord independent of all earthly changes and conditions when he says, "The Lord is our refuge and strength, a present help in time of trouble. Therefore will not we fear though the earth be removed, and though the mountains be carried into the midst of the sea; though the waters thereof roar and be troubled, though the mountains shake with the swelling thereof."[40] His soul was too firmly anchored in God to be dragged from her moorings by the changes of time. The earth itself might vanish away, yet the soul would remain unmoveably fixed upon its center. Such a soul is prepared to enter upon the higher worship of the skies. It is weaned from earth, and joined to eternity.

Oct. 7. I feel a great love for spiritual truth. I love truth as intensely as a miser loves gold. I am not conscious in myself of any prejudice that would prevent my embracing what was clearly true. I long to be perfected by the Holy Spirit in Christian wisdom, and to possess a character and life formed after the image of divine wisdom and truth. I throw open my soul, and turn it imploringly towards the eternal source of light and knowledge, the uncreated Word, with whom are hid all the treasures of wisdom and knowledge. My soul drinks in pure truth, as the thirsty earth imbibes the rain. I find my spirit more and more receptive of heavenly knowledge, and thank the Giver and Source of all good, that I am making some advancement in heavenly wisdom. May my mind become still more fitted to receive the truths of the kingdom of God. One thing is here of fundamental importance. The soul that would advance in knowledge must be holy. It must be conjoined to the Lord in the unity of the same spirit. Mere knowledge separate from God is a lie. Persons who store the mind with mere worldly science, having no relation to the Deity, turn the truth of God into a lie. Knowledge by being disjoined from its Source becomes a falsity. Such wisdom puffeth up; it inflates the mind with mere emptiness and vanity.[41]

Nov. 27. I find myself increasingly in sympathy with the heavenly world. Heaven is not removed from me by distance of place, but by condition of state. If my heart is in a heavenly frame, heaven is near. It is in me, and I am in it. It is as near to me as the soul is to the body. Distance between spiritual existences is not measurable by any material standards, as miles, leagues, &c, but distance, is a dissimilitude of state; and nearness and approximation are a similitude of inward condition. (When my heart is in harmony with Christ, he is brought by that spiritual likeness & sympathy unspeakably near, and in Christ, I have communion, and fellowship, with all that are united to him.)[42] He is the only medium of communication with with the celestial or angelic world. As was taught by the vision of Jacob's ladder, on which the angels of God ascended and descended.[43] This type Christ applied to himself in his conversation with Nathaniel. (Jno. 1:51.)[44] A soul united to Jesus by a vital faith and perfect love, has in him a conjunction with the heavenly realms. Out of Jesus, and sundered from him, the soul may communicate with hell but not with heaven. He is the door. He is the way, the truth: and the life. No man cometh unto the Father but by him.[45]

Dec. 14ᵗʰ. What would once satisfy my soul will not now fill my heart. Every time my heart swells unutterably full of glory and of God, it stretches the soul's capacity for divine enjoyments, and larger measures of heavenly bliss are required to fill its enlarged powers. I have times of heavenly communion that are unutterable, seasons of abstraction {of} from the things of sense, when I am taken in a measure behind the veil, and celestial light breaks in upon my spirit. I am carried away in the spirit to a high mountain, that is my soul is elevated above its natural condition, breaks away from the fetters of its material enthralment, and the scenes of Paradise are unfolded to the partially unrolled spiritual senses. The soul is closed toward earth, and opened towards heaven; the world and all its gilded pageantry disappears, and seraphic pleasures and unutterable delights flow into the heart. When the soul is made receptive of heavenly delights by being emptied of the love of the world and sin, celestial bliss flows in. Immortal life and joy come upon it like the dew of heaven {of} upon a withering flower or a shower of rain upon a thirsty soil. (I pray God to render my spirit more and more receptive of heavenly wisdom and spiritual delights—)[46]

There is a certain experience which is symbolized by a lofty mountain. According to the correspondence which subsists between things in the

natural world and the spiritual world, mountains signify a great elevation in the moral and spiritual condition of man, an elevation of the soul
above the common level of its natural action, to a higher plane of spiritual
activity and enjoyment. Hence the ancients who understood more clearly
the science of correspondence than the moderns, built their places of
worship on mountains, which are called high places in the Scriptures.
Hence Moses went up into a mountain to receive the law, and also when
he died he ascended to the summit of Pisgah, which commanded a view
of the promised land. All this had its symbolical or spiritual sense as
well as {it} its litteral historical meaning. Hence the sermon of Christ
was delivered on a mountain. The prophet also declares that in the latter
days, the Messianic times, the mountain of the Lord's house, the Church,
shall be established on the top of the mountains, that is its spiritual condition shall be greatly elevated, it shall ascend to a higher form of divine
life. Hence when the disciples were to have a glimp[s]e of the celestial
glory, and to have their spiritual senses so far uncovered as to discern
the solid realities of an eternal sphere, they were taken by Christ into an
high mountain, apart by themselves, where he was transfigured before
them. Hence John, when he saw the glories of the New Jerusalem was
transported in spirit, not in body, to a high mountain. When the time
predicted by the prophet shall arive, that the mountain of the Lord's
house, or the Church, shall be established on the top of the mountains, it
will be a glorious era in the history of redemption. The Church will then
enter upon its New Jerusalem stage of developement. Heaven and earth
will be brought into closer connections, and the spiritual and natural
worlds will be brought into a more intimate conjunction. Then we shall
see as the favored disciples did the kingdom of God come with power,
and that extraordinary vouchsafement will become the ordinary experience of the children of God. At present men, and even the Church are so
buried in the things of sense, and so floundering in the dismal swamp of
materialism and Saduceeism, that the spiritual world is a terra incognita,
an unknown land.[47] The age is coming when the two worlds will come
into closer proximity, when we shall say,
"Heaven comes down our souls to greet,
And glory crowns the mercy seat."[48]

(**Jan. 3ᵈ. 1859.** I am entering upon a new epoch in my spiritual history. My future experience I trust will be marked by a closer communion with heavenly things. My spiritual vision is becoming more opened to discern the realities of a higher sphere. I have had some views of heavenly things that are ineffable. I sometimes retire into my spirit, behind the veil of sense, and feel that I am with the Lord; for to be absent from the body is to be present with the Lord. I am not removed from the heavens by spatial distance; but when my soul is in such a moral condition as to qualify me to dwell with Christ and holy angels, then by elevating my spirit above the things of sense, it is present with them. It is in heaven, for they are heaven. Thus have I seen things, mortal eye never beheld—things which I could not imagine. Forms of surpassing beauty and loveliness, mansions exceeding all that was ever conceived. Once I beheld a mansion, which seemed of pure marble, ornamented with gold embossed upon it. The gate leading to it was of gold, and surpassed description. The grounds were ornamented with trees and flowers. My soul had been exalted to a state of presence with the Lord, and I asked of him to show me my heavenly mansion, when this appeared before the eye of my spirit. Sometimes the Lord has illuminated my mind to see truth in a heavenly light, In this way have I come to the conviction that Jehovah Jesus is the only living and true God. That the whole Trinity is in him. This has removed much confusion from my mind.[49]

I am aiming to live the life of heaven upon earth; to walk with God, and to abide in Christ. He knows how ardently I love truth for its own sake, for he himself has given me that love. With Peter I can say to him, Thou knowest all things; thou knowest that I love thee.[50] I give myself to God, to love, and to truth. In the name of God. Amen.)[51]

Jan. 19ᵗʰ. (In my closet I enjoyed a season of intimate communion with the Lord. My soul came into his divine sphere, and seemed to be in his presence. He spoke sweetly and comfortingly to my soul. My soul was drawn out in prayer that he would make me a means of opening blind eyes, and of bringing souls out of the bondage of sense into an interior communion with him, and that I might be employed in this work forever.)[52] It has appeared to me that a new age is about to dawn upon the world; and that the Church is coming into a closer conjunction with Christ and heaven, so that will be realized the passage, "Behold the tabernacle of God is with men, and he shall dwell with them."[53] It seems to me that Christianity was not intended to shut heaven, but to open it. If the most ancient saints saw and conversed with the Lord and with angels, may not a Christian do so? The Christian is come unto an innumerable company of angels. After I rose from my knees, I seemed to be in the midst of angels. It seemed as if I was like Jacob at Mahanaim, who exclaimed this is God's host.[54] I felt around my spirit celestial presences, who embraced me. I saw them not but felt them. Why should I who have been almost a Saducee have such an experience? It does seem to me as if a new day is dawning. I have a kind of prophetic presentiment that those who love God in simplicity and sincerity are coming into closer relations with the celestial hosts. I hear a voice within, saying, "Thou shalt see greater things than these."[55] When this thick veil of sense shall be rent, when this carnal Saduceean spirit shall cease to rest like an incubus upon the souls of the Lords people, they will rise to the communion of the heavenly ones.

(**Claremont. Sept. 19. 1859.**[56] I came to this place about the middle of April last. My health so completely failed me that I could not preach. I have not preached for more than six months. There was a time when I could not so much as read. But during this complete prostration of my nervous system, my soul has tranquilly reposed in God. Far down below my trembling nerves there is a region of soul where all is still and silent. After my health utterly failed, a voice came to my spirit from Christ, "Turn aside with me into a desert place and rest awhile."[57] The thought of dwelling in a desert was at first repugnant to my feelings, but my faith at length with humble boldness replied to the divine voice, "Lord if thou art there, I shall have bread." And I here record to the glory of God, that thus far I have been strangely fed. He has given me food for my family and living bread for my soul. In a beautiful retirement and holy solitude, I have walked with God[.] All things, much of the time, have been radiant with the divine presence. I bought a small cottage with four acres of land. No sooner had I come in possession of it, than in a solemn & sincere spirit, I dedicated every inch of the soil as a temple for the worship of God in Spirit and in truth. And Jesus, who is greater and holier than all temples, has been with me.)[58]

I have recently returned from a Camp Meeting at Springfield Vt. It was a season of great profit. Never did I attend a meeting where so much attention was paid to holiness, and where there was so earnest a striving to reach a higher and deeper experience in the things of God. A gentleman from Boston, a lay member of the Congregationalist Church, by his labors on the subject of sanctification, gave a marked character to the meeting. I have never found a person with a richer experience in the things of God. I have come from the meeting with an increase of that faith that sees the whole Deity in every promise, and appropriates Christ, and all that he is & has, now to the soul. My faith was in danger of becoming a too passive sinking into God, instead of that stubborn faith, which says, the blood of Christ cleanses me from all sin now, and with humble obstinacy will never yield the point. For five or six days God has given me all I could endure of heavenly bliss. It {has} seemed at times as if I should sink, crushed beneath a weight of divine love and glory. I could sympathize with Mr Fletcher, where he speaks of a happiness so intense as to border on misery.[59] But such a weight of glory will enlarge my capacity to enjoy God, & render my soul more receptive of the divine good.

Sept. 25. Sabbath. Last evening had an inquiry meeting at my house in relation to the higher Christian life—a life of full consecration and assurance of faith.[60] It was a season of great interest. About fifty were present. Several persons solemnly consecrated themselves as a living sacrafice to God, and exercised an appropriating faith in the blood of Christ. The influence of the movement was very manifest in the social meetings of today. Several persons have certainly entered upon a higher degree of life—

I have lately come to the conclusion to devote my life and all the strength of my activity to the cause of holiness. It seems to me to be the will of God. Providence has strangely led me to this decision— It appears as I look back upon the past, that God's dealings with me have aimed at this result. Every thing in the past seems connected to bring me to this purpose. If it is my duty, God will restore my bodily vigor. I feel better already. The great aim of the divine government seems to be the creation of the greatest possible amount of holiness in the universe. This is the central idea of the divine administration. This is the key to the mysteries of history sacred

& profane. I have consecrated myself to a life of cooperation with Infinite Love and Wisdom which govern the world with constant reference to this great result. It is a noble work, fit for an angel. May God help me, and make me so far as possible adequate to it.

This word came with power from Christ to me today.

"I have ordained thee to bear much fruit."[61]

For some time my soul has been in travail for others. But tonight I have unutterable rest. I can sympathize with Mr Fletcher, when he exclaims, "O for a gust of praise to fill the whole world!"[62]

Oct 2. Have been detained by sickness from the house of God, yet I have had communion with him who is greater than the temple. (This evening enjoyed a precious season in my closet. Christ was with me and spake with sweetness to my heart, assuring me that he had chosen me for a great work. My soul was in a state of presence with the Lord, and it seemed to me in the society of angels. Heaven was brought nigh.)[63]

A new age is commencing. A new developement of the Church is begun. The different ages and stages of the progress of Christs redemptive work have been characterized by the reign of some great idea. In the age of Abraham and after it was the idea of the divine unity. This stood forth in opposition to the prevailing polytheism of the nations. About 300 yrs after Christ, the reigning idea in the Christian mind was that of a Trinity in unity. This gave character to the age. The Lutheran Reformation brought into prominence the idea of justification by faith. This may have assumed too great an importance—it was sometimes pushed to the extreme of antinomianism. The last 300 yrs have been characterized by the reign of this central idea of Protestantism. But the idea of sanctification by faith is now growing into prominence. (The Church of the future will not find in Christ merely a pardon of guilt, but a new and heavenly life. He will be made unto the believer not only righteousness (justification) but sanctification and redemption. As the Church through the power of a celestial life derived from Christ shall be brought into a state of sympathy with heaven, that world will be brought nigher and will be more and more opened.)

The present is a transition point— Old things pass away. The new age is struggling into birth.

May Christ give me grace to meet the responsibilities of this crisis. He has given me a rich inward experience, not for my own sake merely, but for the good of others. Lately I have prayed for a deeper experience in the things of God, not for my own satisfaction, but that I am impart it to my brethren in the Lord. (All that he gives me, I will give to others.) (A want of this disposition is one reason why some are so little blessed. They make their souls the sepulchre of God's blessings,) just as precious gems are sometimes buried with the great in their tombs. (He will give to us, all we will impart to others.) He that has two coats must give to him who has none.) (I consecrate my soul as the organ of communicating spiritual good from Christ to the church. Though unworthy he accepts me in this use. His kingdom is a kingdom of love, and his government one of use.)

Oct 3. There have been three distinct epochs in my religious history. These have been about equally marked {and} by an inward change. The first commenced with my conversion and continued about three years— This degree of Christian life was increased by faithfulness in prayer, and by a study of the Word. The second epoch commenced with my embracing the doctrine of sanctification as taught at Oberlin, and by Wesley & Fletcher. I no sooner embraced the theory, than I began to seek it as a living experience. I gave myself up to Christ to do his whole will, and by an appropriating faith in the Blood of Christ, I found salvation from sin, as I had already found deliverance from guilt through justification. Thus I entered upon a higher degree of life. Though not always faithful to the grace received, this degree of divine life continued for twenty years. I had seasons of great peace and emotional bliss. Three years ago I was brought into a more intimate union with the God of love than I ever attained before. This is the third epoch. It has been characterized by a deliverance from the bondage of sense, a fuller renouncement of all the creatures and even the gifts of God, as my portion, and inward consciousness of the divine presence, a removal of the sense of distance between my soul and Christ, and an abiding sense of the <u>allness</u> of God, and the nothingness of the creatures. (Prayer has become more a life than a form. Prayer is reduced more and more to the escense of all true prayer—"Thy will be done." Oftentimes I have such a sense of fulness and completeness in Christ, and such a profound contentment that God's will should be done in earth and heaven, that I can make no special requests for myself. Prayer becomes intercession for others, and triumphant praise. My thoughts are taken captive, so that for most of the time for three years it requires a gentle violence to disengage them from their natural center—God and heavenly things. I asked of Christ to show me whether I had really passed through three distinct spiritual changes. Immediately I saw before my minds eye three concentric circles representing three distinct degrees of <u>interiority</u>.)[64] In the outermost circle I remained three years; in the second, twenty years; in the inmost circle, I have now been three years. Christ, in whom is all the fulness of the Deity is the point around which the circles are described. I also saw represented before my spirit, three planes one above the other, to mark three degrees of spiritual elevation. The temple of Jerusalem also represents three distinct degrees of spiritual life. There were the outer courts, or the yards surrounding the sacred edifice. This represents a state of mere justification, and incipient regeneration. Next came the sanctuary or holy place. Here the ordinary priests performed the services of the temple. Here was the table of shew-bread,[65] and the altar of incense. This marks the second discrete or distinct degree of spirituality. Beyond the sa[n]ctuary was the most holy place, where was the ark of the law, the mercy seat, the cherubim, and the visible glory of the Lord. Here the high priest entered only once a year. But Christianity makes general what was special and partial in Judaism. Paul teaches that the holy of holies may now be entered by the believer by a new and living way, that is, the interior experience symbolized by the entrance of the high priest into the inmost apartment of the temple, may now be attained by all who seek it in Christ. Here are marked three degrees of nearness to God and union with him. Three degrees of the death to self are also marked. The last degree of divine life is heaven begun. It is the incipiency of a truly angelic life. This is represented by the cherubim in the most holy place— Heaven has become as near to me as my soul is to my body. I love to retire into the depth of my spirit, losing sight of the world and the things of sense, and communing with heavenly things. The solid realities of the spiritual world, are faintly seen before my spirits eye—

(I trust infinite Love & Wisdom to render my soul still more receptive of heavenly good—)

Nov. 12. Since I have written in my spiritual journal, I have enjoyed many rich experiences of God & heavenly things. Yesterday I returned from Marlow[66] where a week was spent in laboring to assist souls into a higher and deeper life in God. I found the brethren in that state of restless dissatisfaction, and hungering and thirsting after righteousness, which rendered them peculiarly receptive of the truths of the kingdom of God. They drank in the heavenly doctrines, as a man dying of thirst drinks the rain of heaven. I cannot but believe that a large number of persons went up one degree in the scale of spiritual life.

My own soul was in the antechamber of heaven. I had seasons of as intense bliss as I ever enjoyed. I consecrated myself to the love of God and my neighbor. This is to be my experience in the future.

I stood up for Jesus to speak what he should deposit in my heart, and consecrated my soul to be the organ of communicating spiritual truth and divine good to souls. Christ communicated with some souls through me. The sphere of labor which I have chosen seems to me more & more important.

Nov. 21ˢᵗ. For some time past my experience has been that of David as expressed in some of the Psalms—or rather of the soul of Jesus who is speaking in the Psalms. I have been in a state of peaceful inward recollection. It is not merely a meditative state, where the thoughts are directed towards God by an effort of will, and held in that position by a gentle force; for such a state is a labored one and not a spontaneity, and consequently not a state of perfect repose. My soul has been in a state of contemplation, which is one where the mind enters naturally and without effort into the presence of God. It is not engaged all the time in any voluntary conversation with its heavenly Friend, but enjoying the sweet satisfaction of being with him, drinking in his heavenly smiles, as a flower drinks in the light of the morning, which expands its petals to receive it. "Unto thee lift I up mine eyes, O thou that dwellest in the heavens." (Ps. 123:1.) Again says Christ in Ps. 16:8. I have set the Lord always before me. God said to Abraham "Walk before me (or in my presence) and be thou perfect[.]" (Gen. 17:1.) This inward consciousness of the divine presence as a permanent experience, and not a mere transient gleam, is expressed in Ps. 139:1–10. "O Lord thou hast searched me and known me. Thou knowest my down-sitting and my up-rising; Thou understandest my thought afar off. Thou compassest my path, and my lying down, and art acquainted with all my ways. For there is not a word in my tongue, but, lo, O Lord, thou k[n]owest it altogether. Thou hast beset me behind and before, and laid thy hand upon me. Such knowledge is too wonderful for me; it is high, I cannot attain unto it. Whither shall I go from thy Spirit? or whither shall I flee from thy presence? If I ascend up into heaven, thou art there; if I make my bed in hell, behold, thou art there. If I take the wings of the morning, and dwell in the uttermost parts of the sea; even there shall thy hand lead me, and thy right hand shall hold me." The soul may pass into a state where the conscious presence of God is so fixed in the inmost of the spirit, that escape from him is impossible. Outward things do not call off the attention of the spiritual eye. It is permanently <u>converted</u> or turned toward the Lord. Because the interior of the soul is always turned toward the object of the ruling love. If that be self and the world, it never turns any thing but an external gaze toward the Lord. If the ruling love, be love to the Lord, he becomes the center toward which the whole life of the soul flows, and the inmost of the soul is always turned toward him, and there God is truly present. The union here is also a reciprocal one. The soul which has experienced a true <u>conversion</u>, or turning to the Lord, enjoys not only passively the presence of the Lord, as the outward world does, which is full of God; but it reciprocates the conjunction. God is not only present with that soul, (which is true in a certain sense of all men,) but the soul is present with the Lord. It fulfills the command, "Abide in me, and I in you."[67] This being in a state of presence with the Lord as a permanent spiritual condition is a realization of the hidden sense of the words of Christ, "If I go and prepare a place for you, I will come again and receive you unto myself; that where I am, there ye may be also." And, "Lo I am with you always." ["]I will not leave you comfortless; (or in a state of orphanage) I will come unto you."[68] He went away from our outward senses, in order that he might be more really present to our spirits. We are not to wait until the end of the earth, for the fulfillment of these celestial words. He who is in bondage to sense, and is in the lowest degree external and natural, cannot see their spiritual sense, any more than a blind man can see the tints of the rainbow. His mind sees only the outward letter in such promises, just as a child sees the bow in the heavens to be a solid arch. But the more advanced mind sees it to be etherial, but none the less real. Because we know Christ no more after the flesh, is no evidence that we do not know him at all, and must wait until the end of this material world before he comes to us. It is the law of the spiritual world and of our own spiritual natures, that to think interiorly of Christ causes presence. It brings the soul into the presence of the Lord. To think interiorly and from love, causes conjunction. It unites the soul to the object of thought. Nearness between spirits, finite or infinite, is similitude of internal character. Those are near who are grounded in similar love. Distance is dissimilitude of spiritual state. When the soul is created anew into the image of the Lord, and thinks of him interiorly from love, it is brought ineffably near. Such a soul lives and moves in the divine presence.

Some persons in accordance with these mental laws have enjoyed an all-satisfying communion with the Lord, and an inward recollection so deep that nothing outward could disturb it. Francis Losa who wrote the life of Gregory Lopez says of himself, after he attained to this inward consciousness of the divine presence, that "whenever he went through the city, (Mexico,) whether to collect or distribute charity, he felt an inward recollection and prayer, which all the noise and hurry of the city could not interrupt. As if he had been fifty years, in that holy exercise he found himself a new man. Having lost, in a moment, all thoughts of earth, and being filled with heaven alone, he renounced all compliments, visits of form, and needless conversations; and his only joy was to retire into himself, and treat with God upon the affairs of salvation. He began to walk alone, unless he was obliged to go with any one on a work of charity; and the multitude of people whom he met, no more disturbed his attention to God, than if they had been rocks and trees." (*Life of Lopez* p. 71.)[69]

He says of Lopez, that after the reading of the Scriptures in the morning, which was his invariable practice, "he entered into so deep a recollection, that one could not judge by any outward mark, whether he was speaking to God, or God was speaking to him. All one could conjecture from the tranqulity and devotion which appeared in his countenance, was, that he was in the continual presence of the Lord. But that presence of God wherein he lived was not barren and unfruitful, seeing it daily produced more and more acts of love to God and his neighbor—the love which is the end of the commandment, and the sum of all perfection." (*Life of Gregory Lopez*, p. 54.)[70] This state of presence with the Lord is not only fruitful in producing in us the death of self, and the love of God & the neighbor, but by it the soul becomes receptive of the divine wisdom, and truth flows into it from its only Source. We can learn more in this way, in a short time, than we can in a whole life spent in the schools and among books. The soul has conjunction with him who is truth itself. Christ is not only in the word, but is the Word. The Gospel is a manifestation of Christ himself, not in the outward letter, which is only the envelope, but in the living & life-giving spirit underneath the letter.

In order to have a recollected frame of mind, God must be loved perfectly. He must be the only desire of the heart. We must delight ourselves only in the Lord. We must be able to say with David "Whom have I in heaven but thee; and there is none upon the earth that I desire besides thee."[71] The creatures of God are valuable only as they bring God to the soul. They are of worth only sofar as they contain God. Sundered from him, and sofar as they are separate from him, they are evil. If we would be in a perpetual state of inward recollection, we must avoid useless conversation. Nothing sooner uncenters the soul, and removes the consciousness of the Lord's presence than empty and idle words. There must be a deep attention to our words— Silence is often a most important means of grace.

Nov. 22. In my communications with souls, I ought always to remember that the Holy Spirit is never separated from divine truth. I need not pray that he be present with the truths of the Word, for he is the Spirit of truth, and is Truth itself operating in the souls of men. This thought should give me a confidence in my efforts for the good of souls. So far as I announce a divine truth, so far the Holy Spirit is present to accompany that truth. The truth is the Holy Spirit. There is no truth separate from him. Truth is the divine that emanates from the Lord, and is the Lord. The Holy Spirit is the Lord as divine truth operating in the souls of men.

Dec. 18. Preached in the morning on Isa. 1:16, 17, on putting away the evils of our hearts and lives.[72] Enjoyed some freedom of utterance, and do not feel so badly prostrated as I have sometimes. Yet the time has not yet come for me to occupy the pulpit as my sphere of activity.

I consecrate all to God and believe in infinite Love to save me. I can no longer doubt either the presence of the Lord, or his willingness to save me. So far as I dispose myself for the reception of God he will flow into my soul. This I must do as of myself, though it is of the Lord. I must act as if the whole progress of my redemption depended upon myself, yet all the time feeling that it is God who worketh in me to will & to do.

Dec. 26. Yesterday, being Christmas, I preached, on Jno. 17:21.[73]

I have ever looked upon the Incarnation as the great fact of the Gospel, and the central truth of the universe. All other truth revolves around this, as sattelites around their primary. The union of God and man in the person of Jesus is also the patern or model of the conjunction of all holy souls with the Deity.

In order to understand the mystery of the incarnation we must know what the divine Mind is, and what the human mind is. There are two fundamental ideas in the divine Mind, or the divine essence is Love and Wisdom. Love includes his whole moral nature. It is not an attribute, but an essence, the substratum of his attributes. It is the divine substance in which all the attributes inhere. Justice, mercy, long-suffering, &c are only forms of love, or states of the divine substance. The term wisdom includes the whole of the intellectual character of God. His power, his omniscience, his omnipresence, are but attributes of that department of the infinite Mind, which we call Wisdom or Truth. All the love that exists in the universe[74] is from God. So of truth. They are from God, and are God. "Love," says St John, "is of God."[75] Love and wisdom are not creatable. All the love & truth that are in angels & men are from God. Our Savior expressed an absolute truth when he said, God alone is good.[76] All other goodness is not self-originated, but is from God, and is God. So of power. ["]Power belongeth unto God." "There is no power but of God."[77] A man cannot receive anything except it be given him of God. Every good and perfect gift is from above.[78] God is the only Life. He alone has immortality, or life in himself. Man is only a receptacle of the divine Life.

Such is God. He is Love and Wisdom. Man is created in the possession of neither. The human mind is an image of God—that is, it is a form receptive of the Divine Love & the divine Wisdom. It has two capacities by virtue of which it is capable of receiving the Love & Truth of the Deity. One of these capacities is the Will faculty, or the affectional nature, usually called the Sensibility.[79] The term will, in the Scriptures, is used to cover the idea of the sensibility, and not merely the power of volition. The other department of the soul is the understanding, or intellect, and is a capacity receptive of the divine Wisdom or Truth. All the truth that is deposited in it is from Gods truth. (The mind of man starts into existence without one ray of truth in it. It only has a capacity to receive the uncreated Truth, which has eternally existed in the infinite Mind.)[80]

(Christ had a complete humanity, a body and a soul with the two above named capacities. His will-faculty was filled with the infinite Love. His understanding became the habitation of the divine Wisdom. Hence the whole Godhead filled his mind, so that all the fulness of the Godhead dwelt in him bodily. The divine Mind so appropriated the human mind, and filled its two capacities, that all the movements of the one were the movements of the other. God became man, and man became God. Christ is the God-Man and the Man-God. There was a <u>humanization</u> of the Divine, and a <u>deification</u> of the human. All the operations of the Mind of Jesus, were manifestations of the thoughts and feelings of God.) Jesus wept at the tomb of Lazarus, and on the mount of Olives. That a man should weep is nothing. It is no more than millions have done. But when we consider that the human mind of Jesus was the receptacle of the whole divine Mind, which filled all its powers & capacities, then we see that the weeping of Jesus exhibits the feelings of God. So when he loves his country, and his intimate friends, and talks of birds, and flowers, and takes little children in his arms and kisses them. We rejoice to learn that all this exhibits the feelings of God, and that he feels as we do. We cannot divide the personality of Jesus, & make him possess two independent natures that operate separately. The divine Soul & the human soul did not inhabit the person of Jesus side by side, like two individuals dwelling in the same house. But the infinite Mind <u>filled</u> the capacities of the human mind with all its fulness. Is this impossible? (Is there any limit to the mind's power to acquire truth? The more of truth we receive the more we may receive. There is something infinite in the capacities of the human soul. In the Incarnation, that took place <u>at once</u>, which in our case is to be eternally progressive. We are to receive of the divine Love & Wisdom forever. In Jesus, it filled at once & forever all the capacities of his soul, so that he & the Father were one.[81] All the Deity in the Universe was in him. It was not a part of God—a fraction of the divine Nature, but it was

Jehovah himself.) That Jehovah himself descended & became man is evident from many passages of Scripture. Isa. 9:6. "A child is born to us, a Son is given to us; and the government shall be upon his shoulder, and his name shall be called, Wonderful, Counseller, the Mighty God, the everlasting Father, the Prince of Peace." Isa. 40: 3.5. "The voice of him that crieth in the wilderness, Prepare ye the way of Jehovah, make straight in the desert a highway for our God. The glory of Jehovah shall be revealed, and all flesh shall see it together."[82]

Thus God was manifest in the flesh, and we saw the glory of God in the person of Jesus Christ. {Thus God was in Christ reconciling the world unto himself, not imputing their trespasses unto them. (2 Cor. 5:19.) To reconcile is to bring back to union parties at variance. God united himself to humanity and prepared the way for our conjunction with him—}[83]

March. 3 [1860].[84] I have thought much of the power of a living faith, by which I mean a faith that is connected with love, or which proceeds from love. Such a faith is power. And it seems to me that its power is but little understood. In the primitive Church the power of faith was understood. In the Church of the future it will be so again. Once faith had power over disease. Here undoubtedly was no violation of the laws of nature, but the unfolding of a higher law. A law is only the mode of the divine action. Faith once gave the mind power over the material world, to some extent. All causation, all force lies in the spiritual world or in some mind, uncreated or created. Will is the only causal agent in the universe.[85] The phenomena of the outward world are effects, the causes of which are in the world of mind. It is not incredible that in the primitive age of Christianity, when a new influx from God came down to the world, that the minds of the disciples, through faith, affected the natural world. It is something more than an Oriental hyperbole, when Christ says, "If ye had faith as a grain of mustard, ye should say to this mountain, be ye removed hence and it would obey you."[86] So by faith the sycamine tree could be plucked up.[87] It is true there is a spiritual sense to the word mountain and sycamine tree in these passages, but that does not make the natural sense wholly false. (I believe our Savior expresses in these words the law of the souls power over matter. That in the future this law will be more fully developed—

I pray the Lord to increase my faith. To give me a faith that works, or is made energetic by love— Love is life. Love is power. Faith without charity is dead and powerless. May I have faith in God, or as it reads more correctly in the margin, the faith of God. A faith that is an emanation or influx from the Lord. A faith that is thus the gift of God, and is God in us, as nothing proceeds from God that is not God. A faith and love which are the divine proceeding, or the proceeding divine. I will hereafter live by the faith of the Son of God,)[88] that is by a faith that proceeds from the Lord, and of which my soul is only the receptacle. Not a faith that is self-originated. This faith is the secret of power in the ministry— O[m]nipotence in God is the result of faith. So power from on high, is the power of faith that finds the root of its existence in love.

O for a faith that will not shrink,
    Though pressed by every foe,
That will not tremble on the brink,
    Of any earthly woe; —

That will not murmur or complain,
    Beneath the chastening rod,
But in the hour of grief or pain,
    Will lean upon its God; —

A faith that shines more bright & clear,
    When tempests rage without;
That when in danger, knows no fear,
    In darkness feels no doubt; —

That bears unmoved, the worlds dread frown,
    Nor heeds its scornful smile;
That seas of trouble cannot drown,
    Or Satan's arts beguile; —

A faith that keeps the narrow way
    Till life's last hour is fled,
And with a pure and heavenly ray
    Illumes a dying bed—

Lord give us such a faith as this,
    And then, whate'er may come,
We'll taste e'en here, the hallowed bliss,
    Of an eternal home—[89]

March. 9. (Enjoyed a season of intimate communion with the Lord at sunset.[90] My soul is consumed with a deathless thirst for God. I cannot endure the thought of distance between me and him. He is revealing himself more and more to my inward consciousness. (O that I could see him without a veil between. I now but faintly discern the Sun of righteousness. I could not endure his full-orbed glory. May he fill my soul with the fire of his love & the light of his truth. O that my soul was more receptive of the divine life. My soul is turned imploringly toward him without cessation. The affectionate eye of faith looks to him. I am receiving him more & more into my soul. But my spirit sighs to be fully lost in him. Make me one with thee in everlasting love. When shall I come & appear before God— My hope is full of immortality. It reaches beyond the veil—)

March. 10. I find now very much more in the Holy Scriptures than I once discovered in them. I always supposed they were inspired, but of what inspiration was, I had but a vague and indefinite notion. I now not only feel that the Word is inspired but is in its inmost essence no other than the Lord himself.[91] My belief in the inspiration of the Scriptures has risen into a consciousness of their divinity. The Word is not only something from God, but is God. It is a proceeding from the Lord, but nothing emanates from him that is not the Lord. Nothing goes forth from God that is not in its essence divine. The Bible is not a word that has gone forth from Jehovah, and ceased to have any connection with the divine Mind, but is a perpetual and ever present manifestation of the Mind of the Lord. It is not merely a transcript of the divine Mind, an exact copy, but is the original itself.[92] *It is not something that the Lord once spoke, and is now forgotten, and passed out of mind, but is what he utters now. It is a manifestation of the present thought of God. He spake the Sermon on the mount, but the truth was not then created, but it was only a manifestation of uncreated & self-existent truth, which is ever present in the divine mind—*[93]

This important doctrine is plainly revealed in the Gospel of John. "In the beginning was the Word, & the Word was with God, and the Word was God. The same was in the beginning with God. And the Word was made flesh and dwelt among us." (Jno. 1:1, 2, 14.) Here by the Word is meant the Lord as to the divine Wisdom or Truth. It was the uncreated and everlasting Truth itself, manifested to the world in the person of Christ.[94] He is the embodiment and essence of Truth. He is essential, eternal, immutable, necessary, absolute, self-existent, infinite Truth. When the Holy Spirit reveals truth to the soul of the believer, he takes of the things of Christ, and shows them unto us. Christ is the Truth, and all truth is from him, and in its inmost essence is the Lord. The Gospel is the word of Christ, and is a manifestation of Christ. For God was manifest not only in the flesh but as the Word. When I speak of the divinity of the Gospel, I do not mean merely the outward letter, that which is apprehended by sense, but I mean that of which the external letter is only a shadow, the truth of which the outward letter is only the envelope. The Gospel is the expression of the thoughts of God. Now a thought is not anything volatile or floating away from the mind of him who thinks. It is not an exhalation from the mind, which ceases to have any connection with the mind. Thought is a state of the thinking substance, and is in the mind itself. It is so with all the mental operations. Love is not something that issues from the soul, and is disjoined from the soul. It is an internal state of a spiritual substance. Sight & hearing are not out of the mind but in the mind. The Gospel is a manifestation of the wisdom and love of the divine Mind. It is a fixed & perpetual manifestation of the thoughts of the Lord. But the thoughts of Christ are not separate from his mind, but are a state of his mind. The Gospel is not something that has issued from the Lord, and is now separated from him, like a stream continuing to flow after the fountain has dried up. But the Lord is ever present with his truth.[95] By means of the manifested Word, we have access to the Lord, and so far as we receive his revealed truth into our inmost being and incorporate [it] into the very texture of our souls, we have conjunction with him. The Word is the Christian's oracle. By it we inquire of the Lord, and receive the divine response. It puts us into actual connection with the invisible Deity, as much as if we stood face to face with God in the solitude of empty space, and he spake the Word to us for the first time. The Scriptures being a manifestation of the Divinity himself, can never be fully fathomed. Says Dr. Col[l]n of Germany, (["]The simplest sentence that ever fell from the lips of Jesus, contains a depth and fulness of meaning, that we, with all the aid derivived from philosophy and history can never boast of having fully fathomed.")[96] Every verse of the Gospel contains the germ of an infinite developement. The word of God abides forever. It is as well adapted to angelic mind, as to ours, because in its essence it is the uncreated Truth itself. (We never shall outgrow the Bible, either in this world or the next. But as the garments of the Israelites kept even pace with the growth of their bodies, so that they fitted them in childhood & in manhood, so with the Word.)[97] The more the finite mind is developed, the more it finds in the infinite Word. The word of God is Truth itself. May I become more & more imbued with the truth as it is in Jesus, and the truth Jesus is.

("Divine Instructor, gracious Lord,
    Be thou forever near;
Teach us to love thy sacred word,
    And view the Savior there.")[98]

March. 17. The more perfect my knowledge of God becomes, the more easily I can trust in him. A proper knowledge of the divine character is necessary in order to love him, and then the love of God becomes the best school in which to learn God and his truth. Prof Bush, in an article in the *Methodist Quarterly* on the Will of God, has some good observations on the divine character. The will of God, as the phrase is used in Scripture, belongs to the affectional department of the divine mind, and not to the intellectual. He remarks, "The phrase will of God, in common parlance, conveys no very clear or emphatic idea of emotion or affection in the Divine mind, but either that of simple arbitrium, or determinate purpose; whereas will, in the sense of voluntas, points to the affectional state of the willer, and identifies the will with the love."[99] This is founded on a two-fold, instead of the modern threefold division of the mind. The will is the same as the love; for we will what we love, and love what we will. Hence the Greek θελω, signifies besides to will and to be willing, also to wish, to desire, to delight in, to have pleasure in, to love. The emotion indicated by {it} the term may be heightened into a purpose or resolve, but for the most part, a strong affectional propension toward an object is the prominent import of the word. God's will is a form of God's love. He cannot will the death of a sinner, because he cannot love it, and whatever the divine Being cannot love, lies wholly without the range of his will—

Mr Bush remarks, "The truest conception, perhaps, of the Divine nature, is that of an infinite, eternal, irrepresible, and overwhelming loving-ness, which yearns with ineffable longings for the highest good of every creature, and which only fails to realize its desires because it cannot without destroying the highest prerogative of the creature."[100] How dishonorable to God, and how unnatural is a want of confidence in him! What a foundation is there here for the largest trust. He longs to bestow upon me all manner of good, and save me from every form & degree of evil. So far as I dispose myself to receive him, sofar he imparts himself to me. By conforming to the laws of divine order, which are the outgrowth from his love, my soul is made receptive of the divine good.

April 2. I am deeply impressed with the importance of silence as a means of grace. A soul that would enjoy an uninterrupted sense of the divine presence, should never speak except when it is necessary, that is, when the good of our neighbor demands it. An idle word is a useless word, and for all such words we must account in the day of judgment, that is, such useless words leave their impress {of} upon our characters and have an influence in shaping our destiny. Retirement and solitude, for which men sometimes long, derive their profit from silence. Without this, they are of no spiritual worth. He who is silent and recollected in the midst of society or business, will enjoy all the advantage of the most quiet retirement. Silence cherishes the presence of God. We often leave company regretting that we spoke; seldom that we were silent. I feel the importance of attending to this, for I am sure no one can realize the highest results of Christian experience, and an all-satisfying communion with God, who does not attend to his words. "If any man offend not in word, the same is a perfect man and able also to bridle the whole body." (James 3:2.) Therefore I sincerely pray with David, "Set a watch, O Lord, before my mouth; keep the door of my lips." (Ps. 141:3.)

It is the law of our nature, that to express an evil passion by words increases it. Under provocation to anger, we should stand like Christ before the bar of Pilate, in victorious silence. Under great distress and affliction, it is better to keep silent. We need not even attempt to exhibit our humility by speaking humble words. Silence will much better do this. How well does Fenelon say, "Silence and peace under humiliation are the true good of the soul; we are tempted under a thousand specious pretexts, to speak humbly; but it is far better to be humbly silent. The humility that can yet talk, has need of careful watching; self-love derives comfort from its outward words—" (*Spiritual Progress.* p. 191.)[101]

April 12. Yesterday returned home from the Conference, which was held in Manchester. My appointment is at West Unity, with the understanding that I preach but half of the time. I was elected delegate to the Gen. Conf. to be holden in Buffalo in May next. My health is not yet adequate to the full work of the ministry. I long for strength to employ it in the work so dear to my heart. When I am well, it is to me a great pleasure to preach a free & full salvation. It is no cross, when I am in health, to proclaim the unsearchable riches of Christ. I have hope of regaining my former power. The Lord is my strength. He is the health of my countenance and my God. I will find in Christ all that I need. He can cure every form of mental disease, and thus restore the body; for disease originates generally, if not always, in the mind.[102] I lay hold of Jesus as my life & salvation.

April 23. God's divine power has given us all things that pertain unto life and godliness; whereby are given unto us exceeding great and precious promises; that by these we might become partakers of the divine nature. (2 Pet. 1:3.4)[103] The promises are the <u>media</u> through which the divine good, that is, the divine nature is imparted to souls. The good which the promises profer to us is an emanation from God, and is God. They are different modes of communicating to us the divine life itself, and they furnish the soul all the elements of spiritual growth. God is in the promises. He who lays hold of the promises, lays hold of and appropriates God.—

April 26. Started for the General Conference. Came to N. Haven and took the steamer for N. York.

April 27. Am today in N. York City. Find here nothing to attract my attention. My soul amid all the noise and show pines for communion with Jesus.

I long to lose myself in him, and to be everlastingly one with him. Visited Trinity Church, and there raised my soul to him I love. But all places are alike to me. The forest, the mountain top, the bank of the river, or beneath the heavens at night with all their wealth of stars, are to me a temple for the worship of God in spirit and in truth. Those who know little of interior worship, may need gorgeous temples to assist their devotion; but my soul finds God only within. O that he would draw me into a closer fellowship with him. I searched the book-stores to find some good works on the interior life, which, through the influence of the Holy Spirit, might contribute to nourish the spiritual life within me. Found three which I do not possess, viz, *The Spiritual Torrents*, by Madan [sic] Guyon, with parallel passages from the writings of Swedenborg; Arbouin on the *Regenerate Life*; and the *Song of Solomon*, by Adelaide Leaper Newton.[104] These appear to be truly valuable works on the higher forms of Christian experience. But the soul cannot get from books what must come only from God. Good books may be the channel through which the divine good & truth may flow into the soul. Shutting my eyes and ears to all external surroundings I would hold my soul, in adoring silence, in the presence of the Lord, offering no resistence to the divine operations, and purposing to incorporate into my life the truth which may flow into my soul from its source, and consecrating all to the good of others, It is in this way alone, rather than by reading, or reasoning, or active meditation, that my soul is elevated to a divine light. I lay myself upon the altar of God anew this night. May God bless the loved ones at home. __ __ __ __ __ [105]

April 29. The Sabbath in N. York is a day of only <u>comparative</u> stillness. It is not the divine silence of the country on that sacred day, but only much <u>less</u> noisy than other days of the week. In the morning I attended worship at the Swedenborgian temple, and heard a very good sermon from the pastor, on the Way to Heaven, Ps. 37: 3. "Trust in the Lord, and do good; so shalt thou dwell in the land, and verily thou shalt be fed." As I had read nearly all the important works of that strange but good man, Immanuel Swedenborg, I had a desire to witness their order of worship, and to hear one of their ministers preach. I am convinced that a very large proportion of the members of the New Church, as they style themselves, have but a poor comprehension of the spiritual principles, unfolded in the writings of their founder. It seems to me an attempt to work a spiritual system, or to run a spiritual piece of machinery, by a people who are not sufficiently spiritual-ized. There are many things in Swedenborg's writings, which are of great value, but many of these are not new revelations as he claims, but are found in all mystic authors. I can by no means assent to the lofty claims set up for him. I do not see how he can be the founder of a new dispensation, which the original twelve apostles were commanded to preach throughout the spiritual world. They assert that the Church founded by Christ and his apostles is consummated or ended, and only exists now as Judaism did, after the establishment of Christianity. If they are a new Church, and the infancy of a new dispensation, they ought to exhibit a very much higher and holier life, both interior & exterior, than the older Churches. They ought to exhibit a richer experience in religion and a higher consecration to the good of mankind, than such persons as Paul and John, and Kèmpis, Tauler, Fenelon, Lady Guyon, and John Fletcher & his devoted wife, and Bramwell and Payson.[106] It does seem to me that the New Church, as it is called, has not as yet exhibited, a higher love to God and devotion to the good of the neighbor, and realized so celestial an experience, as many in the old Church. This ought not to be if their claim be just. Of what use is a new dispensation if it does not make us more heavenly, and unite to God more intimately than the old one.

There are many things in the theological writings of Swedenborg of enduring value, and it does appear to me, that there is much which might have been better omitted. There is too much of what the angels say, and too little of what Christ says. He solemnly de-avers that he received nothing of his doctrines from the angels, but all from the Lord, who personally appeared to him; and yet he continually brings forward what the angels say. He is too coldly intellectual, and too little devotional. He exalts the intellect and leaves the heart frigid. He neglects prayer, and does not insist upon communion with God. If a sinner should come to me and earnestly inquire what he must do to be saved, and how he may find rest to his burdened soul, I could not put into his hands any work of Swedenborg, or of any New Church Author. It seems to me powerless, inefficient. After a person is advanced in his Christian experience, he may profitably read some of the books of Swedenborg. But it cannot impart life & comfort to souls groaning for deliverance from the weight of their sins. Such persons have no time to go through with a course of theological reading; they must be saved now. Thus Methodism with its doctrine of consecration and trust in the Lord Jesus Christ, or repentance & faith, must be more efficient in saving the million. Swedenborg & Wesley were contemporaries; but what a difference in the result of their labors, and the preaching of their followers. Yet Methodists belong to the old dispensation, and Swedenborgians to the new.

Whatever of truth there is in all systems will live. I find in my heart an ardent desire to <u>know</u> the truth that it may make me free.

My experience today has been at times peaceful and tranquil. At other seasons I have been inwardly disturbed and desolate. I have had some severe encounters with the power of evil; (but thanks be to God who always causes us to triumph in Christ, and who can bring victory out of <u>apparent</u> defeat. I desire that my life may be attended with solid results—that it may be of use to the kingdom of God.)[107]

May 1st. The General Conference commenced today. The delegates are nearly all present.

May 4. I do not feel that interest in the mere outward affairs of the Church, which I once did, nor which many seem to exhibit. But my heart is interested in the spiritual life of the Church. If the Church is right at the root it will be healthy in the branches. If there be purity at the center, it will be seen in the circumference. If the Church has a healthy interior life, it will flow out into a vigorous and efficient outward life. I can but think it would be far better for the kingdom of God on earth, if all the intellectual power, which the General Conference brings together, could be consecrated to the promotion of the spiritual life & inward holiness of the Church.

My soul has great peace in the center, though there [is] often much disturbance at the surface. My nervous system has been so prostrated that trembling seizes upon me in the performance of the simplest services. I know not the occasion of it, nor the remedy for it. But relying on God, from whom is all life and all good, I am resolved to put it away as an evil, that is a sin against God, because it unfits me for his work. I consecrate myself and all that I am & hope to be to the uses of Christ's kingdom. This evil that has almost crushed the life out of me must cease. I will be myself, that is, what God would have me to be.

May 9. Trip to Niagara Falls.[108]

I have seen Niagara Falls. Yesterday, in company with Bro. Howard, I went down to see the Great Cataract— We followed down the noble river which commences at Buffalo, twenty two miles above Niagara. The river is from one to two miles in width, flows smoothly along, and is interspersed with numerous islands. The rapids commence about a mile above the Falls, where the water flows over an unbroken bed of limestone. It is two miles wide at this point. Goat Island divides the stream into two currents, one of them constituting the American, and the other the Canadian or Horse Shoe Falls. The American Falls are 900 feet wide and 163 feet high. The Canadian Falls are 2000 feet wide and 154 feet high. The sheet of water is about twenty feet deep, and over the precipice the water rushes at the rate of one hundred million tons every hour.

On reaching the village we took a carriage for Goat Island. It contains seventy acres, and is covered with a primitive forest of beech and elm. It is a delightful place—a place for meditation and a temple for worship. The deep roar of the Falls is heard like the sound of an immense organ, filling the whole region with its ceaseless hymn of praise. I could have lingered here all the day. The song of birds filled the air, and the ground was covered with the flowers of spring. But we moved on towards the American Cataract. At length through the trees it burst into view. The first feeling was that of disappointment.— It appeared only some fifty feet in height, and only a few rods in width. But the eye had not become accustomed to judge of distance and dimension. In a short time the eye is properly educated, and they stand before you in all their vastness and overwhelming grandeur. I was under the necessity of turning away, overpowered with the emotions that swelled in my heart. Yet my gaze was rivited upon the rushing, foaming, roaring waters. After passing along a short distance, the Canada Falls came into view. The main body of the river passes over this cataract. It is, or was once, in the form of a horse shoe. It is now more in the shape of the letter A. The water is deeper, and descends less broken than the other falls. I could say with Mrs. Sigourney—

"Thou dost speak
Alone of God, who poured thee as a drop
From his right hand—bidding the soul that looks
Upon thy fearful majesty, be still,
Be humbly wrapped in its own nothingness,
And lose itself in Him."[109]

We afterwards passed over upon the Canada side, where you have the best view of the falls, both of them lying before you.

I was disappointed somewhat in the appearance of the falls, though favorably disappointed. The water breaks more than I had anticipated. I had also anticipated seeing simply an exhibition of unlimited power, acting blindly and furiously. Such a view would be only horrible. But in the great Falls the element of terror does not predominate. It is true one is at once impressed with the idea of almost unlimited power; but it is power decked with indescribable beauty. Thus it reveals and exhibits God. I felt to exclaim, God is here! But he is seen not only on the side of his omnipotence, but the magnificent beauty of the scene is radient with love and wisdom. The rainbow which spans the chasm reveals the presence of the God of the Covenant, and dispels your fear.

The American Falls, which are my favorite, are a thing of unearthly beauty. The water is divided by a rock, called Luna Island, into two cataracts, one of them is 660 feet wide and the other 240 feet. It has the appearance of a vast mass of snow crystals rolling over the precipice, or it looks like a white cloud of smoke falling down upon the broken rocks beneath. As you gaze upon the sheet of water, its form seems to change, and then it flashes upon your view the same as before. The bottom of the falls is concealed almost wholly from view by the cloud of mist that lies at its foot. This cloud, which is a constant feature of the falls, seems to have lost its balance in the heavens and fallen to the earth. The sea gulls carelessly dip their wings in the mist and foam.

The sound of Niagara is peculiar. It is not as noisy as some insignificant mill dams; but the sound is deep and solemn, like the voice of God. Great forces are not noisy. They seem conscious of their strength without proclaiming it. St. John must have heard something like Niagara when the "sound of many waters" broke upon his ear.[110] It is not a rattle, but a deep bass, sounding occasionally like the distant booming of cannon, and causing the earth to tremble, as if the Deity himself was marching over the land. It is such a hymn of praise as I never heard nature sing to her Creator. It is not like the roaring of a deep forest at midnight; but more grand and awe-inspiring.

As one stands in the presence of this scene of grandeur and beauty, the soul is inclined to silence and contemplation.— Language is inadequate to express the emotions of the soul. He gazes upon t[h]is exhibition of omnipotent love, and by a mysterious enchantment is fixed to the spot.— Conversation is out of place, and laughter profane. The soul desires to be left alone in adoring silence. The grandest works of art appear as nothing. God alone is great[.] The Suspension Bridge any where else would be worth a journey to see; but here it disfigures the scene.

One of the most beautiful scenes connected with the Falls, is the river below the cataract. I was astonished to observe how soon the river became tranquil. A short distance below the Falls the surface becomes smooth, and flows on slowly yet majestically and powerfully. We walked down on the bank two miles. The chasm through which the river runs is about 250 feet in depth, and from 600 to 1200 feet in width. The walls of solid rock rise nearly perpendicular, and sometimes project over the stream. The channel looks as if cut by design. The water is 300 feet deep. The surface of the green current is smooth, moderately rapid, and, covered with the floating foam, which assumes all conceivable forms, looks like painted glass. At one place two beautiful cascades, with their drops of pearl glittering in the sun, fall over the perpendicular precipice one hundred feet. It was a scene full of poetry and beauty.

The day of my visit to Niagara is a marked day in my history. It is full of great memories. I have seen and enjoyed in my day some scenes of magnificence and sublimity. I have stood on Mount Washington at sunset and sunrise. The impression there is that of vast extent—of immensity. In the distance the heavens and the earth blend into one. It is good to be there, for God, who loves the mountains, is there. I have seen the ocean in a storm make war upon the land, and roll its hostile billows upon the beach as far along the shore as the eye could extend. The scene is sublime, but it is the sublimity of unbounded power, acting blindly and furiously. It strikes terror to the stoutest heart. I have gazed into the clear heavens at midnight, heard them proclaim the glory of God in their awful silence. It is a scene full of quiet grandeur, in which a soul in harmony with all that is divine, loves to revel. But the impression made by Niagara is different from all. It has all the elements of sublimity. Here is vastness, obscurity caused by the cloud of mist, and unlimited power—in fact all that can heighten the idea of the sublime. Its image will never fade from my memory.— Niagara will be to me, I hope, a means of grace. Here virtue seems more divine, and sin more deformed, than in any spot I ever visited. I left the place feeling more than ever that God is supremely good and man selfish and vile. I thank God for this great gift to the world.

May 10. I am never weary in looking upon Lake Erie. Today when not a breeze is stirring, it is the very image of repose. To the left there is seen a long line of forest, just rising above the water—a dark margin of this sea of glass. It is a part of the frame of the picture. The waters are not stirred by a single ripple, but are an emblem of the deepest spiritual repose. Happy is that river, which, after flowing restlessly, through a long and troubled journey spreads out into this tranquil sea, whose waves are of crystal purity. Blessed is that river which loses its turbid waters in the clear waves of the Lake. In front of where I stand the land disappears. The water, in the dim distance meets the heaven. The heavens seem to stoop to meet and embrace the pure wave. The earth & the celestial realms are one. Where one ends and the other begins I cannot tell. I can easily imagine that in the distant horizon is the place where the purified spirit might mingle in society of the angels, and walk with the blessed. There it seems,
        "Heaven comes down the soul to greet
        And glory crow[n]s the mercy-seat."[111]
        The ocean is a symbol of God's eternity. The lake is but the image of the ocean. It can scarcely be distinguished from the sea. In its present tranquil state it represents a soul at rest. A deep lake in perfect stillness is the most expressive image of the profound serenity of a soul restored to unbroken fellowship with God, which nature furnishes. It is like the soul when all its desires and affections and thoughts are <u>fixed</u> upon their divine center.
        While I {looked} gazed upon the lake a dark and threatning storm cloud looked upon it. It cast its gloomy shadow over it; and mingled {the} its soldid darkness with the water, and then turned away without even ruffling its surface. O that thus might be averted from my soul every dark

cloud of temptation which might mar my peace by sullying my inward purity. Would that I was so grounded in the divine love, and rooted and confirmed in all goodness, that the dark powers of hell could not disturb the tranquility of my spirit. I long for solid peace and undisturbed repose.

The lake, so smooth and tranquil, reflects all that is in the heavens above. The sun, the silvery cloud, the moon and stars at night, are seen beneath its surface. But it is only when its waters are pure and peaceful. Could they become turbid, in consequence of a storm, and be defiled with the impurities of the earth, it would no longer reflect the heavenly things. I would that my soul might so abide in the peace and purity of God, that it should bear the permanent impress of the celestial realms, and be a partaker of the beatitudes of the angels. I pray that heaven may be enstamped upon my susceptible heart.

The sun painting the clouds, and making them look like mountains of gold, pours his flame upon the surface of the lake, and then sinks into {the} its bosom and finds the place of its rest. So may Jesus, the great Sun of righteousness, who gives grace and glory, enlighten and warm my soul with his beams, the emanations of his love and truth, and find in my soul a permanent home. Arise, O Lord into the place of thy rest.

The lake in its unruffled stillness is like the Sea of Galilee after the word of of Christ had hushed the storm to silence.

"And the wind ceased—it ceased! That word
  Passed through the gloomy sky:
The troubled billows knew their Lord,
  And fell beneath His eye.

 And slumber settled on the deep,
  And silence on the blast;
They sank as flowers that fold to sleep,
  When sultry day is past."[112]
So may his Spirit calm my soul, and give me a recollection so deep, a peace so divine, that nothing without can disturb.

May 11. My thoughts often turn toward my home in C. It is consecrated ground. Amid all the conflict of opinions and petty ambitions, & the apparent desire to magnify self which I witness every day in General

Conference, my thoughts following[113] the lead of my affections wander away to the loved ones at home. The domestic affections, are it seems to me immortal, especially that holy feeling of the heart, true conjugal love. It has something of God & heaven in it. It is a foretaste of what angelic natures know. It throws over earth a celestial radiance and hue. It is in mercy given to man "to light the wilderness with beams of heaven."[114] It must live in that blessed land where death can never separate kindred hearts.

> "Yes! in the noon of that Elysian clime,
> Beyond the sphere of anguish, death, or time;
> Where mind's bright eye with renovated fire,
> Shall beam on glories never to expire;
> O! there th'illumined soul may fondly trust,
> More pure, more perfect, rising from the dust,
> Those mild affections, whose consoling light
> Sheds the soft moonbeams on terrestrial night,
> Sublimed, ennobled, shall forever glow,
> Exalting rapture—not assuaging woe."[115]

May 13. Been confined to my room by sickness, and have not attended Church. In the almost painful silence and stillness of my room, in the forenoon, had sweet communion with Christ. Felt so weak that I could not walk but little, yet it has been I hope a day of good to my soul. The winter is followed by spring—the ice will yield to flowers. I shall not always go mourning. God is laying waste the life of self. These terrible inward conflicts, and this indescribable desolation of spirit, will be followed by the dawn of the celestial life. A horror of great darkness has for some time come upon me. I have prayed God not to spare me, but let the work be thorough and radical. Underneath all my darkness and below all this surface disturbance there is a faith that this dreadful surgery is to be followed by a higher and healthier spiritual life. Hence I can say I hope with truth in the language of that true female poet, while shut out by sickness from the house of God and six hundred miles from my loved home among strangers,

> "I may not tread
> With them those pathways—to the feverish bed
> Of sickness bound; yet, O my God! I bless

Thy mercy, that with Sabbath peace hath filled
My chastened heart, and all its throbbings stilled
To one deep calm of lowliest thankfulness."[116]

These trials when viewed aright are but the prophecy of future peace and triumph. There has been present to my mind at all times this passage— "I will praise the Lord at all times. His praise shall be continually in my lips."[117]

May 19. Ogdensburgh N.Y. Day before yesterday I left Buffalo for home, in consequence of an attack of fever and ague. Came down to Niagara Falls and stopped the first night.[118]

The night I stopped there we had a severe thunder storm, which in such a place looses all its grandeur. The loudest thunder appears in the presence of the mighty cataract utterly insignificant and is scarcely noticed. In the morning, I walked out to view the rapids below the Suspension Bridge and to see the Whirlpool. The river which flows smoothly and tranquilly for two miles below the Falls, under the bridge commences a rapid descent, and rushes with deafening roar through the narrowed chasm, boiling, leaping, and foaming. The birds were sweetly singing, after the refreshing shower of the previous night. Some could be heard distinctly; others but faintly amid the roaring of the waters. It was the voice of love heard above the discordant raving of unfettered power. It is to the ear what the rainbow at the cataract is to the eye. The language of both is, "Behold the goodness and the severity of God."[119] No one of the attributes of the great Creator acts alone, or is exhibited by itself in the realm of nature. His wisdom, power, and love act in harmony, and are as one.

Niagara is full of beauty and sublimity, and affords nothing but pleasure to the beholder, if one does not violate the laws of God in relation to it. If we invade its rights and come under its power, it has no mercy. A day or two before my visit to the Falls, a boy of ten years of age, carelessly playing on the brink of the river above them, fell in and was seen no more. But the Cataract was made to look at, not to fall into. We must keep within the laws of the divine order, which God has established in relation to it.

The ride from Suspension Bridge to Lewiston, a distance of seven miles, is one of the pleasantest imaginable. You pass along the brink of the chasm, through which the river rushes, so near that it seems as if the cars would leap into it.— The scenery is wild in the extreme, bearing some resemblance to the White Mountain Notch. We passed by the Lewiston Suspension Bridge, which is nearly too [two] hundred feet longer than the one above, but is a much lighter structure. At Queenston on the opposite side of the river, the high table land, which is a horizontal continuation of Table Rock at the Falls, suddenly terminates, and the country sinks some three hundred feet almost perpendicular to the level of the river. On this lofty escarpment, called Queenston Hights, stands Brock's Monument. It is 185 feet in height, and surrounded by a statue of the gallant General, who fell in battle fought at this place in 1812.[120] Niagara Falls, has certainly worn back from this place, and was once a hundred feet higher than at present, as the river descends during the distance of seven miles a hundred feet. I observed that the lower stratum of rock, which at Lewiston appears at the surface, disintegrates upon a slight exposure to the atmosphere. This crumbling stratum runs horrizontally back to the Cataract. It wears away from the action of the water, and the harder rock which lies above being left without support, breaks off. The red shaly sandstone, on which the hard limestone rests, is wearing away more or less every year, and the Falls are gradually receding.

At Lewiston the river becomes perfectly tranquil, spreads out nearly a mile in width, and flows on calmly to the lake[.] It is one of the grandest symbols in nature of a soul, which, after a long inward struggle and combat with the power of evil, has passed into a state of unutterable rest.— You could hardly imagine that this placid current, ever rushed over the precipice, and down the rapids above. The glassy surface reflects the heavens above, just as a soul at rest, after all its wanderings, images the celestial life.

The country on each side of the river is perfectly level, and exceedingly fertile. It is interspersed with villas and cottages, and at this time of the year, the air is laden with the perfume of the millions of blossoms on the fruit trees. It is a picture of Paradise. I have never found a place in all my travels, which I should sooner select as the seat of the original Garden of Delights, where our first parents lived in innocence and bliss.

I started from Queenston, on the steamer Zimmerman, for Toronto at 1 P. M. We touched at the town of Niagara, on the American side, where we caught the first view of the noble lake Ontario. Fort Niagara, around which many historical associations cluster, stands on the bank of the river in the angle which it forms with the lake.[121] The ride from Lewiston to the lake, on the river flowing between two mighty empires, is one of much interest. The view of the lake as you enter it is sublime. It is a sublimity different and more pleasing than that of Niagara. The steamer moved merrily over the waves, enlivened by the strains of a violin in the hands of a blind musician. I sat in the stern of the boat and watched the land we had left as it faded away in the dim distance. The line of the coast became lower and lower, until at length it wholly disappeared, and nothing but the green water was visible. The changeless prospect was varied only by the occasional appearance of a gull or a schooner. The only variety in the view is in the ever changing panorama of clouds, which were quietly floating in the heavens. So to the departing spirit earth fades away from its view. It rises from the realm of sense[.] Time disappears, and a limitless eternity of peace is its portion.

On reaching Toronto, we started immediately for Ogdensburgh, on board the splendid steamer New York, which is a floating palace, and said to be the best boat that runs upon the lake. There were not more than a dozen passengers on board, so that the trip was somewhat solitary, but none the less pleasant. The lake was unusually smooth, so that the motion of the boat was scarcely perceptible. This inland sea of fresh water is 190 miles in length and 55 in width. It is 330 feet below the level of lake Erie, and is 600 feet in depth. The color of the water is peculiar. If you can imagine blue to pass imperceptibly into green, and can arrest the process on the dividing line between blue and green, you will have a conception of the color of these lakes. The water is as pure as crystal, and in the wake of the steamer the foam is white as snow.— When the sun sank into the water in the western horizon, there seemed to be a path of light between us and the descending orb. The deep waters of the lake were tranquil, and the land had wholly disappeared. The watery plain appeared as an immense circle, and the heavens a magnificent dome resting upon it. It was a scene of surpassing grandeur, and a temple for the worship of the Creator and Father of all.

At night the lake is black as the Stygian sea. The heavens were overspread with clouds, and the sparks from the smoke pipes fell like a shower of stars, hundreds in number, and were quenched in the dark flood. It was a splendid exhibition of fire works. At 9 P. M. we passed into a thunder shower. Darkness was upon the face of the deep,[122] the lake was blackness itself. No one can imagine the gloom that settled upon the waters. What would the world be without light! And what would the moral universe be without the Word of God!

At daylight we began to pass among the Thousand Islands of the St. Lawrence. In a distance of twenty seven miles there are said to be 1500 of them. They are of all conceivable forms; some of them contain but a few square rods and are mere naked rocks. Others contain extensive tracts. They are generally covered with trees to the water's edge. The scenery much resembles that of Winnepisseogee lake, only it is on a larger scale.[123] It is a scene of surpassing beauty. A portion of these islands are inhabited, and contain highly cultivated farms, which contrast finely with the un-broken forests which cover most of them. Occasionally you pass an island with a single cottage looking the very picture of contentment. The birch at this season of the year is of a delicate green and shows finely by the side of the more sombre hue of the evergreens. The noble St. Lawrence, as we enter among the Islands, is twelve miles wide, and gradually contracts to three miles.— By the politeness of the Captain, I was invited to take a seat with him on the upper deck, who pointed out to me all the objects of interest. I observed that the roughest men seemed to be affected with the scene of beauty that surrounded us.— It is a scene that even the inhabit-ants of another sphere might be supposed to view with pleasure. I could but imagine with what feelings the French, who are peculiarly susceptible of the emotion of the beautiful, must have gazed upon this part of the St. Lawrence on its first discovery. There is no more delightful trip on the continent. It is one of those many scenes of beauty and loveliness with which the infinite goodness of the Creator has adorned this fair world, which is made for our habitation during the first stage of our existence. Such a spot was not made to be the abode of sin, but of beings made in the image of God.

The river, the morning we passed down it, was of a glassy smoothness, with not a single ripple on its surface, which added much to the quiet beauty of the scenery. The islands seemed to be the abode of Peace itself, and the home of love. One could not help feeling that the Happy Islands, of which the poets and philosophers of the old world loved to dream, were at last found.[124] I left them feeling more deeply than ever that the earth we inhabit needs but little change to make it a suitable residence for holy beings. The world is fair and beautiful, and is everywhere radiant with the wisdom and love of God.

Sept. 8. Returned from Campmeeting at Lebanon.[125] It was a season of spiritual refreshment. Was edified in conversing with Bro N__ of Boston, who has a rich experience in the deep things of God. He is the only man I have ever met who fully understands my own experience. He made the same remark of me.

Sept. 14. Had an overwhelming sense of the love of God. It was all I could endure: My soul almost sunk beneath the weight, overpowered by the immensity of the divine love.

Who could endure to see God as he is. May he enlarge my soul's capacity to receive more of him. By beholding may I be changed more & more into the same image, until all my soul shall be love.

Sept 29. The last three weeks have been among the best weeks of my life. God has been preciously near. These words have often been present to my mind, and have been greatly blessed to my heart,
"O Love, thou bottomless abyss,
My sins are swallowed up in thee."[126]

Oct 26. This has been a memorable day in my spiritual history. The heavenly world has opened down into my soul more than ever before. In the evening I walked out into the field to commune with the Lord in prayer. The moon floated tranquilly through the deep blue aerial ocean. The clouds were tinged with its silvery light. The silence of nature was almost oppressive. In such an hour how sweet to raise the soul from earth to heaven. I seemed to be transported to the spiritual realm, and more amid celestial presences. Never have I felt the heavens so near. The earth seems to me to be the basis and continent of the higher spiritual and celestial creations. Heaven with all it contains is not separated from earth by spatial distance, but only by dissimilarity of state. When that dissimilitude ceases the two worlds are made a one. O that I might be more and more in harmony with the celestial realms, so that I might enjoy "the communion of saints," in all the plenitude of its meaning.

Oct. 27. This evening walked out in the forest to commune with a present God. What a temple for worship is an autumnal forest by moonlight! It far surpasses the grandest cathedral on earth. My whole life is becoming prayer. I do not find myself so much drawn out in supplication for special objects as I once did. My prayer is now more a silent communion with God and the ever present heavens. I am able to abstract my mind from created things at any time and in any place, and center my thoughts upon a present Deity, and elevate my soul to a state of presence with the Lord. This seems to me to be the object & end of prayer. This is _real_ prayer.

Nov. 29. The object of prayer is not to effect any change in the divine disposition toward us, for his infinite love is an infinite and unchanging inclination to impart himself to us, and this he always does according to the receptivity of the creaturely spirit. The idea that prayer or any form of worship effects any objective change in God is only an _appearance_ of truth and not a real truth. It does not bring God any nearer to us, but brings us nearer to Him. It may be illustrated by a man in a boat drawn to the shore by a rope fastened there and which he pulls. This makes no change in the position of the shore, but only in the boatman, though there may be an _appearance_ of motion in the shore, and the effect is the same as if the land itself were moved. Thus in prayer we do not bring God down to us, but only rise to him. There should be no attempt in prayer to bend the divine will to ours, but to bring ours to harmonize or be one with his. Then the obstructing barrier is removed and the divine flows in. On the philosophy of worship, Emanuel Swedenborg has some good thoughts. He says, "The essence of spiritual love is to do good to others, not for the sake of self, but for the sake of others; infinitely more so is the essence of divine love. This is like the love of parents towards children, who do good to them out of love, not for their own sake, but for the sake of their children, as is manifest in the love of a mother toward her children. It is believed that the Lord, because he is to be adored, worshipped, and glorified, loves adoration, worship, and glory, for his own sake; but he loves them for man's sake;

because man thereby comes into such a state, that the Divine can flow in and be perceived, for thereby man removes his <u>proprium</u> (or self-hood) which prevents influx and reception; his proprium, which is the love of self, hardens his heart and shuts it.[127] This is removed by the acknowledgment that from himself nothing is done but evil, and from the Lord nothing but good; hence comes a softening of the heart and humiliation, from which adoration and worship flow." (*D.L. & W.* 335.)[128]

Dec. 1. My religious opinions respecting doctrine have undergone during the last four years a gradual revolution. They have been essentially modified. I have been released from the bondage of litteralism and materialism, and my views have become more spiritual and satisfying. The process of putting off the old sensuous conceptions of religious doctrines has been attended with much inward desolation, and also with great supports and comforts. Any form of Christian doctrine that causes me to think more highly of the necessity of inward and outward holiness, that brings me into a closer conjunction with the Lord, that gives a larger charity to man, and a deeper sense of the value of the divine Word, and causes me to think less of self and the world and more of heaven, cannot be false. It has not the marks, nor does it bear the fruit of falsity. One thing I know, union with Christ is conjunction with the uncreated and imperishable Truth. He whose system of doctrine is not a union with the Lord is in the spirit of falsity whatever he believes. His truth is only a collection of dead ideas, and not the light of life. To divest ourselves of old opinions which have become rooted in the soul's very substance, is a crucifying process. This divesting process brings the soul often into a state of inward <u>vastation</u>. Yet in the case of those who are good at heart, it must be done here or hereafter in the intermediate state, as no falsities can enter heaven, which is a realm of unclouded truth. I love truth as I love God, and love it for its own sake, not for its connection with a creed or sect. I am making advancement in the school of Christ at the feet of the Master. My heart is lifted up to God in deep sincerity, that he will lead me into all truth.

 "If I am right, thy grace impart,
   Still in the right to stay;
 If I am wrong, O teach my heart,
   To find that better way."[129]

Feb. 18 [1861].[130] I sometimes have experiences which are difficult to reproduce in words. A few days ago the Lord was pleased to manifest himself to me as the Word—the imperishable Truth contained in the Holy Scriptures. It seemed to me that in the Celestial world Christ himself is the living Word, to which the angels apply, and which so far as they are receptive of it, flows into their inmost perceptions. In reading the Scriptures I do not read over so much surface as formerly, but confine myself to a few passages, sometimes to a single text. The outward letter is only the continent of the hidden Truth, which is from the Lord & is the Lord. In every passage of the Word, I am put into direct communication with the infinite Mind. I therfore aim to divest myself of all selfish desires in acquiring spiritual truth, and hold my soul in an attitude of consecration to the good of others, and then bring my soul into the presence of God in some passage of the Word. I abstract my mind from all sensible things, and by introversion retire inward, and let the divine Light flow into my inmost perception. The passage of the Bible appears to be the place where the heavens, which are a development of God, open or extend down to my soul. By silent introversion, and perfect self surrender, the communication is formed, and the uncreated Truth, which is an effluence of the Eternal Mind, flows in. In this way unutterable things are seen in a single verse of the Scriptures. In this way the soul finds divine nutriment in the Scriptures. It has union with God through the Word. It makes rapid growth in the knowledge of the truth. Two things must be always attended to by him who would advance in divine knowledge. 1. He must purpose to obey the truth, and thus incorporate it into the inmost life of the soul. 2. He must consecrate all his attainments to the good of others—to the spiritual enlightenment of those who thirst for the light, and are receptive of it. The soul that is in such a state may safely to its eternal interests be taught by the Lord the hidden wisdom. The secret of the Lord is with it. Such a one sees in the divine Word what others look for in vain. God reveals his revelation to him. The seals are broken, and the Book opened. Those who thirst for truth as a means of promoting the spiritual good of others, and not merely as a source of honor, or gain, that is for the gratification of self, obtain from the Lord all that wisdom which they need to accomplish the ends they propose. The Holy Spirit, which is the effluence of the uncreated Wisdom, leads them into all truth. They see truth in its own divine light, receiving it not by reasoning, but by intuition.[131] "They see {them} truths inwardly in themselves, as the eye sees external objects, for the objects of spiritual sight, which is of the interior understanding, are spiritual truths, which are seen by those who are in that understanding, in like manner as natural objects are seen before the eyes."[132]

Feb. 19.[133] Finished today the manuscript of a book to be entitled, *The Celestial Dawn or Conjunction of Earth and Heaven.*[134] Its object is to show how a soul may rise from the ruins of its fallen state to the beginning of a heavenly life on earth, and how in accordance with divine order we may communicate with the heavens. It points out the <u>media</u> of connection between the two worlds. It is designed to satisfy the innate desire to communicate with the unseen world that underlies the modern Pythonism.[135] It has been written in the presence of the Lord, with much prayer, and with a sincere desire to know & make known the truth. A[f]ter finishing it I wrote the title page upon my knees, devoutly thanking the Lord for the assistance rendered me in composing it, and humbly committing it to the stream of his Providence. He has in a very striking manner supplied me with some of the materials. A year ago I published a work on the higher forms of Christian life, called *The Happy Islands or Paradise Restored.* It has met with some favor, and been blessed to the good of some souls. I also published a small work entitled *Divine Order in the Process of Full Salvation.*[136] I have evidence that it has been made useful to souls.

March 2. This evening enjoyed a precious season of communion with God and with heaven. My soul came into a state of presence with the Lord, and the angelic heavens, which appear to me as an unfolding of God, came consciously near. I am not separated from angelic beings by distance of space, (for that is only an <u>appearance</u> as it does not belong to the spiritual world) but by dissimilitude of moral condition. When my soul comes into sympathy with the angelic realms, those heavenly beings come near. Conscious communion with the angels is effected without a miracle in harmony with the laws of mind. Swedenborg has unfolded the laws by which it is effected. There must first be a similarity of state. He says, "Let him know that in the spiritual world all presence is effected by knowledge and acknowledgement, and that all conjunction is effected by affection which is of love; for spaces there are nothing else but appearances according to similarity of minds, that is, of affections and consequent thoughts, wherfore, when any one knows another, either by fame, or report, or by intercourses with him, or by conversation or by relationship, when he thinks of him from an idea of that knowledge, the other becomes present, although to all appearance he were a thousand miles distant; and if any one loves another whom he knows, he dwells with him in one society, and if he loves him intimately, in one house. This is the state of all throughout the whole spiritual world, and this state of all derives its origin from the circumstance of the Lord being present with every one according to faith, and conjoined according to love." (A.R. 937.)[137] The same principles are involved in communing with the Lord, as with his holy angels, who derive all their life and holiness from him. But there can be no fellowship with holy angels, unless we are like them in wisdom and love. If we become grounded in any good we are associated [with] those in the spiritual world who are in the same form of good. If we are in bondage to any particular evil we are in conjunction with those in hell who are in the same evil. Thus we have unseen connection with our like in another world. Death only takes off the bandage from our eyes and shows us where we are, but does not transfer us through space to some other material realm. We are now in the midst of our proper society—are never alone.

East Salisbury Mass—May 23ᵈ 1861.[138] Came to this place five weeks ago today. Have prayed earnestly that divine results might attend my labors here. Through the blessing of God & in answer to prayer my health is improved. I lay hold upon Christ as my life & as the "health of my countenance—and my God."[139] Have found in this place some who are acquainted with the higher forms of Christian experience. May the Lord raise up a spiritual Church.

June 7. The doctrine taught by Swedenborg of the spheres is one of much importance in Christian experience. He teaches that every angel and man is surrounded by a sphere of thought and affection, or a circle within which they impart, (oftentimes silently) their own feelings and thoughts. Thus there are persons who exert a secret and powerful influence over others, who come within the sphere of their spirits. This encircling sphere is more or less extended according as the angel or man is more or less elevated in the scale of life. There are those among the angels whose sphere extends to a great distance. The sphere of the Lord is infinite. I sometimes by abstraction from the world of sense come into the divine sphere of the Lord, or the infinite circle within which the God of love imparts his own divine wisdom and life to the soul. I occasionally have an indefinable, ineffable consciousness, an inmost perception of the divine influx, and the radiations of the divine love & wisdom to my soul. This divine sphere of the Lord, this emanation from the Lord, this divine proceeding or proceeding divine, is the Holy Spirit. The Lord took upon him human nature and glorified it or deified it in order to make it the medium of communicating himself to the souls of men. Hence we see why it was expedient that he should go away from his disciples, or put off his material body, and put on the glorified or divine body. His material form obstructed the divine communications, so that it is said the Holy Spirit was not yet (fully) given, because Christ was not yet glorified. After his glorification of his Human form, the divine life, without obstruction, and without limitation, except our want of receptivity, may be imparted to us. It is the object of _real_ prayer to bring the spirit within the radiating sphere of the Lord, to receive him. For nothing proceeds from God, that is not God. The soul is made to be a receptacle of the Divine. O when will a sensuous church ever come to the perception of their high privilege and true dignity.

We may be partakers of the divine nature—the divine love & wisdom.

Christ is of God made unto us wisdom, and righteousness and sanctification & redemption. All our light & love, all our goodness is an emanation from the Eternal Goodness—it is something of God in us. The soul has attained to the end of its creation only when it becomes a voluntary recipient of the Divinity. For this, it was made an image of God or a form receptive of the divine Life. Our spirits may be the abode of an indwelling Deity. When the soul receives directly from the Lord through the deified human body in which he dwells, it is called immediate influx. When it receives the divine influence, as it often does, through the angelic heavens, or when the soul comes within the sphere of angels, it is secondary or mediate influx. I asked the Lord a few days ago to illuminate my mind so as to see the meaning of the passage, "The angel of the Lord encampeth round about them that fear him."[140] I saw in a divine light that by the angel of the

Lord is meant the angelic heavens, and not an individual angel. It is called an angel of the Lord, because all their light & holiness are derived from God, and are something of the Lord in them. When the angelic heavens enclose our spirits round with their calm & heavenly presence, the angel of the Lord is said to encamp round about us. Sometimes in temptation they enclose us within their sphere, and strengthen us. Thus it is said of Christ, "Angels came and ministered unto him."[141] I would that I might so live, and possess such an interior frame of spirit, as not to repel, but rather attract this celestial angelic influence.

June 22. This afternoon I walked down to the bank of the Merrimack river about one mile above Newburyport. Here under the shade of a cedar tree, had a precious season of communion with the Lord. This passage was applied with divine force to my soul. "The Lord is my shepherd; I shall not want. He maketh me to lie down in green pastures; he leadeth me beside the still waters. He restoreth my soul."[142] The last words came with redeeming power to my heart.

I have seemed to myself lately like Lazarus, raised to life by the Savior. He came forth from the tomb, but was bound hand and foot with grave clothes. So my soul has received life from Christ. I have heard the voice of the Son of God and have lived. But my spirit has been bound with grave clothes. But lately I have heard the word— "Loose him & let him go."[143] I long to emerge into perfect freedom.

July 20. This morning while reading the sixth chapter of Mark, the fiftieth verse came with divine power to my heart— "Be of good cheer; it is I; be not afraid." When Jesus says this to the inmost soul, it enjoys an inward perception of the boundless love of God. All anxieties and fear are removed and the soul subsides into a divine calm. (With Christ to say and to do is one and the same. His word goes forth with creative force. When he says, "Peace be still," he makes a calm.[144] He casts out the evil spirits by his <u>word</u>. (Matt. 8:16.) There is divine power in his word. "For his word was with power." [(] Luke 4:32.) It is of great advantage to the soul to discern by faith a divine power in the words of Jesus. There is wrapt up in them the same power that created & now creates the material universe.)[145] And the creation of the world is symbolical of the higher moral & spiritual creation which takes place in regeneration. We may by faith lay hold of the redeeming power of the words of Christ. We should never forget that saying and doing are one & the same with him.

July 23. I have thought lately of the promise of Christ, "Ye shall <u>know</u> the truth, and the truth shall make you free."[146] There are some three distinct stages or degrees of divine knowledge. 1. The truths of holy Scripture are deposited in the external memory. This is the first dawn of regeneration. It is the transition from heathenism to Christianity. Many go no farther. The truths of the Gospel lie in the external mind. 2. There is a solid demonstration of the reasonableness of those truths. Their beauty and propriety are clearly apprehended, and the soul advances to <u>faith</u>, from its first mere sensual, external view. Here is a state of intellectual illumination. 3. Lastly the soul rises to the <u>Gnosis</u>, an <u>intuition</u> or <u>inward perception</u> of truth. It now shines in its own divine, uncreated light. This is a knowledge for transcending reason or memory. St Paul speaks of this as belonging to the <u>manhood</u> or maturity of the soul. The soul rises above all childish conceptions of divine things. It does not see through a glass darkly. It sees with open or unveiled face the glory of the Lord, or the light of his divine truth. It knows as it is known. Its knowledge is divine. (1 Cor. 13:9–12.) It has attained the all-satisfying truth that maketh free. "Ye shall <u>know</u> the truth and the truth shall make you free."[147] Such a one will have views of truth but poorly apprehended by those on a lower plane of spiritual life. He sees truths in a passage of Scripture that others cannot see, & which may appear fanciful & <u>dreamy</u> to them. Such a one pierces through the enveloping letter to the spirit and life within.

Aug. 9. One of my greatest wants—one that is most deeply felt—is the enjoyment of the society of kindred spirits. I often pine for the fellowship of those who can understand my experience, and are recipients of those views of divine truth which I have been taught by the Holy Spirit. It is but seldom I come in contact with one of like mind and spirit with myself. (I long for heavenly society and the fellowship of the blest.)[148] I now sometimes find myself in a state of sympathy and nearness with the wise and good of different lands & ages. I have felt especially oftentimes a sweet nearness of soul and union of spirit with Neander. There is no one with whose views I more deeply sympathize than with his. Though he has gone before to the spiritual world, and I remain in the natural world, yet we are not sundered by spatial distance. (The spiritual world is (to use the language of Mr Wesley) "all round about us, and yet no more discerned by our natural senses that [than] if it had no being.")[149] My natural senses cannot discern it, but when faith becomes an intuition or inward-seeing, I have an inmost perception of it. I must enjoy the communion of saints, (which according to Bishop Pearson on the apostolic creed, embraces fellowship with those in heaven as well as those on earth,) or feel a restless craving for society which earth seldom satisfies.[150] Union with the unseen is not an imaginary thing, but is in harmony with the deepest laws of our spiritual being. Conversation by spoken words, {nor} and through any material _media_, is manifestly an impossibility. They are pure spirits and have no means of discerning what is material having put off the material organs of sense by which they took cognizance of earthly things. But they may discern by their spiritual senses & perceptions my spirit & read its state. They cannot see my body, but they can perceive my thoughts and feelings. Without this they could not be ministering spirits to the heirs of salvation. (Now between spirits in the other world, language is not merely by uttered words and sounds—for such language is always defective and fails to express all we think or feel—but there is thought—speaking. Were I sufficiently pure to be united with {the}angelic human spirits I might now converse with them _in thought_. They can perceive my thoughts as well as I can hear the words of a friend by my side. It is, perhaps, more true than we imagine, that "our thoughts are heard in heaven.")[151]

When I am in a state of interior thought, I may hold an intercourse with the blest too deep & real for words. They perceive my thought, and cause me to perceive theirs. Another means of conversing with those of a higher realm might be by symbols or correspondences exhibited before the eye of the spirit. In this way the human angel of the Apocalypse, instructed John concerning things present & to come. But this involves a sufficient knowledge of the correspondence between natural & spiritual things, as to be able to interpret the symbol; otherwise it would be speaking in an unknown tongue.)[152] But all men cannot receive these sayings, except they to whom it is given. Men are yet too deeply plunged in materialism and Sadduceeism[153] to understand this. The spiritual world is too unreal to their fleshly mind, to even <u>imagine</u> it to be near. They do not rise above the plane of sense in their conceptions. But this will not always be. (In the new age about to be born, heaven and earth will mingle into one. We shall then believe in the "communion of saints" in all its plenitude of meaning.)[154]

Aug. 10. I have become convinced that in order to find rest, it is necessary that I exercise an active appropriating faith in Christ. There is danger of becoming too <u>passive</u>. A mere sinking into the will of God is not enough when it is alone. It is necessary as a state preliminary & preparatory to an active appropriating faith in God.[155] But we must lay hold of God in all those offices and relations in which we need him at the time. If we are restless & uneasy, we must sink into the will of God and then by faith lay hold of Christ as our peace. "In the world ye shall have tribulation; but in me ye shall have peace."[156] When our faith lays hold of him as our peace, all the bliss of the divine mind becomes ours. It is not enough that a soul remain <u>passive</u>, like clay in the hands of the potter, it must stretch out the arm of faith and take hold of Christ & appropriate him according to the needs of the soul. It seems to me to have been an error in the experience of Lady Guyon, that she was too passive, too quiescent. If active & passive faith had been in due proportion, she would not have been so long in darkness & desolation. In the excess of passive faith over active faith there was a onesidedness in her character. The other fault, where active faith is in excess of passive faith, or a sinking into the will of God, is equally to be avoided, and equally mars the perfect symetry of the Christian character. All God's purity, and joy, and peace and wisdom are mine, when I am conjoined to him by a perfect self-surrender and an appropriating faith. I have often been greatly blessed by apprehending him by faith as I might specially need him. It is not enough to renounce all self-will and relinquish all desire—this must be done, but there must be positive faith. The former state is too negative. It is a state of emptiness, which must precede the experience of the fulness. (For it is only when we are emptied of self, that we can be replenished with God.)[157] Faith in its <u>reality</u> and <u>completeness</u> is a passive surrender, and an active laying hold of God. Lord increase my faith.[158]

It seems to me that most of the mystic authors, have failed here. What they say of self-abandonment, the death of the selfhood, and of inward crucifixion is all true & good. But while all this is accomplished, the soul may remain in a wilderness state, if there is not an active, vigorous, brave & daring faith that siezes hold of God and appropriates his life as the life of the soul. We are not only to die with Christ, but we should rise with him. And when we plunge into "the Godhead's deepest sea,"[159] we are not to wait till we float up to the surface, but we are to raise ourselves in the strength which God supplies. There cannot be a happy experience without active faith.

Aug. 16. In the account of Thomas Walsh, we see an instance of one who enjoyed the internal presence of God, and who had attained to a state of presence with the Lord. It is said, "He walked the streets of great cities absorbed in introspection and prayer, and as unobservant of external things as if he were in the solitude of a wilderness. [. . .] He is represented as sometimes lost in mental absence on his knees, with his face heavenward, and arms clasped upon his breast, in such composure that scarcely could one hear him so much as breathe; as absorbed in God, and enjoying a calmness and transport which could not be expressed; while from the serenity, and something resembling splendor which appeared on his countenance, and in all his gestures afterward, one might easily discover that he had been on the mount of communion, and had descended, like Moses with the divine glory on his brow.

His public prayers were attended with such ardor, pertinence, and faith, that it appeared, says his biographer, 'as though the heavens were burst open, and God himself appeared in the congregation.'

He was sometimes wrapt away, as from earth, in his devotions, being quite lost to himself, and insensible to everything around him, absorbed in the visions of God; and in these profound and solemn frames of mind he has remained for hours, still and motionless as a statue." (Stevens, *History of Methodism* vol. 1. p. 339. 340.)[160] A person in such a state of contemplation and peaceful union with God, will, like St Paul, see and feel ineffable things. In reading the Word of God, in his presence, a divine light illumines the abyss of its spiritual import, and the soul perceives what words but poorly express. Such a state is not designed to be a permanent one, for health and life would fail, if we were always thus absorbed in God. It is not to be entered upon when the higher duties of charity to the neighbor require us to actively labor for his good. (But blessed is the man who can in his seasons of private devotion thus be, as it were, absent from the body, and present with the Lord. It has been given me of the Lord's mercy, in a measure to enjoy that blessedness. Yet to be absorbed in the vision of God, and to be lost in divine contemplation, is not of so much value as charity, the sincere, Christ-like love of the neighbor.)[161]

Aug. 26.[162] We were made sad and lonely by the departure of Franklin, our only son, for the war. He came home, on a visit from his regiment, {Saturday} Friday & spent the Sabbath. We trust in God's divine providence to preserve him. In family prayer we read this morning the 91st Psalm, and felt to trust that it might be realized in his experience.[163]

Sept 2. Had a letter from Franklin. His regiment has gone into camp at Mineola, on Long Island.

Sept. 20. Received a letter from Franklin from Washington.[164]

Sept. 22. Today felt as I never did before the importance of Christ's resurrection. (It seems a great thing that Christ should <u>die</u> for us, but it is a greater thing that he <u>lives</u> for us. He gave himself for us in death and in his life. He died for our sins, and rose again for our justification. The apostle Paul attaches an importance to the <u>life</u> of Christ, which is not common in the faith of the Church. He inquires, "Who can condemn us, since it is Christ that hath died, yea rather that is risen again?["] (Rom. 8:34.)[165] In the economy of salvation, the life of Christ—his resurrection & ascent to the heavens—has as much, yea more to do with our freedom from condemnation than his death. I have felt today the "power of his resurrection" as never before in my experience.)[166]

Sept. 26.[167] The day of the national fast, appointed by the president in view of state of the country. Preached to a large congregation from 2 Chron. 14:11.[168] Also spent some time in private prayer for the country. Felt to cry. Spare thy people, O Lord, and give not thy heritage unto reproach.

Probably a million of prayers were offered unto God today for the country from the pulpit, the family altar, and the closet. O Thou who hearest prayer, save this guilty land.

Sept. 27. Today felt the force of this stanza,
"I hate my sins, no longer mine,
    For I renounce them too;
My weakness with thy strength I join,
    Thy strength shall all subdue."[169]

(All good is from God, and cometh down from the Father of lights.[170] It is an emanation from the Lord. "For a man cannot receive any thing except it be given him from above."[171] It is necessary that a soul <u>feel</u> this so as to ascribe all to its Source. We must not appropriate anything good to ourselves, or feel that we have any merit for it, if we do we defile that which is good, and it ceases to be good. All good is from above. The human soul by creation is only a void to be filled with God, just as the atmosphere is filled with the light of the sun. (Every good thought, every holy feeling, every sacred purpose, is from heaven alone. It is equally important for me to feel that all evil in me is from hell and is a part of hell. When I feel this, and hate and combat it as such,[172] it is not imputed to me as mine. For instance when I feel melancholy, and feel that it is a dark shadow of hell thrown across my spirit, and array myself against it, it is not imputed to me as mine. When the will opposes it, I cease to have any property in it. So of anger, impurity, anxiety and other forms of evil. When my will rises up against it, and I believe that the evil is from beneath, and flows in from the world of darkness, "it is no more I that do it."[173] (Blessed is the man whose iniquity is thus covered, to whom the Lord imputeth not sin.[174] Good is an inflowing from heaven; evil from hell. Evil thoughts may be injected into the mind from the world of evil spirits, and so of feelings. This I cannot avoid. "The first motions of our mind, as it is impossible to hinder them, are reckoned by all divines, not to be sinful, provided we do not encourage them." (Paley's *Works*, p. 239.)[175] When we feel evil thus entering into us from beneath, and intruding itself into the temple of our soul, we should feel that it is not ours; the will should assume an attitude of opposition, and by a mental ejaculation, we should lift up our souls to the

Lord,[176] and in a few minutes, sometimes instantly, it will be removed, and the soul will be left in peace. I deem this a principle of great importance in the spiritual life. I should not appropriate to myself good that belongs to God alone; nor evil which is an inflowing from beneath. This is necessary to my sanctification, my liberty, my peace.[177]

Sept. 28. A genuine Christian experience is one that is derived from the Word of God. Man lives by every word that proceedeth out of the mouth of the Lord.[178] The Bible is fitted to originate and to nourish every degree of the divine life in us. I sometimes ask the Lord to give me a promise adapted to my present wants. Oftentimes some sweet promise is brought to my remembrance by the Holy Spirit, which is full of comfort and support. It often comes luminous with divine light. (May I live more and more on the word of God. Eternal life is in the words of Jesus. They are spirit, and they are life.)[179]

Dec. 2ᵈ 1861.[180] The writings of that remarkable man, Immanuel Swedenborg, have taken a deep hold upon my mind. I must confess that his doctrines and revelations satisfy my reason and meet a long-felt want of my spirit. He who comes to the perusal of them with an unprejudiced mind and a sincere desire to learn the truth for the sake of truth (who love truth for its own divine self,) will not fail, I think, to come to an inward perception of their truth. God has always, in every age of the world raised up men, and endowed them with such gifts & qualifications, as to meet the wants of his kingdom on earth. Their training for the work assigned them is the care of Providence. It seems reasonable to suppose that a new dispensation of the Church will sometime dawn upon the world.*[181]

* It is reasonable to suppose that there will be three dispensations of the Church, corresponding to the three manifestations of God as the Father, the Son, & the Holy Ghost. There has been the dispensation of the Father. In the O.T. how little is said of the Son! It is an age of obscurity. We have had the Age of the Son—the intellectual age, or the dispensation of faith. This has continued until now. The next will be the age of the Holy Ghost—the dispensation of love. In the first the sensuous predominates; in the second the intellect; in the third love & the intuitional.[182]

There have been several successive dispensations of mercy in the history of mankind and the Church. It does not seem reasonable to suppose that the present state of the Church, either Protestant or Catholic, is to be a finality—the last and most perfect stage in the unfolding of the kingdom of God among men. In fact it has long been the belief of the church that a brighter age and a better dispensation would have its birth in the future. This has ever been the hope of the church. This better dispensation has been generally denominated the millennial age. A moments reflection, however, will convince any one that its proper & Scriptural denomination is the New Jerusalem, which term marks the last and most perfect stage in the developement of the Church on earth. Now if there is to be a new dispensation, it is self-evident that it must have a beginning somewhere. If the New Jerusalem is to come down from God out of heaven, there is some one to whom it must first come. This divine influence or effluence from God through the heavens into the church on earth, which is signified by the New Jerusalem coming down from God out of heaven, must find its first receptacle in some soul fitted to receive it and to be the germ of the new age. Look back upon the history of the church through all the past ages, and every dispensation of grace has had its rise and small mustard-seed beginning in some one individual. So it manifestly must be in the New Jerusalem stage of the Church's progress. That Immanuel Swedenborg, servant of the Lord Jesus Christ, was the instrument of Providence in ushering in a new and better age of the church, seems to me clear from the following reasons.

1. He has, like Abraham in a former age, been raised up by the Messiah's Providence to restore to the world & the Church the idea of the unity of God. This idea was fading from the mind of the church, and especially of the learned. With the latter the Trinity had become Tritheism, which is a long step toward Polytheism. Swedenborg has shown from the Word of God, that there is one God in whom there is a Trinity, & that Jehovah Jesus is that God. In him is all the fulness of the Godhead bodily.*[183]

The prophet Zechariah, in speaking of the last age of the church, or the latter day of glory, says that {there} in that day there shall be one Lord, & his name one. (Zech. 14:9.) Before the church can be advanced to a higher life, it must come to the belief of one only God, & that Jehovah Jesus is that

God. Without this the soul remains in the natural plane of life & cannot be illuminated. Why?

2. He has restored to the church the almost obliterated knowledge of the spiritual world. In the unbelieving age in which he lived there was little belief in the reality of man's existence after death. The Church was so sunk in sensualism, and was so floundering in the Dismal Swamp of material-ism,[184] that the faith of man's future existence was so feeble as to have little or no influence. It was becoming the wisdom & goodness of Providence to check the progress of this Sadduceean spirit,[185] lest the church should come to an end & the race perish. It cannot be supposed that the church would be suffered always to live with the spiritual world at so cold a dis-tance, but that the clouds and darkness that rested upon that unknown realm would be removed. In the earliest age, according to the Scriptures, men lived in communication with angels. Is Christianity designed to close heaven entirely? Is it consistent with the known character of God to sup-pose that the spiritual world to which we hasten, would always remain a dark unknown, a terra incognita? Is it not probable to reason that it would sometime be revealed? With regard to the disclosures of Swedenborg, and his teachings respecting the spiritual world, they are in perfect harmony with the laws of human nature. His intercourse with spirits and angels was no miracle. He unfolds the laws of mind in accordance with which it took place. What he did, every soul is capable of doing, if it so pleased the Lord. And in the progress of the New Dispensation, and as soon as it can be done safely to man's regeneration & salvation, intercourse with the ever present heavens will be more frequent. There is no doubt that in {the} this respect, in progress of time, men in the New Jerusalem or mil-lennial age, will commune with angels, as was the case with the men of the church in the Golden Age, or the Paradisiacal state. Swedenborg has shown that every man as to his spirit is already in the spiritual world & his soul constitutes a part of that world. He has shown that time and space are the properties of material things, but do not belong to spiritual things. See Knapp's *Christian Theology* p. 106.[186] And hence, the world of spirits, though a real and substantial world, is not removed by spatial distances from men in the earth.^[187]

^It is an interior world, and is within the material cosmos as the soul is within & animates the body. In searching for the spiritual world, we shall find it just as we find our soul. It is an interior realm. To close the corporeal senses, is to come into it, whether this takes place at death or by an introversion of the mind.

We are already connected by the laws of our inmost being with our like in heaven or hell. Swedenborg has given <u>reality</u>, and consequently influence & power to our conceptions of heaven. Man is such by creation, that he is capable of being among the angels of heaven as to his spirit, while as to his body he is among men of the earth.*[188]

* "By the presence of a spiritual being with us, we mean, that he <u>thinks</u> of us, and in this way acts upon us. But in order to this, we need not suppose his local presence, or the aproximation of the spiritual substance. We are present in spirit with an absent friend, when we think of him, and thus act upon him. Paul says, (1 Cor. V. 3.) 'Absent in body but present in spirit.' We see thus that our minds have an agency different from that of matter, though we are ignorant of the mode of their operation." (Knapp's *Christian Theology*, p. 106.)[189]

He is made to be an inhabitant of both worlds. When men become in their interior state like angels, they may then come into conscious communication with them. Swedenborg says, "It is given to no one to discourse as a spirit with angels and spirits unless he be such that he can consociate with angels as to faith and love; nor can he so consociate, unless he have faith and love to the Lord, for man is joined to the Lord by faith and love to him, that is, by truths of doctrine and good principles of life derived from him; and when he is joined to the Lord he is secure from the assaults of evil spirits from hell: with others the interiors cannot be so far opened, since they are not in the Lord. This is the reason why there are few at this day to whom it is given to speak & converse with angels." (*Earths in the Universe*. No 123.)[190] But in the new dispensation, the quality of the church will be such that it will be one with heaven. This is signified by the measurement of the wall of the city, that it was a hundred & forty four cubits according to the measure of a man, that is of an angel. (Rev 21:17.) That is, the members of that church are such as to faith & love as to be as to their spirits one with the angels.

3. He has given to the church the key to the spiritual sense of the Word of God. He has shown that there is a correspondence between the spiritual & natural world, and that all things in the natural world exist

from & represent things in the spiritual world. The Word of God is written according to this correspondence.*[191]

* In all languages the terms employed to express spiritual things are taken from the material world. The notion of the <u>soul</u>, is expressed in all the ancient languages by terms which originally signify <u>mind</u>, <u>air</u>, or <u>breath</u>. This is the case with the Greek word[s] ψυχή and πνεύμά.[192] The same is true of the Latin word <u>spiritus</u>, (from <u>spiro</u>, to breathe) and <u>animus</u> & <u>anima</u> which are derived from the Greek ἄνεμος, wind.[193] Witness also the words heart, veins or kidneys, bowels (Latin <u>splanctna</u>)[.] It is one of the laws of the mind that it expresses spiritual things by natural things.[194]

The deep spiritual significance concealed beneath the enveloping letter, cannot be seen without a knowledge of the science of correspondence. To restore to the world the lost science of correspondence was the great mission of Swedenborg. He has {that} thus lifted the veil from the abyss of spiritual & celestial truth in the Word, and prepared the way for exploring its hidden depths. He has shown that the Word is holy in every part, that it came down from God through the angelic heavens, and is adapted as well to the highest angels as to men of our earth. It contains the deepest <u>arcana</u> of wisdom—and in fact the wisdom of the angels is derived from no other source. It is the fountain of all spiritual wisdom, and in it are hid all the treasures of wisdom and knowledge. The words of Scripture find the root of their existence in the Divine Mind. The Word, especially in its interior senses is an ever present manifestation of the Mind of the Lord.*[195]

* See A.R. n.959, for a comprehensive view of his doctrine of the Sacred Scriptures.[196]

It is the bond of connection between heaven & earth, and the means of conjunction with the Lord. The means by which the <u>spiritual</u> mind may come into an appropriation of this divine treasure of celestial wisdom is the science of correspondence. In unfolding the spiritual sense of the Word according to the correspondences in which it is written, there is nothing left to mere fancy.

Swedenborg's principle of interpretation is infinitely different from that of Cocceius, who laid down the principle that a passage of Scripture is to be made to mean all that it <u>can</u> be made to signify.[197] This was giving room to float off into an ocean of conjectures and wild fancies. The laws of correspondence as unfolded by Emanuel Swedenborg are as fixed as the laws of Geometry.[198] In fact the science of correspondence may be placed among the exact sciences. The life of the Church is derived from the Word, in which there is spirit & life, and the quality of that life is according to the understanding of the Word.[199]

*Swedenborg has taught that there are three senses to the Word, and whether we come into one or the other of these depends upon our interior state. There are three degrees of the soul or three planes of mental being, the sensual, the intellectual, & the intuitional, or in his terminology, the natural, the spiritual & the celestial.[200] If we read the Word of God from the sensuous plane, we extract from it only the literal sense; if from the stand-point of the Intellect, we perceive its spiritual sense; if we elevate the mind to its highest plane, & from this lofty position contemplate the Word of the Lord; we see its celestial & divine import. The three senses of the Word are thus based upon the necessary laws of our being.

Who then can conceive the influence of this great discovery upon the life of the Church through all the ages of the future? John saw the New Jerusalem radiant with the glory of God, or luminous with spiritual truth from the Lord.[201] It has always been the belief of the pious in every age of the church, that there is a spiritual sense in the letter of the Scriptures. The mystic writers, like Fenelon, Madam Guyon, Tauler, Kempis & others in ancient and modern times, have had glimpses of this spiritual significance; but they had no fixed principles of interpretation. All was left to feeling & to fancy. But with the restoration of the lost science of correspondence, we have a solid basis on which to rest our interpretations. Swedenborgs explanations of the Word are made with mathematical exactness. His works contain a most valuable treasure of spiritual wisdom and philosophy—*[202]

^valuable not merely for what they actually teach, but for what they suggest. And they will be better understood in a future age than they are at present. The more we abstract our minds from the world of sense, and are in an interior (or superior) state, the more we shall <u>see</u> their truth & value, and the infinite sweep of his principles. They are not addressed to the sensuous, but to the spiritual mind, and such a mind spontaneously perceives their truth, and receives them.

But all was derived, as he often asseverates, not from angels, but from the Lord, through the spiritual sense of the Word. The greater portion of his works are designed to unfold the interior sense of the Scriptures; but

150   1861.

significance; but they had no fixed principles of interpretation. All was left to feeling & to fancy. But with the restoration of the lost science of correspondence, we have a solid basis on which to rest our interpretations. Swedenborgs explanations of the Word are made with mathematical exactness. His works contain a most valuable treasure of spiritual wisdom and philosophy. But all was derived, as he often asseverates, not from angels, but from the Lord through the spiritual sense of the Word. The greater portion of his works are designed to unfold the interior sense of the scriptures, but he has only led us into the portico of the heavenly palace, and through the divine mercy of the Lord put the key into our hands and invited us to enter by a life of love & faith, and explore for ourselves.

It is worthy also of remark that he who grasps the idea of correspondence in its amazing sweep and its infinite bearings, will not only find within the Bible a New revelation, but the whole outward

he has only led us into the portico of the heavenly palace, and through the divine mercy of the Lord put the key into our hands and invited us to enter by a life of love & faith, and explore for ourselves.

It is worthy also of remark that he who grasps the idea of correspondence in its amazing sweep and sees its infinite bearings, will not only find within the Bible a new revelation, but the whole outward world will be changed. It was the doctrine of the ancients that "All things which are in the heavens, are in the earth, but in an earthly manner; and all things in the earth are also in the heavens, but in a heavenly manner."[203] Plato expressed the idea in this form— "All natural things, being symbols of the immaterial, are pictures of the divine Mind."[204] He who realizes this will find the outward world itself a book, and hills & mountain, rivers & lakes, trees & forests, and all living & moving forms, will be words and letters full of heavenly import. He will live & move in a new earth & beneath new heavens.^205

^His outward actions, such as giving gold or silver, or food & raiment, to the poor, will be performed with the consciousness of their higher celestial import, through the law of correspondence, and thus he will live a heavenly life on earth. This was actually the condition of man in the Golden Age or Paradisiacal state.

"Earth will be crammed with heaven, & every common bush afire of God."^206

4. From the spiritual sense of the Word he has given us higher views than the Church has hitherto enjoyed of the divine nature and character. The knowledge of God is of fundamental importance in the Christian life. It lies at the basis of the whole Christian character. "This is life eternal that they know me &c[."]^207 And our spiritual state, both in time and eternity, will be according to our knowledge of God. A false view of God, will derange the whole inner life. Union with God, which is salvation, must be based upon a proper knowledge of God. "Acquaint now thyself with him & be at peace with him."^208 This is the law of our spiritual being. The character which men attribute to the God they worship will have a reflex influence upon the worshipper. The human mind never can rise above the character of the Divinity it adores. Of idols the Psalmist says, "They that make them are like unto them. So is every one that trusteth in them." (Ps.)^209 If there is to be a new dispensation of the church, called the New Jerusalem, which is to be characterized by a higher wisdom & spiritual life, it must have as its unshaken basis a better knowledge of the divine nature and character.^210

^It [is] a prominent idea in the old Church that God acts for his own glory, not for our good. Thus making him an infinite Self-Love. E. S. declares that he does nothing for his own sake, but all from the love of others. How difficult it is for us to rise above our selfishness—the root of all evil—when we worship the Divine Being in a character of infinite selfishness. If God acts for his own glory, why may not we? How is it possible to love God for his gifts when we feel that they proceed from a selfish desire of glory. But when we attain to the highest charity, the most self-forgetting love, we are only faint images of the Lord—of his boundless love.

While the church derives all its ideas of the divine character from the letter of the Word, where God is often presented as he <u>appears</u> to the natural man, and not as he really is, no higher life is possible, no advanced stage of the church is attainable. One will not read far in the writings of Swedenborg before they will get higher views of the character of God. The knowledge of God is derived wholly from the Word. It has no other source among angels or men. And the deeper our insight is into the inner senses of the Scriptures, the higher will be our views of God. In the writings of Swedenborg, the divine Being is presented in such a light, as to lead us to worship & obey him not through fear, but from love.

As his character is unfolded there from the spiritual sense of the Scriptures, He is Love itself & Wisdom itself. His essential life is love, and it is the necessary property of that Love, to love others out of itself, to desire to be one with them, and to make them happy from itself. These properties of the Divine Love were the cause of the creation of the Universe & of its preservation, which is but a continued creation. In the writings of Swedenborg, one never meets with such views of the divine Being, as would make the Father an object of dread, while the Son is presented in a more amiable light.^211

^In the older dispensations such views of God have prevailed as to render obedience to him impossible except through fear. We are taught that when the Father bestows a blessing upon us, he does it not for our sakes but for the sake of another divine Personality. What becomes in this case of God's love? Why should we love him in return? This second being, for whose sake the blessing comes to us we can love, but can entertain towards the Father no other feeling than that of aversion & dread. In the light of the New Age we learn that the Lord blesses us for our sakes, not for his own glory, not for the sake of a second Divine Person. "Herein is love."[212] (See this Diary, Jan. 7, 1862.)[213]

But the Father & the Son are one. Jesus is Jehovah made man. Such views are given us of God as lay the foundation for a higher trust in him, & a closer union with him. This was to characterize the new Jerusalem stage of the Church's progress. "Behold the tabernacle of God is with men, and he shall dwell with them."[214] And John saw the New Jerusalem not only as a city, (or a system of heavenly doctrine) but also prepared as a bride adorned for her husband, or in a state of union with God.[215] I think I find in Swedenborg's invaluable spiritual writings those higher views of God which are to constitute the basis of a closer conjunction of the church with the Lord and which render such a state practicable. I confess that to my own mind I find here the principal charm in his teachings. He has taught me more of God, and hence enabled me to love him more. By dispelling the false views of the divine character which I had imbibed from education and tradition, he has advanced me another stage in christian experience— has advanced me from the state of a <u>servant</u> to that of a <u>son</u>.[216]

5. Man is capapable of living on either of three planes of being—a life of sense, a life of intellect, and a life of love.^[217]

^When we are restored from our inverted {of} or fallen condition to the divine order of our being, then we shall be led by love—by heavenly affections. We shall use the Intellect as an eye to <u>see the way</u>. The Intellect will be servant, not the Lord of the Heart, and sense will be the slave of both.

The church may pass through successive dispensations, corresponding to these three degrees of the mind. If there is to be a higher & better age of the Church, called the New Jerusalem, it must be the reign of love. It will be the coming back of the charity of the Golden age.

This predominance of love & charity in the church, by recovering man from the inverted or fallen state of his powers, & restoring the soul to the divine order into which it was created, will elevate his intellect & lower faculties also. In Swedenborg I find the germ of such a state of the church. In no one do we see more fully exemplified the truth of Paul's words— "Now abideth faith, hope, charity, these three; but the greatest of these is charity." (1 Cor. 13:13.) His is emphatically the theology of love. At the time when he arose, faith was elevated to the first place in religion. Perhaps in that stage of religious progress, it was natural to exalt the intellect to the highest place. A man who is in the lowest stage of being and is sensual and material, will make the delights of sense the chief happiness of his life. In philosophy, he will make the senses the foundation & source of all knowledge, as in Locke & Condillac,[218] and before them, in Aristotle.^[219]

^The religion of such a one will be a Pharasaic formalism, a mere mechanism of outward rites.

When the soul of the individual, or of collective man, as existing in a society or church, is advanced to the second stage of progress,—to the predominance of the intellect or of faith, it is natural to make faith of the first importance in religion. The Church during the past centuries of its annals has not risen above the first & second degrees of mental life, except in the case of particular individuals. These sometimes appear like gleams of {heavenly} celestial sunshine in the obscured heavens. The life of faith, Swedenborg denominates the spiritual state; the life of love, the celestial state. Now in his theology, which is the theology of love, I see the dawn of a brighter day—the coming of a, celestial, state of the Church. In his teaching, (and I may say in his life) every thing is {the} to be consecrated to the good of the neighbor. This is the beginning of the heavenly life. He teaches that in heaven all live for the good of each & each for the good of all.^220

^The love of God is an infinite inclination and perpetual endeavor to to impart its own blessedness to beings made capable of receiving it. This is its essential property. When this love is received into the soul, which is a created receptacle of it, it does not lose its necessary property, but becomes in us charity or the love of the neighbor, which is a desire that our own good & truth should be another's. Such a charity is "the life of God in the soul of man."[221]

(See H & H. n. 399, 418, & 413.)[222] Who can imagine the effect such a life in the church would have upon earth?

Such a life of love elevates the intellect to the light of heaven, or to an interior perception of truth." (See this Diary of July 23. 1861.)[223]

6. He has given us from the Word of God a more rational system of salvation. He traces sin to its vital root in the soul, and finds that root to be self-will, or the love of self, and the love of the world for the sake of self. Any remedy that does not weaken & remove the source of depravity, must be inefficient. Now in many of the so called conversions of the present day it is to be feared that the deep seated selfishness of the natural heart is not removed, but is only concealed under other forms of manifestation. We are taught in the doctrines of Swedenborg, that there is a divine order in the process of a soul's salvation.[224] That order is this. Before one can come into the goods and truths of heaven, he must put away the evils & falsities of the soul, and which flow in from beneath. He must put away the falsities of faith in his understanding, by truths derived from the Word of God. He must also put away his evils as sins against God, and for no other reason, than because they are sins against God. If we cease from the outward practice of an evil, for any other reason, as that it is unprofitable or destroys our

reputation, or even because it makes us unhappy, we leave untouched the selfishness from which it proceeds as its vital root. The evil in this case is not effectually removed, but only concealed.

And "he that covereth his sins shall not prosper."[225] Such conversions "heal the hurt of the daughter of my people slightly."[226] If you analyze the state into which vast numbers are brought by the current popular teachings of the day in times of revival, you will find them to be of this character. Appeals are made to the selfishness of the heart, and the outward life is changed from self-love. But we are taught by Swedenborg, (& at the time he arose it was new in the church,) that an evil is to be shunned or put away, because it is a sin against God. As soon as one does this his regeneration commences, because then a death blow is given to his self-will or self-love, which is the essence of all sin. When he does this, he is then to exercise confidence in the Lord Jesus Christ, the only God of earth and heaven. Before coming into this attitude of hostility to evil, and of obedience to God, such a confidence is impossible, and if possible would be of no avail in our salvation. He says. "By faith in him, is meant confidence that he will save, and this confidence is enjoyed only by those who shun evils as sins; with others it does not exist." (A.R. 949.)[227] This is a very different thing from salvation by faith <u>alone</u>.

He teaches that our first duty and the first step in the process of our salvation, after coming to the knowledge of evil, is to combat it and put it away as a sin against God. Having done this the soul becomes receptive of good which flows in from God through heaven. It belongs to man's free will or free agency, to do this, and he must do it <u>as of himself</u>; but all the while acknowledging that it is of God, from whom all good proceeds. When a man puts away evil as sin, he comes spontaneously into the opposite good. This is the reason why the precepts of the Decalogue with two exceptions are given in a negative form. The reason lies in this principle or law of the human spirit, <u>that mind is essentially active</u>. When it ceases from an evil or disorderly activity, it being essentially active, it comes at once into the opposite condition of holy activity. When a man puts away or ceases from the evil of idleness he becomes diligent & industrious. When one ceases from covetousness, he becomes benevolent. When he ceases from the love of self and the world, he comes into the love of God and the neighbor. The Command, "Cease to do evil; learn to do well,"[228] is the divine order of salvation, and is based upon the laws of our spiritual being. That a man can cease from evil, is involved in the idea of free will. M. Cousin, defines a free act to be one that is performed with a consciousness that we had a power not to act.[229] Whether man has a <u>natural</u> ability to cease from evil & do good, is a question that will not require a moment's thought to decide, with one who feels that all good is from God, and that our very life is the constant gift of him, who alone has life in himself. Our regeneration, thus commenced, is {the} to be carried on by successive combats with evil, & with fallen spirits with which our evils connect us.*[230]

* By resistance to evil, we become grounded in the opposite good, according to law of spiritual action & reaction, So by an encounter with doubt, and with the false, we become rooted in the truth. Hence temptation is a necessary part of the regenerating process.[231]

The external man is to be brought into obedience to the internal man. In our natural state the external man rules, & the internal obeys. This is an inversion of the true order of our being.[232] That which was made to serve, is permitted to rule. It is such a <u>vanity</u> of [the] human condition, that Solomon describes. "I have seen servants upon horses, and princes walking as servants upon the earth." (Eccl. 10:7.) This inversion of the order of our being is what Dr Chalmers denominates "the great unhingement of human nature."[233] When man is restored to the true order of his being, which is accomplished by regeneration, he comes into tranquility & peace. "He is also as to his internal nature, consociated with the angels of heaven, into whose society he comes after the disolution of the body, when he is capable of entering on a full enjoyment of the life of heaven, which consists in loving the Lord, in loving the neighbor, in understanding truth, loving good, and perceiving the felicity thence derived." (*New Jerusalem & its Heavenly Doctrines*, 182.)[234] See also farther on the subject of Swedenborg's system of salvation, this Diary at. Sept 27. 1861 (p. 138) Also p. 231. et seq. Also p. 215–223.[235]

It may seem strange that if Swedenborg be the herald of a new dispensation that his doctrines have not made more rapid progress during the last century. But this is no objection to the fact of their being the beginning of a new age of the Church. It is impossible to make mere <u>external</u> proselytes to the system. His doctrines must be received interiorly by those who are in a recipient state. A system that is to be received interiorly makes its way slowly in the world, because few are receptive of it; but it moves forward surely, because it takes a deep hold upon the spiritual life of man.

It is also in accordance with that divine order unfolded in the government of the world, that whatever is to be of long continuance is a long time in reaching maturity. This is the law in the animal & vegetable kingdom, and is illustrated in the history of the world in the rise of the various kingdoms & governments.[236]

It might be thought also that the new dispensation ought to have exhibited a much higher spiritual life than the old Church has exhibited. This has been with me a great difficulty. But I now think that in reality, though not always apparent to the eye of a sensuous world, this has been and is the case. The real Christian life is a conjunction of truth & good, or of wisdom & love, or faith and charity. Swedenborg has shown that where good is not united to truth, as essence is to form, it is not real good but only apparent; and that where truth or faith is disjoined from good in the will, it is by virtue of this disjunction, no longer truth. Much of the goodness that appears in persons of the old dispensation is of this character.^[237]

^It is more a capacity of goodness, or a receptivity of good, than real good.

They do good from a false ground, or from wrong views of God, and divine things. Good done from a false ground is in reality a false goodness.

Swedenborg says, (A.R. 107.) "They who are in works alone, and in no truths, are like people who act and do not understand, and actions without understanding are inanimate."[238] Truth gives quality to goodness. To be good is to act according to truth. Goodness is truth in the life. Hence a life of worship and religion that proceeds from falsities of faith is not in reality good, however it may appear externally. (See on this subject A.R. 97.)[239] Where there are several illustrations of the principle that goodness must proceed from truth, or be one with truth, and truth must be the form of the good. Among them, this: "He who is in this falsity, that he thinks that he does good from himself, from his possessing the faculty of doing good; the good of such a man is not good, because he himself is in it; and not the Lord."*[240]

* See also Divine Providence n. 10–15.[241]

In comparing the Christian life as it is exhibited in the new and old dispensations, we are to decide from these principles. Looking at it from this point of view, we shall find that those who have heartily embraced the spiritual doctrines of Swedenborg, have exhibited as high a life as any in the old dispensation.[242] Yet it does not seem to me that the New Jerusalem, or new dispensation of the Church is to be a <u>sect</u>. It cannot be inclosed within the area of any sect or party. It will gradually descend to all denominations, or there will gradually arise within all of them those who have attained that spiritual position, called the New Jerusalem.*[243]

 * The first <u>stadium</u> in the development of the New Dispensation must of necessity be prominently intellectual. This is indicated by the New Jerusalem being represented to the vision of John as descending first as a city or doctrinal system, and then as a bride adorned for her husband.[244] This is the law of human development—sensual, intellectual, spiritual. Truth must first be received & then <u>done</u>. It then becomes goodness.

The new age is to come forth from the old.[245] Christianity in the apostolic age was not so much a new dispensation, a new spiritual creation, as it was a new development of the old dispensation. Christianity came forth from the envelope of Judaism. The whole Gospel was in the Old Testament, as a precious stone is sometimes found in a rough matrix. So the New Jerusalem or millennial dispensation is to be an unfolding of the present Church. It will come forth from the womb of the present Church; but like Rachel, in giving birth to Benjamin, will itself die. So it has been with every age. The giving birth to the new has alway[s] cost the life of the old.

I have written, & hope to publish, the above views of the doctrines and mission of that most remarkable man, for the reason given by another, for a different work— "It is one of our noble human instincts that we cannot feel within us the glory and the power of a real conviction without earnestly striving to make that conviction pass into other minds."[246]

Jan. 1 [1862]. The last year has been to me a good year—a year of solid advancement in the spiritual life. God has bestowed upon me many blessings of Providence & of grace. It has been a year of ill health, of great trials, and sharp conflicts with the powers of evil. But the Lord Jesus Christ who is to me the only God, has fought for me, and given me some victories over the powers of darkness. To day at noon, I rendered thanks to God for all his mercies to me & my family during the past year, and humbly implored

his merciful loving kindness for the year to come: especially did I make
supplication that my life might be eminently useful to his kingdom & the
souls of men. Hitherto the Ld has been my help, & I trust him for all time
to come.

Jan. 2. Have thought of the expression <u>voice of the Lord</u>, which often
occurs in the sacred Scriptures. It has appeared to me in a new an[d] interesting light. The voice in the spiritual world is the outward expression
of the state of the affections, for it is the law of our being that the tones of
our voice should indicate the state of our love. Each emotion and passion
has its proper tone of voice. It is so even among animals. We soon learn
instinctively to read and interpret the tones of the voice. All men do this
spontaneously, even children. But in this world, the law operates only
imperfectly. We gain only a glimpse of its action. In the spiritual world, it
will act with unvarying uniformity and certainty, so that a man's whole
inward character will be revealed in every sentence which he utters. The
state of the interior life will not only appear in the changes in the expression of the countenance, which is another law of our being, but in the tones
of the voice. So there will be nothing hid that shall not be revealed. The
voice is the index of the affections. When it is said in Holy Scripture, that
the voice of the Lord was heard, it signifies an interior manifestation and
perception of the love of the Lord. It is influent divine truth concerning
the character of God as a Being of eternal goodness. His boundless love
appears in a clear and heavenly light at such times, diffusing through the
soul calmness & peace. Fear is banished, and the soul reposes with confidence on the bosom of the infinite Love. Such voices it has been granted
me to hear, or to experience what is symbolized by them. So Jesus when
entering upon his last temptation & combat with the forces of hell, heard
the voice of the Father. (Jno. 12:28–30.)[247] He also says that his sheep hear
his voice, and know his voice, and discern that voice from the voice of
strangers. (Jno. 10:3, 4, 16, 27.)[248] This voice is not a vibration in the atmosphere affecting the tympanum; but it is a perception of truth concerning
the divine affections or love. It is said also, "That the hour is coming when
the dead shall hear the voice of the Son of Man, and they that hear shall
live.["] (Jno. 5:25.) It is such a voice that raises the spiritually dead. It is
only those who have become spiritual that will be likely to comprehend

what I am saying. By the voice of the Lord, I do not mean anything external, but <u>influent divine truth, and manifest perception of what God is</u>. God delights in this way to converse with those who have an ear to hear, or are receptive of such illuminative communications from heaven. "Sing unto God, ye kingdoms of the earth, lo, he doth send out his voice, and that a mighty voice." (Ps. 68:32, 33.)[249] Such illuminative communications from God, concerning himself & heavenly things, are attended by an elevation of the soul to greater spiritual altitudes. The Revelator in Patmos, heard a voice as of a trumpet talking with him, which said; Come up hither. And immediately <u>he was in the spirit</u>, and saw the wonders of heaven. (Rev. 4:1,2.) Something similar to this every spiritual mind experiences. There is a voice from God out of heaven, or the influent truth from him, illumines the interior of the soul, and then it rises to a holier altitude, and becomes perceptive of heavenly realities. Things that before were involved in impenetrable midnight, are now seen in celestial light. If the church was less selfish and sensuous, such experiences would not be uncomon. Now the light shines in the darkness, but the darkness comprehends it not.[250] In the new age which is now having its birth, we shall see with unveiled vision the living realities of the all-surrounding spiritual realm. What we now deem an extraordinary vouchsafement to prophets & apostles, will be a common experience.

Jan. 6. Today while reading in the Apocalypse had an affecting view of the connection of the Holy Scriptures with the divine Mind. The divine truth or light which they contain in its progression from the Divine Mind to ours, seemed to be changed, so that it reaches us veiled in human forms of expression. Yet by tracing back the rays of this divine effluence we come to the uncreated Wisdom of God; so that by every passage of the Holy Word, we are placed in a vital connection with the Divine Mind, in whom are hid all the treasures of wisdom and knowledge. But in coming to us, the living Word comes, "after the manner of men."[251] It is the Divine in the human, the spirit in the letter. It is heavenly wisdom in the language of men. It is the divine idea descending into time and space, and by rising above those material limitations, to the mount of transfiguration, we see the Son of Man, or the divinely-human Word, in his glory. It is good to be there, to rise above the mists of time and place and see the King in his glory and beauty. The Word of God to me is God. Every sentence opens up into the uncreated fulness of the Divinity. Hence Paul declares, "the Word of God is living & powerful."[252] The Holy Scriptures in their interior senses and in their highest import proceed from God, and treat of God, and are an ever present means of connection & communication with the Lord. They contain a sense adapted to the sensuous or fleshly mind—the mere litteral sense;—and a spiritual sense, adapted to the spiritual mind, and to angels; and a divine sense known fully to God alone, for in its inmost essence the Word is God, and God only knows the mind of God. May the Word of God dwell in me richly in all wisdom and spiritual knowledge. I cannot fully reproduce in words the views I sometimes have been permitted of the Lord to have of the divinity of the Sacred Word.

Jan. 7. The words of the Psalmist (Ps. 5:7.) have been of late deeply impressed upon my mind, "In thy fear will I worship toward thy holy temple." It was the custom of the devout Jews, wherever they were, to direct their prayers towards the temple. In whatever land they were, they faced that way in their public and private devotions. There was profound spiritual significance in this, though perhaps they were not aware of it. The temple spiritually signifies the church, especially the church considered as the depositary of the divine truth. Hence Paul says to the church of Corinth, "Ye are the temple of the living God." (2 Cor. 6:16. See also Eph. 2:21.22.) But in its highest import the temple signifies the divine Humanity,*[253]

*When the Divine assumes the Human, the result must be to make the Human Divine. When the Divinity was <u>humanized</u>, the humanity was <u>deified</u>.

or the human nature as the habitation of all the fulness of the Deity.[254] Christ said to the Jews, "Destroy this temple, and in three days I will raise it up. This he spoke of the temple of his body." (Jno. 2:19.21.) And St Paul asserts that in him dwelleth all the fulness of the Godhead bodily. (Col. 2:19.)[255] In our prayers and in all our worship, we should look to and address the Divine Humanity, for that is the recipient of the Deity in his undivided wholeness, and is the medium of communicating his gifts & his nature to us. The body is the habitation of the soul, (2 Cor. 5:1.)[256] and the means of communicating with the invisible spirit. We speak to a mans body, and not directly to his mind. So the Humanity of Christ is as the body, and the Deity as the soul. In his fear, that is in love to him, we should worship towards this holy temple, for this is the divinely appointed order of approaching Jehovah. The Humanity is the Mediator, or intercessor, that is, it is that which comes between us & the invisible Divinity, the Divine Esse,[257] and is the medium through which the Deity conveys to us his gifts of grace & life. They proceed from the Father into the Son, or Divine Humanity, and emanate from him to us. Now the Son does not intercede for us, by constantly praying the reluctant Father to have mercy upon us, as we sometimes hear it asserted, but simply by being the medium of communication with him. He says, "The time cometh, when I shall no more speak unto you in proverbs, (or parables) but I shall show you plainly of the Father["][258]— (Or in the dispensation of the Holy Ghost, the New Jerusalem or millennial state, he will admit the soul to the spiritual or interior sense of the Holy Scriptures, and to a higher knowledge of God.) "At that day ye shall ask in my name,"[259] (or address the invisible divine Being through the glorified or deified Humanity, just as we speak to a man's soul through his body,)— ["]And I say not unto you, that I will pray the Father for you; for the Father himself loveth you." (Jno. 16:25.26.)[260] And the Father and Son are one, as the soul and body are one in Man, for the Humanity, consisting of soul and body, became the habitation of the whole of His Divinity. When I look toward this holy temple, I should just as much expect to be put into a living and saving connection with the only living and true God, as when I address my words to one's body, I expect to communicate with his soul, for the body is only the external manifestation of the soul.

> "Whate'er the Almighty can
>> To pardoned sinners give,
> The fulness of our God made man
>> We here with Christ receive."[261]

Jan 8. My thoughts are almost perpetually ascending to the Lord. I live in his presence and walk before him. He has given me a great love of spiritual things. These to me are the <u>real</u> things. He has given me an ardent love of <u>truth</u> for its own sake. It seems to me to be something purely divine. It emanates from God, and is something of God. It is a ray from the uncreated Sun. Never did truth seem to me so holy, so <u>divine</u>.

March 30. Sabbath. It is now two months since I have preached, otherwise than in private conversation. I have passed through a painful sickness, and am yet far from being fully restored. I have had some rich experiences of divine things, and some heavenly views. Today my soul has been drawn out in prayer. Every breath has been prayer. God has given me an earnest spirit of supplication for some days past for restoration to health, that I may be made the messenger of good to souls. My faith has grasped Christ as the Life—the eternal Life. My soul lives wholly from him, and my body from my soul. Hence in saving the soul he saves the body. This he did during his fleshly manifestation. And the principles of his government and providence are always the same—immutable as himself. That the body should be saved from an abnormal, disorderly condition by faith, violates no law of nature. For it is the eternal order of God that faith saves the soul, and the body's life is derived wholly from the vital spirit it incloses. The omnipotence of God acts according to the eternal order he has established. This order is expressed by Christ when he said many times to those he healed in soul & thus in body— "Thy faith hath saved thee."[262] In absolute self-despair, I have looked to him who is the only Life. With stubbornness of faith—a faith he has imparted, hence the faith of God—I have said with humble boldness, "I know thou dost save." Like Peter sinking I have siezed hold of him, & how can I die while Jesus lives. Through faith I have conjunction with the one & only Life. I shall yet praise him who is the health of my countenance & my God. I hear his voice, a voice that sent life to thrill through the decaying body of Lazarus, "Go in peace, thy faith hath saved thee."[263] I have no hope from physicians & drugs. They are as powerless as the staff of Elijah in the hands of Gehazi to raise the widows son.[264] May Christ eternally unite me to himself by granting me this great favor.

April 6. This evening while thinking of the blessedness of internal converse with Christ, and the privilege of the redeemed soul to speak familiarly with him, I asked of him to speak some word of comfort to my soul. This word then came with power to my heart, "Be of good courage. Wait thou upon the Lord, and he shall strengthen thine heart. Wait I say upon the Lord."[265] This came as from the lips of God, with all the freshness of a new revelation. He who is himself the living Word spake to my inmost soul. He always speaks in the language of the written word, or at least in perfect harmony with it, when he utters his voice in the soul. Christ and the Holy Scriptures in their inmost essence are the same. They are called the same. On this point thus speaks Mr Adolphe Monod: "We find the same name given to Jesus Christ, and to the Holy Scriptures. Both the one and the other are called <u>the Word of God</u>. The one of these Words, Jesus Christ, is the living Word of God, the personal manifestation of his invisible perfections in the bosom of humanity: the other, the Holy Scriptures, is the written Word of God, the verbal manifestation of these same invisible perfections given by language."[266] The one is the Word, the uncreated Wisdom, the eternal Truth, made flesh; the other is the same Word made writing. They are both <u>living</u>. St Paul says, "The Word of God is living and powerful." (Heb. 6:)[267] Whoever would have access to Christ, the one only God, and would find union with him, must do it through the Word of God, which in its inmost essence is divine. God is manifested in the flesh and in the Word. The same infinite Mind, is the inmost soul or spirit of both manifestations. God was manifest in the flesh. And whoever saw the humanity of Christ saw God. Said Christ, "He that seeth me, seeth him that sent me." (Jno. 12:45.) God was <u>in</u> Christ. So we may find God within the letter of Holy Scripture. Happy was that soul which could discern the invisible Divinity beneath the lowly servant form of the son of Man; flesh and blood did not reveal it to that heart.[268] Equally blessed is that soul, which beneath the sensuous envelope of the letter, perceives the uncreated Word. God came nigh to us by being made flesh; he comes equally near in the Holy Scriptures, the Manifested Word.

Claremont. June 22. 1862.[269] Have been in Claremont since April 19. My health has somewhat improved, though I am not as yet able to preach or even to attend church but once on the Sabbath.

In my religious views I am an Eclectic. Many years ago all prejudice was banished from my mind, and I have sought for truth with persevering earnestness, and have found it everywhere. Victor Cousin of France has shown that philosophy in all lands, and in all ages has appeared under one of the four following forms—Sensualism, Idealism, Mysticism, and Scepticism. Through this cycle it has ever been running. All the philosophical systems of the world belong to one or the other of those forms. The first three forms are based in the principles of human nature. Where the sensuous element, which belongs to our nature is in predominance, philosophy will be sensational, as in Locke and Condillac. Where the intellectual is unharmoniously prominent, as in Plato, Berkley & others, the philosophical system will be Idealism.[270] Where the feelings and intuitions are the ruling element in the mental character, philosophy will be Mysticism. And where neither alone can satisfy the wants of the human soul, Scepticism arises. Now all these systems are true and become false only when they become exclusive. Something similar may be said of religion. It always exists under a few fundamental forms. It is sensuous, as in the Pharasaic formalism of the age of Christ and every age—a bondage to the letter. This is the Jewish element, which has ever been in the Church of Christ.[271] The fleshly, somatic, ritualistic element, mere naturalism. When the intellectual element is pushed to an undue prominence, and is made {the} of primary importance we have another fundamental form of the Church in its historical development. Here we must, for an example, place the Aristotelian Scolasticism of the mediaeval period.[272] This is often seen in individuals and in sects both before, and after, the Reformation. There are others who lay excessive stress upon the emotional and intuitional in religion, upon frames and ecstacies. This form is mysticism. It has produced some of the most finished characters in the history of human redemption.^[273]

^Its maxim is, Pectum est, quod theologum facit.[274]

In the 17th Cen. it had its Fenelon & Madam Guyon, in the 14th, its Kempis & Tauler. Charles Wesley was a mystic. Sometimes in the Christian development of the Church and individuals, the moral or ethical element rises to prominence and we have the other fundamental form of Christian life. These four aspects are the only ones under which Christianity can be viewed. It is either ritualism, or intellectualism, or mysticism, or moral duty & life. These like the four sides of a paralellogram include it. They are represented in the primitive Church, the mustard-seed beginning of the new creation, by Peter, and Paul, by John and James.[275] In fact, the twelve Apostles are arranged by threes under these four divisions. All sects contain truth & good. It is the part of the wise good man of our age to gather up these disjecta membra,[276] these scattered limbs of the body of Christ, into a harmonious unity. All sects are needful; they become sects only by becoming the organized embodiment of some truth or form of Good, which belongs to the Church. It is only when these peculiarities are pushed into undue prominence, and become exclusive that they are heretical. The perfect Christian character, and the glorious Church of the New Jerusalem, when it comes down from God out of heaven, will combine the four fundamental forms of Christian life, into a harmonious whole. There will no longer be any one element pushed to a one sided development, but all will be symetrical.[277] The Christian Eclectic is {the} to reap a rich harvest from all the experiences & teachings of the past. The sects are one sided; the New Jerusalem or Millennial Church will be a perfect harmony. Newton showed that light—the light of the sun—is compound. By means of his prism he separated it into seven prismatic colors. These may still be reduced to some three {four} fundamental colors viz. red, yellow, & blue. These must be combined to form the pure light of the world. The sects each represent a prismatic ray in the light of the Sun of righteousness. We are not to throw them all away, but build the truth & good they contain into a perfect structure. It is said that the human body is a combination of all beautiful forms. So let us build up a Church, a body of Christ, that shall be composed of all the good that has ever appeared in the history of redemption. The kingdom of God is like a net, that gathers of every kind, The good are to be gathered into vessels; the bad thrown away. (Mat. 13:47, 48.) This is the characteristic of the New age that is struggling into birth. It has already dawned.

July 25. Oftentimes some sentence of Scripture, or verse of sacred poetry, will be in my mind for days in succession. A few days ago these lines were in my mind incessantly,
      "The eternal peace that closes
      Round the soul that dwells in God."[278]
      Yesterday the following lines were the expression of my faith,
      "I shall o'ercome through Christ alone,
      And stand entire at last."[279]

July 26. My soul has of late been drawn and in prayer to God for faith. I have realized its power in the life of the soul & even of the body. I have often cried with the disciples, "Lord, increase our faith."[280] May Jesus speak to my inmost soul—and may the word be with power— "Have the faith of God."[281] When I have the faith of God, or a faith divinely imparted is mine, I shall have the life of God; and can say with Paul, "I live by the faith of the Son of God."[282] O for a faith that makes impossibility a practicable thing. A faith like that of God, and a faith emanating from God, quickens the dead, and calls those things that are not as though they were. Man lives by faith, as well in body, as the soul. But the life of faith is love. O for a loving faith, and a believing love.

Aug. 10. Felt the importance of rejoicing always in the Lord. Why go I mourning all the day because of the oppression of the enemy? Had in the evening some joy in the Holy Ghost.

Aug. 11. This has been a remarkable day in my experience—a new epoch in my spiritual history. My faith was put to the trial, and through Christ gloriously triumphed. In the evening I enjoyed an extraordinary season in prayer. Out of the deeps I cried unto the Lord & he heard me. Out of the belly of hell, I called upon him, and have been cast upon the shore. While sinking like Peter, I seized hold of Christ, and walked upon the abyss as if [it] had been marble. I touched him who is the Life, and life thrilled through my whole being. More than twenty years ago after a long season of desolation & self-imposed condemnation, Christ spake me whole, soul and body. There is a faith to which the divine power always responds, "Go in peace; thy faith hath saved thee."[283] With holy violence I laid hold upon him who has become my salvation. I live because Christ lives. Here is the connection of cause & effect. I no longer live but Christ liveth in me. I am dead, and my life is hid with Christ in God.[284] I feel myself saved— perfectly well, soul, spirit, and body. The 11th day of August is laid up in everlasting remembrance. From this time forth I live a life of faith. There is a faith that puts the soul in vital connection with the one only Life. My salvation is no longer a future expectation, but a present reality. I am saved on this eleventh day of August. All is w[e]ll. Christ lives, and I live. To him I commit the <u>keeping</u> of my soul in w[e]ll doing as unto a faithful Creator. He is bringing me up to a higher plane of divine life. I now bid an eternal farewell to the experience described in the seventh chapter of the Epistle to the Romans.[285] The day of freedom dawns at length.

Aug. 12. The Lord manifested himself to me in this passage: "Blessed be God who teacheth my hands to war and my fingers to fight." (Ps. 144:1.) I derived much strength from those words in my internal combat with the forces of hell. They nerved my soul to the battle.

I also felt as I never did before, that while I may have great disturbance in my external mind, (I know not what else to call it.) I may have profound peace within. There is an external and an inmost department of the soul. This we may be certain of in this way. We are conscious that we have certain thoughts in our minds, and there is a department of soul lying farther inward that enables me to see my thoughts, as distinctly as the eye sees material things. So of my emotions, or feelings. In my external mind there may be great sadness, grief, anxiety, and other disturbing elements, yet there is an inmost center of the soul calm as the deep of eternity. Into this evil does not enter. It is appropriated as the residence of God in man. Evil lies farther outward in our nature. If it should once become seated in the inmost deep, the holy of holies of the soul, our salvation would be an impossibility. But into this divine habitation evil is not permitted to enter. If God does not consciously dwell there, it is closed—it is a solitude. Evil enters us from without, by an external way; God from within by an internal way. There are times in my experience, when in my external spiritual nature there is great commotion; but when I flee into the inmost apartment of the temple of the soul there is unutterable bliss & everlasting rest. There is the calmness of the passionless nature of God. There is a region of spirit beyond the reach of storms. Happy the man who has learned to enter into himself, and there commune with God. There the human spirit may mingle with the infinite Spirit, and live eternal life. Oftentimes by retiring inward from the external disturbing elements, the joy & peace that we find within, will diffuse itself over the surface. There is always quiet in the deep. There is the calmness of God. It is within that we must find him.

Aug. 13. The Lord promised to <u>manifest</u> himself to his disciples. This he does in various ways. The particular form of divine manifestation that I enjoyed today was this: I cried in my inmost soul, "Avenge me of my adversaries,"[286] my spiritual foes who have aimed to torment me, if they could not ruin me. The Lord manifested himself in this passage of his Gospel with redeeming power. "Will not The Lord {will} avenge his own elect that cry unto him day and night? I tell you he will avenge them speedily."[287] I enjoyed a great victory over the powers of darkness. The enemy was overthrown, & put to the route. How many times I have had occasion to say in my spiritual combats, "If it had not been the Lord who was on our side, then they had swallowed us up quick, when their wrath was kindled against us. Then the waters had overwhelmed us, the stream had gone over our soul; then the proud waters had gone over our soul. Blessed be the Lord who has not given us as a prey to their teeth." (Ps. 124:1–6.)[288] What a beauty and propriety there are in the Psalms when we perceive that the foes of David were not men, not flesh and blood; but they were interior spiritual enemies, the same that assail us. Here the most vindictive language is the most expressive of our feelings when we array ourselves against them. Paul refers to this state of mind in 2 Cor. 7:11. Speaking of Godly sorrow he says, "What carefulness it wrought in you, yea what clearing of yourselves, yea what indignation, yea what vehement desire, yea what zeal, yea what revenge!"[289] That is the kind of vengeance that breathes in the Psalms.

It is God that fighteth for me. Then I may say with David, ["]The Ld is my light and my salvation; whom shall I fear? The Ld is the strength of my life: of whom shall I be afraid? When the wicked, even mine enemies and my foes, came upon me to eat up my flesh, they stumbled and fell. Though an host should encamp against me, my heart shall not fear: though war should arise against me, in this will I be confident." (Ps. 27:1–3.) In our battles with our spiritual foes, the victory belongs to the Lord alone.

Aug. 17. This has been to me a joyful Sabbath—a delight of the Lord and honorable. The words of the Lord in Jno. 16:22–24, were blessed to my comfort. "Ye therfore now have sorrow: but I will see you again, and your heart shall rejoice, and your joy no man taketh from you. And in that day ye shall ask me nothing. Verily, verily, I say unto you, Whatsoever ye shall ask the Father in my name, he will give it you. Hitherto ye have asked nothing in my name: Ask, and ye shall receive, that your joy may be full." It seemed to me that my soul had been in traivel [travail] for a long time, but now the hour of my deliverance has come. I confidently asked the Father, in the name of Christ, or made my supplication to him by the name of Christ, that my joy might be full. My soul was filled with inward delight, and walked upon the high places. Such joy diffuses life through my whole being.

In the victories I have gained over the powers of hell, All is due to Christ. I wish to record my testimony that his right hand and holy arm hath gotten him the victory. It may seem as if we fought alone, but it [is] Christ who subdueth our foes under our feet. I can adopt the language of the devout Payson: "I have done nothing, I have not fought, but Christ has fought for me. I have not run; but Christ has carried me. I have not worked; but Christ has wrought in me. Christ has done all."[290]

I have felt that the day of freedom has dawned. I shall leave the plain, with its fogs & chills, for the mountain. I shall enter into rest. I long to say with Christopher Hopper, "I have not a doubt, no, not the shadow of a doubt; and as for the enemy, I know not what has become of him. I have neither seen him nor heard from him for some time. I think he has quitted the field."[291]

It is possible to so vanquish the foe that he shall quit the field, and a permanent peace shall be won. The last struggle shall be over, and eternal peace shall be attained. Says Mr Sears in his excellent little book on *Regeneration*, "If any one should object, that it is not given to man here on the earth to pass into those high spiritual frames, or pitch his tent on this mountain of golden peace, we simply take issue upon the fact; for we know those and {we} read of those who have the world under their feet, with whom the struggle is past and the victory won; and God's angels are with them as 'a camp of fire around.'" (*Regeneration* p. 125.)[292]

Aug. 18. My soul was drawn out this morning to pray for faith and faith's increase. In answer to my prayer, my faith has been tried, and increased. It has been a day of deep peace, and at times of unutterable rest. I have calmly, steadfastly, and self-desperately believed. Yesterday I had more of joy; today I have had peace. The difference seems to be this. Joy is more external, more emotional; peace is an interior blessedness—a deep and unutterable contentment and satisfaction in God. It is the inmost blessedness of the soul. It seems to me more divine than joy. It diffuses an unspeakable sweetness through the spirit. I have often felt today,

"There's quiet in the deep."[293]

I have at times felt conscious of a strange calmness, that I shall recognize in heaven. I found it difficult to make supplication in my prayers, for my faith recognized the possession of the good I asked. And after asking my faith spontaneously would say, "I have it." This state of peace & joy in the Lord is to be permanent. "Peace I leave with you—Your joy no man taketh from you," is the word of the Lord.[294] The gifts and graces of God are without repentance. I have passed through several successive stages of spiritual development in my religious history corresponding to the several dispensations of the Church. Now through Christ I enter upon the millennial or New Jerusalem period. The night is far spent; the day is at hand. I have often felt as is expressed by Jean Paul. "But as yet struggles the twelfth hour of the Night. Birds of darkness are on the wing; specters {appear} uproar; the dead walk; the living dream. Thou, Eternal Providence, wilt make the day dawn!"[295]

The morning light is already breaking.

Sept. 13. Returned from Campmeeting at Lebanon N.H. It was to me a profitable meeting. Though not able to preach, the Lord enabled me to communicate spiritual good and truth. I have been in the habit of praying the Lord to bring me in contact with souls that he can benefit through me. He has often answered my prayers. Though to communicate spiritual instruction to a few persons, or to a single individual, in conversation, is not a way of doing good that attracts much notice, yet the influence is permanent & ever widening and opening in extent.

Sept 14. My faith has been much increased of late by reading Müller's *Life of Trust*.[296] The remarkable answers to prayer recorded in the experience of that devoted man establish one thing, viz, that what is utterly impossible according to the ordinary laws of causation, is possible & practicable through the prayer of faith. Faith in God is a higher cause. God governs the moral universe by moral laws; and as man's moral nature is of more importance than physical nature, so moral laws—and such is faith—have the precedence. In one respect his experience is similar to mine. Every morning he reads and meditates upon the word of God, in order to gain nourishment to his soul for the day. He deems it important also to get into a happy frame of spirit in order to be prepared for doing good to others. I fully concur in that. Emotional bliss is not to be sought or asked as an end but as a means of strengthening us & fitting us for communicating good to others.

Faith is a creative power. It was so in God. It is so in us. "Through faith we understand that the worlds were framed by the word of God, so that things which are seen were not made of things which do appear." (Heb. 11:3.) That is, as some interpret it, (among them Prof. Upham,) God made the world by faith.[297] It is according to the order of God that faith calls into being what would have to us no existence without it. So that things which are seen are not made from things which do appear. There is a power in a faith divinely imparted & an importance to it which is but little understood in the Church. Had we the simple faith of apostolic times, we should see equal or greater results.

Sept. 16. Have thought today on the subject of silent, secret influence. It has afforded me much comfort. Every man's soul is a part of the spiritual world, and every man's interior state is a part of the moral universe. If I am in a state of wisdom and love, derived from the Lord, the tendency is to make every other being better & happier, though I may have no verbal communication with any one, and though my name may be wholly unknown. If I am internally evil, the influence is to swell the general current of evil, and make the moral universe worse. Hence the most useful thing one can do for the world is to be holy himself. Our spiritual life is so interwoven with all other being, that our state, of necessity, affects the whole. This law of silent, spiritual influence is as powerful in its operation & as universal as gravitation in the material universe. Hence some persons humbly pious, who daily walk with God, and who make no noise in the world, are far more useful than some who are full of noise & stir. He who is inwardly holy & can do nothing is of more use than he who is not holy within, and who performs never so {much} many pious actions. We are most mysteriously and wonderfully connected by invisible bonds with all other human beings in this world & the next. How far reaching may be the influence of a pious thought, a sacred purpose, a holy emotion no finite mind can guess. It extends through the whole realm of created spirit, and all who are not lost to all that is true & good are made better by it. No good man can live in vain or for himself alone. We should use every opportunity of communicating good to others, & if we do not see so great visible results as we in our unbelief desire, we should remember that the way to be more useful is to be more holy. <u>To be interiorly holy & spiritual and not at the same time useful to the moral universe is an impossibility</u>.

Sept. 20. No books satisfy me now as they used to do, not even the external letter of Scripture. The interior Word, by which I understand the Infinite Understanding, the Divine Mind itself, alone satisfies me. The living Truth is alone able to meet my wants, and satisfy my thirst. Mere dead ideas are like chaff to my soul. It is only by putting my soul into communication with the interior Word, the infinite Intellect, that my spirit can be nourished. Upon that Word I live; by it I am fed. All other books are shadows; this is substance. The Scriptures in their internal spirit are the very heart & mind of God. He who has found this has found infinite treasure. My soul lives upon this just as really as an infant lives from the breast of its mother. Here is more than there is in all the libraries of ancient and modern times. All that there was in the famous libraries of Alexandria and Pergamos that was good was a ray from the Interior Word.[298] Here is the treasure-house of all wisdom. God open it to me more and more, or rather open my soul to receive more of it.

When a dark room is opened to a light that shines without upon it, the light flows in. So when the soul is opened to admit the uncreated Light, it fills our spirits.

We may get some conception of what is meant by the interior Word in this way. The Bible is the Word of God. The words which a person utters are the outward expression of interior thought. Trace the word, either spoken or written, inward, and you find a thought. This thought is in the mind, and is the mind in a certain state—a thinking state. But the thought is the manifestation of a more interior affection. Trace the thought farther inward & you come to its secret spring in the love. Let us take the Words of God, which we find in the Holy Scriptures brought down into the language of men, and into the range of our senses. But they are the words that God continually speaks. Within the envelope of the outward letter is the divine idea—the thought of God. This thought is in the mind of the Lord, and is the Divine Mind thinking. But this thought is only the expression of the divine affection. The thought finds the root of its life in the love of God. Thus we come to the center, as it were of the Divine Mind. Now all beyond the external letter is the interior or living Word. It is the Book of life or the Living Book. (Rev. 20:12.)[299] This we read not with the bodily eye, but with the eye of the understanding. The Bible is not, like an ancient classic, a dead volume, but is living (quick) and powerful. The words of Christ are spirit and life. It is by receiving these living words of God that we can spiritually live. Through the Word of God he imparts to us his inmost life which is love.

The external word enters us through the senses. This is the envelope of the divine, living idea. But this idea is the continent of the divine affection. Thus as Gregory said, the Scriptures are the heart and mind of God.[300] And through his word he conveys to us his secret life which is love. The states of the divine Mind, as joy & peace, are imparted to us, when we put ourselves in communication with him in some passage of the Word of God which contains those states. When we need the peace of God or joy in the Holy Ghost, let us pray that he will,

"Send some message from his Word,
Which shall joy and peace afford."[301]

When we wish to convey our affections & feelings to the mind of another we do it by means of words spoken or written. This is one of the uses of language.

The state of one mind is made that of another mind through words. So the words of Christ, being spirit and life, convey to those, who receive them interiorly, the affections, emotions, and desires of Christ, and we are made to share the blessedness of the Deity himself. When we thus receive the words of Christ—and his word is with power—he can say to us, "Now ye are clean through the word which I have spoken unto you. (Jno. 15:3.)

The external Scriptures are a body; the living spirit that animates it is Christ as the Holy Ghost. There is an outward expression of truth and an inward spirit or life. The Holy Spirit is the spirit of truth. (Jno. 15:26.)[302] The Holy Spirit and the interior Word are one, especially when that Word is imparted to my soul. God gives the Holy Spirit through the Word. This is not the common notion. The external Word is the continent of the living spirit. It is the channel through which the spirit is conveyed to me.[303] The truths which Christ proclaims are called living water. (Jno. 4:10.)[304] The life is in the interior spirit of his words, and not in the letter. The letter is the channel through which it flows, the vessel containing it. My thirsty soul says with the Samaritan woman, "Lord, evermore give me this living water."[305] May God so open my mind's interior eye that I can read the Book of Life or the Living Book. Than [Then] I have in one volume more than all the libraries of the world.

If any one desires an increase of faith, he can obtain it only out of the Word of God. "Faith cometh by hearing, and hearing by the Word of God." (Rom. 10:17.) Faith and truth are one and the same in essence. Hence in the Hebrew language there is but one word to express both truth and faith (the word <u>Amen</u> & <u>Amuna</u>.)[306] Faith in combination with love, or made one with love, is alone saving. They are never in reality separated. Where there is no genuine love there is no real faith; and where there is no real faith there is no genuine love, but only a false love, or love from a false ground. The Word of the Lord is that alone which can originate & nourish faith in us. A real & saving faith can have no other origin or support.

Sept. 28. It is a principle of great importance that there is such a thing as <u>apparent</u> truth and <u>real</u> truth. This principle belongs to that <u>hidden wisdom</u> which Paul spake among the perfect. There is the <u>phenomenal</u>—or things as they appear to the senses of the natural man—and the real, or things as they appear to the spiritual mind and to enlightened reason.[307] Now it makes a vast difference in the appearance of anything when we look at it from the standing ground of the natural man, or the plane of the senses, from what it does when we behold it from the higher plane of our spiritual nature. There are three degrees of soul or three planes of mental life, the natural or sensual, the intellectual or spiritual, the intuitional or celestial. The Word of God or anything else will mean differently to us according as we occupy one or the other of those positions when we contemplate it.

Things are spoken of <u>generally</u> in the Scriptures as they appear to the natural man or the sensuous mind. The divine truth was brought down to the platform of the carnal mind. God condescended to men of low estate. The Word of God was made flesh (Jno. 1:14.), or the divine thought was brought down to the range of the natural man. The celestial descended to the sensual in order to raise the sensual to the heavenly. It is important that we bear in mind that the letter of Scripture is the truth as it is apprehended by the natural man; the spiritual sense is included in it and is the truth as it is cognizable by the spiritual man or the divinely enlightened reason.

This is not peculiar to the Holy Scriptures. So it is with everything contemplated by man. If we see anything with the eye of sense it is different from the same object contemplated with the interior eye. To the sensuous mind it appears (and so it is said even in the word of God) that the sun rises and sets, and revolves around the earth. But it does not only in appearance. How long it took, & how much persecution was suffered, before even scientific men could be raised from the sensuous appearance to the fact in this case—from the the phenomenal to the real.[308] It appears to us, when we look at it from a sensuous standpoint, as if the body had life and feeling, but a moment's reflection will convince us that sensation is a mental state—that all feeling, all sense, all life is in the soul. If we carry this up to a celestial or intuitional position we shall see that the soul has no life in itself, but lives from the one only Life—from Him who is the true God and eternal life. To the eye of sense and the carnal man, death appears as the extinction of life. If we had only our sensuous & animal mind, we could have no possible evidence of or belief in the existence of ourselves or others after death. But to the divinely enlightened reason, death is only the revival of life. It is the transition to a higher form of life. With those who have risen above the rational to the celestial or intuitional, death is a conscious & vital union of our personality with the living God. Paul said, "I no longer live, but Christ liveth in me." "Ye are dead and your life is hid with Christ in God."[309] To the carnal, fleshly mind death is the end of life. To the heavenly mind, it is the highest possible life—life in God.

God is spoken of in the Scriptures as he is apprehended by the natural or carnal mind. But in this sensuous representation, as in an envelope, lies concealed the real & spiritual truth. When we are guilty of known sin, and our wickedness makes us miserable & unhappy, it appears as if God was <u>angry</u>, just as it seemed to the demons at Gadara that Christ had come to torment them, though he came to torment no one.[310] It is evil, every one's own wickedness, and not God, that slays the wicked. (Ps. 34:21.)[311] When it is said that the Lord is angry, that he is a jealous God, that he repents, the expression belongs to the same class as where it is said that the sun rises and sets, and that the earth is a level plain bounded by the ocean—the apparent view taken of it in the Word of God. But let it be well observed that a carnal and wicked man cannot rise above that appearance of God. Such are the laws of our being, that we can never while wicked & impenitent view God otherwise than as angry with us. When we do what we know to be wrong, we can have no confidence in God, & must be jealous of him. This causes him to seem to us as though he were a jealous God. It is one of the deep laws of our spiritual being, that God manifests himself to us, or appears to us, just what we are ourselves. This is said in Ps. 18:25, 26.[312] The real truth is that God is not angry at all or with any one. The Scriptures declare this. "God is love.["] (1 Jno. 4:16.) He says of himself, "Fury is not in me." (Isa. 27:4.) "Say unto them, As I live, saith the Lord God, I have no pleasure in the death of the wicked." (Ezek. 33:11.) But as a wicked man can never in his conceptions of God rise above the sensuous appearance, it has all the use in restraining him from deeper depravity that it would have if the Lord, whose name is Love, were actually angry with him. It will do no harm to proclaim the real truth, for no one will or can come into an inward perception of the truth, until he {is} attains to purity and spiritual mindedness, which is life and peace. But blessed is the man, whom grace has elevated, in his conceptions of divine & heavenly things, above the phenomenal to the real. In the words of our Savior, we are commanded to seek a spiritual standing ground, where we may see truth in its reality. "Judge not according to the appearance (κατ' ὄψιν, the outward appearance only, so Bloomfield),[313] but judge righteous judgment." (Jno. 7:24.)

The principle that there is apparent and real truth is one of vast importance and amazing sweep. It is fundamental to the attainment of a true spiritual knowledge. It is one of the letters of the spiritual alphabet. It is one of the principia[314] of the hidden wisdom. It is one of the ground-works of a living theology. We should never lose sight of it.

Nov. 20. Received today the first copies of my new volume, 'The Celestial Dawn or Connection of Earth and Heaven.'[315]

Nov. 8. 1862. I have seen more clearly than ever before that the spiritual world is an interior world, and is within the material cosmos as the soul is within the body. Not that it lies in towards the center of the earth, or beneath the surface. But material things are the outside circumference of being, or are the ultimates of spiritual things.[316] We are surrounded on every side by the spiritual realm, and its influences press upon the soul, both good & evil. Wherever there is in our soul any evil it forms a point of contact with spirits of darkness. Wherever there is in us any good it is a point of connection with heaven & its holy influences flow in. All illumination comes to us, says Swedenborg, from the Lord through heaven, and enters by an internal way. (*Continuation of Last Judgment*—no. 11.)[317]

As the Holy Spirit signifies the divine influence, or the divine proceeding, so it includes the influences that come to us from God through the angelic heavens. It signifies the divine sphere of the Lord which in reaching us, passes through the heavens, just as light comes to us sometimes from the sun tempered & colored by the transparent media through which it passes. But in this case the light is from the sun; and whatever good we may receive from holy spirits from out the higher or inner world emanates from the Lord alone. When we pray for the Holy Spirit we in reality ask for the enlightening & tranquilizing influences (in & fluo) of the angels. Yet I have no doubt that we may be put into immediate connection with the Lord's Divine Humanity.

Nov. 22. Spent most of the day and yesterday in selling my new book. Met with more success than I anticipated. Enjoyed myself well in the work of selling them. It will give me an opportunity for conversing on spiritual subjects with the people. The whole matter is committed to the care of Providence. My faith apprehends in God all that is implied in "Our Father who is in the heavens."

Nov. 24. The following sentence from St Augustine seems to me to contain an important principle, and one we should never lose sight of in reading the Gospels. Verbum Dei est Christus, qui non solum sonis, sed eliam [etiam] factis loquitur hominibus, Christ is the Word of God, who speaks to men not only by uttered language, but also by things done.[318] He was the Logos or the Infinite Understanding. The divine Love or Sensibility is the Father, and is the inmost esse[319] or life of the Deity. This is the origin of all things, as it is the very life of God. The divine Word or Intellect is derived from it, and is the Son. In this sense the Son of God is eternal. "In the beginning (or in that from which all things proceed, viz. the Divine Love) was the Word (or the Divine Understanding)["] (Jno 1:1.) This Word of God was made flesh and dwelt among us (Jno 1:14) or became man, and lived the Word. In coming down from the top of his divinity to the lowest sphere of humanity, there was a gradual hiding of his glory. In the highest heavens and among the archangels, he was the Angel-Jehovah or the Jehovah-Angel, so often mentioned in the Old Testament. In the middle heavens, he was the Angel of the Presence. In this form and to the angels of the spiritual heavens, his intellectual nature was more manifest, and his infinite love nature was less apprehended, than in the highest heavens.

In the lowest heavens he was apprehended by those who compose that spiritual realm as a mere angel. In the intermediate state and in this world he was as a man. But he fulfilled the Word or the Scriptures, that is he acted out the Divine Word. In the Highest Heavens as the Jehovah-Angel, he lived and acted and spake as the Infinite Wisdom, brought down to that range of life. In this lower or ultimate world he was the same Infinite Wisdom, but the Word here was made flesh. Everything he spake, and did, and all that was done to him had relation to his character as the Word of God, and to the treatment that Word has received from men. His life here was the life of the Word, and was a a great and noble creed. It was just such a life as the same Word dwelling in us will produce.

Dec. 9. I have felt today an unusual desire to be about my Father's business. I earnestly inquired what my peculiar sphere of activity was to be. The answer came from the ever-present spiritual world that I was to be a helping spirit, or that I was to perform the work symbolized by that of the good Samaritan. There are many souls, who in going from Jerusalem down to Jericho have fallen among thieves, or those who deprive men of truths; these have been wounded & stripped of their raiment and left half-dead. The work of the good Samaritan is to put upon them the garment of true doctrine, to bind up their spiritual wounds, pouring in oil & wine—the representatives of good & truth. This is a most Godlike & divine work. It is the highest in the kingdom of God. It [is] the work of the Lord himself. May he help me in so divine a calling. To help souls to rise to a higher spiritual life is a noble work. If I could be of any use even to fallen spirits, I would gladly do it. I feel today a love for even them, and would turn to them a loving heart. Perhaps that is the best way to to be delivered from their disturbing influence. "Overcome evil with good," is a precept truly divine.[320] I am not to fight against evil spirits with any weapon but love, omnipotent love. This idea was suggested to me today by a pious & spiritually minded woman. It seems to me important. I wish to be swallowed up in love. Love is life, & life is divine. Eternal life is everlasting love.

Dec. 20. It is one of the doctrines of Swedenborg relating to the regeneration of man, "That it is a law of the Divine Providence, that man should, as of himself, remove evils as sins in the external man, and that thus and not otherwise the Lord can remove evils in the internal man, and then at the same time in the external." (*D.P.* 91–106.)[321] This seems to me a principle of great practical importance, and is emphatically a doctrine of life—an idea that illustrates the way of life & salvation. Evil is internal and external. So far as it comes forth or is ultimated in the outward act, it is in the external man; so far as it is an inward affection or desire, it is in the internal man. Now it comes within the sphere of free will to prevent the outward manifestation or ultimation of it, and then it is weakened by having no basis on which it may rest. And by looking to the Lord with an affectionate trust, he takes away its interior root, or removes those affections & lusts from which the outward act springs. We are to do this as of ourselves, or in the use of that freedom of will with which we have been created & in which we are preserved by the Providence of the Lord. Also it is ever to be borne in mind, that we are to put away evil in the external man, or prevent its outward manifestation in word or deed, because it is sin against God, and for no other reason. Nothing else goes to its vital root or touches that selfishness from which it proceeds. But when we remove evils from the external man as sins, then the Lord purifies us from the concupiscences of evil or the unclean desires which sustain to the outward act the relation of cause to an effect. Every man is tempted when he is drawn away of his own lust and enticed, and it is as far as free agency can go to prevent its ultimation, and then the Lord purifies the soul from the inward spring of evil. This is all taught by our Savior in that highly symbolic act of washing the disciples feet, and in that strange declaration that he that washes need wash only his feet, and by so doing is clean every whit—an assertion that is not true only in its spiritual significance. The feet represent or correspond to the lowest principles of our mental nature, the mere outward & animal nature. To wash the feet is to put away evils as sins in the external man, and then the Lord's saving power delivers us from the corresponding interior evils, & we are clean every whit, or saved in fulness, externally & internally, body & soul. He who anxiously inquires what he must do to be saved, is directed to a principle that can never fail. Break off from all your sins in outward act, simply & solely because it is sin against God, and look to the Lord Jesus Christ as the one only God, and he washes the heart from {the} its evil affections and desires. When one came to our blessed Savior and asked what he must do to inherit eternal life, He who is the Way, and the Truth & the Life, replied, "Keep the Commandments," refering him to the Decalogue.[322] He did not say believe & thou shalt live. He had not come into such a moral position as to re[n]der it possible for him to have confidence that the Lord saved him. He must first avoid the evils as sins which are forbidden in the Commandments, and so far as he does this, the Lord removes the corresponding inward evils, and the opposite goods flow in from Him. Then & then only may a soul <u>assuredly</u> believe that the Lord saves us. It is one of those far reaching principles, we so often find in Swedenborg, that so far as we shun evils as sins, we have faith. For by so doing we come into a moral attitude in which faith inflows from God, & to us it is spontaneous.

We must beware that we do not invert this divine order and teach men so. We are not to believe that we are saved until we are saved, for that is to believe a lie & such are, according to an apostle damned rather than saved.[323] At some future day (the Lord's Divine Providence permitting) I will record some thoughts on the true idea of Justification by faith, & show what I think Paul means when he says "Being justified by faith we have peace with God." (Rom 5:1.)

Dec. 21. The subject of Justification by Faith has for some time past occasionally occupied my thoughts. I think I have a somewhat clear conception of what is meant by it. In the first place it is evident that faith in us effects no change in God, but only in {us, and} our mode of apprehending God. It is a truth clearly taught by Swedenborg from the Word of God, that the Lord is love itself, & mercy itself, that he condemns no man, but freely forgives all men. Christ, who is the one only God, said to the woman who was accused of crime, "neither do I condemn you; go and sin no more."[324] On the cross he forgave his murderers, who did not even ask the favor of him, or receive it. It would be unreasonable to suppose that he did not feel as merciful to us as he did to them. Paul also declares that "God was in Christ reconciling the world unto himself, not imputing their trespasses unto them.["][325] Now it is the law of our spiritual nature that a heart in a state of conscious disobedience condemns itself. This always must be so. This law is expressed by our Savior when he declares that he came not into the world to condemn the world, but that the world through him might be saved. He that believeth not is condemned already, because he believeth not in the name of the only begotten Son of God.[326] St John also says, "If our heart condemn us not, then have we confidence towards God."[327] It is utterly impossible for a soul in open rebellion against God to apprehend God as forgiving us, or to view him otherwise than as condemning us. That evil state of the will is necessarily followed or attended with the falsity in the understanding that God is angry with us, and will punish us. On the other hand when we put away evils as sins, and do this as of ourselves, or from choice & in freedom, we come into an attitude of submission & obedience to God, and our heart no longer condemns us. For as Swedenborg has taught, "so far as we put away evils as sins, so far we have faith, or a confidence that the Lord saves us.["][328] This right state of the will is always attended with the truth in the understanding that God of his boundless love & mercy freely forgives us, that he is not angry with us & will not punish us. But all this time no change has been wrought in God; but the change in us has affected our conceptions of him. The soul is not pardoned for its faith, & faith effects no change in God, but it is by faith we come to the inward consciousness of the pardon, which the Lord extends to all. Faith includes not only the belief that God forgives, but also that obedience of the will which renders such a belief possible. In the New Testament the word rendered unbelief, is also rendered disobedience. The term in fact includes both ideas. Unbelief is not merely a state of the understanding, but also of the will. So faith is not simply an action of the intellect, but a state of the will. It is a complete self-surrender—a denial of our own will in obedience to the will of God. When a soul is in that moral attitude there flows into it from God the sweet assurance that he forgives & saves. And that is justification by faith. It seems evident to me that Paul uses the term faith in this comprehensive sense, when he declares that "the just shall live by faith, or the justified by by faith shall live."[329] And justification is a being made just or righteous, and not that phantasm called justification, which is being called & treated as if the sinner were righteous. The just man or the righteous man, or justice or righteousness was in the conception of Paul the highest moral position. It was the highest spiritual state. Swedenborg has taught that righteousness refers to the state of the will, and holiness to the state of the intellect. The one is a freedom from evils; the other of falsities. Paul seems also to have thought of the just or righteous man as of one who was in a state of unqualified obedience to God. And this was attained by faith—not a mere belief, but a complete self-surrender, which is always accompanied by the consoling consciousness that the Lord forgives & saves. Thus "Being justified by faith, we have peace with God, through our Lord Jesus Christ." (Rom. 5:1.)[330]

Jan. 16 [1863]. Have been of late much interested in the science of correspondence as taught by that wonderful man Immanuel Swedenborg. My wife is pursuing the study with me. It affords us mutual pleasure and profit. It is the key to the deeper senses of the Holy Scriptures. It is truly science of sciences—a study in which the angels may be supposed to delight. Several years ago while thirsting for a more satisfying knowledge of [the] divine than the current superficial literature of the Church could supply, I was led to pray the Lord most sincerely, to lead me to some book or books which could satisfy this inmost need. I had been previously led to study with interest and profit the mystic authors. From Madam Guyon, Fenelon, Kempis, Tauler, Law[331] and others I found something that was valuable. But all was vague and indefinite. There was no complete system. While in a bookstore in the city of Portsmouth, I saw on the shelf a work entitled "*Athanasia, or Foregleams of Immortality.*"[332] It was deeply impressed on my consciousness that this was an answer to my earnest prayer. I consequently bought two copies, retaining one and presenting another to a brother in the ministry. The views of that excellent little volume came to my soul as rain upon a thirsty soil. In a foot note I observed a reference to the Work of Swedenborg on the *Divine Love and Wisdom.*[333] It was forcibly impressed upon my mind that the views of the book were those of Swedenborg, and that what I had earnestly longed for would be found in him. I accordingly sent to Boston & procured his principal works. I may truly say that what my soul long yearned for I have found. They satisfy both departments of my nature, my Intellect & my Affections. I believed his teachings because I could not do otherwise. I inwardly saw their truth. But to embrace those views has cost me much, and may cost me more (speaking as men speak;) but they are worth all they will cost. Believing them to contain the germ of a new & higher dispensation, and what the Church is dying for the want of, it cannot be doubtful whether it is my duty to teach them to others. "Freely ye have received; freely give."[334] I have already imparted them to some, who have affectionately embraced them. I am settling down into a state of rest in regard to them. My dreadful struggles of soul & combats and desolations are subsiding, and, through the redeeming mercy of Christ, my only Lord, I hope to come into tranquility[335] and peace. Perhaps my Lord, whom I love & serve, has some work for me to do in proclaiming the new dispensation. When the fullness of time comes, he will send me forth. I wait the motions of his will. Some years ago, this passage from the Word of God was deeply impressed upon my consciousness, "I will make of thee a great nation, and I will bless thee and make thy name great; and thou shalt be a blessing." (Gen. 12:2.) It has always followed me, even when I have been laid aside from any active labor in the ministry. I hope God will fulfill this word unto his servant on which he caused me to hope, and fulfill it in its spiritual import. Nations signify those who are in goods of life, or in good works from charity. And greatness according to Swedenborg is only predicated of goodness & hight of truth. A great name is a holy life and character. And blessing is heavenly beatitude. May he make me thus; and many others through me. Thus he will bless & make me a blessing. The Ld. grant it. Amen.

March 14. Many of the philosophical principles, unfolded in the writings of Immanuel Swedenborg, that sounded strange when first published to the world, are now after the lapse of a century beginning to be admitted by scientific men, among them the principle that all things in the planetary worlds that commpose our solar system owe their origin to the sun. I find the following in one of the journals of the day, on the Atmosphere of the Sun. "Recent investigations clearly establish the fact that the atmosphere of the sun holds in suspension or solution many of the substances that exist on our planet only as solids—the metals for instance. Of course, we trace this naturally to the much higher temperature of the sun; and yet the fact is scarcely appreciable to our imaginations, and still more that, being so, we should be able to discover and discuss it intelligibly. A scientific writer on this subject says:— 'Our impoverished atmosphere still contains nothing but the elements necessary for the support of organic life—oxygen, azote,[336] carbon and water—and our understanding can with difficulty accustom itself to the idea of an atmosphere charged with iron, with alkaline metals, with bodies the most different, in a state of combustion. It would require the pen of a Dante to portray that chaotic condition of nature, that rain of metalic fire, those luminous clouds darkened by the contrast of a still intenser light, that incandescent ocean of the sun, with its tempests, its currents, its {gigantic} rushing and gigantic water-spouts; such pictures set at defiance even imaginations the most enamored of the fantastic and the strange, and our streams evaporate as a drop of water before that blazing lava, that focus, that refulgence of the world, source of all warmth, of all movement, of all life.['"][337]

I find also in *The Apocalypse Revealed* (n. 936) a fine illustration of the scientific correctness of {the} Swedenborg's doctrine of correspondence.[338] It is in relation to the correspondence of leaves and flowers. By leaves he remarks are signified rational truths; and rational truths are those which proximately receive spiritual truths, for the rational faculty of man is the first receptacle of spiritual truths.[339] When a soul {has} is able to receive divine truth rationally apprehended, it stands {of} upon the dividing line between the natural and spiritual state. Hence the Lord says, "Come now & let us reason together." (Isa. 1:18.) The leaves of the tree of life are for the healing of the nations, & by those leaves are spiritually signified "rational truths."[340]

The correspondence of flowers is higher, because flowers are more delicately organized than leaves. Flowers signify, "primitive spiritual truths in the rational mind."[341] Leaves represent merely rational truths; flowers the first truths apprehended rationally by the spiritual man. Here is exactly the same difference between the correspondence of leaves & flowers, that there is in their physiological structure. It is a principle, but recently admitted into Botanical science, that the leaf is a "typical form," and all the organs of the flower, such as the sepals, the petals, the stamens and pistils are only modifications of the leaf. They are only the leaf form more delicately organized and metamorphosed into those organs respectively. Whence comes this nice discrimination of the spiritual meaning of leaves & flowers by Swedenborg? Whence this scientific {exactness} correctness of his doctrine of correspondence as applied to those organs of plants. It is not probable that Swedenborg was acquainted with the principle of Botanic Physiology, that the various parts or organs of the flower are only modifications of the leaf, for it is of very recent introduction into Botany. This affords a good example of the almost mathematical exactness of Swedenborg's science of correspondence. And I am fully convinced that the more his teachings are studied in the light of science, the more evidence we shall gain of his divine illumination. The Correspondence between the natural & the spiritual worlds is a divine idea, and one of the loftiest conceptions that was ever uttered by the mouth of man. Its influence both upon the scientific & religious world is only beginning to be felt.[342]

March 19. It seems to me to be one of the mistakes of the old dispensation of religion, that they attempt to make men <u>spiritual</u> before they become rational. This is an impossibility. It is one of the laws of divine order in the process of our recovery from our fallen condition to the heavenly state, that before we can become truly spiritual—can attain to that spiritual mindedness which is life & peace—we must become rational.[343] The latter is the standing-ground on which alone we can rise to the former. In the highest heaven's [heavens] where the true order of life alone prevails, the intellectual views of the angels flow out from their love. Their faith is not the result of a slow process of reasoning, but is an intuition, a spontaneous inward perception. In them the love predominates and governs their whole being. They are moved by their affections and the instincts that belong to them rather than by their ideas. {They use} A celestial love uses the Intellect only as an eye to <u>see the way</u> to the ends of which it aims. The Intellect is the servant, not the lord of the Heart. This is the true order of our being. But we are in a fallen state, and in order to rise to that heavenly condition from which humanity has descended, we go back in an inverted order over the same route {over} through which we descended. Man fell from this high spirituality, through rationality, into sensuality. Hence in returning we must go back over the route—from a state of carnality we

must rise to a state of rationality, and this is the point of transition to a
true spirituality. Now this is exactly the order of the redeeming process as
unfolded by Emanuel Swedenborg. He makes no appeal to the sensuous
& selfish side of our nature. He never asks of us a blind faith in anything,
for he avers that what does not fall into the compass of our understanding cannot be an object of belief. Such are the laws of the mind that we
cannot believe a real or apparent absurdity. It is the tendency of his whole
system to raise man from his low sensuous views & feelings, to a state of
enlightened reason & then to a truly spiritual life. This is the divine order
of our recovery. I do not mean that a soul cannot become <u>religious</u> without
first attaining to rational views of divine truth. The advocates of a blind
faith make their disciples religious. The Pharisees were religious, but they
were carnal & not spiritual. The Athenians, according to St Paul, were <u>very
religious</u>;—for it was easier in Athens to find a god than a man—but they
were far from being spiritual.[344]

  If there is to be a new dispensation of the Church which is to raise man to
a higher spirituality than he has ever attained, it must come with such views
& teachings respecting {all} divine & heavenly things as shall satisfy our reason, and then from this elevated foothold of the Intellect the Heart can rise
to those loftier & holier experiences that belong to the spiritual man. In the
true order of our being light comes through heat—truth through love. In the
inverted order of our being in which we are unhappily placed, heat comes
enveloped in light,—love comes through truth. Swedenborg says: "Rational
truths are those which proximately receive spiritual truths, for the rational
faculty of man is the first receptacle of spiritual truths." (A.R. 936.)[345]

  When a soul attains to that state of mental elevation which may be
called rationality, it becomes receptive of <u>spiritual</u> truth, and will imbibe
it as the dry soil drinks in the rain of heaven. The plan of salvation as
unfolded by the great Swedish theologian & philosopher is in harmony
with the redeeming effort of the Lord, He says, "Come now and let us
reason together." (Isa. 1:18.) A man can never become spiritual, much less
celestial, until he is willing to look soberly, candidly, and from a rational
point of view at the truths & duties of religion. No quantity of dogmas,
blindly received, can make a man truly spiritual in his views & feelings.

  Swedenborg, and the same is true of all his followers, would not have
us receive even those loftier and more satisfying truths & doctrines he

teaches, except so far as they are rationally apprehended by us. For it is only that which we do in freedom according to reason that is appropriated to us, & is of any enduring value. (*D.P.* 78.)[346] It is only in this way that it is really incorporated into the soul's life, and receives the quality of perpetuity. Mere dogmas, blindly swallowed, are like indigestible substances in the stomach. They are not transformed into the living tissue so as so as to become a part of ourselves, and happy for us if their presence in the system is not positively injurious. There are many honest souls in all the older churches that are sincerely seeking for a higher Christian life. They are filled with unsatisfied cravings for a higher position in religion. What they lack is light. I am confident that by a prayerful perusal of the writings of Swedenborg, they would obtain those higher views of divine truth which would raise them to a position of illuminated rationality. Then they would receive from our blessed Lord, those spiritual truths which would satisfy the deepest needs of their natures. By receiving those truths, not merely into the intellect, but embracing them with the will, and incorporating them into the life, they become {true} real goodness, which is truth in this life. Thus they become receptive of still higher and more satisfying views, according to the words of our blessed Savior, "He that doeth the truth cometh to the light, that it may be made manifest that his deeds are wrought in God." (Jno)[347] A person in such a state of rational illumination has an interior perception that all the truth & goodness he possesses is from the Lord & is the Lord in him. And that state becomes as the seed of a richer harvest of Christian experience. For by means of the two faculties of rationality & liberty, man can be so far reformed & regenerated, as he can be led to acknowledge that all the truth and {all} the good which he thinks and does is from the Ld, and not fr. himself. (*D.P.* 87.)[348]

March 23. It is difficult at first to conceive of love and truth as substance. In the philosophy of Swedenborg they are real substance & even form. If we elevate the mind above a mere sensuous range of thought, and look at this matter we see that it must be so. If truth is what it has been defined to be, the reality of things, it must be a substance—a spiritual substance. Both love and truth are viewed in the old theology as a nothing—a nonentity. But that which is anything, that which has any real being, must be a substance. Truth is something most divinely real. God is truth, and all truth in us is of God. It is as real as God's own being. There is emphasis in the words of our blessed Lord, "I am the truth." Also in the declaration "God is love."[349] The verb to be there has a signification it is difficult to conceive & more so to express. Some one a few weeks ago in a conversation respecting the spiritual sense of the Scriptures asked with an air of triumph, what is the spiritual meaning of the verb to be? It was given me immediately to answer that it signifies love. For love is life, & life is love. To be refers to our inmost being, and that is always our ruling love. That love is a substance. It can inflow into other minds. Truth is a substance. It can be imparted to other souls from our own. It is well for us to gain a clear conception of love and truth as a substance the most vitally real of anything in the universe. They are something of God's own life.

March 24. I see how it is that by believing I have the thing for which I am praying, causes me to have it. It is implied that the faith is divinely imparted. It proceeds fr. Gd.[350] Faith is truth, and truth fr Gd. is something real & substantial. If one prays for recovery to health, and the Ld gives him to believe that he is recovering, that faith is only the truth that it is so, received from the Ld. To believe that I am being recovered to health, if that faith is self-originated, accomplishes nothing, But if my belief of it is a truth received fr Gd, or if my faith is the faith of Gd, it becomes a substantial reality. Faith in its essence is truth; and truth is substance. Hence the Author of the Ep. to the Heb. says, "Faith is the substance (ὑπόστασις, Latin substantia) of things hoped for." (Heb. 11:1.) Now if the Ld imparts to {one} me a divine conviction that a certain blessing is mine, that faith being a substantial reality,—being the substance of what I desire—puts me into an actual realization of what I am praying for. But this is all based upon the fact that faith is truth, & truth is a divine substance that finds its first source in the life of Gd.

But one is in danger unless he is truly enlightened of taking mere impressions for a divinely inwrought conviction. How may one know that his belief that a certain thing is so is the faith of Gd, and not a mere impression originating in our own minds or coming fr. evil and false spirits? I do not know unless in this way: what comes fr. Gd carries with it the evidence of its divinity. There is no mistaking what is divine. Gd shines by his own light. We have received the sprt that is of Gd, that we may know the things that are freely given to us of Gd. If He gives any thing, He imparts with it the evidence that it comes fr Him.

July 11.[351] Our only son, Frank H, a member of 3ᵈ Reg. N.H.V, was severely wounded on Morris Island S.C. by a shell fired from Fort Sumter.[352] His right hand was blown off, and he was wounded in both legs, in the right leg severely. But we are consoled by the truth that the Lord never permits an evil come upon us except it be to save us from some greater evil or to accomplish some enduring good. In that case the apparent evil becomes a positive good. The Lord being infinite & eternal, has reference in all that he does to the infinite & eternal. Hence a light affliction is made to work out for us "a far more exceeding & eternal weight of glory.["][353] The Lord always acts in reference to our salvation. Every thing is made to contribute an influence to this end. A few days ago I had an affecting view of the truth that God's power is love. I saw this in a divine light it is not easy to reproduce in words. What he loves he is able to do, & what he is able to do he loves to do. His will is his love. What he loves, he wills, & vice versa. Here is a sure foundation for trust in Him.

Aug. 28.[354] While engaged in prayer, the Lord gave me a most impressive view of my inability to guide myself, & of the blindness of my own understanding when unilluminated by the sun of righteousness. Though it was midday, all was dark as midnight before me. I could not see an inch before me. All was blank darkness. Only near the Lord was there any light. I never felt more like yielding myself to the direction of the Infinite Love. I would put my hand in his, & follow where Wisdom & Love lead. May the lesson never be lost or forgotten.

I have been for some time passing through severe temptations. These I know are necessary, & am fully persuaded that the Lord fighteth for me.[355] He is accomplishing in me the six days work of creation, and then he will sanctify the Sabbath of rest. I have felt uneasy at the thought of my necessary inactivity, not being able to preach at all. But silence is my duty, and I should do it as cheerfully as any duty the Lord lays upon me. The Lord also revealed to me by the Spirit, that the mental struggles and the regenerating soul-agonies that I am passing through are for the good of others as well as myself. Our blessed Lord passed through the same, not only for the glorification of his assumed Humanity, but for the salvation of others, for the accomplishment of which the deification of the Human was necessary. I am following him in the regeneration. "No one liveth unto himself, and no man dyeth unto him[self]."[356] The most useful thing we can do for the world is to suffer ourselves to be redeemed or regenerated. Then, as in the case of our blessed Lord, we become media of transmitting heavenly blessings to others. I would have the Lord finish his work—his six days labor. Then cometh the rest of the holy Sabbath. I am conscious of progress in the redeeming process. He who attains to a celesstial experience on earth, must pay the price. Christ suffered & entered into glory. It is only by suffering with him, that we can be glorified together.

Nov. 17.[357] Today wrote the following letter to Sampson Reed esq of Boston, with whom I have had some correspondence in relation to various matters connected with the doctrines of the New Church.[358] I herein more publicly avow my belief in the doctrines of {the} Swedenborg and my sympathy with those who have embraced them & consecrated themselves to their exemplification in life & their diffusion abroad. I have written in the fear of the Lord, having fully counted the cost, fully realizing that it will probably result in sundering my connection with the M. E. Church. This I do not now so much regret, as my connection with that body is only an external one, my interior state not being in harmony with the prevailing spiritual condition of that Church. I ardently love the doctrines received from the Lord through his eminent servant, Em. Swedenborg. My connection with Methodism is not a living one, but Methodism is to me like the dead & loose bark of a tree. Why should it not fall off? There are many in the church whom I love sincerely, but it does seem to me that the real <u>animus</u> of the body is some form of selfishness or self-love. There seems to be little or no charity, & hence no real internal faith. Its vitality is gone. In the Ld alone is my hope & trust.[359]

CLAREMONT, N.H., Nov 17, 1863.

Sampson Reed, Esq.:

DEAR BROTHER:—Your letter of the 10th ult. was duly received, containing your kind invitation to attend the Social Meeting on Thursday, the 19th. Nothing would give me more pleasure than to do so if it were practicable. I deeply feel the need of the society of New Church people, being entirely shut out from all communication with them except by letter. I have no desire to hold myself aloof from those who I firmly believe are the depositaries, through the Divine mercy of the Lord, of the truths of the new dispensation of grace. On the contrary, I ardently desire to connect myself with them, sharing with them the burden and heat of the day, and consecrating all my remaining energy of body and mind in spreading abroad the glorious and all-satisfying truths of the new age, of which Swedenborg was made the herald. I began to read the works of that most remarkable man some years ago. They came to my soul, filled as it long had been with unsatisfied cravings, like the rain of summer upon the dry fields. I at once embraced the higher views of religion there unfolded, and proclaimed them in private conversation and in the pulpit, and circulated the books among my friends, some of whom have cordially embraced the truths which they teach. I made no public profession of faith in the doctrines of the New Church, for what, at the time, seemed a good reason. I was aware that there was a deep-seated prejudice in the minds even of many honest religious people against everything that emanated from Emanuel Swedenborg. It appeared to me that I might be called by Providence to diffuse those higher views and religious teachings through the church of which I had long been a member and a sincere preacher. It was very natural to suppose that truths which had been so greatly blessed to my comfort would be eagerly embraced by all, as soon as they were made acquainted with them. But I, all the time, labored under the mistake of supposing that the New Church was only another sect, added to the too many already in Christendom, and not, as it really is, a New Dispensation. Many of the early disciples who passed over to Christianity from Judaism, labored under a similar mistake. They supposed that Christianity might be grafted into the old, decayed Judaistic stock, and cause it to bud and blossom again. And it is a fact of ecclesiastical history, that the first eighteen bishops of the church at Jerusalem were circumcised Jews. But I have at length learned a lesson, that ought to have been acquired long ago, that new wine is to be put into new bottles, else the bottles will break and the wine be spilled. The old churches are dead, having lost all that can constitute a real church of Christ—true faith and charity. The attempts to resuscitate the consummated ecclesiastical organizations of the old dispensation with the fresh life of the New Jerusalem, is like the attempt of the prophet's servant to revive the dead body of the widow's son with the staff of Elijah, or like the professor of the dissecting room galvanizing his subject into the appearance of the phenomena of real life. The Old Church sustains the same relation to the New, that Judaism does to Christianity. It is not in accordance with the Divine order that a consummated church should ever be made alive. That which is dead must turn to corruption; but, perhaps, a remnant may be saved.

My reception of the new truths has been attended with severe mental struggles, which I will not attempt to describe, for few perhaps could understand them or sympathize with them. To reconstruct one's system of theology from top to bottom, especially with one who sincerely believed the old system, must be attended with great temptations, wrestlings of spirit, and inward desolations, sometimes sufficient to prostrate the bodily health entirely. All this I have passed through, but through the mercy of our one and only Lord, I hope to enter into rest. The struggles of my soul are subsiding into tranquility and peace. I have a great desire to impart to all receptive souls the spiritual riches which the Lord has, out of the plenitude of His love and mercy, given to me, though all unworthy of the heavenly treasure. We have often felt in our own experience, what is so beautifully and simply expressed by Swedenborg, in H. H. 413. "I observed that when I wished to transfer all my delight into another person, there followed a new influx of delight, more interior and more full than the former; and that in proportion to the amount that I desired to impart, was the amount of that which flowed in; and I perceived that this was from the Lord."[360] Here is unfolded the law of the kingdom of the heavens, as immutable in its operation as the regular succession of phenomena in nature. As citizens of the New Jerusalem, we must give what we have freely received. Jerusalem that was, with her children, was placed in the geographical centre of the old world, that the light of her temple fires might be cast into the profound midnight of Pagandom. So the One Lord of heaven and earth calls upon us to let our light shine, that men may see, not only our creed, but our good works, so that our Father in the heavens may be glorified. The New Church is to be one with the new heavens. The same doctrines that are in the heavens are to be in His New Church, and, what is more, the same life. Christ came the first time to send fire on the earth. He came the second time for the same purpose—to transfer celestial love, which is the life of the heavens, to His church on earth. The Lord has revealed to us, through his eminent servant, Emanuel Swedenborg, the laws of heavenly life, that they may be reproduced and illustrated in the lives of the people of his new kingdom.

I hope sometime to see you and the dear brethren of the New Church face to face, and commune with you on those things that related to his church on earth and in the heavens. I cannot, on the occasion of your social meeting, for reasons I will submit. I have an only son, who, in July last, lost his right arm in the service of his country, in a battle on Morris Island. I have bought for his benefit a periodical business, and am conducting it for him until his arrival home. Also I have charge of the schools in town, and the winter term is now just commencing, and my time is all engaged. In the meantime, I send my cordial greetings and affectionate salutations to the New Church friends in Boston. I hope to be present with you in spirit, and trust I may not be wholly forgotten on that interesting and profitable occasion. My wife joins me in the above.

Affectionately yours,

W. F. Evans.

April 4 [1864].[361] This day has been an epoch in my spiritual history. I have sundered my connection with the M.E. Church. It is not a step that has been hastily taken, but has long been considered. For five years past the providence of the Lord seems to have led me to this result. The failure of my health while preaching at Lawrence. My partial recovery and then after another attempt to preach in the Old Church, the failure of my health again, seemed to me the voice of God, that my labors as a Methodist preacher were by his will closed. My poverty & sufferings while my health would not admit of my laboring, and no help being offered me by the Church for whom I had expended all my energies, served to wean me from it. The suspicion of heresy, & even of <u>insanity</u> that rested upon me for the views expressed in the *Celestial Dawn*, and the cold shoulder that was turned toward me by my brethren, was a part of the permissive providence of the Ld, leading in the same direction. I have been lead to this decision by a higher power, against which it has been vain to struggle. I have felt myself for years floating before a current of providences that was bearing me towards the New Church & out of the Old. I now feel a sense of freedom that is a great relief to my mind. I have been brought by the Divine mercy of the Ld from darkness into light. I wish here to record my grateful sense of the divine goodness to me in all his dealings with me. He has heard my sincere and oft repeated prayer that he would lead me into all truth. I have learned to trust all to his management. I only pray to be of use to the souls of others. I long to impart the divine treasures, in mercy given to me, to all receptive souls.

Today wrote the following letter to the N.H. Conference, which I hope may be received in the spirit in which it is written.[362]

Sundered from Methodist Church

CLAREMONT, April 4, 1864.

REV. JAMES THURSTON,

Presiding Elder, Claremont District:

DEAR BROTHER:—You find enclosed my ordination credentials, which, through you, I wish to deliver to the Conference, and which you will please accept as my withdrawal from the Methodist Episcopal Church. This step is not the result of any sudden caprice, but has been long considered and duly weighed, and is deemed necessary in order to prevent any unprofitable excitement in reference to my case. It is known to most of my brethren that I entertain views of doctrine and religion that are at variance with the standards of Methodist theology. For some years I have been a reader of the writings of that most remarkable man of modern ecclesiastical history, Emanuel Swedenborg. After a careful investigation, conducted with a conscious honesty of purpose, with much prayer for divine illumination and guidance, and I trust a sincere and unselfish love of truth for its own sake, I have come to the conclusion that that eminent servant of the Lord Jesus Christ was raised up by the Lord's divine providence as the herald of a new and better dispensation of the church, known in prophetic language as the New Jerusalem. The reasons on which that opinion is based it is not necessary here to give. They are fully given, so far as they have influenced my judgment, in a work now in press, entitled "The New Age and its Messenger."

The system taught by the great Swedish philosopher, so simple, and yet so profound, so vast and so harmonious in all its parts, containing so many truths of infinite import, which were never before made known to the Christian Church, and which commend themselves with self evident force to the intuitions of the reason, satisfies the deepest wants of my intellect. The spotless and unselfish purity of heart, and constant self-devotion to the good of others, on which he everywhere insists, satisfies the heart's holiest affections. He has taught me more of God, and thus enabled me to love him more. A perusal of his spiritual writings has deepened my love and reverence for the Holy Scriptures, as containing the Word of God, not merely inspired, but divine in every letter and every thought, and being in fact an ever present manifestation of the deity to the world. He has given higher views of the Lord Jesus Christ as the one only living and true God, who is divine even as to his humanity, which is but the evolution of the indwelling divinity.

He has given increased moral force to the great doctrines of the resurrection and the judgment, by not postponing those events, as is done in the old theology, to the indefinite and unknown future, but showing that they follow immediately after death, thus bringing them home to the hearts and consciences of men. He has restored to the church the lost science of correspondences, which demonstrates its truth by giving to the Scriptures an interior spiritual sense, in a connected series, differing from that of the letter, but not contradicting or undervaluing it, and governed by laws in its application to Biblical interpretation as immutable as those of geometry. His works contain a profound system of spiritual philosophy, unfolding the changeless laws that govern the interior life of men and angels. They have poured a flood of light upon the spiritual world, that hitherto unknown realm, to which we all hasten, and whose mysteries we instinctively long to have uncovered. He has disclosed its substantial realities, and shown its vital connections with this lower abode, and our every-day concerns. Yet his teachings are fundamentally and irreconcilably at variance with the modern Pythonism. The so-called spiritualism of the times involves the hurtful falsity of denying the personality of the Godhead, who is made an all-pervading principle, and not a person. It makes of Christ a mere man, and destroys the sanctity of the Word. The first of these errors is really contained in our own articles of faith, which declare that God is a being without *form* or parts. To say that a being is without form, and yet a person, is a contradiction, and of such a being the mind can have no conception, otherwise than as an indefinable principle diffused through all nature, which is Pantheism, and not Christianity.

In the system of Swedenborg, the Divine Being is intensely and infinitely personal, and clothed with such attributes, and invested with such qualities, as to render it possible for us to love him without doing violence to our moral nature, for that God, even in thought, is no other than the Lord Jesus Christ, Jehovah made man. The practical tendency of all his teachings in relation to God, is to lead the soul to a calm and tranquil trust in his boundless love, and to a spiritual life whose every breathing shall be prayer.

For many years it has been my constant study and earnest aim to attain to the higher forms of the Christian life, and the highest results of a truly Christian experience. This inward year[n]ing of spirit to reach a better position in religion, and enter into a solid enduring peace, has lost none of its strength; but the blind instinctive craving of the heart for a better state needs guidance, in order that it may find satisfaction; and it can find only in the uncreated light of the New Jerusalem that which can conduct it to the rest it seeks. Here the laws that regulate the progress of a real regeneration are revealed with unfailing certainty. It is only by a conformity to those laws, in the exercise of our rationality and freedom, that we can rise from our lapsed condition to a state of union with God, and to the commencement of the celestial life, which is the end of the whole redemptive scheme.

During my connection of twenty-five years with the Methodist Episcopal Church, I have lived in peace and harmony with all my ministerial brethren and fellow-laborers in the vineyard of the Lord. The memory of our social intercourse still affords me unalloyed pleasure. So far as I know, I still enjoy your confidence and brotherly affection, which you may be assured is most heartily reciprocated. It is to be hoped that hereafter there may be no controversy between us. The whole land is before us, and there is appropriate work for each of us to do in the kingdom of God. We may each usefully occupy some sphere of Christian activity, perform the part allotted us in the great plan of the Lord's providence, finish the work given us to do, and meet and mingle in a world of light and love, where we shall see eye to eye, face to face, and no longer as now, through a glass darkly. To sunder my connection with brethren whom I have learned to love, gives me pain, and costs me a struggle. I am aware that it is a sacrifice of what the natural man holds dear. Should I consult my temporal and selfish interests, it would lead me in a different direction. But it has been given me of God to love truth for its own divine self, independent of the honors and temporal advantages resulting from its possession. Truth is of God, and he who has it in its reality, has something divine in him. He who gains it, though at the loss of all earthly and transient interests, may yet rejoice in the possession of so divine a prize and heavenly treasure. The Lord has declared himself to be the way, and the truth, and the life, and his Word, as a manifestation of himself, is truth. He who has union with him is in sympathy with all that is true and good in the universe. Sundered from him, the soul is in error and falsity, whatever may be its creed. He who cleaves to the Divine Word with reverence and affection, is in living communication with the fountain of all truly human and angelic wisdom.

It would afford me pleasure to meet with you during the session of the Conference, if circumstances would permit. I trust that the presence in your midst of the great head of the Church will render your meeting both pleasant and profitable.

Affectionately yours,

W. F. Evans.

April 10. Myself & wife were this day baptized by the Rev. Thomas Worcester, D.D. and received into the New Church.[363] Though we are only members at large, and not connected with any particular society. Thus we have come into the visible fellowship of the New Jerusalem. I feel conscious of a living sympathy with the new heavens and with the New Church above. By baptism, according to Swedenborg, we are inserted among Christian spirits in the world of spirits. By baptism in the New Church we are placed in a vital connection with those who compose that Church in the spiritual world, for the reason that the Church on earth & the Church above form a one like body and soul. No one can have any perception of the importance of baptism, who does not come to the knowledge of the living connection of this world with world of spirits. This is just as real as the conjunction of the body and soul in man. In the world above there are societies of Christians, drawn spontaneously & necessarily together by the force of their moral affinities, which force operates as powerfully in the realm of mind as gravitation does in that of mater. Baptism is not a mere <u>symbol</u>; it is more. It is a reality. It brings the subject of it into vital connection with some association of spirits in the other world. And through that society his spiritual life is derived from the Lord. Such is the law of divine order. He who comes into the New Church had better do so by baptism, as it will weaken the power of those spiritual infestations, which previously have so often marred his peace, and strengthen the golden tie that binds him to the new heavens, through which his new life must descend from the Lord. All this I realized in my own experience, within twenty four hours after I received that holy sacrament. The severest struggle of my whole life preceded & attended my reception of that ordinance. It seemed as if all the spirits of darkness had gathered their forces for a final assault. The struggle was short but terrible beyond description. But there was a sweet power in the words of the Lord, "It is finished."[364] There was a consciousness that my union with the new heavens was sealed. And ever after I felt the sympathetic tie that bound me to the old Dispensation gradually loosened.[365] And the <u>spirits</u> that are in the darkness of that age <u>have been removed into a conscious distance</u>. All this I aver from my inmost soul is true. And unto Him who sitteth upon the throne & unto the Lamb, be glory[,] dominion & power forever.[366] Salvation belongeth unto the Ld.[367] He is my God & I am his. All that in me is good & true, is his, yea is Himself. To him I commit the keeping of my spirit. Amen.

Aug 6.[368] For some days these words have been a source of great strength and comfort to me. I have found a Divine nutriment in them. "Thus saith the Lord God, the Holy One of Israel; In returning & rest shall ye be saved; In quietness and confidence shall be your strength." (Isa. 30:15) I desire that the <u>spirit</u> of that text may be more & more incorporated into my soul's life. In quietness, in tranquility of spirit, & in a calm trust in the Lord shall I find strength. I have had some correspondence with the missionary committee of the Mass. Association of the New Church, in relation to being employed as a Missionary & Colporteur. Yesterday I wrote to Dr Worcester, that I would go. I am aware that my health is not sufficient at present. But if the Ld will have me accomplish that use, he will empower me to do it. My consent was based on my confidence in the Lord & in his Word. One thing I know, that sofar as a soul will hold itself in readiness to impart, the

Lord will give. "With what measure ye mete, it shall be measured to you again."[369] I long to engage in some higher use than I have apparently filled the last few years—years of preparation.

Aug. 7. Sabbath. This morning as the first bell was ringing for meeting, I walked to a high hill South of Claremont village, called Flat Rock. It overlooks the entire village, with its churches, & its forest of shade trees. I went to this place about a year ago, but under very different circumstances. I was then in bondage, in deep wrestlings of soul, while old things were passing away, & all things were being made new. I had an impression that when I went to that place again, it would be with different feelings. So it has been truly. I am now out of the Old Church & in the New. My severe temptations & struggles have in a great measure subsided into tranquility of mind. I felt a desire to go to that high eminence & formally thank the Ld of heaven & earth for what he has done for me. It was one of the most remarkable seasons of spiritual refreshment that I ever enjoyed. I read the three chapters of the Word containing the Sermon on the Mount, and the one containing the account of the Transfiguration. I was alone in that great solitude with the Ld & his angels. Both came consciously near. There was a divine sweetness in the Words of Him who spake as never man spake. I prayed extemporaneously concluding with the Lord's Prayer. My soul was truly upon the high places of Israel. The kingdom of God was to me righteousness, and joy, & peace in the Holy Ghost. It will long be remembered as an era in my spiritual life—. These words came with reviving power, "Arise, be not afraid." (Mat. 17:7) I have sometimes felt that [there] was an inherent divine power & living virtue, in the words of the Lord, that create the state they enjoin—as in the words "Peace be unto you."[370] There is in those words a life-giving power that imparts peace to the whole mind. It was one of the most refreshing seasons of worship ever enjoyed by me. I descended {and} refreshed. I must have felt something of what Moses experienced in that state of worldly abstraction & mental exaltation, called being with [the] Lord in the mount.[371] How refreshing is solitude to one who is fitted to enjoy it. Solitude, not as a permanent condition, but as an occasional spiritual luxury, is of great value. The Lord sometimes left the multitude for the stillness & silence of the mountain. He has by his life & example sanctified solitude & silence as a means of grace. But they are to be enjoyed as a needful rest & recreation from more active uses. They are to be a mere episode in the poem of human life—an interlude in life's drama. I can look back upon many such seasons, when I could truly say, "I am not alone, for the Father is with me."[372]

Sept. 1. Have been for some days nearly sick. In a journey to Bath Me., was exceedingly seasick, and it has seriously deranged my stomach.[373] But my trust is in the Lord. At present have no means of living but by faith in the Lords Providence.[374] Yesterday in reading Bryant's lines "To a Water-Fowl," my faith in God was strengthened— The following stanza is peculiarly expressive of Providence, which extends over all the objects of his creative love.

> "There is a Power whose care
> Teaches thy way along that pathless coast,—
> The desert and illimitable air,—
> Lone wandering, but not lost.["][375]

He closes the beautiful poem, with the following stanza's [sic], full of poetical thought, and of a calm trust in the loving care of the Father of All.

> "Thou art gone; the abyss of heaven
> Hath swallowed up thy form; yet on my heart
> Deeply hath sunk the lesson thou hast given,
> And shall not soon depart.
>
> He who, from zone to zone,
> Guides through the boundless sky thy certain flight,
> In the long way that I must tread alone
> Will lead my steps aright."[376]

I have felt the importance of more faith in God, not only in reference to my temporal concerns, but in regard to my personal salvation. I want to say with <u>undoubting confidence</u>, "Behold, God is my salvation; I will trust & not be afraid: for the Lord <u>Jehovah</u> is my strength and my song; he also is become my salvation." (Isa. 12:2.) But how shall I get this faith? It must come from the Source of all good. Faith is the gift of God. If genuine, it is "the faith of God."[377]

The summer is past. Today is one of those clear, calm, still days, that mark the dividing line between summer and autumn, when there seems a Divinity in the light & the air. But soon the winter cometh. Soon we can say,

"Changing, fading, falling, flying,
    From the homes that gave them birth,
Autumn leaves in beauty dying,
    Seek the mother breast of earth.

Soon shall all the songless wood
    Shiver in the deepening snow,
Mourning in its solitude,
    Like some Rachel in her woe."[378]

But we may live above times, & seasons, & place. Living in God, and in the present, neither uselessly regretting the past, nor anxious about the future. Thus the angels live.

July 2 [1865].[379] Have been for some time more & more impressed with a sense of the presence of spirits around me & with me. My mind often turns inward upon itself, & becomes in a degree unconscious of the outer world, the senses being more or less closed, & I pass into a state that maybe [may be] described by saying it is half way between sleeping & waking. It is an interior, or superior state, which means the same. In this state spiritual forms sometimes stand disclosed before my inner sight, sometimes seen more clearly than at other times. Sometimes the scenery of the spirit land opens before me, it[s] mountains, hills, lakes, rivers, forests, & its mansions & paradises. Trees & flowers, such as are not seen in this world are beheld by me, and in the form of their leaf & flowers of surpassing beauty. These are attended with a sense of <u>realness</u>, as much so as objects seen in an earthly landscape. By means of what Swedenborg calls "cogitative speaking" or thought speaking, which is the mode in which angels converse with each other & with men, it has been given me, at times to hold conversation with spiritual beings. Simitarity [Similarity] of affectional state, is nearness among spirits. We are always associated with our like in the spiritual realm. To think of some one of those whom you have known from personal acquaintance or have read or heard of them from others causes that spirit to be <u>consciously</u> present, for thought of another always occasions a sort of spiritual presence.

Then I ask a question & make a remark in thought, which is perceived by the sp. or angel, and he replies in thought, which I intuitively perceive, & sometimes almost seem to hear. This is all effected in accordance with the laws of the mind or spirit. It is no miracle, any more than our daily conversation with our family or neighbors. I receive in this way many important truths of wisdom— Last night or rather this morning at 2 O clock I awoke from sleep & received an important suggestion relating to the removal of diseased conditions from the body. Where a disease tends to produce a particular & unhealthy mental condition, as melancholy or low spirits, by dyspepsia or diseased liver, if the opposite mental state can be induced, it will tend to cure the diseas. This is a principle of great extent. Disease should be studied in relation to its effects upon the mind, & then the states of mind that are antagonistic to the disease may be induced, through the spiritual world.

Nov. 2.[380] For some time past have been much drawn to Jesus. He is becoming more & more the central point of my existence. I have of late had some interesting experiences of interior vision, or intuition. Distance of space is sometimes annihilated, and I see persons & things a hundred miles off with great clearness. This is the Clairvoyant (clear seeing) state, or, as I choose to call it, a state of intuition or perception. It was enjoyed by the most Ancient Church, or the Paradisiacal state of the race. By it also, it is given me to perceive the thoughts and mental states of persons. This is the spiritual gift called <u>Discerning of Spirits</u>, which the apostles possessed. In the intuitional state, one has a clear perception of the nature of the sphere bodily & spiritual, exhaled by persons. Swedenborg speaks of this state as belonging to the angels. (See *Arcana Celestia.* n.)[381] It belongs also to the soul in the New Jerusalem state. The sensuous veil is removed from the interior vision, & we no longer see through a glass darkly, but with open vision—with unveiled face. In this state, my soul sometimes comes into the conscious perception of the Divine sphere of the Lord, and drinks in the life of Jesus. After being affected by the disquieting sphere of other minds, how sweet to be absent from the body & present with the Ld. Then I can say,

Jesus, the name that charms our fears,
That bids our sorrows cease;

Tis music in the sinners ears,
        Tis <u>life</u> & <u>health</u> and <u>peace</u>.[382]

Nov. 4. It is a declaration of Swedenborg, that we have vital communication with the Lord through the Word, He speaks to us by the word, & imparts his life to us, even to the ultimates of our being, by the Holy Scriptures. It is the bond of connection between us & the angelic heavens. Every passage of Scripture is an influx of the Ld's life, through the heavens, into the earth, & has extension into some society of heaven, so that in every passage we find a point where we come into communication with some angelic society, & by means of it the life of that society is imparted to us. It has been given me to have some experience & interior perception of the reality of this. By means of some passage of the Word we come within the sphere of a celestial society whose state is expressed by that passage. This can be made available in the removal of diseased states of the mind. Of this I have had experience. To illustrate this, if the soul is in a state of interior desolation, & there is an absense of all sensible delights, & great doubts & fears, let it slowly read the following verses from Habakuk: "Although the fig-tree shall not blossom, neither shall fruit be in the vine; the labor of the olive shall fail, & the fields shall yield no meat; the flock shall be cut off from the fold, & there shall be no herd in the stalls; yet I will rejoice in the Lord, I will joy in the God of my salvation. The Lord God is my strength, & he will make my feet like hinds feet, & he will make me to walk upon my high places.["][383] The fig-tree is the perception of good or delight in the natural man, the fruit of the vine, the delight, of the spiritual mind, & the labor or fruit of the olive, the perception of delight in the celestial degree of the mind. If all this is absent, then by means of the words following we come into the sphere of angels whose state is thus expressed: ["]I will rejoice in the Lord. I will joy in the God of my salvation. The Lord God is my strength, & he will make my feet like hinds feet, & he will make me to walk upon my high places."[384] Sometimes instantly the soul will feel an influx of calm tranquil joy, that will even ultimate itself in the body, causing a pleasant sensation in the nervous plexus at the pit of the stomach. The feet represent the ultimates of our being, & to make our feet like hind's feet, is to cause heavenly & spiritual delights to pervade with a thrill of life & pleasure the body itself, carrying health to all the organic tisues. To walk upon our <u>high places</u> is significant of peace & internal felicity, which ultimates itself in tranquility & external delight.

In states of great temptation when the soul is assailed by principalities & powers of darkness, let it remember there are angels who minister to the tempted spirit, & whose office it is, & whose delight it is, to disperse evil spirits, & deliver the struggling soul. When the ark set forward in the wilderness, which signifies the progress of the temptation combats, Moses said, "Rise up, Jehovah, & let thine enemies be scattered; & let them that hate thee flee before thee."[385] In these words there is living connection with the hosts of angelic deliverers, before the influx of whose sphere, our spiritual foes will be dispersed, like the stubble before the whirlwind.[386] And we shall have occasion to repeat the formula used, when the ark rested, which signifies the end of temptation, & the return of peace & tranquility to the interior & external man: "Return, O Jehovah, unto the ten thousand thousands of Israel."[387] Saying this, the struggling, disquieted spirit, takes shelter from the assailing storm, within the enclosure of the sphere of celestial hosts. This is not imaginary, but as vitally real as the life of God. There is a power in the Word, but poorly apprehended, & less experienced by the people of God. The Word is the medium of the conjunction of the heavens with man, as Swd has shown, in the *H & H.* 303–310.[388] It is the point where the soul meets the heavens, & mingles its life with the life of angels, & drinks in <u>life</u>, & <u>health and peace</u>.

If we are cast down, & the melancholy shades of the realms of night are thrown across the pathway of our spirit—& who is not sometimes in that state—there is a standing-ground for the soul within the hallowed limits of the Word, where we may commune with a realm, where all is calm & pure, & joyful. There is a door-way for the soul into that blissful clime. "In that day thou shalt say, O Ld, I will praise thee: though thou wast angry with me, thine anger is turned away, & thou comfortedst me. Behold, God is my salvation, I will trust & not be afraid: for the Lord <u>Jehovah</u> is my strength & my song; He also is become my salvation.["][389] Then the singular form of expression is changed to the plural, to indicate that the joys of angels mingle with the delights of our souls, and,

    "scenes of earth
And heaven are mixed, as flesh & soul in man."[390]

"Therefore with joy shall ye draw water out of the fountains of salvation.["] (Isa. 12:1–3.)[391]

"Why not learn to conquer sorrow?
  Why not learn to smile at pain?
Why should every stormy morrow
  Shroud our way in gloom again?

Why not lift the soul immortal
  Up to its angelic hight—
Bid it pass the radient portal
  Of the world of faith & light.

Oh! there is an other being
  All about us, all above,
Hid from mortal sense or seeing
  Save the nameless sense of love.

Not the love that dies like roses,
  When the frost-fire scathes the sod,
But the eternal rest that closes
  Round the soul that dwells in God.

Into this great habitation
  Never tear or sorrow came,
Oh, it is the new creation,
  God its light, his love its flame.

Up, O soul, & dwell forever
  On this hidden, glorious shore;
Chilled by cloud-shade never, never,
  Up & dwell forevermore."[392]

It is through the word, we have vital connection with that happy realm, that summer clime, that blissful shore.

There is also healing power for the body in the divine Word. Here is the tree of life, "& the fruit thereof shall be for meat & the leaf thereof for medicine.["] ["]The leaves of this tree are for the healing of the nations.["][393]

The life of the body is from the soul, & all diseases originate in the mind. The states of the mind are the body's health or malady. The body lives from the soul, and the soul from God, whose life descends through the heavens above. Swd discloses the fact, which the sensuous mind will be slow to admit, & dull to apprehend, that our connection with the angel world is a vital one, & were it sundered for a moment we should cease to live. All thought & affection, which constitute the life of the human spirit, are derived thence, & are an influx from that unseen realm of being. He often asserts that "without communication by spirits with the world of spirits, & by angels with heaven, & thus through heaven with the Lord, it would be utterly impossible for man to live; for his life depends entirely on such conjunction, so that supposing spirits and angels to depart from him, he would instantly perish." (A.C. 50.)[394] But as we have seen, the orderly divine method of communion with the angel world is through the medium of the Word. Here we have access to a realm & sphere of being where all is life. Sickness & sorrow, pain & death, never invade that world of life. Communion with those, who drink in life from its central Source, the Sun of the spiritual world, whose light is wisdom & whose heat is love, will send a thrill of life into even the decaying members of the body. It will cause life immortal to seize & animate our clay. It is a fact, that few will admit, & the truth of which still fewer have any interior perception of, that without the Word, through which the Divine Life & the life of Heaven could desend to this earth, the human race would perish. The Word is as the life's blood of the world. All things were made by it, & without it was not anything made that was made.[395] All diseases, according to Swd, have correspondence with the sp. world & with diseased mind there. States of health have correspondence with the heavens, & with the spirits of the blessed. If by the Word we have communication with a clime, where disease is unknown, & if through that connection we are linked to the Great Central Life, here is revealed a divine method of cure. In that living realm, there are societies whose office & joy it is to minister to minds diseased. The descending influx of those societies, becomes here according to the law of correspondence, the healing of the body. By the Word we may drink in life from such immortal fountains, & be bound in the same bundle of life with the Ld our God & his holy angels. This health-imparting influence descends first to the soul, & then extends outward to the body. Jesus thus healed the sick, restoring soul and body together. From Him went forth healing virtue, first to the soul, & then new life thrilled through all the organs of the physical frame. This is the the Divine Method of cure, & is as available & efficient today as it was eighteen centuries ago.[396] In sickness we may still say, "Why art thou cast down, O my soul, & why art thou disquieted within me? Hope thou in God, for I shall yet praise him, who is the health of my countenance, and my God.["][397] The Lord healed the sick with his Word, & that Word still lives & speaks to men. In it is enclosed the life of God & of angels. If any diseased state of the body is caused by some pre-existing condition of the spirit, to induce upon ourselves the opposite & healthy state of mind, will cure the disease. This can be done by our connection with the angel world through the Word. Here is a remedy always at hand, always safe, always efficient. Here is the voice of the Great Physician, before whose potent words, disease & death retire. His healing power is imparted through faith.[398] "Thy faith hath made the[e] whole," was a declaration he often made to those he healed.[399] The laws of our being are the same today. He is as near to us, as he was to men when he walked over the hills & through the vales of the Holy Land. Faith in him has the same potent efficacy today as then. Had men the same undoubting faith in the power of Jesus to save that the diseased woman had, who said within herself, "If I may but touch the hem or fringe of his garment, I shall be made whole,"[400] the same result would follow.

Nov. 5. Had this evening a most affecting vision of the connection of the Word with the Heavens. The heaven seemed spread out over a wide extended surface, as far as the eye could reach, before my inward sight while I was in the interior state. Its hills & mountains were covered with a soft silvery light, which cannot be described, it was so pure & tranquil. From those wide extended plains there flowed down innumerable rays of light, which all centered upon the Word, & rested upon & terminated in some passage of the Word, to each verse & word a ray. This was like an immense cone of light with its apex resting upon the Holy Volume, & made up of millions of separate rays. Then there extended upward the same number of these celestial rays which centered in the Lord, who appeared as far above the heavens as the Word did below, thus constituting two cones of heavenly radience the bases of which came together on

the celestial plains, showing how each separate ray proceeded from the
Lord through the heavens and terminated in some passage of the Holy
Scriptures. There was also a delightful and ineffable perception of life in
the rays, seeming as if they were life itself—as the Lord said, "The words
that I speak unto you, they are spirit & they are life."[401] Perhaps the vision
would be of no use to any one else, but I can never forget it, nor, I trust,
lose the impression it made upon my mind. It has left upon [my] spirit a
clearer perception & a stronger faith in the Divine vitality of the Word. It
demonstrated to my inner perception, that the Word of the Lord is quick
(or living) & powerful. It is the life of the heavens, & the life of God is in
it, & by it is communicable to us. This is to me a demonstrated fact & not
a mere theory of the intellect.

The connection of the Word with the heavens & through the heavens
with the Lord, also follows from the doctrine of Correspondences according to which it is written, Correspondence is not an imaginary, but
vital relation, being that of cause & effect. Every passage corresponds to
something in the heavens, & in its inmost sense to the Lord.

Nov. 6. There is no doctrine of more importance in the sp. life, than
that the Lord is the one only Life. That we have no life in ourselves, but
live only from a perpetual influx of life from above. Every thought and
affection flow in, & do not originate in us. Should this influx be cut off
& we left to ourselves we should instantly die. All thought & affection
would instantly perish. The proprium or self-hood of man, or the appearance that life is self-originated, is only a mere seeming.[402] It is a fallacy of
the natural mind. God above has proprium or self-existence. All other
beings live from and in him. The angels have an intuitive perception of
this, and so far as we rise toward the celestial state, we are perceptive of
the same infinite verity. This was the Paradisiacal state—the garden of
Eden. It was the Golden Age. It also belongs to the New Jerusalem. Today
I had a clearer perception of this truth than ever before. I seemed to be
annihilated as to my own being. I became as nothing. All love of self was
gone, for I could find no self to love. Never could I say so fully as in that
memorable moment, "I no longer live, but Christ liveth in me."[403] These
words had a clearness, a fulness, a depth of meaning, I never before discerned in them. The original state of man, (or man in Paradise,) was one

of self-annihilation. He appropriated nothing to himself, neither good nor evil. It is the steady aim of the Lords Providence to bring all souls back to the intuition of this one truth, the foundation & the essence of all wisdom. It is the key that unlocks all the mysteries of the Lord's dealings with us. Self-love is the vital root of all evil, it is the essence of all sin. We never can be cured of the love of self, only so far as it is demonstrated to us that our self-hood is a nothing; —that the very idea of self is an infinite falsity—a terrible delusion. The only proprium which any one can claim is a dead capacity—a lifeless receptivity. All its good is an inflowing from Him who alone is good—the Good One. All its evil is an influx from the abyss. He who in the light of the Lord has come to realize this, to whom it is no mere theory but an intuitive fact, claims no merit, feels no guilt. He appropriates to himself neither good or evil. His thoughts are no longer his own, nor his affections, nor his desires.

Himself, redeemed to a dead capacity, claims nothing, owns nothing, merits nothing. He seeks no reward for well doing, fears no punishment for evil. To him all truth in the universe is reducible to two axioms—the all & the nothing—God the All, himself the nothing. The words I, me, & mine, assume another meaning—they lose their significance. They no longer express a truth but a necessary & eternal falsity. But few can understand this. It will be foolishness to some, to others a stumbling block. Only a few souls in this world of sense ever climb up to this celestial hight, when this angelic wisdom flashes upon the illuminated soul. "W[h]osoever hath ears to hear, let him hear."[404]

Nov. 7. Have a great desire to preach the Gospel again. "Who is sufficient for these things?"[405] To be fully prepared for this great use, the highest office in the kingdom of God on earth, I am impressed that two things are necessary. In the first place, in preparing a sermon for the people, the minister must be able to enter the interior state, so that spiritual light may be able to flow into his receptive & divinely illuminated mind. His mind must be open & passive towards the heavens. In this state, through the Divine Mercy of the Lord I have now been for several years. I have seen wondrous things out of the law. Views of heavenly truth ineffable & most glorious. I have been able to sit within the sphere of heavenly radiance. This is a negative or passive condition of the mind. He who can enter into this interior state and exalted condition of the mental powers is divinely fitted to receive. But in order to impart to the famishing multitudes, the minister must possess the power voluntarily to pass into another state while preaching. He must be able to come down from celestial hights to the natural plane, the level & range of the popular mind. And he must be able to bring down in his descent from the mountain summit the <u>law written on tables of stone</u>, as Moses did. Or in other words must be able to present celestial & spiritual truth so that it will be apprehensible by the sensuous mind. Christ taught his favored disciples on the mount, but the multitude, on the sea-shore. The sea signifies the <u>external</u> of heaven & the Church. "Jesus went out of the house and sat by the sea-side. And great multitudes were gathered together unto him, so that he went into a ship, and sat; and the whole multitude stood on the shore. And he spake many things unto them in parables." (Mat. 13:1–3.) From the mount of transfiguration where the sermon is prepared and truth received, the minister must descend to the shore of the sea of Galilee. He must go out of the house,—the interior state, the negative, passive condition of the mind—& by means of figures & illustrations borrowed from the world of sense, present celestial truth in a natural dress. In the receptive state, when the soul is in the spirit, or retired into itself from the realm of sense, like John in Patmos, the fore brain becomes <u>passively active</u>. The back brain is quiescent. But in order to preach to the multitude, the back brain must be called into voluntary action, & its vital force thrown forward. He who can do this, at pleasure, is prepared to preach. He must be able to enter into a state of spirit, or he will receive nothing, & consequently have nothing to give. He must be able to come down from the mount, bringing with him the law written on tables of stone, or he will be out of sympathy with the multitude. From being negative, he must become positive. From being passive he must become active. If he goes before the congregation in the interior state, which is a negative one, & receptive of influx from above, he will be affected by the sphere of his hearers. He must be so positive as to disperse that sphere & cause his own to fill the place & control all other minds.[406]

NOTES

INTRODUCTION

1. For a fuller discussion of the life and significance of Emanuel Swedenborg germane to my remarks here, see Catherine L. Albanese, *A Republic of Mind and Spirit: A Cultural History of American Metaphysical Religion* (New Haven, Conn.: Yale University Press, 2007), 140–42.

2. W. F. Evans, *The Happy Islands; Or, Paradise Restored* (Boston: H. V. Degen, 1860).

3. William J. Leonard, "Warren Felt Evans, M.D.: An Account of His Life and His Services as the First Author of the Metaphysical Healing Movement," *Practical Ideals* 10, no. 3 (November 1905): 21. Leonard produced a four-part series in the New Thought periodical *Practical Ideals* from September–October 1905 through January 1906. Besides using Evans's journals from 1850 to 1865, Evans's published books, and writings by Julius and Annetta Dresser (see below in the text) and their son, Horatio, he relied on personal recollections he received from Julius A. Dresser and John Hamlin Dewey, M.D., a mental-healing author and practitioner. Leonard himself was a minister, but his denomination is unknown. He became secretary of the newly formed New Thought Metaphysical Alliance in 1906. Leonard's earliest sketch of Evans's life was published in an eight-page pamphlet in 1903: William J. Leonard, *The Pioneer Apostle of Mental Science: A Sketch of the Life and Work of the Reverend W. F. Evans, M.D.* (Boston: H. H. Carter, 1903).

4. See William J. Leonard, "Warren Felt Evans, M.D.: An Account of His Life and His Services as the First Author of the Metaphysical Healing Movement," *Practical Ideals* 10, no. 2 (September–October 1905): 6.

5. W. F. Evans, *The Celestial Dawn; Or, Connection of Earth and Heaven* (Boston: James P. Magee, 1862).

6. W. F. Evans, *Mental Medicine: A Theoretical and Practical Treatise on Medical Psychology* (1872; reprint, Boston: H. H. Carter, 1885), 210.

7. Julius A. Dresser, *The True History of Mental Science: A Lecture Delivered at the Church of the Divine Unity, Boston, Mass., on Sunday Evening Feb. 6, 1887* (Boston: Alfred A. Mudge, 1887), 21. Leonard quotes Dresser in "Warren Felt Evans, M.D," *Practical Ideals* 10, no. 3 (November 1905): 2.

8. A.J. Swarts, as quoted in Mitch Horowitz, *One Simple Idea: How Positive Thinking Reshaped Modern Life* (New York: Crown, 2014), 31.

9. See Keith McNeil, *A Story Untold: A History of the Quimby-Evans Debate* (2016), 1172–73, 1246–58, on-line publication at http://ppquimby-mbeddydebate.com/. For some of the chief sources of the traditional account, see Horatio W. Dresser, ed., *The Quimby Manuscripts* (1921; reprint, Secaucus, N.J.: Citadel, 1961), 16; Horatio W. Dresser, *Health and the Inner Life: An Analytical and Historical Study of Spiritual Healing Theories, with an Account of the Life and Teachings of P. P. Quimby* (New York: G. P. Putnam's Sons, 1906), 114–21; Leonard, *Pioneer Apostle*, 1–5 (quoted at length in Dresser's *Health and the Inner Life*); Leonard, "Warren Felt Evans, M.D.," *Practical Ideals* 10, no. 2 (September–October 1905): 1–4; Charles S. Braden, *Spirits in Rebellion: The Rise and Development of New Thought* (Dallas: Southern Methodist University Press, 1963), 90–92. My own *Republic of Mind and Spirit* largely follows the traditional account—see Albanese, *Republic of Mind and Spirit*, 300, 303–5. McNeil lists the historiography much more extensively in *Story Untold*, 1150–53.

10. For evidence of Evans's work as a colporteur, see McNeil, *Story Untold*, 1251.

11. Leonard, "Warren Felt Evans, M.D.," *Practical Ideals* 10, no. 3 (November 1905): 17–18 and n11.

12. Ibid., 2–5.

13. Dresser, *True History*, 21.

14. Keith McNeil suggests an even earlier December 1858 entry because of Evans's mid-month reference to a "lofty mountain" and "the correspondence which subsists between things in the natural world and the spiritual world" (McNeil, *Story Untold*, 1161).

15. Evans, as we shall see, published two books in 1860, the second, most likely, the forty-eight-page *Divine Order in the Process of Full Salvation* (Boston: Henry V. Degen, 1860). While, on first reading, this second work seems overtly closest to Evans's Methodist spirituality, it is actually an exposition of Swedenborgian theological views, without citing the Swedish theologian himself. The autobiographical account of spiritual odyssey makes most sense chronologically as a predecessor of the Swedenborgian *Divine Order*. Moreover, as Keith McNeil has pointed out in personal correspondence, Evans habitually listed his previously published titles in front matter for each new book, beginning with his third, *Celestial Dawn*. The sequence lists *Happy Islands* first and *Divine Order* second.

16. Evans, *Happy Islands*, 3, 14–15, 18–20.

17. Ibid., 26–27.

18. Ibid., 39–40.

19. Ibid., 40–42.

20. Phoebe Palmer, *The Way of Holiness* (New York: Palmer and Hughes, 1845), 60–70. Palmer (1807–1874), with her physician husband Walter Clark Palmer, was drawn to Wesleyan perfectionism and after 1830 promoted her understanding of it. Aside from her writings and travels, she is especially remembered for her leadership of the well-known Tuesday Meeting for the Promotion of Holiness.

21. Evans, *Happy Islands,* 43–44.

22. Ibid., 44–45.

23. Ibid., 167–68.

24. Ibid., 175, 179.

25. Ralph Waldo Emerson, "The Over-Soul," in Ralph Waldo Emerson, *Essays: First Series,* in *The Collected Works of Ralph Waldo Emerson,* ed. Alfred R. Ferguson et al., vol. 2 (Cambridge, Mass.: Harvard University Press, 1979), 159–60.

26. Ralph Waldo Trine, *In Tune with the Infinite* (1897; Indianapolis: Bobbs-Merrill, 1970), 167, 47.

27. Evans, *Happy Islands*, 259–60.

28. Ibid., 246–48.

29. As I have already noted, the autobiographical *Happy Islands* seems the logical predecessor of this work, which—as we shall see—presents a closet form of Swedenborgian theology.

30. Evans, *Divine Order*, 3, 4, 7, 9, 13.

31. Ibid., 17, 24. The holiness movement blossomed fully after the Civil War, teaching the experience of entire sanctification by the Holy Spirit, which brought perfection. Eventually, the movement became the source of a series of denominations, the largest and most well-known being the Church of the Nazarene.

32. Palmer, *Way of Holiness*, 60–70.

33. Evans, *Divine Order*, 24.

34. Ibid., 45.

35. William E. Boardman, *Higher Christian Life* (Boston: Hoyt, 1858).

36. Evans, *Divine Order*, 35, 33, 34.

37. Ibid., 38–39.

38. Palmer herself had claimed an experience of entire sanctification in 1837.

39. Evans, *Divine Order*, 46–47.

40. See Patricia A. Ward, *Experimental Theology in America: Madame Guyon, Fénelon, and Their Readers* (Waco, Tex.: Baylor University Press, 2009), 6, 10.

41. W. F. Evans, *The Celestial Dawn; Or, Connection of Earth and Heaven* (Boston: T. H. Carter, 1864).

42. Evans, *Celestial Dawn* (1862), 79–80, 72, 74, 76. All future references to *Celestial Dawn* will be to the 1862 edition.

43. Ibid., 128–29; Charles G. Finney, *Guide to the Savior; Or, Conditions of Attaining to and Abiding in Entire Holiness of Heart and Life* (Oberlin, Ohio: James M. Fitch, 1848).

44. Evans, *Celestial Dawn*, 127–28.

45. George Berkeley (1685–1753), the Anglo-Irish bishop of Cloyne, taught a doctrine of "immaterialism" or "subjective idealism," denying the existence of matter as a metaphysical substance in an attempt to refute what he saw as the materialism of his age. At the same time, he did not argue against the existence of physical objects.

46. Ibid., 15, 42, 53–54, 103–4, 188–89. Jonathan Edwards found divine truth in the sense experience of nature in his unpublished manuscript "The Images of Divine Things." See Jonathan Edwards, *Images or Shadows of Divine Things*, ed. Perry Miller (1948; reprint, Westport, Conn.: Greenwood Press, 1977).

47. Miller, "Introduction," in Edwards, *Images or Shadows*, 36.

48. Evans, *Celestial Dawn*, 195.

49. Ibid., 264.

50. W. F. Evans, *The New Age and Its Messenger* (Boston: T. H. Carter, 1864). The work was published simultaneously in London by Charles P. Alvey.

51. Ibid., 35.

52. Ibid., 19. Emphasis in original.

53. Ralph Waldo Emerson, *Nature*, in *The Collected Works of Ralph Waldo Emerson*, ed. Alfred R. Ferguson et al., vol. 1 (Cambridge, Mass.: Harvard University Press, 1971), 17–18. Emerson's ideas—and even language—here were influenced by Swedenborgian Sampson Reed.

54. Evans, *New Age*, 21–22.

55. Ibid., 23–25. Emphasis in original.

56. Ibid., 31. Emphasis in original.

57. Ibid., 34. Emphasis in original.

58. Ibid., 71, 87, 94. Emphasis in original. For Swedenborg's journeys to other planets, see Emanuel Swedenborg, *Life on Other Planets* (*De Telluribus in Mundo Nostro Solari, Quae Vocantur Planetae*, 1758), trans. John Chadwick (1997; reprint, West Chester, Pa.: Swedenborg Foundation, 2006).

59. These published works are W. F. Evans, *The Mental-Cure, Illustrating the Influence of the Mind on the Body, Both in Health and Disease and the Psychological Method of Treatment* (Boston: H. H. and T. W. Carter, 1869); Evans, *Mental Medicine* (1872); W. F. Evans, *Soul and Body; or, The Spiritual Science of Health and Disease* (Boston: Colby and Rich, 1876); W. F. Evans, *The Divine Law of Cure* (Boston: H. H. Carter, 1881); W. F. Evans, *The Primitive Mind-Cure: The Nature and Power of Faith; or, Elementary Lessons in Christian Philosophy and Transcendental Medicine* (Boston: H. H. Carter and Karrick, 1885); and W. F. Evans, *Esoteric Christianity and Mental Therapeutics* (Boston: H. H. Carter and Karrick, 1886). The unpublished manuscript (ca. 1883 [McNeil, *Story Untold*, v]) resides in the National Library of Medicine in Bethesda, Maryland.

60. McNeil, *Story Untold*, n133, 1388.

61. Evans, *Divine Law of Cure*, 153. See McNeil, *Story Untold*, 1155.

62. McNeil, *Story Untold*, n2, 1177.

63. Robert Allen Campbell, biographical sketch of Evans, in *The Christian Metaphysician* (November 1888), as cited in McNeil, *Story Untold*, n133, 1389.

64. For example, the 15th edition (a reprint for all intents and purposes) of *Mental Medicine: A Theoretical and Practical Treatise* (Boston: H. H. Carter, 1885) bears the "Rev." on its title page. The first edition was published in 1872.

65. A Christian Scientist, "Evans's Esoteric Christianity," *The Christian Science Journal* 4, no. 5 (August 1886): 105.

66. Ibid., 106.

67. Evans, *Primitive Mind-Cure*; H. P. Blavatsky, *Isis Unveiled: A Master-Key to the Mysteries of Ancient and Modern Science and Theology*, 2 vols. (New York: J. W. Bouton, 1877).

68. Evans, *Esoteric Christianity*, 5, 11–21.

69. Ibid., 15.

70. Ibid., 46.

71. Ibid., 17.

72. Ibid., 46–47. Emphases in original.

73. Ibid., 28. Emphasis in original.

74. Ibid., 23. Emphasis in original. I am indebted to Professor James Lawrence of the Pacific School of Religion for the assessment of complex dualism and integrated monism.

75. Ibid., 16.

76. Ibid., 114.

77. Ibid., 173–74.

78. For biographies of Horace Bushnell from which this summary is drawn, see Mary Bushnell Cheney, *Life and Letters of Horace Bushnell* (New York: Harper and Brothers, 1880); Theodore T. Munger, *Horace Bushnell: Preacher and Theologian* (Boston: Houghton Mifflin, 1899); Barbara M. Cross, *Horace Bushnell: Minister to a Changing America* (Chicago: University of Chicago Press, 1958); Robert L. Edwards, *Of Singular Genius, Of Singular Grace:*

A Biography of Horace Bushnell (Cleveland: Pilgrim Press, 1992); Robert Bruce Mullin, *The Puritan as Yankee: A Life of Horace Bushnell* (Grand Rapids, Mich.: William B. Eerdmans, 2002). See, also, Catherine L. Albanese, "Horace Bushnell among the Metaphysicians," *Church History* 79, no. 3 (September 2010): 1–40.

79. Cheney, *Life and Letters*, 85, 105.

80. Bushnell actually published two works on Christian nurture in 1847: Horace Bushnell, *Discourses on Christian Nurture* (Boston: Massachusetts Sabbath School Society, 1847) was suppressed by the society because it was so controversial; when that happened, Bushnell took its contents and appended a response to the society and other materials in *Views of Christian Nurture and of Subjects Adjacent Thereto* (Hartford, Conn.: Edwin Hunt, 1847). Bushnell's work was later amply revised and enlarged, with the standard edition becoming *Christian Nurture* (Hartford, Conn.: Brown and Parsons, 1861). For his controversial work two years later, see Horace Bushnell, *God in Christ: Three Discourses, Delivered at New Haven, Cambridge, and Andover, with a Preliminary Dissertation on Language* (Hartford, Conn.: Brown and Parsons, 1849).

81. Horace Bushnell, *Christ in Theology: Being the Answer of the Author before the Hartford Central Association of Ministers, October, 1849, for the Doctrines of the Book Entitled "God in Christ"* (Hartford, Conn.: Brown and Parsons, 1851).

82. Ibid., 37–38.

83. Horace Bushnell, *Nature and the Supernatural, As Together Constituting the One System of God* (New York: C. Scribner, 1858); on Davis's comments, see A.J. Davis, "A Letter to Rev. Dr. Bushnell" (Hartford, December 15, 1851), in Andrew Jackson Davis, *The Approaching Crisis: Being a Review of Dr. Bushnell's Course of Lectures, on the Bible, Nature, Religion, Skepticism, and the Supernatural* (Boston: Colby and Rich, 1868), 7–8 (emphases in original).

84. See, for example, Winthrop S. Hudson on "the mediating theology of Horace Bushnell," in *Religion in America* (New York: Charles Scribner's Sons, 1965), 175–78; Cheney, *Life and Letters*, 195; Munger, *Horace Bushnell*, 43; Cross, *Horace Bushnell*, 28; Edwards, *Singular Genius*, 295; Mullin, *Puritan as Yankee*, 6, 126. My own essay in *Church History*, "Horace Bushnell among the Metaphysicians," obviously does explore Bushnell's metaphysical inclinations.

85. See Albanese, "Horace Bushnell," 9.

86. Horace Bushnell, *Nature and the Supernatural, As Together Constituting the One System of God* (1858; reprint, London: Alexander Strahan, 1864), 234, 325–26.

87. Ibid., 226–27.

88. Cheney, *Life and Letters*, 64, 46; see, also, Mullin, *Puritan as Yankee*, 41; Emerson, *Nature*, 10.

89. Thomas C. Upham, *Life and Religious Opinions and Experience of Madame de La Mothe Guyon: Together with Some Account of the Personal History and Religious Opinions of Fénelon, Archbishop of Cambray*, 2 vols. (New York: Harper, 1846). For a discussion of Bushnell's attraction to quietism in a broader nineteenth-century context, see Ward, *Experimental Theology in America*, 178–83.

90. Mullin, *Puritan as Yankee*, 6.

91. Bushnell, *God in Christ*, 30, 78.

92. Frank B. Carpenter, "Studio Talks with Dr. Horace Bushnell," *The Independent* 52, no. 2667 (January 11, 1900): 117, 117–19.

93. "Obituary Record of the Graduates of Bowdoin College and the Medical School of Maine for the Year Ending 1 June 1893," *Bowdoin College Library Bulletin*, no. 4, Second Series: 138; B. F. Barrett, *A Cloud of Independent Witnesses to the Truth, Value, Need, and Spiritual*

Helpfulness of Swedenborg's Teachings (Philadelphia: Swedenborg Publishing Association, 1891), 171.

94. Cheney, *Life and Letters*, 76, 276–77, 516.

95. David L. Smith, *Symbolism and Growth: The Religious Thought of Horace Bushnell* (Chico, Calif.: Scholars Press, 1981), 52, 56; William Alexander Johnson, *Nature and the Supernatural in the Theology of Horace Bushnell* (Lund, Swed.: CSK Gleerup, 1963), 13, 231. For a fuller discussion, see Albanese, "Horace Bushnell among the Metaphysicians," 19.

96. R. Laurence Moore, "The Occult Connection? Mormonism, Christian Science, and Spiritualism," in *The Occult in America: New Historical Perspectives*, ed. Howard Kerr and Charles L. Crow (Urbana: University of Illinois Press, 1983), 135; Fred Somkin, *Unquiet Eagle: Memory and Desire in the Idea of American Freedom, 1815–1860* (Ithaca, N.Y.: Cornell University Press, 1967).

97. Mark Twain and Charles Dudley Warner, *The Gilded Age: A Tale of To-day* (Hartford, Conn.: American Publishing, 1873); Paul A. Carter, *The Spiritual Crisis of the Gilded Age* (DeKalb: Northern Illinois University Press, 1971).

98. Donald Meyer, *The Positive Thinkers: Religion as Pop Psychology from Mary Baker Eddy to Oral Roberts*, 2d ed. (New York: Pantheon Books, 1980), esp. 177–80.

99. Gilbert Seldes, *The Stammering Century* (New York: John Day, 1928).

100. See, for an extended discussion, Robert C. Fuller, *Spiritual but Not Religious: Understanding Unchurched America* (New York: Oxford University Press, 2001).

JOURNAL I (1850–1857)

1. Deleted in ms. Hereafter, as stipulated in "A Note to Readers," use of the symbols {} will signify Evans's deletions.

2. Cf. 2 Chron. 14:11, which Evans modifies. All biblical citations refer to the King James Version, which Evans was using.

3. James Caughey, *Methodism in Earnest: The History of a Revival in Great Britain in Which Twenty Thousand Souls Professed Faith in Christ, and Ten Thousand Professed Sanctification . . . with the Labors of the Rev. James Caughey* (1859).

4. Oliver Goldsmith, *The Captivity, An Oratorio* (1764). Evans quotes from memory and modifies the text.

5. Interspersed throughout Evans's journals are parentheses, the intention of which is not completely clear but which appear to be related to his writing projects, as some evidence in his published works suggests. Sometimes, in fact, there is an opening or closing parenthesis without its obligatory partner. And sometimes, too, the marks are nondescript enough that whether or not they are actually parentheses is not entirely clear. I have opted to treat all such marks as parentheses.

6. Mount Ascutney in southeastern Vermont, 3,144 feet high.

7. Vermont.

8. William Tell, the legendary fourteenth-century figure who is the national hero of Switzerland, was remembered as a mountaineer who stood up to an Austrian Habsburg attempt to seize the forest cantons of his native region.

9. Mount Kearsarge, in Merrimack County, New Hampshire, stands 2,937 feet high.

10. "The men of Nineveh shall rise in judgment with this generation, and shall condemn it: because they repented at the preaching of Jonas; and, behold, a greater than Jonas *is* here." Italics in biblical quotations here and below follow the practice of the King James Version.

11. "What could have been done more to my vineyard, that I have not done in it? where-fore, when I looked that it should bring forth grapes, brought it forth wild grapes?"

12. "Brethren, I count not myself to have apprehended but *this* one thing *I do*, forgetting those things which are behind, and reaching forth unto those things which are before. I press toward the mark for the prize of the high calling of God in Christ Jesus."

13. This is most probably the German Lutheran missionary Christian Frederick Swartz (1726–1798), noted for his work in India. He learned English as well as Tamil to advance his efforts.

14. Professor John W. Webster, who in a sensational case had been indicted before the Massachusetts Supreme Court for the murder of Dr. George Parkman.

15. Evans does not explain the absence of journal entries for more than ten months.

16. An acute febrile condition linked to a bacterially caused inflammation of the skin and subcutaneous tissue.

17. Ps. 116:6.

18. John 1:29, 36.

19. Ps. 127:2.

20. The man was a nineteenth-century Chinese merchant executed for murdering his wife. He died on the nineteenth day. The incident is recounted in Paul Martin, *Counting Sheep: The Science and Pleasures of Sleep and Dreams* (New York: St. Martin's Press, 2002), 71.

21. John Wesley (1703–1791), founder of Methodism.

22. Note the fourteen-month lapse, again without explanation.

23. Concord, New Hampshire.

24. A lapse of almost five months.

25. The Methodist General Biblical Institute functioned as a seminary in Concord, New Hampshire, from 1847 to 1867, beginning in a recently vacated Congregational church. It involved a relocation and reorganization of the Newbury (Vermont) Biblical Institute, with students, library, and finances all transferred to the new institution. Osmon C. Baker, who had directed the seminary program at Newbury, moved to the new institution and taught there until he was elected bishop in 1852.

26. From the poem "Spring" by John Milton (1608–1674). In a practice of intertextuality common at the time, the lines were borrowed by Scottish poet James Thomson in "Spring" (1728), which became part of his larger poetic work *The Seasons* (1730). Evans could have read the lines from either source.

27. Methodist love feasts were intimate rituals combining prayer, hymnody, and a community meal. Practiced among the Moravians and observed by John Wesley, at his direction they became part of Methodist worship—by the nineteenth century typically at quarterly and then annual meetings. Love feasts were times to dissolve all hardness and unforgiveness and to experience and express harmony and unity in Christian fellowship.

28. John 4:34.

29. The Rev. Dr. John Dempster was president and primary teacher of the Biblical Institute at this time. Evans was apparently substituting for him, hearing student recitations while he was away at a Methodist conference.

30. Founded in 1795 in Schenectady, New York, Union College was a nondenominational institution dedicated to liberal arts education.

31. The Mohawk River, with its mouth in the Hudson River, flows through Schenectady, New York. Its supporting canal was and is the Erie Canal.

32. This is the first line of British poet James Montgomery's poem "Friends" (1824). It was at some point set to music as a hymn that Methodists sang.

33. The line is from "Oft, in the Stilly Night (Scotch Air)" (ca. 1806–1807) by Irish poet Thomas Moore (1779–1852).

34. "I am the vine, ye *are* the branches: He that abideth in me, and I in him, the same bringeth forth much fruit: for without me ye can do nothing."

35. The "X"—which appears from time to time in journal entries—appears to be Evans's way of marking an item he deems especially noteworthy, often of a biographical nature. The practice suggests a habit of rereading entries after their first inscription.

36. Georg Christian Knapp, *Lectures on Christian Theology* (trans. Leonard Woods, 1831). Knapp (1753–1825) was a German Pietist who taught theology at the University of Halle. The work was used regularly as a textbook in nineteenth-century American Protestant seminaries. A second edition appeared in 1845, and it is more likely that Evans was using this or a later edition than the first, which was out of print at the time of the journal entry.

37. "Jesus answered and said unto him, What I do thou knowest not now; but thou shalt know hereafter."

38. After a gap of more than three years and three months, Evans here resumes his journal. He had left Concord, apparently in 1854, for a two-year appointment in Lisbon, New Hampshire, where as he now tells his journal he endured a season of spiritual struggle. The manuscript journal leaves a half page empty after his last June 1853 entry in Concord and begins the opposite page with the heading for still another New Hampshire appointment—this time in Claremont.

39. In Matt. 3:11, John the Baptist says to Jesus, "I indeed baptize you with water unto repentance: but he that cometh after me is mightier than I, whose shoes I am not worthy to bear: he shall baptize you with the Holy Ghost, and *with* fire." Evans's reference to the baptism of fire here indicates the attraction he felt for proto-holiness and—if we look toward the end of the century—proto-pentecostal spirituality.

40. This is the famed fifteenth-century devotional classic attributed to Thomas à Kempis (ca. 1380–1471), a medieval German monk, reflecting the evolving contemplative tradition in the Rhineland from the fourteenth century.

41. Significantly, the French quietist author and leader Madame Guyon (1647–1717), or Jeanne Marie Bouvières de la Mothe Guyon, was influenced in part by the work of Thomas à Kempis.

42. Luke 17:20–21.

43. 1 John 4:16.

44. Evans places an "X" above this journal entry, apparently marking it as especially significant. The entry itself suggests the influence of the quietism espoused by Madame Guyon.

45. Johann August Wilhelm Neander (1789–1850), a German church historian and theologian, was influenced by Friedrich Schleiermacher with his emphasis on religious feeling and Christian experience. Neander's greatest work, which stresses religious individualism, is his (English title) *General History of the Christian Religion and Church* (5 vols., 1825–1842), with a sixth volume published posthumously in 1852.

46. S. T. (Samuel Thomas) Bloomfield, Ἡ ΚΑΙΝΗ ΔΙΑΘΗΚΗ: *The Greek Testament with English Notes, Critical, Philological, and Exegetical*, appeared in its first American edition from the second London one in 1837 (Boston: Perkins and Marvin, and Philadelphia: Henry Perkins). Bloomfield (1790–1869) was an English cleric and New Testament scholar whose Greek New Testament was widely used in England and the United States.

47. Although Victor Cousin produced his *Introduction to the History of Philosophy* in 1832, Evans was more probably reading Cousin's later *Course of the History of Modern Philosophy*, translated by O. W. Wight (1852). Cousin (1792–1867), a French philosopher, was probably the most renowned such figure of his age.

48. Matt. 5:8; John 14:23. Evans enumerates and elaborates these three stages in W. F. Evans, *The Happy Islands; Or, Paradise Restored* (Boston: H. V. Degen, 1860), 179–82 and cites them again more loosely ibid., 292.

49. Ideas that ascribe human feelings to God.

50. Cf. 1 Cor. 13:12.

51. Cf. Rev. 1:8–11, with its testimony of Jesus as "Alpha and Omega" and its identification of the Aegean island of Patmos as the place where the author, called John, resided.

52. Evans echoes this verbal formulation in *Happy Islands*, 271.

53. Matt. 27:46, with Jesus quoting Ps. 22:1.

54. From Charles Wesley's hymn "Come, Holy Ghost, All Quickening Fire, Come," verse 2. Evans quotes the four verses of the hymn to conclude *Happy Islands* (333–34).

55. Evans, who is apparently quoting from memory, has transliterated, using Greek characters, the Greek ψυχή, for "flesh," instead of σάρξ, the usual term used in biblical Greek for "flesh." The second Greek term Evans uses, πνευμα, means "spirit." Although Evans's contrast between "psyche" and "pneuma"—to use the English transliterations—may seem a bit odd, it reflects 1 Cor. 15:44–49, in which Paul contrasts earthly ("psychic" or "natural") Christians with heavenly ("pneumatic" or "spiritual") ones. I am grateful to my colleague Professor Christine Thomas for her assistance here.

56. 2 Cor. 4:17.

57. Phil. 4:7.

58. "In those days was Hezekiah sick unto death. And Isaiah the prophet the son of Amoz came unto him, and said unto him, Thus saith the LORD, Set thine house in order for thou shalt die, and not live."

59. John 14:6.

60. Isaac Watts, "Ascending to Him in Heaven," verse 4. This poem appeared as a hymn in *Hymns for the Use of the Methodist Episcopal Church, Principally from the Collection of the Rev. John Wesley, M.A.* (New York: N. Bangs and T. Mason for the Methodist Episcopal Church, 1822), 256.

61. Matt. 11:28–29.

62. This untitled hymn (first line, "Saviour, the world's and mine") may be found in *Collection of Hymns, for the Use of the People Called Methodists, by the Rev. John Wesley, M.A.* (London: John Mason, 1845), hymn 27, verse 5.

63. Greek, "without blame." In Greek mythology, Momos (Momus) was a personification of mockery and complaint. (see Hesiod, *Theogony*, 214). He was expelled from Olympus for ridiculing the gods.

64. Jovinian was a fourth-century Italian who, after 385, was considered a "heretic" for his opposition to monasticism. Neander esteemed him next to Martin Luther for his services to the church. The quotation is from Neander, ostensibly quoting Jovinian's words, although scholars say the words of Jovinian are known only through his opponents. See Augustus Neander, *General History of the Christian Religion and Church*, trans. Joseph Torrey from the 1st rev. ed., and altered throughout according to the 2d ed., vol. 2, *Comprising the Second Great Division of the History* (Boston: Crocker and Brewster, 1848), 275. Evans interpolates the parenthetical "love" in the quotation.

65. According to a tradition that comes from late sources.

66. From the hymn "The Christian Zion," Ps. 48 (first line, "With stately towers and bulwarks strong"), verse 3. It may be found in the denominationally inclusive *A Collection of Psalms and Hymns for Christian Worship*, 13th ed. (Boston: Carter, Hendee, 1834), 272.

67. From the hymn "I Know That My Redeemer Lives," verse 7, in Charles Wesley, *Hymns and Sacred Poems* (1742).

68. See, in the translation from the Latin by John Payne, Thomas à Kempis, *Imitation of Christ*, "Of The Imitation of Christ, Book II (Instructions for the More Intimate Enjoyment of the Spiritual Life. Of Internal Conversation)," 1.

69. William Carvasso (1750–1834), apparently a Cornish farmer, left at his death a memoir of his life that provided important entrée into class-meeting practices in the late eighteenth and early nineteenth century. Edited by his son Benjamin Carvasso, the auto-biographical *Memoir of Mr. William Carvasso: Sixty Years as a Class Leader in the Wesleyan Methodist Connexion* appeared in a second edition by 1835–36 and was subsequently reis-sued thereafter at intervals under the title *The Great Efficacy of Simple Faith in the Atonement of Christ*.

70. Greek, "the beautiful, fair" ("to kalon" in English transcription).

71. Ps. 90:17.

72. Isa. 33:17.

73. This line evokes Song of Sol. 5:10, "chiefest among ten thousand." Perhaps more directly the source of Evans's reference is the hymn "The Lily of the Valley," attributed to Charles W. Fry in 1881, with its refrain, "He's the Lily of the Valley, the Bright and Morning Star, He's the fairest of ten thousand to my soul." Since Evans's entry is from 1856, it seems likely that the hymn, in some form, was part of the public domain before Fry became responsible for its last-ing version.

74. Cf. 1 John 4:13. "Hereby know we that we dwell in him, and he in us, because he hath given us of his Spirit."

75. Here Jesus tells his disciples that it is expedient for him to leave so that the Comforter will come and that when the Spirit of truth comes, he will guide them into all truth.

76. Karl Christian Tittmann's *Meletemata Sacra; Sive, Commentarius Exegetico-Critico-Dogmaticus in Evangelium Joannis* was published in Latin ca. 1786 or 1788 and was among the most popular Johannine commentaries in the United States in the mid-nineteenth century. Evans, however, most likely read the commentary as quoted in the notes to an available Greek New Testament of the period. See Bloomfield, *Ἡ ΚΑΙΝΗ ΔΙΑΘΗΚΗ*, 1:419–20 n7, where the parenthetical reference to "v. 12, 24, 16" is a giveaway.

77. Ibid., 420 n7 (continued). Euthymius Zigabenus (fl. 12th cen.), a Byzantine theologian and scriptural exegete, wrote commentaries on the four Gospels as well as on the Psalms and Paul's epistles.

78. "THEREFORE leaving the principles of the doctrine of Christ, let us go on unto perfection; not laying again the foundation of repentance from dead works, and of faith toward God."

79. Evans generalizes this experience in his small book *Divine Order in the Process of Full Salvation* (Boston: Henry V. Degen, 1860), 35: "Full salvation . . . may exist when we have no emotion, when the soul is plunged into the night of naked faith."

80. François de Fénelon (1651–1705), the famed French archbishop of Cambray, theologian, and writer, admired Madame Guyon and supported her quietist mysticism against charges of heresy. His spiritual writings were later often read for their advocacy of quietism. See Patricia A. Ward, *Experimental Theology in America: Madame Guyon, Fénelon, and Their Readers* (Waco, Tex.: Baylor University Press, 2009). Evans uses this material in *Happy Islands*, 132–33 and includes there, too, his earlier reference to "naked faith." See,

also, Evans, *Divine Order*, 35 (see Journal I n79 above), which suggests the influence of Fénelon.

81. The quotation and final "Amen" conflate various scriptural sources, echoing in part 2 Tim. 2:15, 2 Cor. 12:10, 1 Cor. 1, and Gen. 17:5.

82. See August Neander, *General History of the Christian Church and Religion*, trans. Joseph Torrey, 1st Amer. ed., vol. 4 (Boston: Crocker and Brewster, 1851): 216. Joachim of Fiore (1132?–1202) has often been cited for his millennial vision of history as comprising three ages—of the Father, Son, and Holy Spirit.

83. "I say the truth in Christ, I lie not, my conscience also bearing me witness in the Holy Ghost, / That I have great heaviness and continual sorrow in my heart. / For I could wish that myself were accursed from Christ for my brethren, my kinsmen according to the flesh."

84. Raymond Lull (ca. 1232–1316) expounded Neoplatonic religious philosophy and was both a mystic and missionary to the Arabs. He wrote numerous works; his *Book of Contemplation* (ca. 1272), originally in Arabic and then translated into Catalan, is the first medieval theological work not composed in Latin.

85. Evans is quoting Lull's *Liber Proverbiorum* (Book of Proverbs) from Neander, *General History*, 4:310 and 7:430. I have been able to locate the material in vol. 7 in a "new" revised edition (London: Henry G. Bohn, 1852). Evans uses this passage and related material in this journal entry in his later book *The Divine Law of Cure* (Boston: H. H. Carter, 1881), 32–33.

86. Bernard of Clairvaux (1090–1163), the famed Cistercian founder of the monastery at Clairvaux, was known for his mystical writings. Anselm of Canterbury (ca. 1033–1109) is best known as an early Benedictine scholastic, but he also composed devotional writings. Richard of St. Victor (d. 1173), who inhabited the famed monastery of St. Victor in Paris, was a disciple of the mystic Hugo of St. Victor. Richard authored dogmatic, exegetical, and mystical works.

87. Evans quotes this material again in *Happy Islands*, 95–96, where he identifies his source as Neander, citing volume and page (4:307), with an incorrect title attribution (*History of Christianity and the Church*). The quotation may be found in Neander, *General History*, 4:307.

88. Cf. 1 John 1:1.

89. Cf. Luke 24:32.

90. The unidentified couplet may be found (in quotation marks) in Letter of John Wesley to Charles Wesley, London, Feb. 12, 1767, in John Emory, ed., *The Works of the Reverend John Wesley, A.M.*, 7 vols., vol. 6 (New York: B. Waugh and T. Mason for the Methodist Episcopal Church, 1835), 669; and Francis Asbury, *Journal of Rev. Francis Asbury, Bishop of the Methodist Episcopal Church*, 3 vols., vol. 1 (New York: Lane and Scott, 1852), 134 (entry for November 1774).

91. Bernard of Clairvaux, as quoted in Neander, *General History*, 4:263.

92. Evans used this material in *Happy Islands*, 96.

93. Cf. "Then go, plunge yourself in the Godhead's deepest sea; be lost in his immensity," in C. H. Spurgeon, "The Immutability of God: A Sermon Delivered on Sabbath Morning, January 7th, 1855 . . . at New Park Street Chapel, Southwark," http://www.spurgeon.org /sermons/0001.htm.

94. Bernard of Clairvaux, as quoted in Neander, *General History*, 4:372. Evans uses this material from his journal in *Happy Islands*, 97–98.

95. Evans's reference is essentially correct. The source is Neander, *General History*, 4:412.

96. Cf. Heb. 11:1.

97. Miguel de Molinos (ca. 1640–1697) taught the complete passivity of the soul before God in his well-known *Spiritual Guide* and was later jailed by the Inquisition for views considered heretical. The German Lutheran Johann Lorenz von Mosheim (1694–1755) has been cited as the founder of modern church history because of his insistence on objectivity and critical scrutiny of sources, but his *Institutiones historiae ecclesiasticae* (Institutes of Ecclesiastical History, 1726) was written under Pietistic as well as Enlightenment influence. Mosheim apparently also wrote the shorter, two-volume *Ecclesiastical History, from the Birth of Christ to the Beginning of the Eighteenth Century*, an English translation of which, by Archibald Maclaine, appeared in London in 1842. Evans is probably quoting an edition of the latter. Evans quotes this material on Molinos, with a few editorial changes, in *Happy Islands*, 120.

98. Cf. Eph. 3:19; 1 John 3:24, 4:16.

99. See Journal I n82 above for a reference to Joachim.

100. Cf. Jer. 31:33, "After those days, saith the Lord, I will put my law in their inward parts, and write it in their hearts."

101. Evans's citation is correct for volume 4 of the 1851 edition of Neander's *General History*.

102. Ps. 63:1.

103. Job 23:3.

104. Guigo I (1083–1136), also called Guigues du Chastel, was the fifth prior of the Carthusian Grande Chartreuse monastery. His *Meditations*, comprising 276 aphorisms or thoughts that combined theological reflection with personal experience, was composed after 1109. Evans's reference to Neander is correct.

105. Guigo I, *Meditations*, as quoted in Neander, *General History*, 4:413.

106. Louis Bautain, *An Epitomé of the History of Philosophy. Being the Work Adopted by the University of France for Instruction in the Colleges and High Schools*, trans. C. S. Henry (New York: Harper and Bros., 1841–1842), 1:60. The parenthetical material is Evans's interpolation. Evans uses the quotation, with a tense change, in *Happy Islands*, 308.

107. Cf., in the 1897 edition, Jeanne Marie Bouvier de La Motte Guyon, *Autobiography of Madame Guyon*, trans. Thomas Taylor Allen (London: Kegan Paul, Trench, Trübner and Co.), 2:331.

108. Evans elaborates on the contents of this paragraph in *Happy Islands*, 308–9.

109. Bautain, *History of Philosophy*, 1:109, as cited by Evans. The Bautain volume omits a quotation mark at the beginning of the material but supplies one at the end. Pythagoras (ca. 580–500 BCE), a pre-Socratic Greek philosopher from Samos, founded an Italic school teaching the immortality of the soul, its reincarnation, and the need for purification to escape the reincarnational cycle. Evans uses this material in *Happy Islands*, 313–14.

110. Plotinus (ca. 205–270), Porphyry (ca. 232–ca. 304), and Proclus (ca. 410–485) were all memorable leaders of the Greek Neoplatonic school of philosophy, which taught a path of mystical ascent from the Many to the One. Plotinus is regarded as the founder of the school, centered in Alexandria, Egypt.

111. Evans did not write in his journal for an interval of nearly three weeks.

112. The phrase "full redemption" presages Evans's invocation of "full salvation" in the title of his 1860 book *Divine Order in the Process of Full Salvation*.

113. Richard Baxter (1615–1661), who earned notice as a nonconformist and Presbyterian minister during the period of the English Civil Wars, published his classic devotional work *The Saints' Everlasting Rest* in 1650. John Wesley abridged it in 1754. Evans uses this material in *Happy Islands*, 104.

114. Evans probably read *The Saints' Everlasting Rest* in the Benjamin Fawcett abridgment: Richard Baxter, *The Saints' Everlasting Rest: Or, A Treatise on the Blessed State of the Saints in Their Enjoyment of God in Heaven* (London, Edinburgh, and New York: T. Nelson and Sons, 1856). The Fawcett abridgment appeared in Boston as early as 1811 and was also published by the American Tract Society in the 1840s and appeared in other editions. The reference to Section 2 corresponds to the Fawcett abridgment. The quotations may be accessed in the 1856 edition in Baxter, *Saints' Everlasting Rest*, 24–25, http://books.google.com/books? id=nv8CAAAAQAAJ&. In the second quotation, Evans has changed the references from the second-person "thy" to the third-person "his." Evans uses this journal entry on Baxter, with a few changes, in *Happy Islands*, 104.

115. Ibid., 247 (Chapter 13).

116. Ibid., 207. Evans uses part of this quotation in *Happy Islands*, 173.

117. The phrase is from John Milton, *Paradise Lost*, Book 11.

118. Baxter, *Saints' Everlasting Rest*, 258.

119. The parenthetical "father" is Evans's interpolation.

120. "Let him kiss me with the kisses of his mouth: for thy love *is* better than wine."

121. Baxter, *Saints' Everlasting Rest*, 244–45.

122. Madame Guyon's *Moyen court et très facile de faire oraison* (A Short and Easy Method of Prayer) was originally published in 1685 as a primer on contemplative prayer as "prayer of the heart." Evans uses the sentence in *Happy Islands*, 309–10.

123. See Spurgeon, "Immutability of God," http://www.spurgeon.org/sermons/0001.htm. This is Evans's second use of the quotation (see Journal I n93 above).

124. See Gal. 2:20; Col. 3:3. Evans places an "X" after "dead," as if to mark the passage.

125. Thomas à Kempis, *The Imitation of Christ. In Three Books*, trans. John Payne and ed. Howard Malcolm (Boston: Gould and Lincoln, 1855), 148 (Bk. 3, Chap. 14). Evans uses the quotation, citing an apparently different edition (*"Imitation of Christ*, p. 206") in *Happy Islands*, 315–16.

126. Cf. 1 John 4:16.

127. Cf. Kempis, *Imitation of Christ*, 168 (Bk. 3, Chap. 22): "To be able, therefore, in peaceful vacancy, and with all the energy of my mind to contemplate thee, and know that thou infinitely transcendest the most perfect of thy works, it is necessary that I should rise above all created beings, and utterly forsake myself."

128. The lines are attributed to Mary Ann Serrett Barber, opening the third verse of the hymn "Prince of Peace, Control My Will." According to Charles S. Nutter (*Hymn Studies: An Illustrated and Annotated Edition of the Hymnal of the Methodist Episcopal Church*, 4th ed. [New York: Eaton and Mains, 1900], 183 n463), the hymn first appeared in the *Church of England Magazine*, Mar. 3, 1858. Evans's recall of the lines here suggests that the hymn was popularly sung before that. He quotes the four verses of the hymn, including the two lines cited here, in *Happy Islands*, 325.

129. The lines are Charles Wesley's, the fourth verse in the hymn "Saviour of the Sin-Sick Soul." See Nutter, ed., *Hymn Studies*, 297 n486.

130. Cf. Exod. 15:9, Num. 31:27, Prov. 16:19.

131. Evans omits parts of John 17:21, 22, and 23, focusing exclusively on the theme of oneness and avoiding other ideas.

132. "But he that is joined unto the Lord is one spirit."

133. Cf. Matt. 28:20, the last verse of the Gospel of Matthew and part of the Great Commission of Jesus: "Lo, I am with you alway, *even* unto the end of the world." On sitting upon the

throne of Jesus, cf. Matt. 19:28: "When the Son of man shall sit in the throne of his glory, ye also shall sit upon twelve thrones, judging the twelve tribes of Israel"; and Rev. 3:21: "To him that overcometh will I grant to sit with me in my throne."

134. The Urim and Thummim were objects used for divination by the high priests of ancient Israel. They were enclosed in a breastplate or breastpiece worn by the priest. See Exod. 28:15–30 and Lev. 8:8.

135. "Having predestinated us unto the adoption of children by Jesus Christ to himself, according to the good pleasure of his will."

136. The material may be accessed in C[arl] Ullmann, *Reformers before the Reformation, Principally in Germany and the Netherlands,* trans. Robert Menzies (Edinburgh: T. and T. Clark, 1855), 2:140–41; available at http://books.google.com/books?id=Us9CAAAAIAAJ& pg=PA140&lpg=PA140&. Ullmann is quoting Thomas à Kempis, *The Imitation of Christ* here. Evans later uses the Ullmann quotation in *Happy Islands,* 321–23.

137. See Ullmann, *Reformers before the Reformation,* 142–43. Again, this is a quotation from Kempis, *Imitation of Christ.* Likewise, Evans reproduces the Ullmann quotation in *Happy Islands,* 321–23. Still more, all of the February 18 entry until this point is reworked and edited in ibid., 319–23.

138. The quoted words appear to be a summary of the teaching of Kempis in *The Imitation of Christ.*

139. Cf. Luke 14:33.

140. See Ullmann, *Reformers before the Reformation,* 137. Evans uses the quotation again in *Happy Islands,* 294.

141. Prov. 8:22–29 is part of the well-known hymn/poem of a personified Wisdom: "The LORD possessed me in the beginning of his way, before his works of old. / I was set up from everlasting, from the beginning, or ever the earth was. . . . / When he gave to the sea his decree, that the waters should not pass his commandment: when he appointed the foundations of the earth."

142. "But we speak the wisdom of God in a mystery, *even* the hidden *wisdom,* which God ordained before the world unto our glory."

143. John 1:5.

144. "But unto them which are called, both Jews and Greeks, Christ the power of God, and the wisdom of God."

145. "But of him are ye in Christ Jesus, who of God is made unto us wisdom, and righteousness, and sanctification, and redemption."

146. Cf. Col. 2:9.

147. See John Langhorne and William Langhorne, trans., *Plutarch's Lives of Illustrious Men* (Cincinnati: H. S. and J. Applegate, Publishers, 1850), 60; available at http://books.google .com/books?id=n-PVAAAAMAAJ. Numa Pompilius (753–673 BCE), according to tradition, ruled Rome as its second king, succeeding the fabled Romulus. Plutarch's life of Numa was written ca. 75 CE.

148. Rom. 8:2: "For the law of the Spirit of life in Christ Jesus hath made me free from the law of sin and death." Matt. 16:24: "Then said Jesus unto his disciples, If any *man* will come after me, let him deny himself, and take up his cross, and follow me."

149. Ralph Cudworth (1617–1688) was one of the so-called Cambridge Platonists. His major work, *The True Intellectual System of the Universe: The First Part, Wherein All the Reason and Philosophy of Atheism Is Confuted and Its Impossibility Demonstrated,* was published in 1678

and aroused considerable controversy. John Laurence Mosheim produced a two-volume Latin translation of this work as *Systema Intellectuale Huius Universal* in 1733, and Evans was probably quoting from a later edition of this Latin work. Evans uses the quotation in *Happy Islands*, 119.

150. Kempis, *Imitation of Christ*, 30 (Bk. 1, Chap. 3).

151. Evans faithfully records the emphases in the Neander text, which is quoting Anselm as in turn quoted in Eadmer, *Vita S. Anselmi* (Life of St. Anselm, ca. 1124). Evans uses the material on Anselm and the lengthy quotation in *Happy Islands*, 296–98.

152. Evans's quotation from Archbishop Fénelon may be found in [François de Salignac de la Mothe Fénelon], *Pious Thoughts concerning the Knowledge and Love of God and Other Holy Exercises* (London: W. and J. Innys, 1720), 4; available at http://books.google.com /books?id=4bQHAAAAQAAJ.

153. Song of Sol. 2:16.

154. Cf. Gen. 15:1: "After these things the word of the LORD came unto Abram in a vision, saying, Fear not, Abram: I *am* thy shield, *and* thy exceeding great reward."

155. Ps. 48:14.

156. The quoted material, with two small changes, may be found in Elizabeth Rowe, *Devout Exercises of the Heart, in Meditation & Soliloquy, Prayer and Praise* (1737), abridged ed. (New York: D. Hitt and T. Ware for the Methodist Connection in the United States, 1813), 86; available at http://www.archive.org/details/devoutexercisesoooinrowe. Elizabeth Rowe (1674–1737) was English, a poet and novelist who felt the burden of an early widowhood and subsequently composed prose works of a devotional nature.

157. The quoted material may be found in Frederick von Schlegel, *The Philosophy of History, in a Course of Lectures, Delivered at Vienna*, trans. James Burton Robertson, 4th ed., rev. (London: Henry G. Bohn, 1846), 160. See http://books.google.com/books? id=W8AIAAAAQAAJ. There are nonsubstantive errors in the Evans transcription.

158. The "highest good."

159. Note the lapse of over a month.

160. Cf. Ps. 23:2.

161. Cf. Song of Sol. 1:7.

162. Evans leaves a full manuscript page blank before this entry, suggesting the significance of the Conference and reappointment to Claremont for him.

163. Evans is quoting Augustus Neander, *The Life of Jesus Christ in Its Historical Connexion and Historical Development*, trans. from 4th German ed. John M'Clintock and Charles E. Blumenthal, Part 2, Ch. 5, Art. 95, which may be accessed in the London edition of Henry G. Bohn in 1852, 146. See http://books.google.com/books?id=WdhGAAAAIAAJ.

164. See ibid., 146–47. Evans is paraphrasing very closely, with a number of phrases that are actually direct quotations, but the reference to Pentecost is his own.

165. Ibid., 147 (with some small changes in punctuation). For Jesus's estimate of the centurion's faith, see Matt. 8:10.

166. Cf. John 20:29.

167. Evans is quoting the King James Version from memory.

168. See August Neander, *General History of the Christian Religion and Church*, vol. 5, trans. Joseph Torrey, comprising the 6th vol. of the original (Boston: Crockett and Brewster, 1854), 402. The material may be accessed at http://books.google.com/books?id=QGoPAAAAYA AJ&pg=PA402&. Ruysbroch (alternately spelled Ruysbroeck or Van Ruysbroeck) is Blessed

John of Ruysbroeck (1293–1381), most esteemed of the Flemish mystics and called "Admirable Doctor" and "Divine Doctor." He countered the radical mysticism of the Brethren of the Free Spirit in his writings.

169. See Heb. 10:9.

170. See 2 Cor. 5:14.

171. The quotation is part of a hymn that may be found as Hymn 405, "Jesus hath died that I might live," in *Church Pastorals: Hymns and Tunes for Public and Social Worship*, coll. and arr. Nehemiah Adams (Boston: Ticknor and Fields, 1864), 169; available at http://books .google.com/books?id=7HcOIX4v-woC&pg=PA169. Evans's source was obviously earlier, and he may have been quoting from memory because of slight differences in punctuation and capitalization. For the reference to "Godhead's deepest sea" in the May 30 entry (above in the text), see Spurgeon, "Immutability of God," http://www.spurgeon.org/sermons/0001.htm. This is Evans's third echo of the quotation (see above in the notes).

172. S. T. Bloomfield, *Recensio synoptica annotationis sacrae: Being a Critical Digest and Synoptical Arrangement of the Most Important Annotations of the New Testament* (London: C. and J. Rivington, 1826–1828), 3:595n. See http://books.google.com/books?id=BdEtAAAA YAAJ&pg=PA595. The *Recensio synoptica*, which preceded Bloomfield's Greek New Testament, was an eight-volume work produced between 1826 and 1828.

173. Phil. 4.11.

174. Evans was quoting from a digest of Archbishop François Fénelon's *Explication des Maximes des Saints* (Maxims of the Saints, 1697), which may be found in Thomas C. Upham, *Life and Religious Opinions and Experience of Madame de La Mothe Guyon: Together with Some Account of the Personal History and Religious Opinions of Fenelon, Archbishop of Cambray* (New York: Harper, 1847), 2:246, which is transcribed by Evans exactly from "Article Thirty-Sixth." The material may be accessed in http://books.google.com/books?id=gBAsAAAAYAAJ& pg=PA246. Evans uses the quotation again in *Happy Islands*, 282.

175. See Job 35:10.

176. See http://books.google.com/books?id=gBAsAAAAYAAJ&pg=PA236. The source is, again, Upham's digest of Archbishop Fénelon's *Maxims* (see Journal I n174 above), in this case "Article Twenty-Seventh."

177. "One God and Father of all, who *is* above all, and through all, and in you all." Evans has slightly altered Eph. 4:6 to his point.

178. Evans's quotation begins with the end of 1 John 5:20 and excises the "Amen" from 1 John 5:21.

179. The lines form the last verse of Charles Wesley's hymn "O Love Divine, How Sweet Thou Art," alternately "This Better Part" or "Desiring to Love."

180. Cited in Isa. 34:5, Idumea, or in Hebrew Edom, lay south of Judea and was traditionally thought to be settled first by the descendents of Jacob's brother Esau.

181. The direct quotation is actually taken from Isa. 34:16, with the previous verses paraphrased.

182. See Isa. 40:7.

183. A simoon, or simoom, is a desert wind from Asia, Arabia, or Africa that is hot, strong, dry, and dust- or sand-laden.

184. See Rom. 8:11.

185. See Thomas Jackson, *Memoirs of the Life and Writings of the Rev. Richard Watson, Late Secretary to the Wesleyan Missionary Society* (New York: B. Waugh and T. Mason for the Methodist Episcopal Church, 1834), 203; available at http://books.google.com/books? id=kDYFAAAAYAAJ&pg=PA203.

186. David Hartley (1705–1757), a British philosopher and practicing physician with multiple interests including what today would be called neurology, psychology of religion, and spirituality, wrote *Observations on Man, His Frame, His Duty, and His Expectations* (1749). Its universalist theological vision saw people as participants in the divine nature, who grew in "theopathy," or the feeling of piety engendered by the contemplation of God, and who also grew in the moral results therefrom.

187. Johannes Tauler (ca. 1300–1361), a Dominican and well-known fourteenth-century German mystic, was read and admired by Martin Luther. For the quotation, see Johannes Tauler, "Sermon for the Second Sunday in Advent, in [Gottesfreund, Rulman Merswin], *The History and Life of the Reverend Doctor John Tauler of Strasbourg; with Twenty-Five of His Sermons*, trans. Susanna Winkworth (London: Smith, Elder, 1857), 188; available at http://books .google.com/books?id=Dk-HH7gwxRUC&pg=PA188. "An one" is traditional usage.

188. Evans quoted this passage, with a few minor changes, in *Happy Islands*, 85–86, where he lists the source as Fénelon's *Pious Thoughts*, 40–41. The material may be found in a slightly different translation in [Fénelon], *Pious Thoughts concerning the Knowledge and Love of God*, 16–17; available at http://books.google.com/books?id=4bQHAAAAQAAJ&pg=PA16. I have been unable to locate the exact edition of Fénelon's work that Evans was using, but as Ward explains in *Experimental Theology*, Fénelon's *Pious Reflections* (Réflexions saintes pour tous les jours du mois, 1704) was readily available in translated editions in the United States. See Ward, *Experimental Theology*, 88, 99, 107, 118, 257.

189. See [Fénelon], *Pious Thoughts concerning the Knowledge and Love of God*, 18; available at http://books.google.com/books?id=4bQHAAAAQAAJ&pg=PA18.

190. See Jeremy Taylor, *The Rules and Exercises of Holy Living*, in Reginald Heber, *The Whole Works of the Right Rev. Jeremy Taylor, Lord Bishop of Down, Connor, and Dromore, with a Life of the Author and a Critical Examination of His Writings*, rev. Charles Page Eden (London: Longman, Brown, Green, and Longmans, 1850–1856), 3:156; available at http://books.google.com /books?id=0BiRRWOzKIMC&pg=PA156. Evans uses the quotation in *Happy Islands*, 222. Jeremy Taylor (1613–1667), known—because of his poetic style of writing—as the "Shakespeare of divines," gained renown during the Cromwell regime in England. His *Rules and Exercises of Holy Living* was a devotional favorite.

191. See Mark 12:30–31, which Evans is conflating; see, also, Matt. 22.37–39, Luke 10:27, and, in the Old Testament, Deut. 6:5 and Lev. 19:18.

192. Evans is paraphrasing François de Fénelon, significantly in the context of a discussion of "naked faith." See [Francois de Salignac de la Mothe Fenelon and Jeanne Marie Bouvier de La Motte Guyon], *Spiritual Progress: Or, Instructions in the Divine Life of the Soul. From the French of Fenelon and Madame Guyon*, ed. James W. Metcalf (New York: M. W. Dodd, 1853), 46–47; available at http://books.google.com/books?id=G3wuAAAAYAAJ&pg=PA46.

193. See James Hervey, *Meditations among the Tombs*, in *The Whole Works of the Rev. James Hervey, A.M., Rector of Weston-Favell, Northamptonshire*, 6 vols., vol. 1 (London: Printed for Thomas Tegg, 1825), 32, which Evans has edited slightly. The material may be accessed at http://books.google.com/books/about/The_whole_works_of_the_late_Reverend_Jam .html?id=6XsuAAAAYAAJ. James Hervey (1714–1758), English cleric and writer, belonged to the famed Holy Club organized by John and Charles Wesley.

194. Luke 7:36–50.

195. Cf. Deut. 6:5. Evans omits "heart" and "soul."

196. The passage from the Gospel of Matthew that Evans is paraphrasing and elaborating upon begins, in his own text, from "Thus we are commanded to love our enemies."

197. The "xxxxx" functions for Evans as ellipsis points, since he has omitted material from the Neander text (see the next note).

198. Evans's source for the quotation from Abelard is Augustus Neander. See Neander, *General History of the Christian Religion and Church*, trans. Joseph Torrey, vol. 8 (Edinburgh, Scotland: T. and T. Clark, 1852), 127; available at http://books.google.com/books?id=q4 QOAAAAQAAJ&pg=PA127.

199. 1 John 4:18.

200. Evans edits this passage slightly and uses it (beginning from "God becomes the center of our thoughts") in *Happy Islands*, 239–40.

201. John 14:15.

202. Evans echoes this statement in *Divine Order*, 30: "Obedience is not in the outward act, but is a state of the will."

203. See Phil. 4:4 and 1 Thess. 5:16, 18.

204. See Taylor, *Rules and Exercises of Holy Living*, in Heber, *Whole Works of the Right Rev. Jeremy Taylor*, 3:28; available at http://books.google.com/books?id=0BiRRWOz KIMC&pg=PA28. Evans supplies "spiritual enemies" for the "ghostly enemies" of the Taylor/ Heber text. Taylor also quotes Phil. 4:4 immediately before this quotation in his work. Evans cites Taylor's "spiritual mirth" in *Happy Islands*, 248.

205. I am not able to locate the exact edition that Evans was using, but the material may be accessed in Joseph Benson, *The Life of the Rev. John W. de la Flechere: Compiled from the Narratives of the Reverend Mr. Wesley; the Biographical Notes of the Reverend Mr. Gilpin; from His Own Letters; and Other Authentic Documents* (New York: N. Bangs and T. Mason for the Methodist Episcopal Church, 1820), 361; available at http://books.google.com/books? id=ck5OAAAAYAAJ&pg=PA361. John W. Fletcher (1729–1785), whose original surname was de la Fléchère, was John Wesley's clerical contemporary; he was a foremost Methodist theologian of the period and also cited for his piety. Evans used this material in *Happy Islands*, 97.

206. See Benson, *Life of the Rev. John W. de la Flechere*, 98; available at http://books.google .com/books?id=ck5OAAAAYAAJ&pg=PA98. Evans used this material in *Happy Islands*, 97.

207. See Thomas Cogswell Upham, *The Life of Faith: In Three Parts; Embracing Some of the Scriptural Principles or Doctrines of Faith, the Power or Effects of Faith in the Regulation of Man's Inward Nature, and the Relation of Faith to the Divine Guidance* (New York: Harper, 1852), 427; available at http://books.google.com/books?id=3eYOAAAAIAAJ&pg=PA427. Evans is paraphrasing/editing Upham, especially in the last sentence.

208. From 1760 to 1785, the Swiss-born Fletcher was vicar of the industrializing congregation at Madeley, in Shropshire, in the West Midlands part of England. He had disdained a more prestigious appointment to serve there.

209. See Benson, *Life of the Rev. John W. de la Flechere*, 358–59; available at http://books .google.com/books?id=ck5OAAAAYAAJ&pg=PA358. Material in square brackets is my restoration of the online Benson text, in places where Evans differs. Various editions of the works of John Wesley also incorporated Benson's *Life of Fletcher*.

JOURNAL II (1857–1865)

1. In the upper right-hand corner, Evans inscribed a triangle, base down, with a horizontal line drawn across parallel to the base of the triangle. This is followed by "1.1." Beneath both, he drew a solid line. The intention of this symbol is not clear.

2. Left-side page is left blank.

3. Ps. 7:12.

4. Leonidas Lent Hamline (1797–1865), whose collected sermons were published in 1869, was a Methodist Episcopal bishop and also a lawyer. He was a member of the General Conference that in 1844 drew up a plan of separation for the northern and southern church over the issue of slavery. Later, he provided inaugural funds for the foundation of Hamline University in St. Paul, Minnesota.

5. New Hampshire.

6. New Hampshire.

7. New Market (or Newmarket) and Newport are both towns in New Hampshire. Evans leaves the right-hand page blank after this brief chronology of his life.

8. Left-hand page is blank. Evans begins numbering pages in the upper right-hand corner. The manuscript page numbers extend to 288. Likewise, Evans writes the year as a running head at the top of each journal page.

9. Evans is quoting traditional Chapter/Section 38 of Lao Zi, *Dao De Jing* (Lao-Tzu, *Tao Te Ching*). The translation he is using is difficult to determine, since its text does not follow the English transliterations that became available in the late nineteenth century. However, excerpts from the Chinese text appeared in the Transcendentalist periodical *The Dial* (1840–1844), indicating that some materials were already available at midcentury and earlier.

10. "Forasmuch as this people refuseth the waters of Shiloah that go softly, and rejoice in Rezin and Remaliah's son; / Now therefore, behold, the Lord bringeth up upon them the waters of the river, strong and many, *even* the king of Assyria, and all his glory: and he shall come up over all his channels, and go over all his banks:" The parentheses around this passage appear to be a later addition.

11. See James Thomson, "Hymn," in *The Works of Mr. James Thomson: With His Last Corrections and Improvements* (London: R. Baldwin et al., 1802), 1:177; available at http://books.google.com/books?id=CGg1AAAAMAAJ.

12. Greek and Latin, respectively, for universe or world, with the implicit meaning of order and perfection of arrangement. Evans has transcribed the wrong character for sigma ("s") in the middle of the word (a different character from the sigma at the end), but he has preserved the accent mark over the omicron ("o").

13. In 1777, John Hulse endowed Cambridge University with funds for a series of lectures on Christianity, scripture, and the evidences of revealed religion. The lectures began in 1820. Evans does not supply enough information to locate the specific lecture to which he is referring.

14. See James Montgomery, *Lectures on General Literature, Poetry, &c: Delivered at the Royal Institution in 1830 and 1831* (New York: Harper, 1853), 52; available at http://books.google.com/books?id=4rpUAAAAYAAJ&pg=PA52. British James Montgomery (1771–1854) wrote poetry and hymns and was also a newspaper editor.

15. The lines are from Philip James Bailey, *Festus: A Poem*, in 3d London ed. (Boston: Benjamin B. Mussey, 1853), 421; available at http://books.google.com/books?id=gAYPAAAAYAAJ&pg=PA421.

16. See Alexander Smith, "A Boy's Poem" (Part II), in *City Poems* (Cambridge: Macmillan, 1857), available at http://books.google.com/books?id=Ymk-AAAAYAAJ&pg=PA147. Both the Scottish Smith (1830–1867) and the English Bailey (1816–1902), above in Journal II n15, were grouped by critics in what was derogatively, if humorously, dubbed the "Spasmodic School." Spasmodic poets were characterized by their composition of lengthy verse dramas with extended inward-turning monologues, often thought to be bombastic and/or egotistical.

17. Evans edits and refines this journal entry, including the quotation from Archbishop François Fénelon, in W. F. Evans, *The Happy Islands; Or, Paradise Restored* (Boston: H. V. Degen, 1860), 42–43. For the quotation, see [François de Salignac de la Mothe Fénelon], *Pious Thoughts concerning the Knowledge and Love of God and Other Holy Exercises, by the Late Archbishop of Cambray . . .* (London: W. and J. Innys, 1720), 77; available at http://books .google.com/books?id=4bQHAAAAQAAJ&pg=PA77.

18. Heb. 4:9 ("There remaineth therefore a rest to the people of God").

19. From a verse in the hymn "Prince of Peace, Control My Will." The words appeared in the *Church of England Magazine*, March 3, 1858; variously attributed to Mary Ann Serrett Barber or Mary S. B. Shindler. Evans reproduces the entire hymn in *Happy Islands*, 325.

20. See Charles How[e], *Devout Meditations: A Collection of Thoughts upon Religious and Philosophical Subjects*, CXIII, in John Jebb, *Piety without Asceticism; or, The Protestant Kempis: A Manual of Christian Faith and Practice, Selected from the Writings of Scougal, Charles How, and Cudworth* (London: James Duncan, 1830, 369; available at http://books.google.com /books?id=EHhAAAAAYAAJ&pg=PA369. Howe (1661–1742) was a devotional writer at the English court.

21. The lines are from an Isaac Watts hymn on Ps. 139. See James M. Winchell, *An Arrangement of the [P]Salms, Hymns, and Spiritual Songs of the Rev. Isaac Watts, D.D.* (Boston: James Loring, and Gould, Kendall, and Lincoln, 1832), 39, no. 41; http://books.google.com /books?id=owlEAAAAYAAJ&pg=PA39.

22. I have not been able to locate the quoted phrase; for gold tried in fire, see 1 Pet. 1:7.

23. Evans is alluding to what American religious historians later called the "businessmen's revival" of 1857–1858, begun in New York City with a series of prayer meetings and spreading elsewhere.

24. Parentheses appear to have been added later.

25. The lines come from the fourth verse of the hymn "Of Him Who Did Salvation Bring," which may be found in various hymnals of the eighteenth and nineteenth century, including, notably, William M'Kendree et al., eds., *A Collection of Hymns for the Use of the Methodist Episcopal Church, Principally from the Collection of the Rev. John Wesley, M.A.* (New York: N. Bangs and T. Mason for the Methodist Episcopal Church, 1821), 174; available at http:// books.google.com/books?id=LJIQAAAAIAAJ&pg=PA174.

26. See Gal. 3:26, "For ye are all the children of God by faith in Christ Jesus."

27. Rev. 3:20.

28. 2 Cor. 6:16.

29. A reference to the traditional history recalled in the Jewish feast of Hanukkah. Antiochus IV, the Syrian-Greek monarch who ruled Jerusalem in 165 BCE, attempted to transform the Jewish Temple into a shrine to the Greek God Zeus (Roman Jupiter). Judas Maccabeus, his brothers, and other followers drove the Greek troops away and purified the Temple so that traditional services could be restored.

30. Isa. 65:4; 1 Cor. 3:17.

31. Ps. 90:1; Ps. 91:1.

32. An allusion to a line from Charles Wesley's hymn/poem, originally titled "Pleading the Power of Salvation": "Now let me gain Perfection's Height! / Now let me into Nothing fall! / Be less than Nothing in Thy Sight, / And feel that Christ is All in All." The lines may be found in John Wesley and Charles Wesley, *Hymns and Sacred Poems* (Bristol, Engl.: Felix Farley, 1742), 264; available at http://books.google.com/books?id= CGoFAAAAQAAJ.

33. Cf. Eph. 3:19: "the love of Christ, which passeth knowledge."

34. Matt. 28:20.

35. Evans partially quotes and partially paraphrases a quotation from German professor of theology Daniel Georg Konrad von Cölln. He likely found the material in Augustus Neander, *The Life of Jesus Christ in Its Historical Connexion and Historical Developement*, trans. John M'Clintock and Charles E. Blumenthal (New York: Harper and Bros., 1855), 89n, or another English edition of this work; available at https://books.google.com/books?id=xjg_ AAAAYAAJ&pg=PA89. Von Cölln (1788–1833) spent much of his career at the university at Breslau and published a series of theological works in German.

36. Evans reworks this discussion, using some of the same language in W. F. Evans, *The Celestial Dawn; Or, Connection of Earth and Heaven* (Boston: James P. Magee, 1862), 127–28.

37. The lines form a verse in the hymn by Charles Wesley, "I Know That My Redeemer Lives" (originally titled "Rejoicing in Hope"). See John Wesley and Charles Wesley, *Hymns and Sacred Poems*, 182; available at http://books.google.com/books?id=CG0FAAAAQAAJ.

38. Phil. 4:6.

39. The account may be accessed in Joseph Benson, *The Life of the Rev. John W. de la Flechere: Compiled from the Narratives of the Reverend Mr. Wesley; the Biographical Notes of the Reverend Mr. Gilpin; from His Own Letters; and Other Authentic Documents* (New York: N. Bangs and T. Mason for the Methodist Episcopal Church, 1820), 370. Evans was recalling the narrative from memory, since Fletcher's words in the *Life* are recorded as "I want a gust of praise to go to the ends of the earth." See http://books.google.com/books?id=ck5OAAAAYAAJ &pg=PA370.

40. See Ps. 46:1–3.

41. 1 Cor. 8:1: "Knowledge puffeth up, but charity edifieth."

42. Parentheses appear to have been added later.

43. See Gen. 28:10–22.

44. John 1:51 reads, "And he saith unto him, Verily, verily, I say unto you, Hereafter ye shall see heaven open, and the angels of God ascending and descending upon the Son of man."

45. Cf. John 14:6.

46. Parentheses appear to have been added later.

47. The Sadducees, who flourished at the time of Jesus, were strict literalists in accepting only the written Mosaic law and rejecting oral interpretation; Evans's allusion is a metaphor for a sterile literalism and thus materialism. Evans uses this essential analysis but inverts it to find its resolution in the teachings of Emanuel Swedenborg in W. F. Evans, *The New Age and Its Messenger* (Boston: T. H. Carter, 1864), 15.

48. This entire passage, beginning from "There is a certain experience which is symbolized by a lofty mountain" is reproduced, with some elaborations and editorial changes, in *Happy Islands*, 167–70. The ending verse (not in the *Happy Islands* version) is from "Lines from Hugh Stowell's Hymn/Poem 'The Mercy Seat' ('From Every Stormy Wind That Blows')," published in [E. Littell], *The Religious Magazine; Or, Spirit of the Foreign Theological Journals and Reviews*, vol. 1 (Philadelphia: E. Littell, 1828), 104; available at http://books.google.com/books?id =gG42AAAAMAAJ&pg=PA104.

49. Evans explains this realization again and uses some of the same language regarding "Jehovah Jesus" (a Swedenborgian concept), in Evans, *Celestial Dawn*, 76.

50. John 21:17.

51. Parentheses appear to have been added later.

52. Parentheses appear to have been added later.

53. Rev. 21:3. The quotation from the Book of Revelation highlights the millennial character of this journal entry as well as a previous one on December 14, 1858. Swedenborgian influence seems indicated by the reference to a "new age."

54. A reference to Gen. 32:2: "And when Jacob saw them [the angels of God], he said, This *is* God's host: and he called the name of that place Mahanaim."

55. Cf. John 1:50.

56. Note the passage of nine months since the previous journal entry.

57. Cf. Mark 6:31.

58. Parentheses appear to have been added later.

59. Cf. Benson, *Life of the Rev. John W. de la Flechere*, 61: "Let the intenseness of our happiness border on misery, because we can make him no return" (in a letter to two "pious women"); available at http://books.google.com/books?id=ck5OAAAAYAAJ&pg=PA61.

60. The line is repeated in W. F. Evans, *Divine Order in the Process of Full Salvation* (Boston: Henry V. Degen, 1860), 45. William E. Boardman's book *The Higher Christian Life* (Boston: Hoyt, 1858) was *the* basic document of the "higher-life" movement, a Reformed articulation of sanctification and Christian perfection. The meeting seems to be a result of Evans's camp-meeting experience with the Boston Congregationalist (reported in the previous journal entry).

61. Cf. John 15:8 and John 15:16: "Herein is my Father glorified, that ye bear much fruit"; and "Ye have not chosen me, but I have chosen you, and ordained you, that ye should go and bring forth fruit, and *that* your fruit should remain."

62. See Benson, *Life of the Rev. John W. de la Flechere*, 370: "I want a gust of praise to go to the ends of the earth." See http://books.google.com/books?id=ck5OAAAAYAAJ&pg =PA370. This is Evans's second allusion to the remark (see Journal II n39 above).

63. These and the succeeding sets of parentheses in this journal entry appear to have been added later.

64. This and a second set of parentheses in this journal entry appear to have been added later.

65. "Shewbread" (King James Version), or "showbread," is a term that designates bread placed on a special table in the Temple of Jerusalem. It is, literally, "presence bread," since in Exod. 25:30 God commands that it always be present on a table before him.

66. New Hampshire.

67. John 15:4.

68. John 14:3; Matt. 28:20; John 14:18. Evans's interpolation in the last quotation—"in a state of orphanage"—is etymologically correct; newer translations supply "orphans" in place of the "comfortless" of the King James Version.

69. Francisco de Losa (1536–1634), a Roman Catholic priest, encountered Gregorio López (1542–1596) in Mexico, remained with López until he died, and subsequently produced *La vida que hizo el siervo de Dios Gregorio López, en algunos lugares de esta Nueua España* in 1613. An English-language edition was available in the United States by 1841, when John Eyre printed it in New York with a preface of his own. Evans was reading an edition of the Eyre version, from which the quotation is taken (Evans has interpolated "Mexico" and not followed punctuation exactly). See [Francisco de Losa], *The Life of Gregory Lopez, A Hermit in America* (Boston: Henry V. Degen, 1856), 70–71; available at http://books.google.com /books?id=1IsxAQAAMAAJ&pg=PA70. Significantly, this edition bears on its title page an enthusiastic endorsement by the "Rev. John Wesley": "For many years I despaired of finding

any inhabitant of Great Britain that could stand in any degree of comparison with Gregory Lopez." Evans reproduces the entire passage in *Celestial Dawn*, 122.

70. See *Life of Gregory Lopez*, 54–55; available at http://books.google.com/books?id=1 IsxAQAAMAAJ&pg=PA54. Evans has supplied "the Lord" for "God" of the original and has also misspelled its "tranquillity."

71. See Ps. 73:25.

72. "Wash you, make you clean; put away the evil of your doings from before mine eyes; cease to do evil; / Learn to do well; seek judgment, relieve the oppressed, judge the fatherless, plead for the widow."

73. "That they all may be one, as thou, Father, *art* in me, and I in thee, that they also may be one in us: that the world may believe that thou hast sent me."

74. Evans inserts an "X" over the top of this word and another at the end of the paragraph after "divine Life." This may indicate a passage that he intends to use as sermon material.

75. 1 John 4:7.

76. Cf. Mark 10:18.

77. Ps. 62:11; Rom. 13:1.

78. Cf. James 1:17.

79. In his book *Divine Order*, 32–33, Evans calls the "faith of the *heart*" what "mental philosophers call the sensibility."

80. These and the succeeding sets of parentheses in this journal entry appear to have been added later.

81. Cf. John 10:30.

82. Significantly, Evans here twice substitutes "Jehovah" for the "Lord" of the King James Version.

83. Evans has marked a large "X" over this section.

84. Evans has not written in his journal for well over two months.

85. In *Celestial Dawn*, 203, Evans identifies "spirit" as the "only causal agent."

86. Cf. Matt. 17:20.

87. Cf. Luke 17:6. And it is, indeed, a "sycamine" tree, probably one of the two types of mulberry that grow in Palestine.

88. Parentheses appear to have been added later.

89. Evans places an X mark at the beginning and end of this hymn, as if selecting it for later use. "O for a Faith That Will Not Shrink" was first published in 1831, authored by Church of England priest William Hiley Bathurst (1796–1877). It is found in frequent iterations in hymn collections, often with the title "The Power of Faith."

90. This single parenthesis and the later set in this journal entry appear to have been added later.

91. Evans reproduces this line in *Celestial Dawn*, 138.

92. Evans reproduces this material in *Celestial Dawn*, 140.

93. The material between the asterisks appears in the side margin. Evans offers no indication of the exact placement of the marginal material on the page itself.

94. Evans reproduces the line, with some slight changes, in *Celestial Dawn*, 140. Still more, this entire passage is reworked and elaborated in *Celestial Dawn*, 138–41.

95. Material beginning with "the Gospel is the expression of the thoughts of God" is reproduced with some changes and elaborations in *Celestial Dawn*, 143–44. The most notable change is the substitution of "Bible" there for the "Gospel" of the journal.

96. This is the second appearance, in Evans's journal, of the quotation/paraphrase from Da-viel Georg Konrad von Cölln, as reproduced in Neander, *Life of Jesus Christ*, 89n. See Journal II n35 above. Parentheses appear to have been added later. All of this material is reworked and elaborated in *Celestial Dawn*, 145–46.

97. This and a subsequent set of parentheses in this journal entry appear to have been added later. For the reference to the Israelites, cf. Deut. 8:4: "Thy raiment waxed not old upon thee, neither did thy foot swell, these forty years." Evans repeats some of this material in *Celestial Dawn*, 146–47.

98. The lines are from the hymn "Father of Mercies, in Thy Word," attributed to Anne Steele (1716–1778), which appears in numerous hymnals of the period and later. See *Hymns for the Use of the Methodist Episcopal Church: With Tunes for Congregational Worship* (New York: Carlton and Porter, 1857), 236; available at http://books.google.com/books?id=lrM0AAAAMAAJ &pg=PA236.

99. George Bush, "The Will of God," in *Methodist Quarterly Review*, 41—4th series, 11 (1859), D. D. Whedon, ed. (New York: Carlton and Porter, 1859), 289; available at http:// books.google.com/books?id=17URAAAAYAAJ&pg=PA289. George Bush (1796–1859), a biblical scholar and Presbyterian minister until his conversion to Swedenborgianism (significant for Evans's later trajectory), taught Hebrew at New York University for many years and was well-known as a public lecturer. His full-length work *Mesmer and Sweden-borg* (1847) attempted to bring the two together to the chagrin of many Swedenborgian clergy.

100. Bush, "Will of God," 295; http://books.google.com/books?id=17URAAAAYAAJ &pg=PA295.

101. [François de Salignac de la Mothe Fénelon and Jeanne Marie Bouvier de La Motte Guyon], *Spiritual Progress: Or, Instructions in the Divine Life of the Soul. From the French of Fé-nélon and Madame Guyon*, ed. James W. Metcalf (New York: M. W. Dodd, 1853), 191; available at http://books.google.com/books?id=G3wuAAAAYAAJ&pg=PA191. Evans has traced over his writing for virtually all of this paragraph, as if underlining its importance.

102. Evans echoes this sentiment in *Happy Islands*, 247: "A large portion of the diseases which assail us have their origin in the mind."

103. "According as his divine power hath given unto us all things that *pertain* unto life and godliness, through the knowledge of him that hath called us to glory and virtue: / Whereby are given unto us exceeding great and precious promises: that by these ye might be partakers of the divine nature, having escaped the corruption that is in the world through lust."

104. Likely editions that Evans found are Madame J. M. B. de La Mothe Guyon, *Spiritual Torrents: With Parallel Passages from the Writings of Emanuel Swedenborg*, trans. and ed. A. E. Ford (Boston: Otis Clapp, 1853); James Arbouin, *Dissertations on the Regenerate Life: In Harmony with the Theological Views of Emanuel Swedenborg, the Undoubted Messenger of Our Lord's Second Advent* (Boston: Otis Clapp, 1841); and [Adelaide Leaper Newton], *The Song of Solomon Compared with Other Parts of Scripture*, 2d ed. (London: James Nisbet, 1852).

105. Evans has marked this passage with a vertical line in the left margin, beginning with all but the first syllable of "meditation" and continuing to the end.

106. John Fletcher's wife was Mary Bosanquet Fletcher (1739–1815), a Methodist class leader and preacher, although her sermons do not survive. She is considered one of the first Meth-odist deaconesses and is known for her devotional diaries and pamphlets. William Bramwell (1759–1818) was an English Wesleyan minister. He excelled as an evangelical preacher and holiness advocate for the twenty-five years after Wesley's death. Edward Payson (1783–1827)

was an American Congregationalist preacher well-known in the first half of the nineteenth century. He was extolled for his life of prayer and functioned as a highly successful evangelist in the Second Great Awakening.

107. Parentheses appear to have been added later.

108. Here, in what follows for the May 9 entry, Evans pastes into his journal a newspaper clipping, apparently written by himself, that recounts the trip. The source is not given but may be a denominational newspaper or, also likely, his own press, since later—when he purchased a press for his son returned from the Civil War—he seemed familiar with presses. Evans pastes the newspaper clipping on the right-side pages of his journal only, leaving left-side pages blank. He leaves a full left-side page blank after the end of the clipping, and then resumes his regular journal on a right-side page.

109. Lydia H. Sigourney, "Niagara," in *The Female Poets of America: With Portraits, Biographical Notices, and Specimens of Their Writings*, 3d ed., ed. Thomas Buchanan Read (Philadelphia: E. H. Butler, 1850), 56; available at http://books.google.com/books?id=f3YaAAAAYAAJ&pg=PA56. Sigourney wrote a series of poems on Niagara.

110. Cf. Rev. 1:15: "And his feet like unto fine brass, as if they burned in a furnace; and his voice as the sound of many waters."

111. The lines are from the hymn "The Mercy-Seat" by Hugh Stowell and can be found in a series of nineteenth-century denominational hymnals even as it remains popular today. See Charles S. Nutter, *Hymn Studies: An Illustrated and Annotated Edition of the Hymnal of the Methodist Episcopal Church*, 4th ed. (New York: Eaton and Mains, 1884), 266; available at http://books.google.com/books?id=UDLNEiK7KvkC&pg=PA266.

112. See Felicia Dorothea Browne Hemans, "Christ Stilling the Tempest," in *The Works of Mrs. Hemans, with a Memoir by Her Sister, and An Essay on Her Genius by Mrs. Sigourney*, ed. Felicia Dorothea Browne Hemans and Harriet Mary Browne Owen (Philadelphia: Lea and Blanchard, 1840), 4:343; available at http://books.google.com/books?id=aDQXAAAAYAAJ&pg=PA343. The poem also appears in various hymnals.

113. Beginning here and continuing to the penultimate sentence of this paragraph, Evans has marked the left margin of his journal with a more or less continuous solid line, as if to underline his expression of sentiment. "C." above in his journal is Claremont.

114. See Felicia Dorothea Browne Hemans, "The Domestic Affections," in Hemans and Owen, *Works of Mrs. Hemans*, 7:321; available at http://books.google.com/books?id=MyckAAAAMAAJ&pg=PA321.

115. Ibid., 335; http://books.google.com/books?id=MyckAAAAMAAJ&pg=PA335.

116. See Felicia Dorothea Browne Hemans, "Sabbath Sonnet," in Hemans and Owen, *Works of Mrs. Hemans*, 1:314; available at http://books.google.com/books?id=HiwXAAAAYAAJ&pg=PA314. This was apparently a death-bed sonnet dictated by Hemans to her brother.

117. Cf. Ps. 34:1: "I will bless the LORD at all times: his praise *shall* continually *be* in my mouth."

118. There follows a newspaper article, apparently written by himself, that Evans has pasted into the journal. Although the piece is very lyrical, as in the previous newspaper account Evans's newsprint column exhibits his eye for detail and mind for statistics.

119. Cf. Rom. 11:22.

120. This tall column at the top of Queenston Heights (Ontario, Canada) honors Major General Sir Isaac Brock (1769–1812), a Canadian hero in the War of 1812. He died leading British and Canadian forces against American infantry.

121. With an original structure built by the French in 1678, Fort Niagara played an important role in the contest of French, British, and American forces for control of the Great Lakes region. It also impacted the Iroquois Six Nations and the Canadian nation itself.

122. Cf. Gen. 1:2: "And the earth was without form, and void, and darkness *was* upon the face of the deep."

123. Now known as Mirror Lake, this was a historic lake in central New Hampshire, named for the Indians in the area.

124. Cf. the title of Evans's book published the same year—*The Happy Islands; Or, Paradise Restored.*

125. In western New Hampshire, south of Hanover and close to the Connecticut River.

126. These lines can be found as "Hymn 399" in the 1821 hymnal M'Kendree et al., eds., *Collection of Hymns for the Use of the Methodist Episcopal Church,* 343; available at http://books.google.com/books?id=LJIQAAAAIAAJ&pg=PA343.

127. Evans repudiates the *"proprium"* in a somewhat different context in *New Age,* 31.

128. See Emanuel Swedenborg, *Angelic Wisdom concerning the Divine Love and the Divine Wisdom,* trans. James John Garth Wilkinson, pt. 4 (Boston: Otis Clapp, 1843), art. 335, 122; available at http://books.google.com/books?id=Yzo_AAAAYAAJ&pg=PA122.

129. See Alexander Pope, "The Universal Prayer," stanza 8, in Pope, *Essay on Man, and the Universal Prayer* (London: Whittaker, 1860), 46; available at http://books.google.com/books?id=VlwCAAAAQAAJ&pg=PA46.

130. Over two months have elapsed since Evans last wrote in his journal.

131. In *New Age,* 35, Evans attributes this state to the angels.

132. See Emanuel Swedenborg, *The Apocalypse Revealed, Wherein Are Disclosed the Arcana There Foretold, Which Have Hitherto Remained Concealed,* rev. ed. (Boston: Otis Clapp, 1836), art. 920, 3:214; available at http://books.google.com/books?id=5aYQAAAAYAAJ&pg=PA214. Evans has departed slightly from the translated text in the first parts of the quotation, but the alteration is not substantive.

133. There is an "X" mark at the beginning and end of this entry as well as a solid line marking it in the left margin, suggesting that this, for Evans, is a significant biographical entry.

134. This was actually published as *The Celestial Dawn; Or, Connection of Earth and Heaven.* See Journal II n36 above.

135. Constructed from the Greek word for "spirit of divination," *Pythonism* in the strict sense refers to the prediction of events on the model of Pythia, the Delphic oracle of Apollo, who offered prophecies capable of being read in different ways because of their ambiguity. More generally, the term encompasses any act of divination. Here Evans was probably distinguishing Christian from contemporary (pagan as he saw it?) divination as it flourished in the mass spiritualism of the day. Evans alludes to the "modern Pythonism" in similar terms in his preface to *Celestial Dawn,* v, and elsewhere in the volume, as well as in *New Age,* 19.

136. *Happy Islands* has been cited in full above in Journal II n17; Evans, *Divine Order* has also been cited in full in Journal II n60 above. The reference to *Divine Order* in second place, along with Evans's "also," constitute additional evidence that *Divine Order* was Evans's second published work.

137. See Swedenborg, *Apocalypse Revealed,* art. 937, 3:234; available at http://books.google.com/books?id=5aYQAAAAYAAJ&pg=PA234.

138. Evans places two "X's" at the top of this entry and one at the end, indicating its biographical significance for him. Almost two months have elapsed since his last journal entry.

139. See Ps. 42:11 and Ps. 43:5.

140. See Ps. 34:7.

141. See Matt. 4:11.

142. See Ps. 23:1–3.

143. See John 11:44.

144. See Mark 4:39.

145. The parentheses around this passage—"With Christ . . . material universe"—appear to have been added later.

146. See John 8:32.

147. Ibid.

148. Parentheses appear to have been added later.

149. The quoted text is from John Wesley's Sermon 43, "The Scripture Way of Salvation" (Thomas Jackson numbering). See http://wesley.nnu.edu/john-wesley/the-sermons-of -john-wesley-1872-edition/sermon-43-the-scripture-way-of-salvation/.

150. Bishop John Pearson (1612–1686), bishop of Chester (England) from 1672, published his *Exposition of the Creed* in 1659, based on his preaching to his congregation at St. Clement's in Cheapside. The work is considered one of the most important treatises on the Apostles' Creed within Anglicanism.

151. See William Wordsworth, "By the Seaside" (1833): "Ye mariners, that plough your onward way, / Or in the haven rest, or sheltering bay, / May silent thanks at least to God be given / With a full heart; 'our thoughts are *heard* in heaven.'" In William Wordworth, *The Complete Poetical Works of William Wordsworth*, vol. 8, 1823–1833 (Boston: Houghton Mifflin, 1919), available at https://books.google.com/books?id=w6QVAAAAYAAJ&pg=PA280 &lpg=PA281 The parentheses in the text appear to have been added later.

152. There is a parenthetical mark here that appears to have been added later; there is no opening mark to complement it.

153. Here those denying a perspective beyond the present and the tangible (such as belief in an afterworld and afterlife as well as in angels and spirits).

154. Parentheses appear to have been added later.

155. Evans elaborates on these sentiments regarding "appropriating faith" in *Divine Order*, 23.

156. A reversed and conflated echo of John 16:33: "These things I have spoken unto you, that in me ye might have peace. In the world ye shall have tribulation: but be of good cheer; I have overcome the world."

157. Parentheses appear to have been added later.

158. Luke 17:5: "And the apostles said unto the Lord, Increase our faith."

159. The phrase first appears as part of "Hymn to the Holy Ghost," in *Hymns and Sacred Poems*, ed. John Wesley and Charles Wesley (London: William Strahan, 1739), Pt. 2, 184. See http://quod.lib.umich.edu/e/ecco/004800840.0001.000/1:5.51. Cf. "Then go, plunge yourself in the Godhead's deepest sea; be lost in his immensity," in C. H. Spurgeon, "The Immutability of God: A Sermon Delivered on Sabbath Morning, January 7th, 1855 . . . at New Park Street Chapel, Southwark," http://www.spurgeon.org/sermons/0001.htm. This is the fourth time Evans has alluded to "the Godhead's deepest sea" in his journals. Obviously the phrase was deeply meaningful to him.

160. Thomas Walsh (1730–1759) was an Irish Methodist convert from Roman Catholicism, who labored with John Wesley in Ireland and in London, even living in Wesley's home. Walsh was renowned for his piety and rigorous asceticism. See Abel Stevens, *The History of the Religious Movement of the Eighteenth Century, Called Methodism* (New York: Carlton and Porter, 1858),

1:337–340; available at https://books.google.com/books?id=ZitOAQAAMAAJ&pg=PA337 and following pages. Evans excludes about a page of text, which includes the following: "This habitual self-absorption, added to excessive labour, produced the usual consequence of such errors; his health failed, and his nervous sensibilities suffered tortures which he too often ascribed to demoniacal agency." Stevens contrasts Wesley, who took care of himself, with Walsh, who did not; but Stevens adds that Wesley "did not interpose his authority, if his advice were unavailing, to rescue this young and splendid victim," and remarks that Wesley regarded Walsh with reverence, if not awe" (338). Evans reproduces the entire journal passage regarding Walsh with some slight changes in *Celestial Dawn*, 123–24.

161. Parentheses appear to have been added later. The entire passage is reworked slightly to appear in *Celestial Dawn*, 124–25.

162. Evans inserts an "X" before this entry and after the next two entries, as well as a line in the left margin for all three entries. It is unclear whether he wishes to mark this more strongly or target it for later excision as personal and historical.

163. Psalm 91 begins, "He that dwelleth in the secret place of the most High shall abide under the shadow of the Almighty."

164. The second "X" comes at the end of this entry.

165. Evans is apparently quoting the King James Version from memory, as there are small differences in the recorded verse.

166. Cf. Phil. 3:10. The parentheses from the beginning of the second sentence to the end of this entry appear to be a later addition.

167. Evans inserts a line in the left margin to mark this entry and also an "X" before the first word of the beginning sentence.

168. "And Asa cried unto the LORD his God, and said, LORD, *it is* nothing with thee to help, whether with many, or with them that have no power: help us, O LORD our God, for we rest on thee, and in thy name we go against this multitude. O LORD, thou *art* our God; let not man prevail against thee."

169. The hymn, including the stanza Evans quotes, is titled "Psalm CX. 1" and may be found in J. Wesley and C. Wesley, *Hymns and Sacred Poems*, 90 and later Methodist hymnals; available at http://books.google.com/books?id=CG0FAAAAQAAJ&pg=PA90. Evans places an "X" over the "no" in the phrase "no longer mine."

170. Cf. James 1:17: "Every good gift and every perfect gift is from above, and cometh down from the Father of lights." Evans placed a parenthetical mark—apparently later—before the beginning of this sentence.

171. Cf. John 3:27: "A man can receive nothing, except it be given him from heaven."

172. With the phrase "as such," which appears at the head of a new journal page, Evans draws a vertical line in the left margin, apparently later, to mark the entire page.

173. See Rom. 7:17.

174. Cf. Ps. 32:1–2: "Blessed *is* he *whose* transgression *is* forgiven, *whose* sin *is* covered. / Blessed *is* the man unto whom the LORD imputeth not iniquity, and in whose spirit *there is* no guile." Evans, apparently later, placed a parenthetical mark at the beginning of this sentence.

175. See William Paley, *The Works of William Paley, D.D.*, new ed. (Philadelphia: Crissy and Markley, 1850), 239; available at http://books.google.com/books?id=eQ8RAA AAYAAJ&pg=PA239. Paley (1743–1805) was a leading English exponent of natural theology. In post-Enlightenment Britain, his moral, political, and philosophical views were deeply influential.

176. Here ends this page of Evans's manuscript journal and thus the vertical mark in the left margin.

177. Evans reworks the material beginning from the Charles Wesley hymn quotation to this point in *New Age*, 57–59.

178. Cf. Deut. 8:3 and Matt. 4:4.

179. Cf. John 6:63. The parentheses enclosing the last three sentences appear to have been added later.

180. This entry extends from pp. 141–66 of Evans's journal. It is a long discourse on Swedenborg, which Evans says at the end he hopes to publish. He writes vertically in eighteen of the twenty-six left margins of the journal book to add to the points he is making. He did publish the material after editing and reworking it in Evans, *New Age*, passim.

181. Evans here inserts an asterisk to correspond to an asterisk in the left margin. The paragraph that follows is his marginal addition to the journal.

182. Here ends Evans's marginal interpolation. His explanation follows, to some extent, the views of Joachim of Fiore (see above in notes). Emanuel Swedenborg saw a similar plan operating in the world's history, and Evans here is reiterating Swedenborg. I have introduced succeeding material as a new paragraph to mark the end of the interpolation.

183. Evans here inserts an asterisk, and the paragraph that follows is his marginal addition to the journal.

184. A possible reference to the swampy region in southeastern Virginia and northwestern North Carolina, first surveyed by George Washington in 1763. Regarded by some as a natural wonder of the world, the Dismal Swamp was the subject of a poem by Thomas Moore that Evans may have known—"A Ballad: The Lake of the Dismal Swamp." Or this may be an oblique reference to Paul Bunyan's allegorical Slough of Despond in his classic *Pilgrim's Progress* (1678)—the bog into which the "Christian" of the story, weighted by sin, is ever more deeply submerged.

185. In this context, materialistic. The Sadducees rejected belief in the resurrection of the dead, and as priests their passion and preoccupation was with the material details of ritual.

186. Knapp warns against "predicating of God what can only be said of the presence of body. This caution is particularly necessary here, since we are apt to transfer the forms of time and space, which are applicable only to the sphere of sense, into the world of spirits; and in so doing, to come to conclusions which are false and contradictory, and dishonourable to the purely spiritual nature of God." See George Christian Knapp, *Lectures on Christian Theology*, trans. Leonard Woods, 2d Amer. ed. reprinted from last London ed. (Philadelphia: Thomas Wardle, 1845), 106; available at http://books.google.com/books?id=WH5CAAAAIAAJ&pg =PA106.

187. Evans here inserts a caret to correspond to a caret in the left margin. The paragraph that follows is his marginal addition to the journal.

188. Evans here inserts an asterisk to correspond to an asterisk in the left margin. The paragraph that follows is his marginal addition to the journal.

189. Knapp, *Christian Theology*, 106; at http://books.google.com/books?id=WH5CAAAAIAAJ &pg=PA106. Evans translates Knapp's Greek transcription of Paul's words into the English of the King James Version.

190. Evans's transcription agrees with that of the following edition: Emanuel Swedenborg, *Concerning the Earths in Our Solar System Which Are Called Planets; and Concerning the Earths*

in the Starry Heavens; Together with an Account of Their Inhabitants, and Also of the Spirits and Angels There, trans. from the Latin of Emanuel Swedenborg, originally published in 1758 (Boston: Otis Clapp, 1839), 78; available at http://books.google.com/books?id=uNTrqGI5iz4C &pg=PA78.

191. Evans here inserts an asterisk to correspond to an asterisk in the left margin. The paragraph that follows is his marginal addition to the journal.

192. Greek, respectively, for "soul" and "spirit." Evans has no accent over the final character of the latter word and has a straight line over its fourth character.

193. "Anima" is the Latin word for soul.

194. Evans repeats the material in this paragraph in *New Age,* 21.

195. Evans here inserts an asterisk to correspond to an asterisk in the left margin. The sentence that follows in a separate paragraph is his marginal addition to the journal.

196. See Swedenborg, *Apocalypse Revealed,* art. 959, 3:259–60; available at http://books .google.com/books?id=5aYQAAAAYAAJ&pg=PA259.

197. Johannes Cocceius (1602–1669) was a Dutch theologian and biblical scholar specializing in exegetical readings of the Hebrew scriptures that highlighted their Christian signification.

198. Evans repeats the material in this sentence and the previous two in *New Age,* 24.

199. There is an addition regarding the "Word" in the left margin with an asterisk preceding it but no corresponding asterisk in the body of the journal page. Context suggests that the additional material be placed here, and accordingly I have inserted it in a separate paragraph below.

200. Evans repeats this basic formulation in *New Age,* 29–30.

201. See Rev. 21:1–7.

202. Evans here inserts an asterisk to correspond to a caret in the left margin. The material that follows in a separate paragraph is his marginal addition to the journal.

203. The quotation is part of a close paraphrase of material in a sermon reproduced in *The Divine Word Opened: Sermons of the Rev. Dr. Bayley* [ed. Jonathan Bayley] (London: William White, 1858), 7; available at https://books.google.com/books?id=T5gRAAAAIAAJ &pg=PA7. Jonathan Bayley (1810–1886), as a Swedenborgian minister, presided over the Argyle Square Church in London. He had at least eight published works to his credit.

204. Again, the quotation is part of a close paraphrase of [Bayley], *Divine Word Opened,* 7.

205. Note the scriptural echoes of Acts 17:28 ("in him we live, and move, and have our being") and Rev. 21:1 ("And I saw a new heaven and a new earth"); Evans here inserts a caret to correspond to a caret in the left margin. The material that follows in a separate paragraph is his marginal addition to the journal.

206. The quotation (inexact) is from Victorian poet Elizabeth Barrett Browning, in her lengthy novel-like *Aurora Leigh* (1856). "Earth's crammed with heaven, / And every common bush afire with God."

207. Cf. John 17:3: "And this is life eternal, that they might know thee the only true God, and Jesus Christ, whom thou hast sent."

208. Cf. Job 22:21: "Acquaint now thyself with him, and be at peace: thereby good shall come unto thee."

209. Ps. 115:8 and Ps. 135:18. Evans leaves the number and verse citation blank.

210. Evans here inserts a caret to correspond to a caret in the left margin. The paragraph that follows is his marginal addition to the journal.

211. Evans here inserts a caret to correspond to a caret in the left margin. The paragraph that follows is his marginal addition to the journal.

212. 1 John 4:10, which continues, "not that we loved God, but that he loved us, and sent his Son, *to be* the propitiation for our sins."

213. This is clear evidence that Evans revisits his journal and ponders its entries, suggesting that the marginal additions were composed at a later time than the original entries.

214. See Rev. 21:3.

215. Cf. Rev. 21:2.

216. Material beginning from item "4" in Evans's list of points is reproduced, reworked, and elaborated in *New Age*, 41–44.

217. Evans here inserts a caret to correspond to a caret in the left margin. The material that follows is his marginal addition to the journal. Evans uses the formulation of the three planes of being and expands on these ideas in *Celestial Dawn*, 57–65.

218. John Locke (1632–1704), the British empiricist philosopher and medical researcher, is associated with classical liberal views. The French philosopher Étienne Bonnot de Condillac (1715–1780) was also an exponent of empiricist views of the mind and went further than Locke in rejecting innate shapings of the human mind.

219. Evans here inserts a caret to correspond to a caret in the left margin. The material that follows is his marginal addition to the journal.

220. Evans here inserts a caret to correspond to a caret in the left margin. The material that follows is his marginal addition to the journal.

221. *The Life of God in the Soul of Man* (1677), authored by Scotch minister Henry Scougal (1650–1678), was a letter of spiritual counsel to a friend who had lost his faith; it was strongly extolled by John Wesley.

222. See Emanuel Swedenborg, *Heaven and Its Wonders, the World of Spirits, and Hell: From Things Heard and Seen* (1758), trans. Samuel Noble (New York: American Swedenborg Printing and Publishing, 1857), art. 399, 418, 413; available at http://books.google.com/books?id=2UItAAAAYAAJ. Evans gives the numbers of the articles to which he refers. Article 399 cites the delights of heaven as shared, in emulation of the "Lord" who shares with all (Evans's last sentence preceding the caret—about each and all—in fact echoes part of this article, which cites the heavenly "communication of all with each, and of each with all"). Article 418 posits heaven as a reflection of a single divine man (Swedenborg's divine human). Article 413 sees the joys of heaven as particularities becoming a generality and the joys of heaven as joys of the heart.

223. Again, we have evidence here of Evans's reading practice of returning to his journal. Evans reworks the material under item "5," quoting freely from his journal, in *New Age*, 45–48.

224. Note how close this title is to the title of what was most probably Evans's second book—*Divine Order in the Process of Full Salvation* (1860).

225. Prov. 28:13.

226. Jer. 8:11 and 6:14.

227. See Swedenborg, *Apocalypse Revealed*, art. 949, 3:250; available at http://books.google.com/books?id=5aYQAAAAYAAJ&pg=PA250.

228. Isa. 1:16–17.

229. Cousin put together a philosophical structure from the work of others that may be called a systematic eclecticism. It moved French thought toward idealism, even as Cousin sought evidence for God in historical events.

230. Evans here inserts an asterisk to correspond to an asterisk in the left margin. The material that follows in a separate paragraph is his marginal addition to the journal. Evans reworks

the material from the beginning of item "6" to this point, quoting freely from his journal, in *New Age*, 51–55.

231. Evans uses this short passage, with editorial changes and elaborations, in *New Age*, 57.

232. Evans repeats this material nearly verbatim in *New Age*, 61.

233. Cf. Thomas Chalmers, "Sermon VII," in *The Works of Thomas Chalmers, D.D., Minister of the Tron Church, Glasgow* (Hartford, Conn.: George Goodwin, 1822), 2:150: "The fall of Adam is represented, in the Bible, as that terribly decisive event, on which took place this deep and fatal unhingement of the moral constitution of our species"; available at http://books .google.com/books?id=q4QAAAAMAAJ&pg=PA150. Thomas Chalmers (1780–1847) was a Scotch cleric renowned as a moral philosopher and theologian and a leader of the Free Church of Scotland.

234. See Emanuel Swedenborg, *On the New Jerusalem, and Its Heavenly Doctrine, As Revealed from Heaven: To Which Are Prefixed Some Observations Concerning the New Heaven and the New Earth* (London: James S. Hodson, 1841), art. 182, 94; available at http://books.google .com/books?id=7uRKa7gCkRwC&pg=PA94.

235. These journal entries are for the dates March 19, 1863 ff. and December 20 and 21, 1862.

236. Material beginning from the reference to Swedenborg above in Evans's journal is reproduced and expanded by Evans in *New Age*, 87–88.

237. Evans here inserts an asterisk to correspond to an asterisk in the left margin. The material that follows in a separate paragraph is his marginal addition to the journal.

238. See Swedenborg, *Apocalypse Revealed*, art. 107, 1:119; available at http://books.google .com/books?id=JaYQAAAAYAAJ&pg=PA119.

239. See Swedenborg, *Apocalypse Revealed*, art. 107, 1:113, which addresses the falsity of mere external forms; available at http://books.google.com/books?id=JaYQAAAAYAAJ&pg=PA113.

240. See ibid., 113–14; available at http://books.google.com/books?id=JaYQAAAAYAAJ &pg=PA113. Evans here inserts an asterisk to correspond to an asterisk in the left margin. The material that follows in a separate paragraph is his marginal addition to the journal.

241. See Emanuel Swedenborg, *The Wisdom of Angels concerning the Divine Providence* (1764), [trans. N. Tucker], 2d ed. (London: Gale and Curtis et al., 1810), art. 10–15, 40–46; available at http://books.google.com/books?id=nGIUAAAAQAAJ&pg=PA40.

242. Material beginning with the reference to the "real Christian life" above in his journal is reworked and reproduced by Evans in *New Age*, 90.

243. Evans here inserts an asterisk to correspond to an asterisk in the left margin. The material that follows in a separate paragraph is his marginal addition to the journal.

244. Rev. 21:1–2. Evans repeats this material, beginning with the reference to the "first stadium," in *New Age*, 89–90.

245. Material from this point to the end of this paragraph is reproduced by Evans in *New Age*, 69.

246. Evans did indeed publish this material, lifting and reworking extended passages from his journal, in his book *New Age*. The quotation comes from the "Biographical Introduction" in G[eorge] H[enry] Lewes, *Comte's Philosophy of the Sciences: Being an Exposition of the Principles of the* Cour de Philosophie Positive *of Auguste Comte* (London: Henry G. Bohn, 1853), 1; available at http://books.google.com/books?id=AiMRAAAAYAAJ&pg=PA1.

247. John 12:28–30: "Father, glorify thy name. Then came there a voice from heaven, *saying*, I have both glorified *it*, and will glorify *it* again. / The people therefore, that stood by, and heard *it*, said that it thundered: others said, An angel spake to him. / Jesus answered and said, This voice came not because of me, but for your sakes."

248. John 10:16 actually has a different message: "'And other sheep I have, which are not of this fold: them also I must bring, and they shall hear my voice; and there shall be one fold, *and* one shepherd."

249. Evans has excised material and conflated the two verses.

250. Cf. John 1:5.

251. Cf. Rom. 6:19, 1 Cor. 15:32, and Gal. 3:15.

252. See Heb. 4:12.

253. Evans here inserts an asterisk after his comma to correspond to an asterisk in the left margin. The material that follows is his marginal addition to the journal. This is his first use of the phrase "divine Humanity," a basic tenet of the teachings of Emanuel Swedenborg.

254. This phrase completes the sentence that Evans has interrupted with his asterisked marginal addition.

255. Evans is in error here, and the citation should be to Col. 2:9.

256. "For we know that if our earthly house of *this* tabernacle were dissolved, we have a building of God, an house not made with hands, eternal in the heavens." The invocation of the "Divine Humanity" makes the Swedenborgian influence clear.

257. Latin "to be."

258. John 16:25. The allusion to "Divine Humanity" and then "New Jerusalem" below again underlines Evans's Swedenborgianism.

259. John 16:26.

260. Actually John 16:26–27.

261. The lines are from a hymn in John and Charles Wesley, *Hymns on the Lord's Supper* (1745). See http://www.divinity.duke.edu/sites/default/files/documents/cswt/27_Hymns_on_the_Lord%27s_Supper_%281745%29_mod.pdf, where the hymn is listed as #81.

262. Cf. Luke 7:50.

263. Evans has confused the Lazarus story (John 11:38–53) with Luke 7:50, in which a woman, deemed sinful, anoints the feet of Jesus.

264. The servant of Elisha (not Elijah), Gehazi, was powerless to bring the child back to life with the staff. See 2 Kings 4:25–31. Evans repeats the line in his small book *Divine Order*, 8, but there "They" refers not to "physicians & drugs" but to words heard "from the lips of God's servant."

265. Ps. 27:14.

266. See Augustus Clissold, *Inspiration and Interpretation: Being an Enquiry into Their True Principles* No. 2 (Oxford: Henry Hammans, and London: Whittaker, 1862), 20, in which Adolphe Monod is quoted; available at http://books.google.com/books?id=3-cCAAAAQAAJ&pg=RA1-PA20. Monod (1802–1856) was a Reformed cleric and theologian, considered the foremost French-speaking preacher of his time and, it has been claimed, all time.

267. Evans does not supply a verse number. The source is Heb. 4:12: "For the word of God *is* quick, and powerful."

268. Cf. Matt. 16:16–17, in which Simon Peter acknowledges Jesus as "the Christ, the Son of the living God" and Jesus blesses him, saying "flesh and blood hath not revealed *it* unto thee."

269. Over two months have elapsed since Evans's last journal entry.

270. Plato (ca. 423–347 BCE) taught a philosophy of idealism in which it is the eternal and immutable Forms that have true reality, while our manifested world consists of copies of

them that are deficient and changing. For Berkeley and his "immaterialism" or "subjective idealism," see Introduction n45 above.

271. Evans here reflects his cultural context in his negative assessment of Judaism.

272. Thomas Aquinas (1225–1274), arguably the leading medieval Scholastic philosopher, has frequently been called a baptized Aristotle. His rationalistic approach, based on natural theology and natural law, is still fundamental in Roman Catholic theology. Again, Evans reflects his cultural context in an implicit suspicion of things medieval (and Catholic).

273. Evans here inserts a caret to correspond to a caret in the left margin. The sentence that follows is his marginal addition to the journal.

274. Latin *Pectus est, quod theologum facit*—"it is the heart that makes the theologian." Supposedly, this was the favorite motto of Augustus Neander, whose work deeply influenced Evans.

275. This long passage, beginning from the reference to Victor Cousin, is reworked and substantially reproduced by Evans in *New Age*, 81–83.

276. Latin "scattered members."

277. Evans borrows loosely from his journal entry beginning from the reference to "disjecta membra" in *New Age*, 83.

278. I have been unable to locate the source of this quotation.

279. The lines are from a hymn by Charles Wesley, popularly known as "Soldiers of Christ, Arise." It was originally published under the title "The Whole Armour of God" in *Hymns and Sacred Poems* (1749). For a later edition, see Elijah Hedding et al., eds., *Hymns for the Use of the Methodist Episcopal Church*, rev. ed. (New York: Lane and Scott, 1840), 433; available at http://books.google.com/books?id=tLwYAAAAYAAJ&pg=PA433.

280. Cf. Luke 17:5.

281. Cf. Mark 11:22, which in literal Greek may be translated "have the faith of God."

282. Gal. 2:20.

283. Cf. Luke 7:50. Evans's declaration suggests perhaps an earlier physical healing he may have experienced. According to William J. Leonard, Evans's metaphysically oriented friend J. H. Dewey, M.D., claimed that Evans was healed of "a most aggravated and obstinate dyspepsia" before he had completed his studies and entered ministerial work. The healing had been a "prayer cure" or "faith cure." See William J. Leonard, "Warren Felt Evans, M.D.: An Account of His Life and His Services as the First Author of the Metaphysical Healing Movement," *Practical Ideals* 10, no. 3 (November 1905): 4–5.

284. Cf. Gal. 2:20; Col. 3:3.

285. Rom. 7 is Paul's meditation on his inner conflict between the law of God and "the law of sin" (Rom. 7:25).

286. Cf. Luke 18:3; Isa. 1:24.

287. Cf. Luke 18:7–8.

288. Evans omits a few words from the psalm that do not comport with his reading, which follows.

289. Evans omits a reference to fear ("yea, *what* fear") from his transcription of the verse.

290. See Asa Cummings, ed., *Memoir, Select Thoughts and Sermons of the Late Rev. Edward Payson, D.D.* (Philadelphia: J. and J. L. Gihon, 1851), 1:413; available at http://books.google.com/books?id=nAZMAAAAYAAJ&pg=PA413.

291. The quotation may be found in Stevens, *History of the Religious Movement of the Eighteenth Century, Called Methodism*, 1: 364 n17; available at https://books.google.com

/books?id=ZitOAQAAMAAJ&pg=PA364. There is no available biography of Christopher Hopper. The only data I have been able to locate suggests he lived from 1680 to 1762 and died in Flushing, New York. See http://records.ancestry.com/Christopher_Hopper_records .ashx?pid=912557.

292. Edmund H. Sears, *Regeneration* (Boston: Crosby, Nichols, and Co., printed for the American Unitarian Association, 1853), 125; available at http://books.google.com /books?id=7D46KxBLiWQC&pg=PA125. Edmund Hamilton Sears (1810–1876) was an American Unitarian minister considered conservative, since he did not agree with radical or "broad-church" Unitarian views. Still, his theological writings influenced Protestant liberals whether they were Unitarian or not.

293. The line appears twice in the third verse of John G. C. Brainard's poem "The Deep." Brainard (1796–1828) studied law but turned to poetry until his early death from consumption. See *The Poems of John G.C. Brainard: A New and Authentic Collection, with an Original Memoir* (Hartford, Conn.: S. Andrus, 1847), 117; available at http://books.google.com /books?id=3bUoAAAAMAAJ&pg=PA117.

294. Evans here conflates parts of John 14:27 and John 16:22.

295. It is virtually certain that Evans read these words as quoted by Thomas Carlyle, who was influenced by Jean Paul Richter and quoted Richter's *Hesperus* in various works. See, for example, Thomas Carlyle, *The Works of Thomas Carlyle*, ed. Henry Duff Traill, vol. 28, *Critical and Miscellaneous Essays* (1899; reprint, Cambridge: Cambridge University Press, 2010), 3:32; available at http://books.google.com/books?id=vJY-COOkrxIC&pg=PA32. The German early Romantic novelist and humorist Jean Paul Richter (1763–1825) wrote using the pen name Jean Paul.

296. Evans was likely reading George Müller, *The Life of Trust: Being a Narrative of the Lord's Dealings with George Müller*, ed. and abr. H. Lincoln Wayland (Boston: Gould and Lincoln, 1861). German-born George [Johann Georg Ferdinand] Müller (1805–1898) was an evangelist in England, reputed for his foundation of orphanages and schools.

297. Evans is referring to Thomas C. Upham, *The Life of Faith, in Three Parts; Embracing Some of the Scriptural Principles or Doctrines of Faith, the Power or Effects of Faith in the Regulation of Man's Inward Nature, and the Relation of Faith to the Divine Guidance* (Boston: Waite, Pierce, 1845). Harper and Brothers published this work in New York a number of times, one of them in 1862.

298. The famously destroyed library of Alexandria, Egypt, was reputed to have been the most significant library in the ancient world, housing from 400,000 to 700,000 parchment scrolls at its height. The library of Pergamon, in Turkey, said to contain some 200,000 papyrus rolls, was also highly esteemed.

299. "And I saw the dead, small and great, stand before God; and the books were opened: and another book was opened, which is *the book* of life: and the dead were judged out of those things which were written in the books, according to their works."

300. "Gregory" is Pope St. Gregory I (540–604), also known as Gregory the Great, and one of the four Latin Fathers or Doctors of the Church. While he was abbot of the monastery of St. Andrew in Rome, he was reputed to have spent much time lecturing to the monks on the scriptures. In one of his letters, Gregory wrote, "Learn the heart of God in the words of God, that you may sigh more eagerly for things eternal, that your soul may be kindled with greater longings for heavenly joys." *Letters*, 5, no. 46.

301. Lines from a familiar hymn of the era and usually transcribed as "Send some message from thy word,/ That may joy and peace afford." See, e.g., Abraham M. Engle et al. (Brethren in Christ Church), *A Collection of Spiritual Hymns, Adapted to the Various Kinds of Christian Worship*, 2d ed. (Lancaster, Pa.: Brethren in Christ Church, 1874), 35; available at http://archive.org/stream/collectionofspiroobreth/collectionofspiroobreth_djvu.txt.

302. "But when the Comforter is come, whom I will send unto you from the Father, *even* the Spirit of truth, which proceedeth from the Father, he shall testify of me."

303. In *Divine Order*, 39, Evans calls faith the "channel" for the "divine life and the divine good."

304. Jesus answered and said unto her, If thou knewest the gift of God, and who it is that saith to thee, Give me to drink; thou wouldest have asked of him, and he would have given thee living water."

305. Cf. John 4:15.

306. The standard transliteration is "emunah."

307. Evans's distinction between the phenomenal and the real is basic to his analysis in *New Age*, 33–34.

308. Evans repeats this material regarding the "sensuous mind" in *New Age*, 31.

309. Cf. Gal. 2:20 and Col. 3:3.

310. See Mark 5:1 and Matt. 8:26 with their mutual reference to the "country of the Gadarenes" where Jesus encounters the demonic. Evans repeats the line in *New Age*, 32.

311. "Evil shall slay the wicked: and they that hate the righteous shall be desolate."

312. "With the merciful thou wilt shew thyself merciful; with an upright man thou wilt shew thyself upright; / With the pure thou wilt shew thyself pure; and with the froward thou wilt shew thyself froward."

313. Evans quotes the phrase exactly from Samuel Thomas Bloomfield's Greek New Testament. See Bloomfield, *H KAINH ΔIAΘHKH: The Greek New Testament, with English Notes, Grammatical, Scholarly, and Elementary* (London: Longman, Rees, Orme, 1837), 218; available at http://books.google.com/books?id=2FoEAAAAQAAJ&pg=PA218.

314. Latin "foundations."

315. See Journal II n36 above. Evans probably inserted this entry here because there are a few empty lines at the bottom of this page, and he apparently added it later since the date makes that of the next entry out of order.

316. Evans repeats the line in *New Age*, 17.

317. See Emanuel Swedenborg, *A Continuation Concerning the Last Judgment, and Concerning the Spiritual World* (1763; New York: American Swedenborg Printing and Publishing Society, 1865), no. 11, 497; available at http://books.google.com/books?id=8vRfmn_6bCwC&pg=PA497. Evans's "illumination" is there rendered as "enlightenment."

318. Evans repeats this material in *New Age*, 30.

319. Latin "to be."

320. Rom. 12:21.

321. See Swedenborg, *Divine Providence*, subject heading preceding art. 100; available at http://books.google.com/books?id=nGIUAAAAQAAJ&pg=PA122. Evans gives inclusive article numbers that do not correspond exactly to those in the translation cited above.

322. Matt. 19:17.

323. Cf. 2 Thess. 11–12. This lengthy entry for December 20 is substantially repeated by Evans in *New Age*, 61–63.

324. See John 8:11.

325. 2 Cor. 5:19.

326. Cf. John 3:17–18, which ascribes activity to God, who sends his son into the world. In keeping with Swedenborgian theology, Evans conflates Father and Son into the Son/Savior.

327. See 1 John 3:21.

328. This is apparently a paraphrase of Swedenborgian doctrine and not an explicit quotation.

329. Cf. Rom. 1:17 and Gal. 3:11, neither of which include Evans's second clause.

330. This long entry for December 21 is reworked and substantially reproduced by Evans in *New Age*, 65–68.

331. William Law (1686–1761) was an English cleric and mystic, whose writings on themes of piety, prayer, and the like were well-known.

332. Edmund H. Sears, *Athanasia: Or, Foregleams of Immortality* (Boston: American Unitarian Association, 1858). Listings in WorldCat show that the book appeared in multiple editions in 1857 and 1858 and continued to be published thereafter. Evans is referring to Portsmouth, New Hampshire.

333. Swedenborg, *Angelic Wisdom concerning the Divine Love and the Divine Wisdom*. See Journal II n128 above for an American edition available online. The earliest American edition was published in Boston by Otis Clapp in 1835.

334. Matt. 10:8.

335. Evans here marks an "X" in his journal, as if to make note of this statement.

336. Nitrogen.

337. See Auguste Laugel, "The Sun: Its Chemical Analysis, according to the Recent Discoveries of M. M. Kirchoff and Bunsen," trans. for the Smithsonian Institution from the *Revue des Deux Mondes*, Paris, January 15, 1862, in *Annual Report of the Board of Regents of the Smithsonian Institution* (34th Congress, 2d Session, House of Representatives Misc. Doc. No. 77) (Washington: Government Printing Office, 1862), 184; available at https://books .google.com/books?id=7l9UAAAAcAAJ&pg=PA184. Evans makes at least two small transcription errors.

338. See Swedenborg, *Apocalypse Revealed*, art. 936, 3:231–33; available at http://books .google.com/books?id=5aYQAAAAYAAJ&pg=PA231.

339. Ibid., 3:232.

340. Ibid., 3:231.

341. Ibid., 3:232.

342. This March 14 journal entry is reproduced, edited, and elaborated by Evans in *New Age*, 103–7.

343. Evans reiterates this basic analysis in *New Age*, 36.

344. Evans repeats this material concerning the Pharisees and Athenians in *New Age*, 36.

345. See Evans, *New Age*, 36. Here and in what follows, Evans repeats material he has already expressed in his previous journal entry for March 14.

346. Swedenborg, *Divine Providence*, art. 78, III, 99–100; available at http://books.google .com/books?id=nGIUAAAAQAAJ&pg=PA99.

347. John 3:21. Evans was quoting from memory and left a blank, no doubt intending to fill it in later. The latter part of the verse reads, "that his deeds may be made manifest, that they are wrought in God."

348. Swedenborg, *Divine Providence*, art. 87, V, 107–8, which Evans is quoting; available at http://books.google.com/books?id=nGIUAAAAQAAJ&pg=PA107. The long passage from

the reference to the Pharisees and the Athenians to the end of the paragraph is repeated, with some editing and elaboration, in *New Age*, 36–39.

349. See John 14:6 and 1 John 4:8.

350. Here and above in his journal, Evans seems increasingly comfortable with the use of abbreviations. He may be using them because he is writing in a hurried manner, pressed with other obligations.

351. It is almost four months since Evans last wrote in his journal.

352. The 3d New Hampshire Volunteer Regiment, in which Evans's son Franklin served, was organized in Concord, New Hampshire, and active from 1861 to 1865. It included over a thousand officers and men who spent most of their time on the Atlantic Coast in the Carolinas.

353. See 2 Cor. 4:17.

354. Over a month has elapsed since Evans's last entry.

355. Cf. Exod. 14:25.

356. Cf. Rom. 14:7: "For none of us liveth to himself, and no man dieth to himself."

357. Again there is a fairly long lapse in Evans's journal—this one almost two months.

358. Evans writes in the left margin "Letter To Sampson Reed Esq of Boston." Sampson Reed (1800–1880) was a Harvard student when he became a disciple of Emanuel Swedenborg, devoting himself to the Swedish seer instead of becoming a Unitarian minister. His *Observations on the Growth of the Mind* (1826) deeply influenced Ralph Waldo Emerson and other Transcendentalists, as did Reed's writings in the Swedenborgian *New Jerusalem Magazine*, which he cofounded.

359. Below Evans pastes into his journal a letter to Sampson Reed printed in two columns. The letter extends to the following manuscript journal page, effectively filling it. There is no information concerning a journal, magazine, or newspaper, if any, in which the letter appeared. The press that produced the letter may actually have been Evans's own, as the letter itself suggests below, with its reference to a "periodical business" purchased for his son.

360. Swedenborg, *Heaven and Its Wonders, the World of Spirits, and Hell*, art. 413, 221; available at http://books.google.com/books?id=2UItAAAAYAAJ&pg=PA221.

361. Almost five months have elapsed since Evans pasted the Reed letter into his journal.

362. Here Evans pastes a newsprint letter addressed to Rev. James Thurston, Presiding Elder, Claremont District, and dated Claremont, April 4, 1864. On the left side margin, he writes "Sundered from Methodist Church." Two X's, one on the left margin and one on the right, probably indicate that he wished this title to head the printed letter that follows—produced again, probably, on a press he owned himself.

363. Thomas Worcester (1795–1878) moved from an activist and reformist Unitarianism to Swedenborgianism and for well over forty years (1821–1867) served as pastor of the Church of the New Jerusalem in Boston. He was also president of the New Church Theological School from 1866 until his death.

364. John 19:30.

365. The "ever after" in this line suggests that Evans may have written this considerably later than the dated entry.

366. Cf. Rev. 5:13.

367. Ps. 3:8.

368. Note the passage of nearly four months since Evans's last stated journal entry.

369. Matt. 7:2.

370. Luke 24:36.

371. A reference, probably, to Exod. 24:12ff., in which Moses follows divine command and ascends Mount Sinai to receive the Ten Commandments; or, alternately, to Deut. 34:1, in which Moses ascends Mount Nebo and is divinely shown "all the land of Gilead, unto Dan."

372. Cf. John 16:32.

373. Bath, Maine, is 33.8 miles from Portland, where Phineas P. Quimby was practicing his mind-cure medicine at the time. It is likely that Evans had combined a visit to Quimby with the trip to Bath. Evans's journal is silent regarding Quimby.

374. In reports to the General Convention of the Swedenborgian New Church, Evans indicates that he began acting as a missionary and colporteur for the Massachusetts Association of the New Church on October 1, 1864. He visited towns in Vermont, New Hampshire, and Massachusetts, fifty-two all told. His income from book sales would not have been great. See Keith McNeil, *A Story Untold: A History of the Quimby-Evans Debate* (2016), 1251–52, online publication at http://ppquimby-mbeddydebate.com/.

375. William Cullen Bryant, "To a Waterfowl" (1815), verse 4.

376. Ibid., verses 7 and 8.

377. Cf. Mark 11:22.

378. William Newell, "Consecration of Cambridge Cemetery" (1854), verses 1 and 2. See Alfred P. Putnam, ed., *Singers and Songs of the Liberal Faith; Being Selections of Hymns and Other Sacred Poems of the Liberal Church in America* (Boston: Roberts Brothers, 1875), 178; available at http://books.google.com/books?id=iM8yAQAAMAAJ&pg=PA178. William Newell was pastor of the First Parish in Cambridge, Massachusetts, from 1830.

379. Ten months have passed since Evans last wrote in his journal, and it is midpoint in a new year. The long lapses perhaps indicates a new level of spiritual peace.

380. Note the lapse of four months since Evans's last entry.

381. Evans leaves the reference blank. Spiritual discernment is a frequent theme in Swedenborg's *Arcana Coelestia* (1749–1756), eight volumes interpreting the biblical books of Genesis and Exodus according to the theory of correspondence.

382. Charles Wesley, "O for a Thousand Tongues to Sing," a well-known Methodist hymn. See M'Kendree et al., eds., *Collection of Hymns for the Use of the Methodist Episcopal Church*, 7; available at http://books.google.com/books?id=LJIQAAAAIAAJ&pg=PA7.

383. See Hab. 3:17–19.

384. Ibid. 3:18–19.

385. Num. 10:35.

386. Cf. Job 21:18; Ps. 83:13; Isa. 40:24.

387. Cf. Num. 10:36. Evans is supplying the literal translation for "thousands" in his "ten thousand thousands."

388. Swedenborg, *Heaven and Its Wonders, the World of Spirits, and Hell*, art. 303–310, 149–55; available at http://books.google.com/books?id=2UItAAAAYAAJ&pg=PA149. The articles constitute a section subtitled "Of the Conjunction of Heaven with Man by Means of the Word."

389. Isa. 12:1–2. Evans underlines "Jehovah" twice to indicate its uppercase transcription in the King James Version.

390. From Bailey, "Proem," in *Festus*; available at http://books.google.com/books?id=gAYPAAAAYAAJ&pg=PA16. Evans uses the quotation, too, in the preface to his *Celestial Dawn*, v.

391. Actually, Isa. 12:3. Evans supplies "fountains" for the King James Version's "wells."

392. George Lansing Taylor, "Conquer and Rest," which may be found in his volume *Asters and Golden-Rod: And Other Poems* (New York: Eaton and Mains, 1904), 126–27; available at

http://books.google.com/books?id=BM0YAAAAYAAJ&pg=PA126. The poem had already been set to music as a hymn in 1865. See Silas J. Vail, ed., *The Diadem: A Collection of Tunes and Hymns for Sunday School and Devotional Meetings*, no. 90 (New York: Horace Waters, 1865), 88; available at http://www.hymnary.org/hymnal/D1865. Evans liked the poem so well that he used it as a concluding flourish in *Celestial Dawn*, 265–66, and in his *Esoteric Christianity and Mental Therapeutics* (Boston: H. H. Carter and Karrick, 1886), 174. Taylor himself (1835–1903) was an itinerant Methodist clergyman with a Doctor of Divinity degree from Syracuse University (1876). He wrote poetry, published sermons and pamphlets, and contributed articles to magazines.

393. See Ezek. 47:12 and Rev. 22:2, which Evans has here conflated.

394. See Emanuel Swedenborg, *Arcana Coelestia: The Heavenly Arcana Which Are Contained in the Holy Scriptures or Word of the Lord Unfolded, Beginning with the Book of Genesis*, vol. 1 (London: James S. Hodson, 1837), art. 50, 27; available at http://books.google.com/books?id=FEA9AAAAcAAJ&pg=PA27.

395. Cf. John 1:3, which Evans here echoes and appropriates to his own purposes.

396. Evans uses some of the language and concepts here in W. F. Evans, *The Mental-Cure, Illustrating the Influence of the Mind on the Body, Both in Health and Disease, and the Psychological Method of Treatment* (Boston: H. H. and T. W. Carter, 1869), 266; and W. F. Evans, *The Divine Law of Cure* (Boston: H. H. Carter, 1881; reprint, New York: Cosimo, 2007), 301.

397. Cf. Ps. 42:11 and Ps. 43:5.

398. Evans here skips a page in his manuscript numbering of the pages of his journal, going from page 276 to 278.

399. See Matt. 9:22, Mark, 5:34 and 10:52, and Luke 17:19.

400. Cf. Matt. 9:21. The King James Version reads, "If I may but touch his garment, I shall be whole." The reference to "hem or fringe" suggests that Evans may have been reading a commentary.

401. John 6:63.

402. In *New Age*, 31, Evans—propounding his understanding of Swedenborgian theology—calls death "the extinction of the *proprium* or selfhood."

403. Cf. Gal. 2:20.

404. Cf. Matt. 11:15 and 13:9; Mark 4:9.

405. 2 Cor. 2:16.

406. Evans's analysis of negative mind echoes mid-nineteenth-century spiritualist notions of the passive and receptive mediumistic state, based on theories of electromagnetism as related to mesmerism. See, for example, Andrew Jackson Davis, *The Philosophy of Spiritual Intercourse: Being an Explanation of Modern Mysteries* (New York: Fowlers and Wells, 1853), 96–100. With this quasi-spiritualist reflection, Evans's journal ends. There are enough blank pages left in the volume in which he was writing to make it clear that he had no further entries for the year. If he started another journal in 1866, it has so far not been located.

INDEX

Note: The abbreviation "WFE" refers to Warren Felt Evans.

Abelard, 115

affirmation, 25, 29

Alexandria, Egypt, 213, 287n298

allness and nothingness, 87–89, 99, 107, 127, 141, 250, 268n177

altar theology: of Phoebe Palmer, 15, 16, 19–20, 22; WFE's use of, 16–17, 19, 20, 52, 156

American Unitarian Association, 11

angels: Swedenborg on, 157, 173–74, 185, 186, 196, 243, 247; WFE on, 26, 138, 140, 142, 147, 173, 174, 175–76, 178, 242–43, 245, 248

annihilation, 75, 84, 88–90, 100, 249–50

Anselm of Canterbury, 11, 16, 80, 97, 263n86, 267n151

antinomianism, 140

Antiochus IV (Syrian-Greek monarch), 130, 272n29

Arbouin, James, 156

Aristotle, 193, 205, 286n272

Arminianized perfectionism, 11

Asian philosophies, 1, 31, 33–34, 44

atheism, 32, 33, 88

Augustine, Saint, 218

Bailey, Philip James, 126, 245, 271nn15, 16, 291n390

Baker, Osmon C., 56, 259n25

baptism of fire, 63, 260n39

Baptist Church, 20

Barber, Mary Ann Serrett, 265n128, 272n19

Barrett, Benjamin Fiske, 39–40

Bartol, Cyrus, 37

Bath, Maine, 241, 291n373

Bathurst, William Hiley, 150–51, 275n89

Bautain, Louis, 264n109

Baxter, Richard, 16, 23, 84–86, 87, 264n113, 265n114

beauty, 72–73, 76

Berkeley, George, 25, 30, 205, 255n45

Bernard of Clairvaux, 11, 16, 80–81, 263n86

Bible: Finney on, 24; Swedenborg on, 187–89, 236, 244; WFE on Christian experience and, 183; WFE on correspondence in, 187–91; WFE on divine mind and, 200–201, 213–14; WFE on heaven and, 248–49; WFE on inspiration of, 151–53; WFE on truth and, 172, 177, 215–17; WFE on Word of God in Bible, 203–4, 213–15, 218–19, 244, 245, 246–47, 248, 249

biblical quotations in WFE: on allness and nothingness, 89, 107, 268n177; on angels, 138, 274n54; on divine humanity of Jesus Christ, 149, 201; on divine manifestation, 209; on divine mind, 152; on divine union, 63, 86, 91, 104, 176, 265n131;

CATHERINE L. ALBANESE

is J. F. Rowny Professor Emerita and Research Professor in the Department of Religious Studies at the University of California, Santa Barbara. She is former department chair (2005–2010) and former president of the American Academy of Religion (1994). Her award-winning book, *A Republic of Mind and Spirit: A Cultural History of American Metaphysical Religion*, was published in 2007. She is the author of numerous other books and articles, including *America: Religions and Religion*, now in its fifth edition (2013). In 2014, she was elected a member of the American Academy of Arts and Sciences.